5TH EDITION

Turning on Learning

Five Approaches for Multicultural Teaching Plans for Race, Class, Gender, and Disability

CARL A. GRANT
University of Wisconsin-Madison

CHRISTINE E. SLEETER
California State University, Monterey Bay

WILEY

JOHN WILEY & SONS, INC.

KH

To the many teachers who have found this book helpful and supportive

VICE PRESIDENT & PUBLISHER	Jay O' Callaghan
AQUISITION EDITOR	Robert Johnston
PRODUCTION MANAGER	Dorothy Sinclair
SENIOR PRODUCTION EDITOR	Sandra Dumas
MARKETING MANAGER	Danielle Torio
DESIGNER	Hope Miller
COVER PHOTO	Corbis/SuperStock
MEDIA EDITOR	Lynn Pearlman
EDITORIAL ASSISSTANT	Carrie Tupa
PRODUCTION MANAGEMENT SERVICES	PineTree Composition Services

This book was set in 10/12 New Caledonia by Laserwords Private Limited, Chennai, India and printed and bound by Malloy Lithographing, Inc.The cover was printed by Malloy Lithographing, Inc.

The book is printed on acid-free paper. ∞

To order books or for customer service please, call 1-800-CALL WILEY (225-5945).

Library of Congress Cataloging-in-Publication Data:

Grant, Carl A.; Sleeter, Christine, E.
Turning On Learning: Five Approaches for Multicultural Teaching
Plans for Race, Class, Gender, and Disability, Fifth Edition

978-0470-38370-4

Printed in the United States of America

10 9 8 7 6 5 4 3 2 1

10/27/10

Preface

This book is the practical, lesson-based companion to *Making Choices for Multicultural Education: Five Approaches to Race, Class, and Gender* (Wiley, 2009). *Turning on Learning* grew out of the requests of teachers and preservice education students for specific illustrations of how to work with diversity, excite and improve the academic achievement of their students. Over the years, we have communicated with many teachers, administrators, teacher educators, and teacher education students around the country who have repeatedly challenged us to show them how to apply our ideas in their classrooms. Theories have value only when they can be demonstrated and used in daily practice and when they offer concrete possibilities. This book provides these possibilities.

The text is grounded in theories and philosophies supporting multicultural education. Attention is given to classroom concerns related to race, class, gender, disability, language, religion, sexual orientation and social justice.

Turning on Learning contains many lesson plans that cover a variety of subject areas and grade levels 1 through 12, as well as action research activities that investigate the various dimensions of teaching. Many of the lesson plans are written by classroom teachers, and all of them have been examined by practicing teachers. But the book is more than a how-to manual. Rather, it is designed to help the teacher or teacher education student teach from a multicultural perspective. Most lesson plans offers a "Before" version—the lesson as it is usually taught—and an "After" version—how the lesson can be improved to "turn on" learning. A discussion explaining why the changes were made follows each lesson plan.

▶ NEW TO THIS EDITION

In this fifth edition, we added some new lessons. These new plans strengthen the Human Relations Approach and the Multicultural Education Approach. Throughout the book we have added new resource materials, up-dated information where necessary, up-dated termonology and changed the Table of Content to make it more user friendly. Over the life of the book, we have seen much more multicultural material become available, we have careful seleleted the best of the best to include.

It is hoped that readers will use not only the lesson plans in this book but also the process for modifying teaching in their own daily curriculum and instruction. We are confident that, in the process, more students will become excited about learning and enthusiastic about living in and bettering their world.

▶ ACKNOWLEDGMENTS

We are indebted to a great many people who contribute and continue to contribute valuable ideas to *Turning on Learning*. Our sincerest thanks go to the following educators for the lesson plans, ideas, and information they provided: Chris Aamodt, Claire Alldred, Natalie Bernasconi, Deborah Bicksler, Kristen Buras, Karen Campion, David Castaneda, Joya Chavarin, Jennifer Clayton, Margaret Conway, Felix Cortez-Littlefield, Larry Escalada, Carolina Evans-Roman, Linda Endlich, Anne Fairbrother, Lola Ferguson, Diana Flores, Maureen Gillette, Dorothy Goines, Jill Moss Greenberg, Kathleen Horning, Derek Jennings, Virginia Kester, Jacquelyn King, Ozetta Kirby, P. Lloyd Kollman, Lisa Loutzenheiser, Jill Moss Greenberg, Gloria Nájera, Connie Olson, Debra Owens, Therese Pipes, Jo Richards, Linda Roberts, Linda Luiz-Rodrigues, Henry St. Maurice, Sue Senzig, Cherri Sistek, Bob Suzuki, Abigail R. Reuler, Kathro Taylor, Paoze Thao, Yer Thao, Amanda Werhane, Robin White, Margaret Whiting, Kimberley Woo, and Lynette Selkurt Zimmer.

We are grateful to numerous practicing teachers and preservice education students who reviewed the lesson plans and gave us their reactions and valuable suggestions. We thank our undergraduate and graduate students at the University of Washington, the University of Wisconsin—Madison, the University of Wisconsin—Parkside, and California State University—Monterey Bay, as well as teachers with whom we shared drafts of the lesson plans in workshops across the country. We owe much to our colleagues who reviewed the manuscript and offered numerous suggestions for improvement: Barbara Kacer, Western Kentucky University; Angela Clark Louque, University of Redlands; Alba Rosenman, Ball State University; Will Roy, University of Wisconsin—Milwaukee; and Vilma Seebert, Kent State University, Abby Potter University of Wisconsin-Madison.

Finally, we owe deep thanks to those who have keyed, reviewed, given suggestions, and helped get this manuscript together. We especially appreciate Chris Kruger's work in making revisions. We also appreciate the help and feedback of Lola Ferguson, Joy Lei, and Michael Tucker on drafts of earlier lesson plans.

Carl A. Grant
Christine E. Sleeter

Contents

► **CHAPTER 6**

Multicultural and Social Justice Education 259

CHAPTER 1

What Turns Your Students On?

Can you imagine what it would be like to be a student in your own classroom or in one with which you are familiar? If you are like most educators, you probably find it difficult to imagine yourself as the student. You may have trouble remembering who you were as a student and realizing that a full quarter century may have elapsed since you were the age of students now in school. Even if you are now a college student, your elementary, middle, and high school years probably seem like a long time ago.

Placing ourselves in the role of student often involves more than a leap across time to a role we no longer occupy. For many of us, it involves trying to identify with someone who visibly differs from ourselves and who is growing up in and influenced by a world that brings challenges, the likes of which we did not have to deal with when we were young. Some of these challenges are caused by globalization, technology, and circumstances from the tragic and horrifying events of September 11, 2001. In addition, as we look at the multitude of ethnicities, people stratified by economic conditions, and people who live, behave, or dress according to a particular culture or lifestyle that is different from our own, we wonder what ideas we should put into practice. For many of us these challenges threaten our ideas of a "good" world. Add to that the unresolved issues surrounding immigration that influence many schools; and how and what to teach become a big mystery.

Compounding our wonderment is the stark reality that we don't have many reference points. We have few human resources—such as fellow teachers from different ethnic and cultural groups—that we can turn to for answers or suggestions. This is so because there is about an 85 percent chance that you, the reader, are White and female. According to the National Center for Education Information report in 2005, the K-12 public school teaching force in the United States is getting older, more female, slightly less White, and more experienced. The Report notes that in 2005 the teaching profession was 85 percent White and the percentage of teachers of color had increased over the previous few years, especially with an increase in Hispanic teachers. Many of you live in middle-class conditions and have never experienced poverty. Most of you are privileged without realizing all of the options that you take for granted, and many of you have rarely—if ever—been in a daily situation where you are the minority, the only person who represents your ethnic, racial, or sexual orientation group. Very few of you were ever in special education. Most of you were educated your entire lives in your first language.

The gap between your own experiences and personal identity and those of your students may be small, or it may be tremendous. But there is a gap, and it will continue to grow as the student population becomes more diverse. The Children's Defense Fund (1998) reports the following information about children born in the United States:

- 1 in 2 will live in a single-parent family at some point in childhood.
- 1 in 3 will be poor at some point in childhood.
- 1 in 3 is behind a year or more in school.
- 2 in 5 will never complete a single year of college.
- 1 in 5 was born poor.
- 1 in 5 has a foreign-born mother.
- 1 in 7 has no health insurance.
- 1 in 24 lives with neither parent.
- 1 in 60 sees his or her parents divorce in any year.
- 1 in 1,056 will be killed by gunfire before age 20.

Also, "it is estimated that 750,000 school-age children live in shelters, cars, parks, abandoned building door stoops, or with other families" (West, 2001, p. 1). For these students, "it means growing up with a future dimmed by an 'abundance of nothing.'" Now add to this the following, also provided by the Children Defense Fund:

Each Day in America
March 2008

2 mothers die from complications of pregnancy or childbirth.
4 children are killed by abuse or neglect.
5 children or teens commit suicide.
8 children or teens are killed by firearms.
32 children or teens die from accidents.
78 babies die before their first birthdays.
155 children are arrested for violent crimes.
296 children are arrested for drug crimes.
928 babies are born at low birthweight.
1,154 babies are born to teen mothers.
1,511 public school students are corporally punished.*
2,145 babies are born without health insurance.
2,467 high school students drop out.*
2,421 children are confirmed as abused or neglected.
2,483 babies are born into poverty.
3,477 children are arrested.
18,221 public school students are suspended.*

*Based on calculations per school day (180 days of seven hours each)

Our intent is not to cause alarm, but if we provoke you, that is good. Our intent is to invite you to examine how you are meeting and working with students; we also invite and, indeed, encourage you to become aware of what life in today's schools is like from students' perspectives. We have observed teachers who are willing to learn from their students, who view teaching and learning as a two-way interchange. As "students of their students," these teachers do an excellent job of building instruction around their students' interests and perspectives. Their classrooms are exciting places because they "turn on" learning. These teachers have not become enslaved by the accountability and high-stakes tests mania. They teach students so that they will be successful on standardized tests without forgetting that schooling and education are much more than the score on an achievement test.

On the other hand, we also have observed some teachers who ignore all else, and their teaching is designed solely to help students do well on standardized tests. We see other teachers who tend to overlook their students' identities and experiences, who teach as if their students were just like themselves. Still other teachers ignore and marginalize students who are different from themselves, or who are academically challenging. When the gap between teacher and student is not bridged, learning gets "turned off." Motivation to learn and to pass tests, including achievement tests, wanes. In the upper grades, thoughts about leaving school increase. In these circumstances, students are as much "pushed out" of school as they drop out. Symptoms of turned-off learning include students' seeming inabilities to grasp concepts, to exert effort, and to display enthusiasm; repeated lateness or absence; boredom; avoidance; and sloppy or poor-quality work. Furthermore, gifted and talented students tend to underperform, doing just enough to get by. When students are turned off, teaching feels like a chore or even a battle.

Unfortunately, the latter type of teaching approach is more common than the former, and with the student dropout rate increasing—between 347,000 and 544,000 tenth-through twelfth-grade students dropped out over the last decade (National Center for Education Statistics, 1999). In other words, if you teach high school, according to estimates from the National Education Association (NEA 2004) you may expect about 30 percent of your students to drop out before graduation, meaning about one million students fail to graduate from high school every year. In addition, only five in ten Black and Hispanic students graduate on time with a standard diploma, and fewer than half of American Indian and Alaska Native students complete high school. Further, NEA reports that each class of high school dropouts costs the nation more than $200 billion in lost wages and tax revenues, as well as spending for social support programs.

The situation is not likely to get better unless an effort is made to improve it. We term this ineffective teaching approach "business as usual," and its frequent use has been documented by recent studies of schools, in which researchers have observed classrooms and interviewed teachers and students (Anyon, 1981; Cuban, 1993; Everhart, 1983; Goodlad, 1984; Grant & Sleeter, 1996; Lareau, 2000; Oakes, 1985; Payne, 1984; Solomon, 1992; Valli, 1986; Weis, 1990; Schultz, 2008). Teaching strategies using the business-as-usual approach are fairly standardized and routine: teachers talk, and students sit and listen or read and complete worksheets. Teaching to pass high-stakes tests takes over most of the school day. Students are tested mainly on what they have memorized and are usually marched through the material with few, if any, adaptations for their individual learning styles, rates, skills, and interest. Although there is some variety and individualization at the elementary level, there is very little at the secondary level.

Furthermore, course content is fairly uniform among schools and is not selected on the basis of student interest or experiential background; instead, it is selected according to that material deemed necessary to pass tests. In fact, course content becomes increasingly removed from students' day-to-day experiences as they progress through the secondary grade levels, even though older students become more concerned about their personal identities and their relationships with their immediate environment. Course content also tends to emphasize the White, wealthy male experience, or it presents information in a sterile, passive manner that neither invites nor encourages student participation. Also, content is taught in English, with the assumption that academic learning can take place only in English. Although attempts during the past three decades to make curricula multicultural, bilingual, and nonsexist have removed many blatant omissions and stereotypes and have added culturally diverse pictures, examples, and some story content, most texts have not substantially enlarged the center of attention beyond European Americans and, to a lesser extent, African Americans.

In the business-as-usual approach, students tend to be grouped for instruction in ways that reproduce social stratification patterns in the larger society. For example, in the elementary grades, ability grouping in reading and math usually reinforces race and social class differences, and groups are usually taught in ways that help them become increasingly segregated over the years. The use of tracking is widespread in our secondary schools. In tracking, certain students—primarily those of White and middle- or upper-class backgrounds—are taken from their elementary school ability groups and prepared for college; other students—primarily those of lower-class and minority backgrounds—are prepared for blue- or pink-collar labor; yet others are prepared for the "general" labor market. We need to note here that some Asian American students are performing excellently in school, but not all groups of Asian Americans or immigrants from Southeast Asia are doing so. The model minority slogan attached to Asian American students can cause teachers to miss instructional opportunities by assuming that the students know more than they actually do and that all Asian Americans students are high achievers.

Special education often constitutes a track below the lower track for students whom the regular program is unable to accommodate, whereas gifted programs offer the most socially advantaged children the best instruction. Students who manage to be placed in the upper groups are often similar to their teachers and are more likely to find school stimulating. Other students—the numbers increase in the higher grades—often find school boring and irrelevant. However, it is not the idea of education that turns students off, for most recognize the value in learning and want to learn. What turns many students off is teaching that is routine and passive, course content that is unconnected to daily life, curriculum and pedagogy that do not meet their language needs, lack of accommodation to different learning styles, and a lack of intellectual challenge.

We interviewed students who were from a working-class background and attended a desegregated school, and asked them about their perceptions of school (Grant & Sleeter, 1996). We found them critical of what the typical classroom offers but cognizant of what makes them want to learn. Regarding the business-as-usual teaching approach, students made the following comments:

JODY: I got science first hour, and you know you're gonna be doing an experiment or taking notes or something. It's one of three things: you take notes, you read, or you do an experiment, and that's it. And you know what's coming up and it's not no fun, it's better if you get surprised.

SHIRLEY: We always do a certain thing through the week [in English]. Like the first day we do these little things, we read and then we have to answer questions about it. And the second day, he's got it planned day through day so if you miss Tuesday you know what you did Tuesday because you always do the same thing. Tuesday we have to work out of a workbook. And Wednesday we finish up the workbook, turn in the assignment, and start on our spelling test. Like, we write down words and get their meanings and stuff. And it goes on like that. It's boring in his class.

ANGELA: Social studies was boring because I just sat there. We just sat down and listened to him and that gets boring.

PHIL: A lot of the reason why the kids screw up in class is because they can see no practical use for what they are learning.

The students also appraised various teaching strategies for us, indicating which ones helped them to learn and which ones turned them on to learning (see Table 1.1). (Although different groups of students may rate activities differently, teachers are often unaware of or overlook students' appraisals.)

As noted earlier, some teachers stimulate student learning effectively, and students know which teachers do so. The students we interviewed (Grant & Sleeter, 1996) commented about the classes in which they felt they had learned the most. For example, one student commented on teaching strategies and curriculum content:

KRISTEN: Multicultural [education] I like because it's different and [I like] publications because it's fun.

RESEARCHER: What makes publications fun?

KRISTEN: You get to go out and report and interview people, write stories to put in the [school newspaper].

RESEARCHER: Why do you like multicultural education?

KRISTEN: You get to study all the different people and stuff you never knew before—things that people say about people that are in books and

Table 1.1   Students' Appraisals of Classroom Activities

Like, Learn From This Activity	Neutral or Mixed Appraisals	Don't Like, Don't Learn From This Activity
Small-group projects Whole-class discussions in which kids do most of the talking	Independent project Recitation (teacher asks questions and kids respond)	Listening to lecture without taking notes Watching films (especially science films) Interviewing people
Listening to speakers Doing handouts Reading, then answering questions	Taking lecture notes Labs, experiments	Reading

Source: Adapted from Grant & Sleeter (1996), p. 139.

stuff that you think is true, and we learn the truth about it. Like how the whites treated the Indians a long time ago. (p. 162)

Grace spoke with us about tests, and her comments may come as a surprise:

RESEARCHER: What do you think about those kinds of tests that you got today? You have to write definitions and then answer questions on the last part. They weren't really questions that you could answer by giving one or two words. It looked like they were questions you really had to think about.

GRACE: Yeah. We had to write long definitions for them and then you had to write what you thought on the last ones.

RESEARCHER: Would you rather have a test like that where you write down what you think or where you write down answers?

GRACE: What I think.

RESEARCHER: In other classes, are you asked to write down what you think like you were in this one?

GRACE: No, in most of the classes they give you notes, and you have to study those notes, and then what is in those notes you have to write on the test.

RESEARCHER: What is different about the class you were just in?

GRACE: I guess it's harder. (p. 167)

Hal expressed a definite interest in being able to formulate questions to direct his learning:

RESEARCHER: So you feel that interviewing is a good way to learn?

HAL: Yeah, because you're asking questions that you want to know and they're giving you answers that are interesting about what you're asking and stuff.

RESEARCHER: How about listening to speakers in class?

HAL: Yeah, because again you're asking questions that you want to know. One of my friends' dad came here and he was from Lebanon and we got to ask questions about it. It's easier to remember than learning from a book because they're telling us stuff that you really don't care about. This way you're asking what you want to know. (p. 168)

Lupe underscored the value of active participation in learning:

LUPE: In our government class we have to take a vote and the whole class is all together in it. We make up our own tests and take votes and stuff. That was only in one class. We only did it one time.

RESEARCHER: What did you think about that?

LUPE: I like it because that way you get more ideas. (pp. 168–169)

Finally, Alvin emphasized the importance of curriculum content being multicultural:

RESEARCHER: Do you think it's important for other kids here to know about what the blacks do, who the heroes are, the contributions made?

ALVIN: Yeah, because some people think that blacks are troublemakers. They don't know what they do or nothing. (p. 171)

Consider again the question with which we opened this chapter: What would it be like to be a student in your own classroom or in one with which you are familiar? What is school like for Brad, or Juanita, or Yvonne, or Carlos, or Ngoc? Does it turn them on to learning, or does it teach them routines and ignore the importance of using their own minds? If this first chapter has stirred some emotion, we encourage you to study this book carefully and to use it to help you examine and experiment with your own teaching.

▶ CONCERNS AND CHALLENGES

A concern you may have is that the home and neighborhood circumstances of some students make it hard for them to concentrate on school. Some students have personal problems that can frustrate the patience and creativity of dedicated teachers. For example, it is hard for a student to get turned on to math if he or she is hungry, worried about a problem at home, homeless, believes she or he is incapable of doing well in school, feels intimidated by high-stakes tests, doesn't understand the language of instruction, feels abandoned by a loved one, is worried about being pregnant, is concerned about his or her safety in traveling to and from school, or is preoccupied with being popular. Other students may have less intense personal problems, such as being overly clothes conscious, that can also frustrate a teacher. Although this book does not deal specifically with the problems that students bring to school, it is important to consider carefully how these factors can limit students' abilities, as well as the extent to which teachers use them as excuses for not trying to turn students on to learning.

Consider the following example: Several years ago one of the authors took up ice skating during a stressful period. The author would often arrive at the ice rink feeling moody, depressed, and preoccupied. After an hour of intense skating instruction and practice, the author would discover that personal problems had drifted to the back of the mind, while the activity and fun of the immediate learning situation took over. Skating instruction not only pushed aside personal worries for a while, but it also left the author with a refreshing feeling of having learned something new, having accomplished something. Thank goodness the skating instructor never labeled the author as too "emotionally disturbed" (not to mention too old!) to learn! In fact, the skating instructor's skill, enthusiasm, persistence, and interest contributed to the author's sense of well-being by providing a delightful alternative to the author's problems for an hour and by helping the author achieve something in spite of whatever else might have been going wrong that day. So it is with good teaching. It may not solve a student's problems, but it may partially divert a student from them by providing an opportunity for the student to develop self-respect and to enjoy life and companionship for several hours a day.

Entertainment should not be confused with teaching; during the 1960s through the early 1980s, for example, such was often the case. Teachers at that time were overly concerned with making students like them and with showing students that they liked them. The affective side of teaching is important, but the cognitive side—helping students to develop to the best of their academic ability—is equally important.

▶ THE PLAN OF THE BOOK

This book is chock-full of insightful curriculum and instruction ideas. A close reading of the different phases of the lesson plans will add to teachers' pedagogical knowledge and skills. The book does not use a "recipe" approach to turning on learning. Although it contains many practical and useful ideas for successful teaching, its primary intent is to help you develop your own analytical and creative teaching skills.

In the remaining five chapters of *Turning on Learning*, we provide a framework for examining five different teaching approaches that address human diversity—race, ethnicity, gender, social class, disability, and sexual orientation. In our work with teachers, we have observed that they have varying perspectives of human differences and of how to handle them in the classroom. Their perspectives can be grouped into five approaches, each having its own distinct goals, assumptions, and practices.

Chapter 2, "Teaching the Exceptional and Culturally Different," addresses the issue of how to help students who do not succeed in the existing classroom or societal mainstream. The approach discussed here builds bridges between the capabilities of the student and the demands of the school and wider society, so that the student can learn to function successfully in these contexts.

Chapter 3, "Human Relations," is concerned with helping students to get along better by appreciating each other and themselves. This approach concentrates on building positive feelings.

In Chapter 4, "Single-Group Studies," groups that tend to be left out of the existing curricula are discussed. This approach teaches students about groups such as women, Arab Americans, African Americans, Asian Americans, people with disabilities, and people who are gay or lesbian.

Chapter 5, "Multicultural Education," combines much of the first three approaches. It suggests changes to most existing school practices for all students so that the school and classroom may become more concerned with human diversity, choice, and equal opportunity. It is hoped that such changes will bring about greater cultural pluralism and equal opportunity in society at large as today's students become tomorrow's citizens.

Finally, Chapter 6, "Multicultural and Social Justice Education," addresses social inequalities among groups in society at large as well as in students' own experiences, power, and social justice. The primary goals of this approach are to prepare students to work actively in groups and individually, to deal constructively with social problems, and to take charge of their own futures. To this end, the intersectionality of social constructs such as race, gender, class, sexual orientation, and the effects of power are used as the framework for teaching, research, learning, and social action.

We encourage you to read all of the chapters. Unless a particular chapter title strikes you as especially interesting, you will probably find it most helpful to read the chapters in sequence, since the approaches build on each other. Once you have finished reading the book, you will probably find that one approach appeals more to you than the others, although you may also like aspects of other approaches. The approach that appeals to you the most should provide a point of departure for your own professional growth. Study that approach; work with its ideas; make it as much a part of your teaching as you can. If after you have worked with the approach you find it limited in ways you did not recognize initially, you may wish to reconsider the other approaches.

You need not practice only one approach. However, if you find yourself drawing bits and pieces from all the approaches without giving careful thought to any one approach in particular, ask yourself whether you are really engaging in business as usual. We have found that teachers who believe they are eclectic actually either prefer business as usual or simply have not spent enough time studying and applying each approach. We also encourage you to read our companion book, *Making Choices for Multicultural Education: Five Approaches to Race, Class, and Gender* (2009), to investigate further the thinking behind each approach.

▶ THE ORGANIZATIONAL PLAN

Each chapter begins with an explanation of the teaching approach. Next are Action Research Activities that investigate some aspect of teaching that helps to implement the approach (and possibly subsequent approaches). The activities can help you to gather information about students, the curriculum, the school, or the school's community that will enable you to examine your classroom behavior and to teach more effectively. Following the activities are several pairs of sample lesson plans that are written in a before-and-after format. The "Before" lesson plans represent samples of curriculum and instruction as they usually exist: business as usual. Because they are based on the observations of teachers, popular curriculum guides and textbooks, and lesson plans developed by teachers, they may be familiar to you. The "After" lesson plans illustrate ways that existing curriculum and instruction can be changed to implement the approach described in each chapter and to turn on learning. Finally, each "After" lesson plan is followed by a discussion of why the plan was changed.

The primary goal of this book is to help you examine existing patterns of curriculum and instruction and then learn how to change them to respond better to human diversity—to turn on more learning. By studying the lesson plans and discussions of changes carefully, you will learn how changes to business as usual can enable you to reach more students and to make a positive difference. You will also benefit from examining your own curriculum and instruction. Take a lesson or unit that you are planning to teach next week or next month and treat it as a "Before" plan. Then think of as many ways as possible that you can change the plan to implement the approach described in the chapter.

Spend time developing a good, workable "After" plan for yourself, and then try it out in the classroom. Do this over a period of time with several lessons and units, until you get the feel of the practices described in each chapter and until you can see what changes are improving your own teaching. As you become comfortable with some new ideas, try out additional ones.

Do not limit yourself to studying the lesson plans in your own subject area or grade level. The lessons in this book are illustrations of ideas; they are not simply recipes to follow. For example, if you teach ninth-grade math, you may find some good ideas about adapting instruction to students' learning styles in an elementary social studies lesson. Think about how you can use those ideas to help teach ninth-grade math.

We also encourage you to work with your colleagues. Discuss with them the approaches that make the most sense to you and why. You may not reach consensus, but you will probably find yourself thinking about what you are trying to accomplish when you teach. Exchange ideas. Observe each other teach, if possible, when trying something new. When you collaborate with a colleague, it provides an opportunity for a scaffolding of knowledge and for more in-depth learning for teachers and students. Throughout the book, we demonstrate the importance and value of students' learning to work cooperatively; the same can be said of teachers. Finally, do not feel that you have to master all the ideas in the text. Rather, use the book as a tool to help you grow.

References

Anyon, J. (1981). Social class and school knowledge. *Curriculum Inquiry, 11*, 3–42.

Children Defense Fund. (2008). *Each Day in America*. Retrieved July 2008. www.childrendefense.org/site/Page Server?pagename = research_national_data_each_day.

Cuban, L. (1993). *How teachers taught* (2nd ed.). New York: Longman.

Everhart, R. (1983). *Reading, writing, and resistance*. Boston: Routledge and Kegan Paul.

Goodlad, J. I. (1984). *A place called school*. New York: McGraw-Hill.

Grant, C. A., & Sleeter, C. E. (1996). *After the school bell rings* (2nd ed.). New York: Falmer.

Lareau, A. (2000). *Home advantage* (2nd ed.). London: Falmer Press.

Martinez, S., & Dahl, K. (Eds.). (1998). *The state of Americas children yearbook: 1998*. Washington, DC: CDF Publications.

National Center for Education Statistics. (1999). *Dropout rates in the United States 1999*. Washington, DC: Author.

National Center for Education Information. (2005). *Profile of Teachers in the U.S. 2005*. Washington, DC. Author. Retrieved December 30, 2007.

National Education Association (2004). NEA on Dropout Prevention: Make High School Graduation a National Priority. Washington, DC: Author.

Oakes, J. (1985). *Keeping track*. New Haven, CT: Yale University Press.

Payne, C. (1984). *Getting what we ask for*. Westport, CT: Greenwood.

Schultz, B. (2008). *Spectular things happen along the way: Lessons from an urban classroom*. New York: Teacher College Press.

Sleeter, C. E., & Grant, C. A. (2006). *Making choices for multicultural education: Five approaches to race, class, and gender* (5th ed.). Hoboken, NY: Wiley.

Solomon, R. P. (1992). *Black resistance in high school*. Albany, NY: SUNY Press.

Valli, L. (1986). *Becoming clerical workers*. Boston: Routledge and Kegan Paul.

Weis, L. (1990). *Working class without work*. New York: Routledge and Kegan Paul.

West, E. (2001). *Imagine the possibilities: Sourcebook for educators committed to the educational success of students experiencing homelessness*. San Francisco: Author.

CHAPTER 2

Teaching the Exceptional and Culturally Different

How can you maintain a high level of teaching performance in the following situations?

- You are Latino/a or African American and some of your colleagues, who are of the same ethnicity, are buying into the argument that Black and Latino/a students' major difficulties for learning are based in their culture and family organization.
- You have a new student who recently moved to the United States from Bosnia. She speaks only a handful of English words, and her life experiences are quite different from yours as well as from those of the other students in the class.
- Three of your students spend a portion of their school day in learning disabilities classes, one attends a class for the emotionally disturbed, and another is visually impaired.
- Most of the students in your class are Mexican Americans (and you are not). Some of their manners of responding to you are unfamiliar to you.
- You are transferred to a new school, and most of your students live at or below the poverty level, which is different from your own socioeconomic background.
- A group of students in your class seems tuned out, unmotivated, and academically behind.

Most teachers encounter situations like these during the course of their careers. The situations share a common characteristic: One or more of the students differ from students the teacher is used to and familiar with. As a result, old routines and strategies do not work well. For example, students may be unable to read the material that the teacher is accustomed to assigning, or they may find the material uninteresting and irrelevant to their own experiences and goals. Students may speak a language or dialect foreign to the teacher and sometimes use it when the teacher feels they should use Standard English. Students may "act out" when the teacher does not expect it, but they themselves may not consider it to be acting out. Students may not participate in classroom activities that the teacher believes to be motivating; they may talk or whisper among themselves when the teacher expects silence, or sit passively when the teacher is trying to conduct a discussion. Perhaps they find the subject matter boring or fail to understand explanations the teacher thought made sense.

Increasingly, teachers are being held accountable for student learning. The best teachers actively take responsibility for student learning and search for strategies that will enable students in their classroom to succeed. This chapter addresses these kinds of situations. It involves changing one's instructional patterns and classroom procedures to fit the students and to facilitate their academic success. (Chapter 2 of *Making Choices for Multicultural Education* [Sleeter & Grant, 2009] develops debates and theoretical ideas behind this approach in some detail.) We use the term *exceptional* to refer to students in special education, but the term can also refer to any student who is not succeeding academically. The term *culturally different* refers to a student whose cultural background—race, ethnicity, language, or social class—differs from that of the teacher. The term also implies that there is sufficient cultural difference between the teacher and the students that effective teaching and learning break down—although, of course, this does not necessarily happen when the teacher and students differ racially or ethnically.

All five approaches in this text emphasize processes for identifying and building on students' strengths. All students have learning strengths—they come to our classrooms having already learned a good deal in their lives. The long-term goal of the approach in this chapter is to enable students to succeed in learning the traditional curriculum in traditional classrooms for school district achievement tests, and later to succeed in the existing society. Success is enabled by building on strengths students bring. Approaches in later chapters also build on the goal of student achievement but at the same time question what counts as traditional learning, test-driven learning, and cultural assimilation.

▶ BRIDGES TO THE CURRICULUM

The approach in this chapter involves building that enable students to succeed and to adapt to the requirements of the traditional classroom. It takes as a given the curriculum defined by state curriculum standards or school district curriculum frameworks, adapting that curriculum somewhat to relate it to the students. In some cases, the bridges are temporary; in other cases, building these bridges entails broadening a teacher's repertoire of what counts as "normal" ways of teaching and learning.

Expectations for High-Level Learning

Teacher expectations are the linchpin of student achievement. When teachers expect students to learn—not simply hope that they do but expect that they will—they take responsibility for making sure that learning happens. They find out what works for their own students and what doesn't, they figure out how to fill in gaps in learning or supports for learning, and they routinely communicate to students that they believe in the students' capacities to learn at high levels (Haberman, 1995). Teachers who hold low expectations for students often present—not necessarily consciously—boring or demeaning schoolwork, which discourages students from wanting to participate. The students get turned off and react accordingly, which the teacher then sees as evidence of their inability to learn. This sets up a cycle that is hard to break. One way of breaking that cycle is to ask yourself how you would teach your students if they were gifted—and then teach that way.

Holding high expectations for students means expecting, not only that they will be able to learn academic skills for their grade level, but also that they have both the capacity for postsecondary education and the commitment and desire to graduate; and should be prepared accordingly. For example, algebra may not seem practical in everyday life, but knowledge of algebra is useful if one wants to attend college. Moses and Cobb (2001) argue that mastering high-status knowledge such as algebra, which opens doors to further opportunities, is a very important civil rights issue. Teachers with high expectations strive to guide their students toward acquiring the knowledge that will help them later in life: at the next grade level, in preparation for college, and ultimately in the kinds of life opportunities that their communities desire for them. When your students leave high school, they will compete with other students for college entrance, jobs, and scholarships, and teachers need to prepare them for these challenges. Students' low expectations of their abilities or teachers' overconcentration on teaching them about their own cultures to the exclusion of the mainstream "culture of power" can be detrimental to these students. Ideas for teaching traditionally hard subjects more effectively are presented in the lesson plans in this chapter, such as "Functions" (p. 55), "Polymers" (p. 58), and "Writing a Five-Paragraph Essay" (p. 51). In addition, teachers with high expectations do not assume that some other staff members are informing students about the courses they should take in order to get into college without a detour to the community college to take courses not taken in high school. A quick story here will help to illuminate our point.

During the holiday, while standing in line to return gifts, one of the authors struck up a conservation with an African American mother who was accompanied by her two sons. As inquisitive and friendly as always, he soon discovered that one of the sons was a sophomore in a high school just outside Madison. He said to the highschooler—let's call him Paul—"I know you are planning to go to college, but have you decided which one?" Paul stated that he had not decided. The author quickly said, "that's OK, you have time—and please consider UW–Madison." He then asked, "What courses are you taking to prepare for the competition of college entrance?" The author discovered from Paul and his mother that they had received only minimal information about higher education and Paul's preparing for it. The author quickly explained to the mother and her sons about college requirements including the need for years of language, mathematic, science, English, community service, and so forth and encouraged them to set up an appointment with the school counselor.

The point of this story is that having high expectations, being a bit inquisitive, and not assuming that some other faculty member has "covered" that area of schooling will probably be helpful to your students.

Learning Styles

What is your preference for learning something new and a bit difficult? Do you prefer reading, viewing photos, videos, PowerPoint, discussion, worksheets, or working in groups? Common sense and the education literature tell us that our students have different learning styles. Students who differ from ourselves, in particular, may prefer to learn in ways that differ from our own preferences. For example, some students learn a concept better when they read about it, others when they actually observe the concept (e.g., oxidation of material), and still others when they use a combination of modalities, such as discussing, touching, and writing. We also know that some students need a great deal of structure (such as a time schedule, a task schedule, or writing guidelines), whereas other students prefer little structure, employing their creativity when doing an assignment.

Learning style is a complex idea and involves how people perceive, process, store, and retrieve information. In a learning situation, what cues does an individual attend to? How does the individual connect cues? What strategies does the individual use to make sense of new information or ideas? With what "old information" in the individual's head is the new information connected and stored? Everyone develops ways of approaching these information-processing tasks, but we all do not develop the same ways (Hollins, 1996). What is your preference for learning something that is new and/or difficult? Do you prefer reading, pictures, videos, discussion, worksheets, and/or working in a small group with others?

Howard Gardner's (2000) idea of multiple intelligences is not the same thing as learning style, but gets at the idea of multiple strengths for knowing the world. According to Gardner, there are at least eight different kinds of intelligence, and everyone has a profile of strengths and weaknesses. These include linguistic intelligence and logical-mathematical intelligence (which schools focus on most heavily), musical intelligence, interpersonal intelligence, intrapersonal intelligence, spatial intelligence, bodily-kinesthetic intelligence, and naturalist intelligence. Students who are not as strong in verbal skills as they are in other intelligence areas often do not do as well in the classroom as they might if classrooms were to support other intelligence areas as well as they support verbal skills. Gardner (1995) recommends that teachers delve deeply into fewer rich topics, rather than covering many topics superficially, and in delving, approach topics through a variety of ways of knowing that will engage the variety of students they are teaching.

Learning styles overlap somewhat with cultural background and gender. Although not all members of a cultural or gender group learn in the same way, patterns exist concerning how members of different groups tend to approach tasks. These patterns develop because of factors such as child-rearing practices and the roles that children are expected to occupy as adults (Boykin & Allen, 1988; Fennema & Peterson, 1987; Hale, 1982; Levinsohn, 2007; Pallapu, 2007; Philips, 1983; Shade, 1989). Rather than generalizing about your own students based on research on group differences, however, it is much more useful to investigate directly your own students' learning style preferences.

Action Research Activity 2.1 can help you to begin to examine your students' learning styles. Based on your discoveries, you probably will want to emphasize teaching strategies that involve students more actively. In other words, we all can afford to cut back on the routines of lecturing, reading the text, and answering the questions. Instead, we should teach students the benefits of working cooperatively with others.

Once students learn to work together, they are much more likely to be academically successful, and you will enjoy the intrinsic rewards that come from your effort. Multimedia computer programs such as HyperStudio lend themselves very well to increased student involvement and appeal to multiple learning styles. Examples of adaptations to student learning style are found in several lesson plans in this chapter: "Sentences, Subjects, and Predicates" (p. 28), "Word Usage" (p. 42), "Mong History" (p. 46), "Functions" (p. 55), "Polymers" (p. 58), and "Cardiovascular Health" (p. 62).

Relevant Curriculum

Students must have a firm grasp of the basics—reading, mathematics, and writing. Good teachers know how to identify topics, examples, or introductions to lessons that are relevant and of interest to their students. They are good at locating and using curriculum materials that make the students want to learn. They know how to start where students are, and develop skills and concepts they are expected to teach, in a way that students see as relevant. For example, in their study of high-performing Hispanic schools, Reyes, Scribner, and Scribner (1999) found that teachers used culturally responsive pedagogy. This means that the teachers viewed their students as capable of high levels of achievement and considered their cultural background to be a valuable resource on which to build. They took students' interests and questions seriously, and they regarded what students learned in their homes and communities as a "fund of knowledge" on which new academic learning could be built. In classrooms, teachers engaged students in dialogue with peers, as well as with the teachers, around higher-order thinking. Honoring students' interests, questions, language, and culture did not mean not teaching them, but rather using these as springboards for complex, new academic learning.

There are many ways to find out more about your students' experiential backgrounds and interests and the community-based funds of knowledge they bring. Action Research Activity 2.2 is one tool you can use. Examples of lesson plans on how to relate curriculum more directly to students' backgrounds include "Our Grandparents Will Always Be Special" (p. 23), "The Research Presentation" (p. 34), "Word Usage" (p. 42), "Functions" (p. 55), and "Cardiovascular Health" (p. 62).

Skill Levels

In any given class, some students are performing below and some above grade level. How can you accommodate a range of skill levels? Should you teach to the midrange of the class? refer some students to special education? seek the help of parents or an aid?

We have observed teachers who work successfully with a wide range of student skill levels, and one of their keys to success is using others—parents, older students, student teachers, and aides—to help meet students at their varying levels of competence. They also use varied grouping patterns rather than permanent ability groups (e.g., to teach specific skills such as spelling, temporary skill groups can be formed), and often group students heterogeneously to encourage tutoring and high aspirations among low-achieving students. Furthermore, they use various forms of assessment to guide instruction more than to assign grades or describe achievement levels. They constantly monitor students' learning so that they can tailor instruction to students' skills and build those skills intentionally.

We stress the importance of teachers meeting the skill level of students because we still observe students who, for example, read at a fourth-grade level but are asked to learn new material from seventh-grade textbooks. Furthermore, these students may try to hide their learning problems from teachers. For instance, they may carry around the seventh-grade textbook because they are embarrassed to let their friends know they are reading a fourth-grade textbook. Teachers must be alert to these tendencies and at the same time help students to raise their skill levels. The lesson plans "Polymers" (p. 28) and "Cardiovascular Health" (p. 62) demonstrate adaptations for diverse skill levels.

Language

Bilingual education and non-Standard English dialects have been the subject of heated debate in the media and throughout society. Many of these debates have been guided by the assumptions that monolingual people commonly make rather than by research on language and learning.

The child who understands little English will not learn new academic content taught in English, nor will the child demonstrate academic competence in tests given in English. If we want children to learn academics, as much as possible we need to teach in ways that are comprehensible to the child. The child's first language is generally the child's strongest language foundation; however, that language needs to be built academically if children are to continue to learn in it. Teachers can use many strategies to make academic content in English more comprehensible. Peer tutors can be helpful not only for translation and communication but also as language role models who can convey to students a sense of friendship—that is, that the teacher cares enough to provide a friend the student can consult when language problems arise. Cooperative learning activities give students an opportunity to process material with each other in their own language as well as in English. Visual cues, such as demonstrations and pictures, give students nonlinguistic sources of information to bolster their newly acquired English vocabulary. Physical activities (such as Total Physical Response strategies (Asher, 1966)) help children connect English with what they know.

One of the myths of bilingual education is that it does not help students learn English. In contrast to this myth, bilingual programs are required to include instruction in English language development; however, many bilingual teachers find it difficult to do this in segregated contexts in which the teacher is the student's only English role model. English as a Second Language (ESL) and bilingual teachers are excellent professional resources to whom the teacher should not hesitate to turn when necessary. Generally, students respond positively to teachers who are interested in learning about their backgrounds. Teachers who have difficulty working with students who speak little English, or who are unprepared to teach non-English-speaking students, can learn to do so successfully. One of our colleagues periodically consulted with ESL and bilingual teachers to discuss ideas and events that would help her to understand better how to work with limited-English-speaking students. The lesson plans "Our Grandparents Will Always Be Special" (p. 23), and "Cardiovascular Health" (p. 62) show how to work with students who are in the process of learning English.

Because limited-English-speaking students are likely to be the major persons responsible for English communication in their families, teachers of these students should prepare notices for home in both languages. In addition, teachers should ask the home–school coordinator or a bilingual staff member to help encourage parents to meet with them to discuss classroom goals and activities. We once spoke at a PTA meeting with an audience of over one hundred parents. About one-third were European American, one-third African American, and one-third Mexican American, many of whom did not speak English and did not attend school meetings regularly. We spoke in English but with an ongoing translation in Spanish. Both the English-speaking and the Spanish-speaking parents told us they found the experience gratifying. The next PTA meeting drew an equally diverse parent group; the large turnout of Spanish-speaking parents was attributed mainly to the bilingual format of the previous meeting. When the school discontinued bilingual PTA meetings, the Spanish-speaking parents stopped coming, because they could not follow the discussion or participate.

English-speaking students who do not speak Standard English need to learn how to speak it. It is likely that they can understand Standard English when it is spoken to them, even though their teachers may have difficulty understanding the students' dialects. Action Research Activity 2.3 will help you identify linguistic patterns your students have mastered to assist you in teaching them a second dialect: Standard English. Teaching the new dialect is much like teaching a foreign language: The differences between the two "languages" must be made clear, and continued practice is essential (see the lesson plan "Word Usage" on p. 42). However, teachers must be careful not to punish or criticize students for having mastered their home dialect; rather, they should view it as a language base on which mastery of an additional dialect can be built. Some teachers choose to explain to students that there is "everyday talk" (or "street talk") and "school talk" (or "formal talk"). Delpit (1995) reports that one teacher of Athabaskan Indians referred to the student talk as "Heritage English." This teacher helped the students to appreciate their language by savoring the words and discussing the nuances of their language. However, it must be made clear that "everyday talk" is to be used with friends or outside of school and "school talk" must be used in school. Most students accept this distinction as long as they are not asked to choose one dialect as the "correct" way to talk in all situations.

Success Stories

The ultimate goal of this approach to teaching the exceptional and culturally different is to incorporate all students into the U.S. mainstream. Students who do not do well in school need extra help and encouragement. Role models can help: For example, low-income students can learn about successful people who had grown up in poverty, female students can learn about successful women in various fields, and students of color can learn about successful people from their own communities. Role models like these can encourage students to become part of the mainstream and can discourage them from giving up (see "Mong History," p. 46, and "Polymers," p. 58).

Relationships With Students

For many students, a caring relationship with the teacher is a prerequisite to learning. If the teacher does not seem to like the student personally, some students will not try in school. In many classrooms, teachers establish caring relationships with all their students, but in many others, teachers expect students to care about academics without necessarily having a warm relationship with the teacher. Students then tune out, and the teacher becomes frustrated because they are not working. Jaime Escalante (1990), who achieved acclaim for his success in teaching college-level math in an East Los Angeles barrio high school, attributes part of his success to his loving his students and teaching them accordingly. His students knew he cared about and believed in them, so they worked for him.

We know quite a few teachers who would like to establish warm relationships with students but are bothered by students' classroom behavior. They become frustrated when students talk out of turn, jostle each other as they walk down the hall, blurt out answers, and so forth. Differences in communication and interaction styles can short-circuit good classroom relationships as teachers interpret student behavior as disruptive, aggressive, passive, cold, and so forth. And when teachers are frustrated or irritated with students, students know it and react accordingly. Action Research Activity 2.4 has helped many teachers become sensitive to communication and cultural patterns their students use in the classroom, as well as cultural patterns the teacher uses and considers "normal." Becoming aware of how cultural differences in interaction style play out in the classroom will not by itself make you care about your students, but it can help you get past feelings of frustration that hinder many caring relationships in developing.

Connections With the Home and Community

Although space does not permit us to fully develop the idea of making connections with students' homes and the community, its importance needs to be emphasized. Teachers should familiarize themselves with the communities in which they teach by spending time there, getting to know parents, and finding out what parents want for their children. It is also useful to compare parents' wishes regarding schooling with your own or your parents'. In general, parents in all socioeconomic and cultural groups want their children to receive the best education possible. Also inquire about the system parents use for making sure homework gets done; if they do not have a system, help them develop one, and if that does not work, identify a community organization that can help with homework. Tell parents about what goes on in your classroom, and make sure your conversations with them are two-way interchanges and that you speak in a way they can understand. We have talked with many teachers who believe that home–school relationships are important but expect this to mean only that the parents come into the school and mostly listen to the teacher.

It has to be a two-way street: Teachers who expect parents to come into the school need to be willing to spend time in the parents' community and also to listen to the parent. Making the effort to get to know parents and other community members on their "turf" eventually pays off immensely in terms of student engagement and learning.

▶ ACTION RESEARCH ACTIVITY 2.1

Learning Styles

This activity is an introduction to investigating learning styles. The following items describe things to investigate, but you need to decide how to investigate them. Collect the requested information on several students, using the record sheet shown in Figure 2.1. You may notice patterns based on gender and ethnic background, but do not stereotype

For each student, record data you collect about the following items related to the student's preferred style of learning.

Student's name _____

		Method of Data Collection	Findings
1. Style of working:	Alone With others		
2. Learning Modality:	Watching Reading Listening Discussing Touching Moving Writing		
3. Content:	People Things		
4. Need for Structure:	High Low		
5. Details Versus Generalities			

Figure 2.1   Learning Styles Record Sheet

certain groups as learning a certain way. Use the patterns you discover in your students' learning style preferences as guides for selecting teaching strategies.

Working Alone Versus Working with Others

Many students work best cooperatively with a partner or small group, whereas others work best individually. The student's preference should be respected; however, those who have not learned to work cooperatively may enjoy and benefit from the experience.

Preferred Learning Modalities

The term *preferred learning modalities* refers to the sensory channels or processes that students prefer to use for acquiring new information or ideas. They can be investigated in the following ways:

- Give students choices, and record which ones they choose most often.
- Record the success with which students have learned under each condition.
- Ask students which they prefer to use for gaining or expressing new ideas or information.

Content About People Versus Content About Things

Students' interest in content can be investigated in the following ways:

- Offer students choices (e.g., a story topic or math story problems), and observe which one they select most often.

- Ask students which topic they usually prefer (but do not force them to choose—for some, it makes no difference).

For each student, record data you collect about the following items related to the student's preferred style of learning.

Structured Versus Nonstructured Tasks

Some students prefer tasks that are structured, whereas others prefer to create their own structure. The best way to investigate this preference is to give the student choices between highly structured work and open-ended work and determine which is chosen most often. Sometimes the teacher may simply ask students, particularly older students, but other students may not completely understand the teacher's question. Students who seem lost or do poorly on open-ended assignments probably need structured work; those who seem bored with structured assignments probably need open-ended work.

Details Versus the Overall Picture

Some students do meticulous work well, are attentive to details, and can work through small steps to arrive at the larger idea; other students need to view the larger, more general picture first and may become bored or lost with details or small steps. For instance, when writing stories, some students use grammar and mechanics correctly, but their stories may not have much point. Other students may produce good overall story ideas, but their first drafts are weak in grammar and mechanics. Students' preferences for details or generalities are best investigated through observation. Although all students eventually need to work on both details and generalities, some will have trouble learning these concepts if the teacher emphasizes one or the other prematurely.

▶ ACTION RESEARCH ACTIVITY 2.2

Students' Experiential Background

Spend time in the neighborhood where your students live, observing and listening. Look and listen for things you can use as examples or as lessons to help teach concepts in your curriculum. It may be difficult to refrain from making judgments, but the more open you are, the more you will find you can help the students. Pay attention to such things as geometric shapes in building designs, the kinds of plant life and rocks that are present, the types of stores that are present, the styles of music played, the kinds of games children play, and so forth. Record your observations in Table 2.1.

▶ ACTION RESEARCH ACTIVITY 2.3

Dialect Difference

If your students speak a dialect of English with which you are unfamiliar, this activity can help you gain some understanding of its linguistic patterns. (A dialect is not the same thing as an accent or partial mastery of English by a speaker of another language.) Listen closely to how people say things. Below you will find a list of things to listen for.

Table 2.1

Observations	Related Academic Concepts	Ideas for Using Observations
1.		
2.		
3.		
4.		
5.		
6.		
7.		
8.		
9.		
10.		

See how many patterns you can detect. You may notice patterns that are not listed; if so, keep track of them also.

Phonemes (sounds)

- Are some consonant sounds pronounced differently than you are used to? Does it matter if the sound is at the beginning, middle, or end of the word?
- Are some vowel sounds pronounced differently than you are used to?
- Are consonant sounds that you pronounce dropped when they appear in certain places in words (such as at the end)?

Grammar

- Compared with the way you speak, are there differences in the way the past tense is indicated?
- Are there differences in the way the possessive is indicated?
- Pay attention to how the words *do* and *be* are used; look for patterns that differ from what you are used to.
- Are there differences in word order?
- Pay attention to patterns indicating the negative.
- Are there differences in the use of pronouns?
- Are there differences in the use of adverbs or adjectives?

Vocabulary

- Listen for words you are unfamiliar with; find out what they mean.
- Listen for words you are familiar with but seem to have a different meaning from what you are used to.
- Listen for phrases you are unfamiliar with or you do not use.
- Pay attention to words and phrases you use regularly that are not used regularly by the students you are working with.
- Pay attention to figurative or creative use of language.

Nonspoken Language

- Are facial expressions used differently than you are used to?
- Are gestures used differently than you are used to?
- Are voice inflections used differently than you are used to?
- Is rhythm or speed of talking different than what you are used to?
- Does the person prefer to be at the same distance from you that you are used to? closer? farther away?
- Does the person talk as loudly/softly as you are used to?

Social Context

Does the person switch dialects around different people or in different settings? If you notice a pattern and feel comfortable doing so, find out if he or she is aware of doing this.

▶ ACTION RESEARCH ACTIVITY 2.4

Interpersonal Communication Style

This activity is appropriate when observing two or more members of the same sociocultural group interacting with each other. Watch people on more than one occasion to discern communication patterns that are commonly used. Watch people talking naturally, and if you can do so unobtrusively, write descriptions of their behavior as they talk. Look for things such as the following:

- What distance do they maintain between themselves?
- What kinds of gestures are used?
- In what contexts do people touch each other? How do they touch, and where? (Some cultural groups touch a lot, others very little.)
- What do they do to indicate they are listening?
- How does a person "get the floor" when he or she wants to speak? (Does the person simply start talking? wait for an opening? use a hand gesture?)
- What level of loudness or softness of speech do people maintain?

If possible, watch an adult giving directions to, or reprimanding, a child who is a member of the adult's same sociocultural group.

- What does the adult say?
- What nonverbal behavior does the adult use?
- How does the child respond?

Compare the patterns you observed with patterns you expect or take for granted from your own cultural background. How do you react when students exhibit interaction patterns you observed? All of us can learn to code-switch between two different cultural patterns. In what ways might your students need to learn to code-switch when in school, and how can you help them learn to do this? In what ways might you need to learn to code-switch?

▶ LESSON PLAN[1]

Our Grandparents Will Always Be Special

BEFORE

Subject Areas: Social Science, Literature, and English Language Development

Grade Level: K–1

Time: Two lessons, two days

Students: English language learners whose primary language is Spanish, receiving English-only instruction

Objectives

1. Students will use the vocabulary words *grandfather*, *grandmother*, and *grandchild* in English.
2. Students will value grandparents in their own families.
3. Students will connect literature to their personal lives.

Suggested Procedures

1. Clarify expectations to students: "We will learn about grandparents so that you can know them better and continue to give them respect and love. You will write about your grandparents in your journals and apply the information we learned on 'caps' and periods in your writing."

2. Introduce the vocabulary words *grandmother*, *grandfather*, *grandchild*, *grandchildren*, and *great-grandparents*.

3. Select one of the following books and read it to students:

   Grandfather's Trolley by Bruce McMillan

   This book, in English, presents a photo essay about a little girl who goes for a ride in her grandfather's trolley car in the early 1900s.

   I Love Saturdays y Domingos by Alma Flor Ada

   This book tells the story of a little girl who visits her European American grandparents on Saturday and her Mexican American grandparents on Sunday. The story explains that, although the grandparents are different in many ways, they have much in common, in particular their love for their granddaughter.

4. In a whole group or in pairs, ask students to answer simple questions in English about their own grandparents. Ask questions such as, Do you know your grandparents? How many grandparents do you have? Where do your grandparents live? How are grandparents related to your mother and father? Do you know their grandparents? What do you like to do with your grandparents? Do you have nicknames for your grandparents?

5. The next day, read to the class *Just Grandma and Me* by Mercer Mayers. In this story, the main character and his grandmother spend a day at the beach.

[1] *Source:* Carolina Evans-Roman, Watsonville, California.

6. After discussing the book, have students draw pictures of themselves and their grandparents in their journals.

7. Ask each student to tell you about his or her picture in English.

Evaluation

1. Assess if students are able to use vocabulary words in the description of their pictures.

2. Assess if students are able to extend the literature and concept of grandparents to their own family in their journals.

Resources

Literature
Ada, A. F. (2002). *I love Saturdays y domingos*. New York: Atheneum.
McMillan, B. (1995). *Grandfather's trolley*. Cambridge, MA: Candlewick Press.
Mayers, M. (1997). *Just grandma and me*. Novato, CA: Living Books. (Available in multiple languages.)

Nuestros Abuelos Son Especiales (Our Grandparents Will Always Be Special)

AFTER

Subject Areas: Social Science, Literature

Grade Level: K–1

Time: Five lessons, five days

Students: English language learners whose primary language is Spanish, receiving bilingual instruction with literacy in Spanish

Objectives

1. Students will use vocabulary words to describe family members and elders in Spanish.

2. Students will explain why elders are important in their lives through discussion and recall of experiences with their grandparents.

3. Students will connect experiences with their grandparents to literacy and demonstrate this connection through writing.

4. Students will compare and contrast how their own local culture and the dominant culture perceive family and community elders.

5. Students will learn that, although their grandparents may be of different ethnic groups, their elders adore them equally as much.

Suggested Procedures

1. Prior to this unit, email or send a letter home to parents explaining the unit and asking if their child's grandparents live locally. Ask students' parents to write a short biography of or experience with their own parents and send a picture of them, if possible. Send a communication to grandparents who live locally, inviting them to a celebration honoring them and asking if they can share a story or skill with the class.

2. The first day of the unit, clarify expectations of the unit to students: "Vamos a aprender de sus abuelitos para que ustedes los puedan conocer mejor y seguir dándoles repecto y amor. Ustedes van a escribir de sus abuelitos en sus diários usando todo lo que saben de la escritura." ("We will learn about grandparents so that you can know them better and continue to give them respect and love. You will write about your grandparents in your journals and use all that you know about writing.")

3. Read to students *Amalia y Sus Primeras Tortillas* by Jerry Tello and Chon Bribiescas. In the story, a young girl tells about her grandmother who teaches her how to make tortillas "con cariño" (with affection). With the whole group, introduce the book's title and author and make predictions based on the picture on the cover. Then read the book aloud. Discuss questions such as the following:

> *¿Qué te ha enseñado tu abuelita?* (What has your grandmother taught you?)
> *¿Porqué es importante conocer a tus abuelitos?* (Why is it important to know your grandparents?)

After relaying your own memories, have students share their memories in pairs. Then have three or four students share memories in large group.

4. Model writing by modeling the thinking process in construction of an authentic sentence on chart paper, such as, *Las abuelitas siempre hacen las tortillas con cariño* ("Grandmothers always make tortillas with affection"). Focus students' attention on various concepts of print, such as capital letter, initial letter sound, spacing, and so on. Have the whole group reread. Point to the words, left to right and one by one. Have students individually locate a word, letter, or punctuation to be reinforced and circle it. Draw a picture to go with the story to reinforce picture and text correspondence.

5. Ask students to think of what they will write today in their journal about their grandmothers. Have each student share with a partner what he or she will be writing, and then have students each write and draw a picture. Ask students to share their pictures and writing with you, with another student, and/or with the whole class. As needed, scaffold writing with individual students: that is, individually assist a student by working within the student's Zone of Proximal Development, using the student's known knowledge to extend to new knowledge. Teacher and student write the student's story together, with the student writing what he or she can do and the teacher assisting with the student's unknown.

6. The second day, read *Los Regalos de Mi Abuelito* by Kratky and Ortiz, in which a little boy tells about the gifts his grandfather has given him, like his smile and his nose. Before reading the book, take a "picture walk": Tell the story through pictures to implant meaning and difficult vocabulary. Have children locate frequently occurring words they may know, such as *me, mi,* and *la.* Read with students, pointing to each word one by one. Using a discussion process similar to that of the first day, discuss questions such as the following:

> *¿Qué es algo que tu abuelito te ha dado?* (What is one thing your grandfather has given you?)

¿Porqué es importante respetar y querer a sus abuelitos? (Why is it important to respect and love your grandparents?)

7. Model writing using the same process as previously. Have students individually locate a word, letter, or punctuation to be reinforced and circle it. Draw a picture to go with the story to reinforce picture–text correspondence. Then have students write in their journal about their grandfathers, using a process similar to that of the day before. As needed, scaffold writing with individual students.

8. The third day, read aloud the book *Un Regalo para Abuelita/A Gift for Abuelita* by Luenn and Chapman. In this book, Grandmother dies, and Rosita misses her very much until her grandmother visits her on *Día de los Muertos*/Day of the Dead. Discuss the book by asking students to share memories of their grandmothers.

9. Using the same process as before, model the construction of a sentence on chart paper, have students each locate a word, letter, or punctuation mark, and have them each draw a picture to go with the story. Also, as before, have students draw pictures, write about their grandmothers or grandfathers in their journals, and share them with another student and/or the whole class.

10. The fourth day, read aloud *Guillermo Jorge Manuel José* by Fox and Vivas. In this book, a little boy befriends an elderly person and helps her recover her memory through different mementos. Discuss the book by asking students, "¿Cómo se sienten de estos ancianos? ¿Porqué?" ("How do you feel about these elderly people? Why?") "¿Cómo son diferentes de tus abuelitos?" ("How are they different from your own grandparents?"). Have students share their answers with a partner; then have three or four students share their answers in the large group. This book presents a view of older people as losing faculties and needing help, in contrast to the respectful view in the previous books. See if students notice the contrast, and if so, ask them what they think about it.

11. As before, model writing on chart paper. Draw a picture to go with the story, have students come up individually to locate a word, letter, or punctuation to be reinforced, and have students write in their journals about their elderly people, share their stories with partners, and draw pictures.

12. The fifth day of the unit is *Día de los Abuelitos*/Grandparents' Day. Have each student introduce his or her grandparent. Ask each grandparent to share a story or skill with the class. Have students whose grandparents do not live locally each share a photo as the teacher reads the story of the grandparent written by the parents. Culminate the celebration with food such as *pan dulce* (sweet bread) and *chocolate caliente* (hot chocolate). For this day, have literacy centers such as the following:

   Art—Make tissue paper flowers to give to grandparents.
   Writing—Write a poem about grandparents. Write a thank-you card to their grandparents.
   Computers—Abuelita y Yo, Mercer Mayers, Living Books
   Cooking—Ask a grandmother to come to class to make tortillas with the students.

13. Finally, ask students if some members of their family are half-brothers or half-sisters to each other, therefore making one of their grandparents different. If so, discuss the idea of the blend family with them.

Evaluation

1. Teacher observes students writing in their journals about their grandparents, looking at their uses of writing conventions and vocabulary, and their ability to connect experiences with grandparents with literacy.

2. Through discussion, teacher assesses students' grasp of the concept of elders.

3. Teacher observes students' ability to connect experiences with literacy.

Resources

Literature

Fox, M., & Vivas, J. (1988). *Guillermo Jorge Manuel José*. Caracas, Venezuela: Ekaré-Banco del Libro.
Kratky, L. J., & Ortiz, J. (1995). *Los regalos de mi abuelito*. Carmel, CA: Hampton Brown.
Luenn, N., & Chapman, R. (1988). *A gift for Abuelita/Un regalo para Abuelita*. Flagstaff, AZ: Rising Moon.
Tello, J., & Bribiescas, C. (1995). *Amalia y sus primeras tortillas*. New York: Scholastic.

Additional Suggested Literature in Spanish

Almada, P. (1994). *Igual a mi abuelo*. New Zealand: Shorthand Publications Ltd.
Castañeda, O. S., Sanchez, E. O., & Marcuse, A. (1993). *El tapiz de Abuela*. New York: Lee and Low Books.
Chavarría-Cháirez, B., Vega, A., & Castilla, J. M. (2000). *Magda's tortillas*. Houston: Piñata Books.
Delacre, L. (2000). *Salsa Stories*. New York: Scholastic.
Galindo, M. S. (2001). *Icy watermelon/Sandoa fria*. Illustrated by P. Rodgiquez Howard. Houston: Pinata Books.
Herrera, J. F. (2005). *Downtown Boy*. New York: Scholastic.
Hughes, J., & Garay, L. (1996). *Un puñado de semillas*. Caracas, Venezuela: Ekaré-Banco del Libro.
Perera, H., & Rodero, P. (1999). *Pepín y el abuelo*. Cón, Spain: Editorial Everest.
Ryan, P. M. (2000). *Esperanza Rising*. New York: Scholastic.
Ryan, P. M. (2005). *Mice and Beans*. New York: Scholastic.
Ryan, P. M. (2001). *Arroz con frijoles ... y unos amables ratones*. Illustrated by J. Cepeda. New York: Scholastic.
Torres, L. (1998). *Las abuelas de Liliana*. New York: Farrar, Straus and Giroux.
Wolff, B. M. (1991). *Mi abuelito y yo*. New York: Scholastic.

Nuestros Abuelos Son Especiales (Our Grandparents Will Always Be Special)

WHY THE CHANGES?

Language

The "Before" lesson is taught exclusively in English. Conceptually, it is simple—it is at a level of English language usage that the children can understand. The "After" lesson builds on students' knowledge in Spanish to extend their language skills and conceptual knowledge. Students who come to school speaking a language other than English need rich concept and language development instruction in their primary language while they are in the process of learning English. This rich conceptual knowledge can then be extended to the students' early literacy instruction in their primary language. The students' connections and motivation can be the catalyst for the stories they tell, draw, and write. These connections can also facilitate their instruction in English language development by providing the necessary prior knowledge and experience for instruction in the new language. This literacy knowledge and second-language learning will then, in time, transfer to their literacy instruction in English.

Relevance

This unit provides the opportunity for Latino students, receiving their literacy instruction in Spanish, to identify with culturally relevant literature that depicts grandparent–child relationships. It encourages them to recall memories and stories about their own grandparents and to use these to connect with their instruction in literacy. The concept of family, especially the extended family, is influenced by culture.

The choice of materials and literature must be culturally relevant in order for students to make the desired connections, and it is essential that the presentation of these culturally relevant materials and literature be conveyed in the students' primary language. Students who have not yet mastered their second-language fluency sufficiently cannot be asked to perform high-level thinking tasks such as comparing and contrasting cultural values.

Connection with Home and Community

Elders in nondominant cultural groups traditionally receive respect and status for their wisdom and experience. Children of these groups come to the educational experience with these positive attitudes toward the elders in their lives. If these students remain in the educational system, they will inevitably encounter contradictions to these values. The dominant culture's attitudes toward its elderly are influenced by the capitalistic system. This influence serves to diminish the respect and status of its older citizens. In order to give validation to the students' world, the school must provide a culturally relevant curriculum that fosters the continuance of these worthwhile values. The "After" plan does this.

Relationships with grandparents give children an essential connection with the past by providing the security of people who love and care for them in the present. Exploring these relationships within the school setting affirms for all children that these relationships are important, that their grandparents are special, and that the elders in their lives deserve respect and love. Importantly, the "After" plan honors the students' grandparents by inviting them to share their experiences and to celebrate their importance and significance in the lives of their grandchildren, families, and communities.

▶ LESSON PLAN

Sentences, Subjects, and Predicates

Subject Area: Language Arts

Grade Level: 2–4

Time: Two class periods

Objectives

1. Students will distinguish a complete sentence from a phrase and demonstrate this ability on a worksheet of phrases and sentences.
2. Students will identify sentences, subjects, and predicates.

Suggested Procedures

1. Explain to the class that today they will learn what a complete sentence is and that it has two parts: a subject and a predicate.

2. Write the following sentence on the board: *The girl is sitting on the bench.* Ask students who or what is doing the action [the girl]; explain that the subject is who or what the sentence is about. Ask the students what the girl is doing [sitting on the bench]; explain that the predicate tells what the subject does.

3. Go through several similar sentences on the board, asking students to identify the subjects and the predicates. When students gain an understanding of these concepts, give them a worksheet and have them underline the subject and circle the predicate of each sentence.

4. Display several pictures around the classroom. Tell the class they will practice how to distinguish between a complete sentence (which has both a subject and a predicate) and a phrase (which does not have both of these). For the first picture, ask the class to suggest a caption; write it on tagboard beneath the picture. Have students identify whether the caption is a complete sentence or a phrase. Then have the class suggest another caption that is a phrase if the first caption was a sentence, or a sentence if the first caption was a phrase.

5. Go through the pictures, calling on individuals to suggest captions and identify whether the caption is a phrase or a complete sentence. Each picture should acquire two captions: one sentence and one phrase.

6. Hand out a worksheet with some complete sentences and some phrases. Ask students to identify whether each item is a complete sentence or a phrase. Have students underline the subjects and circle the predicates of the complete sentences.

Evaluation

Assess individual mastery of concepts by evaluating each student's worksheet and responses when called on to perform orally.

Sentences, Subjects, and Predicates[2]

Subject Area: Language Arts
Grade Level: 2–4
Time: Two class periods

Objectives

1. Students will distinguish a complete sentence from a phrase and demonstrate this ability on a worksheet of phrases and sentences.

2. Students will identify subjects and predicates of sentences.

[2]Source: Karen Caupion, Milwaukee, Wisconsin.

Suggested Procedures

1. Explain to the class that today they will learn what a complete sentence is and that it has two parts: a subject and a predicate.

2. Randomly choose ten students to be subjects and another ten to be predicates.

3. Hand out one large flashcard to each child. Students who are subjects receive flashcards that say "SUBJECT" on one side and display a specific subject on the other side. The ten subjects are

   a. the chair
   b. my sister
   c. a yellow car
   d. all giraffes
   e. this book
   f. the football game
   g. smoke
   h. a clown
   i. the sky
   j. storms

   Students who are predicates receive flashcards that say "PREDICATE" on one side and display a specific predicate on the other side. The ten predicates are
   a. has a broken leg
   b. looks just like me
   c. ran out of gas
   d. have long necks
   e. was hard to read
   f. ended in a tie
   g. rose from the chimney
   h. has a big red nose
   i. is blue today
   j. scare me

4. Explain to students that they are only half of a sentence and need to search for their other half to be complete. If they are a subject, they need to search for their missing predicate. If they are a predicate, they need to search for their missing subject.

5. Students search around the class for their missing half and sit down next to each other when they have found them. When the entire class is seated, students are ready to present their sentences to the rest of the class.

6. Choose one pair of students to come to the front of the class. The two students stand next to each other and hold up their flashcards to make a complete sentence. The class reads the sentence out loud (e.g., "The chair has a broken leg").

7. Explain to students that the subject is who or what the sentence is about. Ask the subject in the pair of students to raise his or her hand. Explain to the class that the predicate tells what the subject is about or what it does. Ask the predicate in the pair of students to raise his or her hand.

8. Have either the subject or the predicate student move to the corner of the room, and ask the class to read what is on the flashcard (e.g., "has a broken leg"). Explain that, without the subject, the predicate is lost—or is not a complete sentence. Subject and predicate need each other for the whole sentence to make sense.

9. Have another pair of students come to the front of the class and repeat steps 6–8, but instead of continually explaining, change the questions. For example, ask what a subject is. Do this until all the pairs of students have come before the class.

10. Review or close the lesson by practicing with sentences on the board. Each student circles the subject and underlines the predicate of his or her own sentence on the board. The teacher evaluates and assists when necessary.

11. Pair students randomly. List topics on the board, such as animals, people, jobs, games, and weather. Have pairs of students choose topics, and provide them with scissors and old magazines. Ask the students to cut out magazine pictures related to the topic they chose. Ask one student from each group to write a caption that is a phrase, not a sentence. Ask the other student to write a caption that is a complete sentence. Students need to cooperate with each other and share ideas. The teacher should give assistance if needed, especially to students writing phrases. The students are asked to glue their pictures on colorful construction paper and to attach the captions underneath them.

12. Each pair of students then shows their pictures to the group and reads the two captions they wrote. The other children are asked to decide which caption is a complete sentence. After they have chosen the correct one, the class decides what is the subject and what is the predicate. Pictures and captions remain hanging on bulletin boards for visual reinforcement.

13. Hand out a worksheet with some complete sentences and some phrases. Read the directions to students, and have them determine whether the items are complete sentences or phrases; then have them point out the subjects and predicates.

Evaluation

1. Assess group learning by presentations and by class response to questions during the activity.

2. Assess individual mastery by evaluating each student's worksheet.

Sentences, Subjects, and Predicates

WHY THE
CHANGES?

Learning Style

The "Before" lesson plan requires students to learn mainly by observing a demonstration and then performing it alone. The modalities used are mainly reading and writing, although the pictures provide some nonliterary visual stimulus. The recitation format in procedure 5 introduces some competition, since each individual's performance is publicly evaluated and the peer group determines who knows the answers and who does not. Although these strategies work for some students, they do not work well for many others. The "After" lesson plan makes several adaptations for the learning style of the students in the teacher's class, which the "Before" plan does not do. The activities involve everyone, with as little lecturing as possible. The lesson uses a people-oriented rather than a task-oriented approach. The learning is from whole to part, in that the lesson teaches a complete sentence by having each part find its partner. It also emphasizes cooperating and sharing information by having students work together and present their results to the class, and it incorporates more visual learning with the poster and magazine activity.

The "After" lesson would probably interest most students because it involves them actively and it offers alternatives to board work and worksheets. Both lessons teach the same concepts in roughly the same amount of time; however, academic integrity and time constraints are not sacrificed in making a more interesting lesson.

▶ LESSON PLAN

The Importance of Math to Everyday Life

Subject Area: Mathematics

Grade Level: 4–8

Time: About 20 minutes

Objective

Students will appreciate the importance of mathematics in daily life.

Suggested Procedures

1. Ask students to list at least five uses of math in everyday life (e.g., making coin change, converting cooking measurements, figuring mileage, appraising, computing, measuring, traveling).

2. Ask each student to provide three examples of where and how math use occurs. For example, if a student lives in the mountain time zone, and if he or she wishes to watch a program on MTV scheduled for 9:00 P.M. eastern time, what mathematical concept would be used to determine the time that the program would air in the Mountain Time zone?

Evaluation

1. Assess students' understanding of math use through discussion.

2. Assess students' appreciation of the importance and usefulness of math through the seriousness with which they apply themselves.

The Importance of Math to Everyday Life

Subject Area: Mathematics

Grade Level: 4–8

Time: One or two class periods

Objectives

1. Students will appreciate the importance of mathematics in daily life.
2. Students will learn that the ability to use higher levels of math often helps one acquire a prestigious and high-paying job.

Suggested Procedures

1. Ask students to list at least five uses of mathematics in everyday life (e.g., making coin change, converting cooking measurements, predicting, determining value, computing, measuring, traveling).
2. Ask students to provide examples (evidence) of where and how these uses occur. Ask students to provide examples of who is mostly responsible for using math in this manner. On the board, develop the chart shown in Table 2.2.
3. Ask students to analyze the chart to determine the following:
   a. Have they seen both men and women performing the job? If so, which gender performs it the most?

Table 2.2   Chart for Using Math Daily

Uses of Math	How	Kind of Math	Person Using	Schooling	Salary
1. Navigation	Airplane	Geometry	Pilot	College and flight school	Beginning annual: $55,000
2.					
3.					

   b. Have they seen people of color perform the job? If so, who?
   c. Which jobs pay the most? Which race(s) and gender mostly occupy the jobs?
4. Discuss with students that one reason white, European American males dominate some of the higher-paying jobs is that they tend to continue with math use through high school and college. Help students to realize that both sexes and any race can hold any of these jobs, but that acquiring a good math background is a prerequisite, and now is a good time to start doing that.
5. Ask students to choose the jobs on the list that they would most like to have and to investigate further the math they would need to know to do the job.
6. Group students across race, gender, and class lines (where possible) to discuss the use of math in daily life and how it affects their ability to attain the profession they chose.

Evaluation

1. Assess students' understanding of math through discussion.
2. Assess students' appreciation of the importance and usefulness of math through the seriousness with which they apply themselves.
3. Through discussion, assess students' understanding of how knowledge of math influences the achievements of groups of people.

The Importance of Math to Everyday Life

Relevance

Students often view upper-level math skills as useless because they believe such skills are not useful in everyday life. The students being taught in this sample lesson plan seem uninterested in mathematics. The "Before" lesson plan inspires students to take math more seriously in the present, which is good.

The "After" lesson plan also connects math with students' futures, to help students realize how knowledge that has no immediate practical use can still be useful later in life. Often students do not realize the extent to which subject matter can relate to future job opportunities, nor do they often have much knowledge of the range of job options or salaries. By providing students with such information, the "After" lesson plan makes math useful for students' futures as well as present lives.

Role Models

The "After" lesson plan has students identify the race and gender of role models in math-related careers and critically think about the role models with relationship to math study. Females and students of color tend to take less math in school than White European American males, which has consequences for the jobs they are able to attain. The "After" plan helps students see a link between the presence or absence of role models available to them and what people do to achieve certain roles. The idea is to encourage students not to be limited by an absence of role models in areas of interest to them.

▶ LESSON PLAN

Scientific Problem Solving

Subject Area: Science
Grade Level: 5–8
Time: One week

Objectives

1. Students will use scientific processes to solve problems.
2. Students will design, set up, and perform a science experiment correctly.
3. Students will write up a science experiment using the appropriate format.

Suggested Procedures

1. Discuss with students the meaning of the scientific method or process by demonstrating several experiments. For example, make a battery or show the principles of a jet engine. While demonstrating the experiment, display a write-up of the steps and procedures on an overhead projector for students to follow.
2. Set up an experiment. For example, use a pulley to show how to lift heavy objects. Provide an outline of the procedure for conducting the experiment on a worksheet, and have students complete the write-up.

3. Provide students with illustrations of science experiments, and have them write up the procedures and results of the experiments.

4. Provide students with a science question that can be investigated by experimentation. Show them a variety of laboratory materials, and explain how the experiment would be set up to investigate that question.

5. Provide students with science questions to be investigated using available laboratory materials. Ask each student to select one question, set up and conduct an appropriate experiment, and write up the procedures and results.

Evaluation

Observe each student's experiment, and check the correctness of his or her write-up.

Scientific Problem Solving

Subject Area: Science
Grade Level: 5–8
Time: Ongoing

Objectives

1. Students will appreciate science concepts as useful.

2. Students will understand that thinking like a scientist means solving problems in an orderly manner.

3. Students will show how scientific processes apply to their everyday lives.

4. Students will design, set up, and perform a science project, device, or experiment correctly.

5. Students will present a science project or experiment in a scientific manner.

Suggested Procedures

1. Discuss with students the importance of a knowledge of science in everyday life. Have students brainstorm applications of science in their own lives; make a list on the board.

2. Take a field trip to a local site at which students can observe the application of science principles (e.g., a farm, lake, hospital, health club, city power plant, water filtration plant). Through discussion of what students observe, make sure they see the connection among some natural resources, scientific knowledge, and their everyday lives.

3. Bring to class a car battery, chain and pedals from a bicycle, a nutcracker, a flush pump from a toilet, a motor from a refrigerator, and so on. Use these items to illustrate science principles that will be or have been taught in class. Ask students to explain, using these examples, how science affects their everyday lives. Make sure they understand the principles of science used in each device.

4. Review the science principles you have taught in class, such as the use of a fulcrum and lever or direct versus alternating electrical current. Organize

students into groups, and have each group locate in their home environment and bring to class an example of how at least one of these principles is used in everyday life. Ask each group of students to present the examples to the class and to explain the science principles that the devices use. Make certain that the student groups include both boys and girls, and discuss the gender neutrality of the materials they bring to class. For example, a car battery or an iron is gender neutral regardless of its connection to particular sex roles in the past.

5. Have students work in small groups to construct a project, device, or experiment that uses science principles to meet an everyday need. The small groups can each work collectively on a project, or the individuals within each group can work on their own projects using the other group members as consultants. For the students conducting the experiments, plan to spend time helping them formulate hypotheses, identify variables, and the like. Use the problem they have selected to investigate as a context for teaching them how to think like a scientist.

6. Have each student or group present their project to the class. During the presentation, students should explain to the class the science principles involved and how they relate to everyday life. Students should use this presentation time to talk and act in a formal manner—like a scientist.

Evaluation

1. Assess students' appreciation of the usefulness of science through discussions of the field trip as well as students' ability to locate and discuss examples of science from their own everyday lives.

2. Assess students' skill at designing and carrying out science applications through their projects.

3. Assess students' skill at formally presenting science projects through their oral presentations.

Scientific Problem Solving

WHY THE CHANGES?

Learning Style

The students being taught seem uninterested in science and don't see the point in studying it. In the "Before" lesson plan, students observe the teacher and then work individually on worksheets and experiments. The "After" lesson plan encourages cooperative learning, active participation, oral presentation, and hands-on activities. Many students find these active, collaborative teaching strategies much more engaging.

Relevance

The "Before" lesson plan teaches important concepts for students to learn. However, the "After" lesson plan relates scientific inquiry not only to experiments done in school but also to everyday life. The "After" plan shows students how science functions in their own environment and emphasizes that it is used to make life more understandable and convenient. The "After" plan discourages students from viewing science as a mystery or as the sole domain of a specialized group of people.

Students need to learn the more traditional kinds of classroom experiments and procedures for writing up experiments. The "After" plan does not stress this as heavily as the "Before" plan. The "Before" plan is best taught to students following the "After" plan—that is, after students have internalized the idea that science is useful to them, interesting, and accessible. When teaching the more traditional experiments and skills, the teacher should continually relate them to everyday life to reinforce their usefulness. The teacher should also continue to use teaching procedures that match students' learning styles, such as cooperative learning.

► LESSON PLAN[3]

A Cultural Human Being Presentation

Subject Areas: Computers, Social Studies
Grade Level: 5–12
Time: Ongoing

Objectives

1. Students will design, produce, and present a multimedia presentation making use of the speaker's notes, bullets in slides, images, and sounds.
2. Students will use and integrate computer presentation skills for the project.

Suggested Procedures

1. Select a research project that students have completed for social studies.
2. Using the information in "Basic Procedure for MS PowerPoint" on p. 39, help students to summarize and synthesize research work into a comprehensive multimedia presentation in Microsoft PowerPoint.
3. Have students create slides or pages that represent the key points, incorporating any relevant images and including art, color, music, sounds and design.

Evaluation

1. Research information is integrated into the speaker's presentation.
2. Slides have key points summarized as a bulleted list.
3. Images and sounds are added to the presentation.
4. Design principles, transitions, action, and sound are used.
5. Student uses rehearsal feature in the PowerPoint presentation to control the timing.

A Cultural Human Being Presentation

Subject Areas: Computers, Social Studies
Grade Level: 5–12
Time: Ongoing

[3]Source: Felix Cortex-Littlefield, California State University-San Luis Obispo

Objectives

1. Students will design, produce, and present in PowerPoint a multimedia presentation, "Yourself as a Cultural Being," making use of speaker's notes, bulleted list, images, and sounds.

2. Students will use and integrate computer presentation skills for the project.

Suggested Procedures

1. Have students think critically about questions such as the following, and collect research and data for a presentation and report:
   - Take a look at how things are in your own cultural group: your family.
   - What is the family structure? What members make up the family, and who plays what role in your family?
   - Who makes the decisions in the family and who plays subordinate roles?
   - How is leisure time spent? What individual and group hobbies does the family share?
   - Does religion play a role?
   - What amount and type of reading do members of your family engage in? Does your family watch or get involved in other media forms, computers, music, or art?
   - Who works in your family? What kind of work?
   - Does your family share set goals, especially education goals?
   - How are the standards for conduct set in your family?
   - What kind of language is spoken in your house?
   - What is the dining culture in your home? (e.g., Do family members eat together? watch TV while eating? etc.)
   - Is "time" important in your household? How do you deal with time?
   - How is affection shown in your family?
   - How are arguments handled?

   These are questions that focus on at-home culture. They will need to be modified for the grade level of the students, and students should not be compelled to address family matters if they would prefer to remain private.

2. After answering questions such as those above, students will have the foundation for a cultural research project and the background to create a digital project. All questions should be answered using a word processor.

3. Every family has many stories to tell; thus, digital media are a positive way to collect and transport stories and history to be passed down and shown to family members, in a way not unlike the oral stories of times past. Yet, digital stories do not replace oral traditions. Rather, they support and stimulate dialogue for a newer generation, one that has grown up with technology and movies. Help students to create a family tree chart in their presentation, tracing back as far as they can. Collect stories from individual family members, and connect these stories to the family member. Stories can be individual slides (miniprojects) with images and sounds or just a page with the story written in biographical form.

4. Help students to summarize and synthesize research work into a comprehensive multimedia presentation in PowerPoint.

5. Have students prepare a "talk" in which they relate the important points of their research. Students will need to take pictures or video slides that represent the key points, along with any other relevant images.

6. Students may create distinct projects that are relevant to them, as time permits.

Evaluation

1. Are the projects relevant to the students' lives? Did the students enjoy and get involved in the projects? Was there family participation in the projects?

2. Research information is integrated into the speakers' presentation.

3. Slides/pictures have key points defined into bulleted lists.

4. Images and sounds are added to the presentation.

5. Reasonable design principles, transitions, action, and sound are used.

6. Student uses rehearsal feature in PowerPoint to stay within time limits.

A Cultural Human Being Presentation

WHY THE CHANGES?

Relevance

In the "Before" lesson, students are taught to use the computer as a tool, but unless they have found their research project to be relevant, many students will not find the computer particularly useful. Computers are not creative or critical thinkers. However, given the opportunity, students are creative and can think critically and imaginatively. This high point is reached when a student changes her or his thinking from just following the procedures to asking, What can I create with these procedures? If we teach only the application software, then we teach our students only to be machines of replication and not thinking human beings. Within the multicultural paradigm, one teaches students how to apply their knowledge within a larger cultural perspective about themselves and others. The larger the perspective, the more useful the tool becomes to them and their world.

PowerPoint is just one of the many marketed multimedia software applications that allows students to create presentations that can incorporate text, images, sound, and movement. Without the ideas from the student there is no story to tell. The message becomes relevant when students present their lives, personal stories, and family histories.

Basic Procedure for MS PowerPoint, Skill Base General by Linda Endlich, Director IMDC, University Wisconsin–Madison

1. Launch the PowerPoint program of application either from All Programs in the Start Menu on a PC or from the menu bar on a MAC. If you cannot find PowerPoint, perform a Find or Search for Files to find the application software location in either platform or double-click on a PowerPoint icon to open.

2. The next step depends on your level of experience: If your computer is configured correctly, a dialogue box will appear to ask you if you want to create a new presentation.

▶ PC

New Presentation

> *Blank*
> *From Design Template*
> *From AutoContent Wizard*

▶ MAC

Project Gallery

AutoContent Wizard

Blank Documents (examples (Figure 2.2): Calendar Event, PowerPoint Presentation)

Templates (Presentations)

AutoContent creates a presentation with step-by-step instructions and limited options. The student adds the text details into fill-in boxes. The Blank option is for advanced users who want to created a custom presentation from scratch. The Template option allows the choice of different backgrounds and formats with placeholders that can be filled in.

For a quick start, the AutoContent Wizard is a fine place to begin one's journey. However, Templates are fun because this option allows more visual choices.

3. Do not let all the jargon bother you; we will use the Wizard only as an example or skeleton of your own project.

4. The AutoContent Wizard generates a project for us; now it is up to us to fill in the content and create the project. There are five views appearing from left to right: Normal view, Outline view, Slide view, Slide Sorter view, Slide Show.

5. Click on each view to see an example of each. (Press Esc to get out of the Slide Show if it takes up your whole screen.) The Normal view shows all of your options at once. You can work on an outline that automatically appears on the slide, type right onto a slide, or rearrange the order of your slides in the Slide Sorter view by clicking and dragging a slide into a new spot.

Figure 2.2

6. Change text. There are multiple ways to change text:
    a. By clicking and highlighting text while in the Normal view and adding or deleting text.
    b. By clicking on the Slide view and changing the text.
    c. By going to the top menu bar > Insert > Textbox.
    d. By editing in the Outline view (text only), which automatically places text onto the slides. If you change the text in the outlines, it will change the Slide view text.

    Remember to save! PowerPoint tends to crash as files grow larger.

7. Insert images as shown in Figures 2.3 and 2.4.
    a. Go to the top menu bar, choose > Insert > Picture, and specify if picture is from a file or is clip art.
    b. Highlight and copy each image from another program and paste it into your project.

    Scanned images should be 72 dpi or screen resolution for presentations to keep the file's size smaller.

8. Insert movies and sounds.
    a. From the top menu bar choose > Insert > Movies and Sounds.
    b. Choose Sounds, CD, or Track (microphone needed).

9. Use drawing tools.
    a. First make sure your drawing and other important toolbars are selected.
    b. Play around with the Auto Shapes; Paint Bucket, Lines, and Rotating

10. Use transitions.
    a. From the menu/choose Slide Show, than select Transitions.
    b. You can choose from different effects that will change one slide into the next. [2.4]
    c. You can also add sound to accompany the transition.
    d. You can even set the show to automatically advance after a chosen number of seconds or to advance on a mouse click.
    e. You can transition choices to apply to each slide individually or to all the slides.

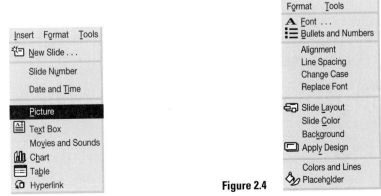

Figure 2.3

Figure 2.4

11. Use animations and builds.
    From the menu choose Slide Show, then select Custom Animation. Then choose the animation you would like to preview.

12. Move slides around.
    a. In the Slide Sorter view, click a slide (hold down the shift key and click several slides to select more than one slide at a time) and drag and drop the slide into its new position. An insert line will appear to the left or right of another slide to show you where you are placing the slide.
    b. From the outline, click and drag the slide, an insert line will appear above or below to show you where you are placing the slide.

13. Format backgrounds and color schemes.
    On the top menu bar click the Format menu, then click on your formatting option of choice (e.g., Design, Layout, Color Scheme, or Background).

14. Create stand-alone presentations and Web pages.
    a. On the top menu bar select Save As, then Save File Type As .pps (Power-Point Show) .html (HyperText Markup Language).
    b. The. pps option creates a stand-alone presentation that can be viewed on many operating systems.
    c. The html option creates automatically generated webpages and images that can be used on the Internet.
    Some basic PowerPoint tips:
    a. From the View menu you can find all of the tools and palettes you need to customize your project.
    b. Don't overdo the animations and transitions.
    c. Using templates saves time.
    d. Entering text into the outline makes slide changes easier.
    e. Keep text at 20 pt or higher.
    f. Be sure to check your presentation if you have crossed from PC to MAC or vice versa.
    g. Fonts appear larger on the PC than on the MAC.
    h. Don't run text too close to the outer edges of the slide.
    i. Keep the amount of text on each slide reasonable.
    j. JPEG images at 72 dpi work best for slide shows.
    k. JPEG images at 150 dpi work best for converting electronic files into actual photographic slides.

▶ LESSON PLAN

Word Usage

Subject Area: Language Arts
Grade Level: 6–12
Time: Ongoing
Students: Those who do not habitually use Standard English in their daily speaking and writing

Objectives

1. Students will use correct Standard English.
2. Students will refrain from using incorrect Standard English or slang.

Suggested Procedures

1. Explain to students that the slang they use when speaking is not correct and that the class will learn and practice correct English.

2. Throughout the school year, spend time on one part of speech at a time: Show correct usage, have students practice locating and correcting errors, and ask them to use correct sentences both orally and in writing. For example, if you are working on correct verb usage, use an overhead projector to show sentences in which there are errors. Sentence by sentence, ask the class to identify the errors and to offer corrections. Create worksheets of incomplete sentences in which students are to fill in blank lines with the appropriate verbs; offer three or four verb choices for each item. Once students have completed the worksheets, review them orally in class. Then ask students to write an essay, "My Favorite Saturday," in which they are to pay particular attention to verb usage. Students who make excessive errors in their essays should correct them with the teacher's help and rewrite their essays. You may also assign additional exercises from a grammar book.

3. Correct students regularly when they lapse back into their earlier speech patterns. Continue to emphasize the importance of always using correct Standard English.

Evaluation

1. Assess mastery of word usage through quizzes and essays.
2. Assess word usage carryover into daily life through oral usage.

Word Usage

AFTER

Subject Area: Language Arts

Grade Level: 6–12

Time: Ongoing

Students: Those who do not habitually use Standard English in their daily speaking and writing

Objectives

1. Students will learn what it means to code-switch and when it is useful to do so.
2. Students will use correct Standard English in circumstances in which it will be to their benefit.

Suggested Procedures

1. Ask students to suggest situations in which they might want to persuade the following audiences: peers, adults in their neighborhood, and authority figures

in the wider society. Ask them to describe differences in the style of speech used by these different audiences and to discuss how people react if one uses the wrong style of speech with the wrong audience. Point out how the concepts of dialect and language difference apply to the situations that students suggest; stress that one dialect or language is not inherently better than another but that one's purpose and audience should help determine which dialect or language one uses. Explain that code-switching means switching from one dialect or language to another, depending on one's purpose and audience.

2. Have students suggest an issue or concern they wish to address to the three audiences. Ask them to role-play orally how they would persuade each audience. (If word processors are used to teach language arts, consider the possibility of using global search-and-replace functions to code-switch. Also, with some spell-checking software, custom dictionaries can be built for each code.) Then have each student write a persuasive paragraph addressed to each audience, using the dialect or language style most likely to achieve the most positive reaction by each audience.

3. Divide students into small reading groups, and have them critique each other's papers. Pay particular attention to the papers that use Standard English; provide correct usage for phrases that the group is unable to provide. Based on feedback from the group and yourself, students should rewrite the papers. If you are using word processors, present different drafts using different codes. Plan rewrites for each draft. Since rewriting with word processors is less demanding, you can ask for more versions and drafts.

4. Collect the papers. Evaluate them, paying particular attention to Standard English usage in paragraphs directed toward authority figures. If there are errors that most students are making, have whole-class lessons on these and repeat this sequence. Have students work individually or in small groups on specific errors that individual students may be making. When teaching specific Standard English patterns, first show students how Standard English differs grammatically, phonetically, and syntactically from their dialects. Then have them practice translating back and forth between dialects. Use games for any drill that may be needed on specific skills.

5. Ask each student to identify a particular authority figure whom he or she wishes to persuade to a particular point of view, either orally or in writing: for example, persuading a prospective employer to hire oneself, persuading the principal to handle a school problem in a certain way, or persuading the city council to deal with a particular problem. Ask students to construct a persuasive argument, in Standard English, that they will deliver either orally or in writing. Provide help as needed.

Evaluation

1. Assess students' understanding of code-switching through the first written assignment.

2. Assess students' ability to use Standard English through each oral and written assignment.

3. Assess students' enjoyment through the effort they put into the assignments.

Word Usage

WHY THE CHANGES?

Learning Style

The "After" lesson plan adds the features of oral language use, role-playing activities, and working cooperatively with peers to the individual writing used in the "Before" lesson plan. These features are important for two reasons: First, social situations require more oral than written language; second, most speakers of non–Standard English dialects prefer oral learning and working with others.

The "After" plan also encourages students to work together and to critique and give feedback to each other on language use, rather than having them receive all information and feedback from the teacher. Again, this makes use of a preference for learning with others. It also attempts to teach non–Standard English speakers to help each other code-switch appropriately rather than rely on someone else for direction.

Word processors can facilitate both practice and collaborative learning, as noted in the "After" lesson plan.

Relevance

The "Before" lesson plan does not make use of students' prior knowledge of language other than their knowledge of Standard English. It also runs the risk of boring students because it overuses worksheets, establishes a weekly routine for teaching discrete skills, and has little connection to students' own language use.

The "After" lesson plan builds in a good deal more relevance, however. It uses students' awareness that people speak differently in different contexts and uses their collective prior experience with Standard English. Since most or all students will have had considerable exposure to Standard English (e.g., through the media), they probably know more about the subject than they use. In addition, the teacher uses the language that students already know to teach elements of a dialect they have not yet mastered. The "After" plan involves students actively in role-playing real situations and invites them to help define what kinds of situations would be real.

The "Before" plan implicitly teaches students that the language spoken in their home and community is wrong, bad, and inferior. Often this forces students to do things either the teacher's way or their home's way, and many students reject the teacher's way if forced to make a choice. The "After" plan teaches that both ways are acceptable in the right context; emphasis is placed on judging context, learning a new dialect (Standard English), and learning to code-switch.

Skill Levels

The "Before" plan assumes that students do not know a skill until it is taught to them. The "After" plan requires the teacher to pay attention to students' oral and written language, spending time teaching only those skills that students have not already mastered on their own.

▶ LESSON PLAN[4]
Mong History

Subject Area: Social Studies
Grade Level: 8–12
Time: Five class periods
Students: Culturally and linguistically diverse, with some Mong students in the class

Objectives

1. Students will explain who the Mong are, where they came from (geography) and when and why they came to the United States (history).
2. Students will describe early Mong history.
3. Students will describe present-day Mong history.
4. Students will identify the major events that are shaping Mong society.
5. Students will pinpoint the geography or the areas of concentration where the Mong lived and are now living.
6. Students will take accurate notes during lectures and films.

Suggested Procedures

1. Have a world geography map available for each appropriate class period, to draw students' attention to the subject matter. Start eliciting students' prior knowledge (elaboration) about who the Mong are. Have students contribute information they already know about the Mong and their relations with the United States. Write their contributions on the board, and highlight new vocabulary as it arises.

2. Explain to students that they will hear a short lecture on the earlier Mong history (previewing and advance organization). They will listen, take notes, compare their notes with their classmates, and then write short summaries (summarizing) of the lecture. The lecture they will hear is normally organized into three parts: introduction, content, and conclusion. Use the following steps:
   a. Read a paragraph to students and have them take notes.
   b. Check their comprehension of the paragraph and ask them for the meanings of the new words (inferencing) presented, and relate the words to what the students already know.
   c. Read the second paragraph and ask students to repeat the second step.
   d. Read the third paragraph and ask students to repeat the second step.
   e. Read the entire short lecture. Ask students to take notes. Tell the students about the importance of linguistic markers. Write some of them on the board as they hear them in the lecture. For example, "Today, I'm going to talk about..." indicates the topic. When they hear the word "important," it means that the following statement is the main idea (selective attention).

[4]Source: Paoze Thao, California State University–Monterey Bay.

3. Explain to students that they will hear a short lecture on recent Mong history. Students should use a Timelines List (T-List) to take their notes (note taking). Ask students to follow procedure 2. Then explain the T-List procedure to students. In this T-List, students will write the main ideas (selective attention) on the left-hand side and the corresponding details on the right-hand side of the T-List.

4. Explain to students that they will continue to hear a short lecture on the major events and activities that are shaping Mong society. Tell students to jot down phrases and make abbreviations when taking notes (note taking). Tell them to practice taking notes by eliminating words unnecessary for comprehension. Show the videos *Journey From Padong* and *The U.S. Secret Army in Laos*. Have students continue to take notes using the T-List format.

5. Have students identify and pinpoint the area of concentration for the Mong that students already know. Then lecture on the demography of the Mong. Students continue to take notes.

Evaluation

1. Divide students into small groups of three to six (maximum) to compare their notes, discuss the lectures, pool information, and fill in any missing information on the T-Lists.

2. Ask students to answer the self-evaluation questions. These questions relate to the parts of the lecture that are easy or difficult to understand (visualizing or making mental pictures).

3. Ask students to write brief summaries based on their notes. Then ask them to work in pairs to revise and edit their summaries.

4. Assess students' additional sources of information about the relations between the Mong and the United States during the Vietnam conflict.

Mong History

AFTER

Subject Area: Social Studies

Grade Level: 8–12

Time: Six class periods

Students: Culturally and linguistically diverse, with some Mong students in the class

Objectives

1. Students will explain who the Mong are, where they came from (geography) and when and why they came to the United States (history).

2. Students will describe early Mong history.

3. Students will describe recent Mong history through oral history accounts.

4. Students will pinpoint the geography or the area of concentration where the Mong lived and are now living.

5. Mong and non-Mong students will cooperate with each other to complete a task.

6. Students will gather information about Mong people from Mong sources.

7. Mong students will participate actively in the classroom discussions.

8. Students will take accurate notes during lectures and films.

Suggested Procedures

1. Have a world geography map available for each appropriate class period, to draw students' attention to the subject matter. Start eliciting students' prior knowledge (elaboration) about who the Mong are. Have students contribute information they already know about the Mong and their relations with the United States. Encourage the Mong students to share a specific episode of their own history with the entire class (elaborating prior knowledge). Write their contributions on the board, and highlight new vocabulary as it occurs.

2. Explain to students that they will hear a short lecture on the earlier Mong history (previewing and advance organization). They will listen, take notes, compare their notes with their classmates, and then write short summaries (summarizing) of the lecture. The lecture they will hear is normally organized into three parts: introduction, content, and conclusion. Use the following steps:
   a. Read a paragraph to students and have them take notes.
   b. Check their comprehension of the paragraph and ask them for the meanings of the new words (inferencing) presented and relate the words to what the students already know.
   c. Read the second paragraph and ask students to repeat the second step.
   d. Read the third paragraph and ask students to repeat the second step.
   e. Read the entire short lecture. Ask students to take notes. Tell the students about the importance of linguistic markers. Write some of them on the board as they hear them in the lecture. For example, "Today, I'm going to talk about..." indicates the topic. When they hear the word "important", it means that the following statement is the main idea (selective attention).

3. Explain to students that they will hear a short lecture on recent Mong history. Students should use a Timelines List (T-List) to take their notes (note taking). Ask students to follow procedure 2. Then, explain the T-List procedure to students. In this T-List, students will write the main ideas (selective attention) on the left-hand side and the corresponding details on the right-hand side of the T-List.

4. Show the videos *Journey from Padong* and *Education at the Crossroads: Needs for Professional Development* (Thao, 1996). Tell students to take notes.

5. Divide students into small groups of three or four (cooperating). Half the class will be responsible for ethnographic interviews with Mong parents and Mong community leaders and tape-recording their oral histories. In their small groups, have the students design the questions (questioning for clarification) that will be used. (You will need to have arranged ahead of time for individuals to be interviewed.)

6. Have the other half of the class do research on the Internet for information on the Hmong culture. Students can also search for Laos history on the Internet. Useful Web sites include www.hmongnet.org and www.laogate.com.

7. Then ask students to report back to the whole class.

8. Encourage students to attend the Mong New Year celebration that takes place every year in about November and December in major cities, where tens of thousands of Mong gather together (e.g., Twin Cities, Minnesota; Fresno, Sacramento, and Merced, California; and Milwaukee, Sheboygan, Eau Claire, Wausau, Green Bay, Appleton, La Crosse, and Oshkosh, Wisconsin). The purpose is to get students to see the dynamics of the Mong communities in the United States.

Evaluation

1. Assess students' general understanding of the specific episode of Mong history that was assigned for each group. Assess the quality of students' oral presentations, the ethnographic interviews collected, and the amount of information students obtained from research through the Internet.

2. Through oval discussion or a quiz, assess students' understanding of earlier Mong history and recent history, as well as their ability to connect parents' contributions to the Vietnam conflict with the ideas in the video *The U.S. Secret Army in Laos*.

3. Ask students to identify the geographic areas where the Mong lived and are now living.

4. Assess Mong students' active class participation through anecdotal observations.

Mong History

WHY THE CHANGES?

Learning Styles

The Mong have long been influenced by the French educational system. During colonialism (1892–1947), the French introduced the European model, which was implemented in Laos for nearly fifty years. The system was highly centralized and very selective. Curricula were based on the French educational pattern, and instruction was conducted in the French language. Since education was focused mainly on the elite carrying out services for the French functionaries, only a few Mong benefited from this system. Because of this influence, Mong parents were instructed by the teacher-centered "rote memorization method"—there was very little interaction between teachers and students. Many Mong parents attained one to two years of formal education in Laos, and the French educational system still influences the way some Mong parents want their children to be taught. Many Mong students thus lack the kinds of learning strategies, higher-order thinking skills, research skills, and critical reasoning skills that are absolutely necessary for high academic success in schools and beyond.

Traditionally, ESL and content-area instruction have functioned independently. That is, ESL has not been integrated with content-area instruction. Although many Mong students were born in the United States, they are still being classified as limited-English-proficient (LEP) students. To implement a successful program for Mong students, there is an urgent need for ESL or bilingual teachers to collaborate with content-area instructors to carry out the instruction. The intent is to accelerate the process of learning and teaching to make a smooth transition from the Basic Interpersonal Communication Skills (BICS) to the Cognitive Academic Language Proficiency (CALP), as defined by Cummins (2000), as soon as possible.

Both the "Before" and "After" lesson plans are designed to prepare all students, including the culturally and linguistically diverse student population, to achieve high academic excellence in the content areas. The "After" lesson plan integrates ESL with the content areas within the context of the Cognitive Academic Language Learning Approach (CALLA). The heart and soul of this approach is to teach students three types of learning strategies: metacognitive (advance organization, selective attention, organizational planning, self-monitoring, and self-assessment); cognitive (resourcing, elaborating prior knowledge, taking notes, grouping, making inferences, summarizing, imagery, and linguistic transfer); and social/affective (questioning for clarification, cooperating, and self-talk).

In addition, the "After" lesson plan provides an opportunity for mainstream students and other culturally and linguistically diverse students to gain a better understanding of their peers' historical background and the reasons why their Mong classmates are in the United States today. This lesson also provides an opportunity for Mong students to experience their history through their ethnographic interviews, with a direct connection to their parents and community leaders. This will motivate the Mong students (some of whom may not know their own history), to have self-esteem, self-worth, and pride as part of American society.

Resources

National Clearinghouse for Bilingual Education (NCBE)
1118 22nd Street NW
Washington, DC 20037
(800) 321-6223
www.ncbe.gwu.edu
email: askncbe@ncbe.gwu.edu

Literature

Cummins, J. (2000). *Language, power and pedagogy*. Buffalo: Multilingual Matters, Ltd.
Kraus International Publications. (1993). *English as a second language curriculum resource handbook: A practical guide for K–12 ESL programs*. Millwood, NY: Author.
Quincy, K. (1995). *Hmong, history of a people*. Cheney, WA: Eastern Washington University Press.
Thao, P. (1994). *Mong resettlement in the Chicago area (1978–1987): Educational implications*. Unpublished doctoral dissertation, Loyola University of Chicago.

Audiovisual

Thao, P. (Writer) (1999). *Mong education at the crossroads: Needs for professional development*. Sacramento, CA: California State University, Monterey Bay.

▶ LESSON PLAN[5]

Writing a Five-Paragraph Essay

BEFORE

Subject Area: Intermediate levels of ESL

Grade Level: 9–12

Time: Two to four 50-minute periods

Students: Multiethnic class of students who are in the process of learning English

---

[5]*Source:* Anne Fairbrother, Del Norte High School, Albuquerque, New Mexico.

Objective

Students will write a traditional five-paragraph essay.

Suggested Procedures

1. The teacher puts the essay form on the board.

2. The teacher gives students a list of essay topics, the kinds of topics that are found on state competency tests: What is your most embarrassing moment? Tell what, when, and why. Who is your hero? Tell who and why. What are you most proud of in your life? Tell what, when, and why.

3. The students choose their topics. The class discusses possible introductions for the topics.

4. The students write their thesis statements and brainstorm from their thesis statements so that they will be ready to write the body paragraphs.

5. The students write the body and the conclusion.

6. The students work in pairs to peer-edit and check that all the pieces of the formal essay are there, completing a peer response checklist. The students write a second draft if necessary.

7. The teacher edits the drafts for grammar and spelling, and gives them back to students to rewrite.

8. Students write a polished second draft and turn it in.

Evaluation

The essays will be graded for content, form, and conventions. The grade for form will reflect the correct construction and placement of a thesis statement, the development of three supporting paragraphs, each of which has a topic sentence, and the development of a concluding paragraph.

Writing a Five-Paragraph Essay

Subject Area: Intermediate levels of ESL

Grade Level: 9–12

Time: Two to four 50-minute periods

Students: Multiethnic class of students who are in the process of learning English

Context

Students watch the movie *Where the Spirit Lives*, about the boarding school experience of Native American students in Canada. Before watching the movie, the students brainstorm what constitutes culture (responses usually include language, religion, clothes, food, music, traditions, stories, values, and history). During and after watching the movie, the class notes how the children's culture was stripped away, by taking away language, religion, clothes, and so on.

Objectives

1. Students compare and contrast their home culture with aspects of what they perceive as American culture.
2. Students will write a five-paragraph essay.

Suggested Procedures

1. The teacher reminds students about their definitions of culture—if necessary, the list is again put on the board.

Introduction **Thesis: 1, 2, 3**
1.
2.
3.
Conclusion — including restated thesis

2. The teacher writes the question on the board: What is the difference between your culture and American culture as you understand it? The teacher could preface this activity with some words about the complexity and diversity of American culture, while acknowledging that the popular and pervasive perception of the dominant culture is what many people often think of as American culture.
3. Using a Venn diagram, students compare their heritage culture and what they perceive as American culture (see Figure 2.5). They write in the outer parts of

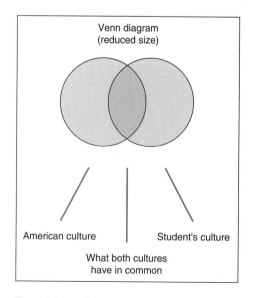

Figure 2.5 Culture Venn Diagram

the circles, showing aspects of American culture that are different from their home culture, and showing, where the circles overlap, what both cultures have in common.

4. When students have a lot written, they can compare their work with other students' work to get more ideas and to express ideas more clearly.

5. The teacher asks students to look at their ideas, and then the class discusses if there are more similarities or more differences.

6. The teacher asks students to complete the following sentence: in response to the question, "What are three things you particularly like about your culture?": "Three things I really like about my culture are...". Students each select three aspects of their culture that they really like from the chart. Students will choose from, for example, food, music, cities, traditions, people, and holidays.

7. The teacher points out that each student now has a thesis statement.

8. The teacher asks students to brainstorm details and examples about each of the three aspects they chose, so that they will have a lot to say about each (see Figure 2.6).

9. The teacher shows students the structure of a five-paragraph essay. The teacher explains that this is not the only way to write about their opinions and ideas, but this is the way teachers in high school expect students to write. The teacher tells the students that they are going to master this form so that they will do well in classes taught in English. The teacher explains that this way of writing involves the following steps: Tell them what you are going to tell them, then tell them what you told them you would. How boring is that?! The teacher explains how they will benefit in school from knowing how to write a five-paragraph essay.

10. The teacher shows the students that the thesis statement is placed at the end of the first paragraph. The class discusses what could go into the introduction: sentences that introduce the topic, general statements, and background information.

11. The students have time to write the first paragraph: the introduction with the thesis statement at the end.

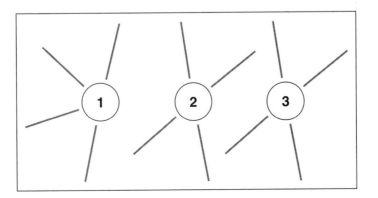

Figure 2.6

12. The students have time to write the body of the essay. They will take points 1, 2, and 3 in turn, and, using their brainstorms, write three paragraphs (Figure 2.6).

13. The class talks about the conclusion. The thesis statement should be repeated, and there should be some concluding comments to wrap up the essay.

14. Students write their first draft. After peer review and some teacher editing suggestions (not everything needs to be corrected), the students write a second draft and turn it in.

Evaluation

1. Students can be graded on the steps of writing the essay: the Venn diagram, the thesis statement, the brainstorming, the first draft.

2. Students will receive two grades on the final draft, one for interesting content and one for using the essay form. The grade for form will reflect the correct construction and placement of a thesis statement, the development of three supporting paragraphs, each of which has a topic sentence, and the development of a concluding paragraph.

Writing a Five-Paragraph Essay

WHY THE CHANGES?

Expectations for High-Level Learning

English as a Second Language (ESL) students need to learn the five-paragraph essay, so that once they are transitioned from ESL they can do well in mainstreamed classes. It is probable that students from Mexico, China, and Vietnam, for example, will have learned to write using different discourse patterns, so they will need to learn how to write in the discourse pattern valued by U.S. high schools and colleges. It is important to let students know that this is just one discourse pattern, one way to write. It may be a totally new discipline for them, so they will need structured help at every step.

Relevant Curriculum

The lesson was changed so that students would have culturally relevant content to work with. The task is a difficult one, and if the content they work with is familiar, relevant, and inherently interesting to the students, it will be easier—and there will be more incentive—to present their opinions and experience in the required form. Students still acquiring English are learning how to talk and write about a subject that is meaningful to them, and there is incentive to express themselves in English. In the "Before" lesson, the emphasis is simply on the skill being taught, and little meaning can be made of the content by the students beyond their desire to do well on the assignment. In the "After" lesson, the content is highly personal and culturally relevant; thus the skills will be more easily learned as students strive to express their opinions and feelings in English, using the form being taught.

This lesson works particularly well if students in the ESL class come from a variety of cultures so they can learn about each other's cultures.

What students understand as "American culture" needs to be examined critically. It is true that students in non-ESL classes too easily equate "American culture" with the dominant culture—and part of the goal of multicultural education is to challenge that assumption. However, newcomers (ESL students in high school who are relative or recent newcomers) also seem to have an image of American culture. It's the mainstream culture they see around them in the media, in the movies, in the schools, and so on. In fact, it is only with the more advanced ESL students (who have been here the longest) that the idea of Chinese American or Mexican American really makes sense.

The students of the teacher who wrote this lesson are from Mexico; they see themselves as *puro mexicano*. Ideas throughout this book, particularly in the chapters that follow this one, can be adapted to help students critically examine who is part of the "American culture."

Language

Because of students' developing facility with the English language, and in order to use the teaching of the essay form as a language-rich experience to promote language development, it is important that students have built prior knowledge and the language to express it through watching the movie *Where the Spirit Lives* and discussing the role of culture within the movie. Students with different levels of language acquisition can all benefit from this lesson. Students with very little English can generate a few words, perhaps broadening them into ideas. Students who are advanced students of English can write a more complex essay, with more emphasis on sentence structure, spelling, usage, and expression. Students with intermediate levels of English can all do well with this assignment. The step-by-step instruction on how to write the five-paragraph essay will be easy to grasp, because the content is familiar and relevant and because students are motivated to write about what they love—and often miss. They will be able to write a multiple-page essay because they have already generated a lot of ideas. They will have a lot to write about because they are writing about their own lives and expressing their feelings about what have been their home countries for most of their lives.

Resources

Audiovisual

Pittman, B. (Director), & Leckie, K. (Writer). (1989). *Where the spirit lives [Motion Picture]*. Oakville, ON: Amazing Spirit Productions.

▶ LESSON PLAN

Functions

Subject Area: Algebra
Grade Level: 9–12
Time: One class period

Objectives

1. Students will explain what the term *function* means in algebra.
2. Students will identify domain and range, given sets of quantities that vary together.
3. Students will construct statements using functional notation.

Suggested Procedures

1. On the board, write the following:

   income, amount of tax
   height, weight
   time elapsed, distance traveled

   Using an overhead projector, show sets of numbers for each pair on the board. Explain that, although all three examples are different, they have something in common; that is, they are sets of two numbers that vary together. Explain that a mathematician needs to focus on both sets simultaneously. For example, an accelerating car travels distance over time; one cannot understand this if one pays attention only to distance or only to time.

2. Define the three items in a function: domain, range, and rule.

3. Show how mathematical sentences can be constructed. For example, I = income, T = tax; the tax on an income of \$15,000 is \$3,025; T(\$15,000) = \$3,025. Have students help construct additional sentences, using the sets of numbers on the projector. Stress that any letters can be used as long as students agree on what they stand for.

4. Explain that mathematicians have agreed on three letters to express functional relationships: x, y, and f. Write $f(x) = y$ on the board and read it aloud. Show how the equation applies to relationships expressed in the previous step.

5. Assign homework.

Evaluation

Assess students' mastery of objectives through homework problems that require them to identify domain and range and to construct statements using functional notation.

Functions

AFTER

Subject Area: Algebra

Grade Level: 9–12

Time: One class period

Objectives

1. Students will compare and contrast street language with mathematical language.
2. Students will explain what the term *function* means in algebra.
3. Students will identify domain and range, given sets of quantities that vary together.
4. Students will contrast statements using functional notation.

Suggested Procedures

1. A day or two before the lesson, ask students for the names of four (or more) popular musicians. Ask them to describe in a phrase or two each musician's career (e.g., length of career, frequency of new recordings, number of times songs have hit the top-40 charts, and so on). Write the phrases on the board and save them. Then ask for volunteers to research the careers of these musicians.

Name of musician	Total number of songs produced	Total number of songs in Top 40

Figure 2.7

For each musician, students are to complete the chart shown in Figure 2.7, providing the number of songs recorded and the number of songs that made the top-40 charts. The teacher should point out that the numbers in each column of the chart are to be cumulative.

2. The day of the lesson, have volunteers put the chart for each musician's career on the board. Explain that their careers can be described in street language and in mathematical language. Review the street language phrases provided earlier; discuss the extent to which they convey precision.

3. Explain that mathematical language uses a different vocabulary and set of symbols: functional notation. On the charts on the board, point to the domain and the range; discuss the fact that these vary together. Also point out that the exact relationship varies over time and varies among musicians. Point out street-language words that students use to express this.

4. For each musician, have students select letters to represent the domain and range and write sentences such as $P(17) = 2$, where $P =$ the number of songs produced. Explain how parentheses are being used.

5. Explain that functional relationships generally have three parts (domain, range, and rule) and that they are expressed with the letters x, y, and f. Write $f(x) = y$ on the board, and explain the relationship to the preceding step. Read this statement mathematically.

6. Explain how to solve for f and express f graphically. Students should learn to graph the musicians' careers and to write formulas describing them.

7. To make sure that students understand, ask for other sets of two quantities that vary together, such as age and height. Ask students to write formulas expressing these relationships.

Evaluation

1. Assess students' comprehension of the term *function* through oral work.

2. Assess students' skills through homework problems that ask them to identify domain and range and to construct statements using functional notation.

Functions

WHY THE CHANGES?

Learning Style

The students being taught here are inner-city students, mainly from poverty-level homes. They are not yet sure why they should be learning algebra and how it relates to anything. They also find many traditional teaching strategies to be passive and boring.

The "Before" lesson plan asks the teacher to explain and demonstrate as students watch. In contrast, the "After" plan invites active student participation, as students gather data and suggest descriptions. Active participation helps most students to learn.

Relevance

The "Before" plan does not suggest to students why they would want to know this information. The teacher attempts to make the lesson applicable to real life by using examples of income tax, height and weight, and acceleration, but students may or may not find the examples relevant or interesting. In the "After" lesson plan, however, the teacher capitalizes on students interest in music. Furthermore, by inviting students to gather information on musicians, the teacher has (1) used the lesson to show students a use for data they care about and (2) allowed students to contribute expertise in an area they probably know more about than the teacher.

In the "After" plan, the teacher asks students to generate other sets of quantities that vary together to make sure students understand the concept. The "Before" plan requires them merely to apply a rule to examples provided by the teacher.

Expectations

The "Before" plan allows more time for students to complete homework in class, which has the advantage of making the teacher available for help. It does this, however, at the expense of interesting instruction that involves students actively. Perhaps the teacher does not expect much homework to get done at home and therefore streamlines whole-class instruction to allow class time for homework. The "After" plan allows more opportunity for the teacher to note and correct mistakes during the lesson, when everyone can benefit from additional explanation. The teacher of the "After" plan expects that students will complete homework at home and therefore uses class time for active instruction of everyone. If the teacher follows through on homework, assigns reasonably interesting work, and explains it thoroughly, it is quite likely to get done.

Language

In the "After" plan, the teacher also makes use of street language, offering mathematical language as a different, more precise, but less colorful alternative. Again, the lesson takes a familiar part of the students' world—their language—and relates it to algebra.

▶ LESSON PLAN

Polymers

Subject Area: Chemistry

Grade Level: 11–12

Time: Two class periods

Students: Those of varying academic skill levels, many below average; those who seem uninterested in chemistry

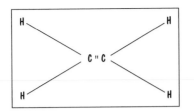

Figure 2.8   Ethylene Monomer

Objectives

1. Students will explain the meaning of the term *polymer*.
2. Given a monomer, students will diagram the polymer chain that forms (see Figure 2.8).
3. Students will learn to identify common materials that are polymers.

Suggested Procedures

1. Review orally the concept of double bonding. Explain that polymers are organic molecules that form when double carbon bonds are converted to single bonds and a long-chain molecule with single carbon–carbon bonds is created.
2. Have students read pages in a textbook on additional polymers.
3. Review the main concepts on the board, asking questions frequently to make sure students understand. Start with the conversion of ethylene to polyethylene; diagram this. Then discuss and diagram polyvinyl chloride, polypropylene, polystyrene, Plexiglas, and Teflon.
4. Show examples of these materials; discuss their uses.

Evaluation

1. Assess students' understanding of polymers and chemical bonding changes through class participation in review.
2. Through a quiz, assess students' understanding of a polymer chain and their memory of common materials that are polymers.

Polymers

Subject Area: Chemistry

Grade Level: 11–12

Time: Three class periods

Students: Those of varying academic skill levels, many below average; those who seem uninterested in chemistry

Objectives

1. Students will explain the meaning of the term *polymer*.
2. Given a monomer, students will diagram the polymer chain that forms.

3. Students will learn to identify common materials that are polymers.

4. Students will enjoy chemistry and consider it as a career option.

Suggested Procedures

1. On a table, have the following items: film, floor tile made of polyvinylchloride (PVC), beakers, Lucite, Teflon bearings, and a Teflon frying pan. Ask students what all these materials have in common; students should figure out that all are forms of plastic and all are either manufactured or naturally produced.

2. Note that some software programs for educational computers simulate the bonding process and permit students to control the steps (e.g., Molecular Editor for Macs). If you cannot gain access to a sophisticated visual resource, use a metal board with magnetic letters, numbers, and sticks to make the formula for the monomer ethylene shown in Figure 2.8. Point out the double-carbon bond, and review the concept of double bonding. Explain that this is a monomer, in which *mono-* means "one." Put another ethylene monomer on the board and ask students how these might be joined. Lead students to see how polymers are constructed when double bonds break and monomers link in a chain. Point out that the prefix *poly-* means "many." (Whether using computer displays or magnetic pieces, all parts, including chemical bonds, must be used in linking monomers to form polymers; point out that pieces do not drop out and new pieces do not appear.)

3. Diagram the monomers vinyl chlorine, propylene, methyl methacrylate, and tetrafluoroethylene on the board. Have students work in pairs to figure out diagrams for polymer chains of each. (Students may use computer displays or magnetic pieces if this helps.)

4. Provide a study sheet on additional polymers; instruct students to read the pages and to complete the study sheet with a partner or alone.

5. With the whole class, review the polymer chains that students constructed in pairs, using students' input.

6. Have students suggest questions they would like to ask a chemist who works with these materials; make a list of students' questions. Encourage questions related to what the chemist does, how the chemist works with the materials, differences a chemist can see between monomers and polymers, what it is like to be a chemist, and so forth. On a subsequent day—after the chapter on polymers is completed—invite a female chemist as a guest speaker and allow students to ask questions.

Evaluation

1. Assess students' understanding of a polymer and of the chemical bonding changes that occur when monomers form by observing student pairs working on problems, through whole-class review, and through items on a quiz.

2. Assess students' understanding of monomers and polymers and of materials that are polymers through study guide answers.

3. Assess students' interest through their questions and reactions to the guest speaker.

Resources

Software
Molecular Editor.
Kinko's Courseware
4141 State Street
Santa Barbara, CA 93110
(800) 292–6640

Polymers

Learning Styles

The "After" lesson plan uses a greater variety of teaching procedures than the "Before" plan. In addition to lectures and textbook readings, it includes a visual diagram and cooperative problem solving. Cooperative problem solving helps students who learn better working with others.

Relevance

Both lesson plans try to relate polymers to daily life by showing items made with polymers. However, the "Before" plan waits until the end of the lesson to do this, whereas the "After" plan begins by introducing familiar, everyday items.

Skill Levels

This type of class is not one in which the teacher can assign a grade-level text and expect students to learn from it. The teacher in the "After" plan has made three adjustments for diverse skill levels. The first adjustment involves utilizing a computer display or magnetic board rather than writing formulas on the board. The magnetic board and computer display allow the teacher and students to move elements and bonds around to create polymers, which makes it easier for students to see the relationships between them. In the "Before" plan, in which the teacher writes formulas on the board, this relationship is not made as clearly.

The second adjustment is the use of peer teaching. The "After" plan asks students to work on polymer chains in pairs and to complete study sheets with partners. The teacher should make sure pairs actually work together; he or she should re-pair students as needed.

The third adjustment involves choosing which monomers and polymers to study. Formulas for monomers and polymers in the "Before" plan vary, and some are quite complex. They are selected on the basis of the textbook and because they are more common materials. However, for students who find the main idea confusing in itself, this variety of formulas only adds to their confusion. Although the "After" plan also selects monomers and polymers from the textbook, those selected have formulas similar enough so that the main idea can be seen more clearly.

Expectations

The "After" plan spends more time than the "Before" plan on emphasizing students' mastery of the material. If the students become interested enough in chemistry and successful enough in learning it, the extra effort is worthwhile.

Success Stories

The "After" plan tries to make the field of chemistry more relevant to students by inviting a guest speaker with whom some of them can identify. The speaker should be someone who can provide a positive role model for students who do not see chemistry as relevant to their lives. Students themselves write the questions for the speaker to address, which bridges the identification and communication gap between the students and the speaker.

▶ LESSON PLAN

Cardiovascular Health

BEFORE

Subject Area: Health
Grade Level: 10–12
Time: Five class periods
Students: Several Spanish-English bilingual students, as well as a few students from a learning disabilities (LD) class

Objectives

1. Students will identify the main parts of the cardiovascular system and their functions.
2. Students will describe several heart diseases or conditions and their causes.
3. Students will learn a healthy dietary and exercise program.

Suggested Procedures

1. Explain that the class will spend the next few days studying the cardiovascular system, related diseases, and disease prevention.
2. Assign pages in the textbook on the structure and function of the cardiovascular system and risk factors.
3. Review the major concepts in a reading assignment, asking questions frequently to check comprehension. Show the film *The Circulatory System: Two Hearts That Beat as One.* Encourage students to take notes on the discussion of the textbook assignment and the film.
4. Assign pages in the textbook on heart attack and heart disease.
5. Review the major concepts in the reading assignment; give a mini-lecture, elaborating on what physicians do when someone has a heart attack.

6. Invite the school nurse as a guest speaker to talk about how exercise and diet can promote cardiovascular health.

Evaluation

Evaluate each student's mastery of the objectives through a quiz.

Resources

Audiovisual

Kennand, D. (1997). *The circulatory system: Two hearts that beat as one*. Princeton, NJ: Films for the Humanities and Sciences. custeserv@films.com web address http://ffh.films.com

Cardiovascular Health

AFTER

Subject Area: Health

Grade Level: 10–12

Time: Five class periods

Students: Several Spanish-English bilingual students, as well as a few students from a learning disabilities (LD) class

Objectives

1. Students will identify the main parts of the cardiovascular system and their functions.
2. Students will describe several heart diseases or conditions and their causes.
3. Students will learn a healthy dietary and exercise program.

Suggested Procedures

1. Invite students to share the experiences of family members or friends who have heart disease. Explain that the class will study the cardiovascular system, diseases, and disease prevention.
2. Divide the class into three groups based on students' reading levels. Have three sets of reading materials ready. One set, written at a lower reading level, describes heart diseases. A second set, written at an intermediary level, describes the circulatory system. A third set, written at a more difficult level, describes the parts of the heart. Distribute the appropriate reading materials to each group. Have students read and then quiz each other until all group members have mastered the material.
3. Regroup students into four groups, so that each new group contains two or three members from the first group. Assign each group one of the following problems or tasks to complete collaboratively:
   a. Explain what types of exercise contribute to the health of the cardiovascular system. Suggest an exercise program for persons ages 15 to 25 that will promote cardiovascular health; give reasons for your suggestions.

    b. Explain what cholesterol does to the cardiovascular system. Develop European American and Mexican menus that are low in cholesterol.

    c. Develop a Spanish-English dictionary to help Spanish-speaking people with limited English communicate with an English-speaking doctor about common heart problems.

    d. Determine and describe the functions an artificial heart must perform. Describe the conditions under which one might be helped by an artificial heart.

    Have available any resource materials the groups might need, such as nutrition guides or newspaper articles on the artificial heart.

4. Have each group orally present its completed project to the class. Encourage students to use relevant diagrams, charts, or activities to involve the class. Make duplicated copies of students' exercise programs, menus, and dictionaries for the entire class.

5. Provide a study guide on the material students should know, as well as additional copies of the first reading assignment for students who wish to read what other groups read. Encourage students to study together and to quiz each other on the study guide.

Evaluation

1. Evaluate students' comprehension of main ideas through group projects.

2. Evaluate students' mastery of the objectives through a quiz.

Cardiovascular Health

Learning Style

Many students tend to learn better through cooperative learning than through individualistic learning. Cooperative learning also fosters peer tutoring, which helps low-achieving students. The "Before" plan does not use cooperative learning. The "After" plan uses quite a bit of it; however, only in procedures 3 and 4 do all students participate—they have a choice in the other procedures. In the "Before" plan, the main role students occupy is as passive recipients. In the "After" plan, students are active participants in learning, which tends to promote better achievement.

The "Before" plan uses various teaching-learning strategies: reading, discussing, watching a film, listening to a speaker. In the "After" plan, the film and speaker are removed only for lack of time; both leave students passive, and a choice was made to increase time on active involvement. Films, videos, and speakers can be useful reinforcers or sources of new information, however, and should be left in if time permits.

Relevance

Little attempt is made in the "Before" plan to relate the curriculum to these particular students. The "After" plan includes several attempts: the introductory discussion, the use of the Spanish language in one project, the use of Mexican foods in a group project, and the invitation for students themselves to figure out a dietary and exercise program.

Skill Levels

The "Before" plan makes no provision for students' diverse skill levels, whereas the "After" plan does, in two ways. First, reading assignments are made according to students' reading levels, but students later have to teach each other about what they read, so no one misses content areas. Second, students are encouraged to study together with a study guide to direct work.

Language

The Spanish-English dictionary assignment helps bilingual students acquire English words. It can also sensitize English-speaking students to language barriers.

References

Asher, James J. (1966) The learning strategy of the total physical response: A review. *The Modern Language Journal, 50*(2) 79–84.

Boykin, A. W., & Allen, B. (1988). Rhythmic-movement facilitated learning in working class Afro-American children. *Journal of Genetic Psychology, 149*, 335–347.

Cummins, J. (2000). *Language, power and pedagogy*. Buffalo, NY: Multilingual Matters.

Delpit, L. (1995). *Other people's children*. New York: New Press.

Escalante, J. (1990). The Jaime Escalante math program. *Journal of Negro Education, 59*(3), 407–423.

Fennema, E., & Peterson, P. L. (1987). Effective teaching for girls or boys: The same or different? In D. C. Berliner & B. V. Rosenshine (Eds.), *Talks to teachers* (pp. 111–125). New York: Random House.

Gardner, H. (1995). Reflections on multiple intelligences. *Phi Delta Kappan, 77*(3), 200–208.

Gardner, H. (2000). *Intelligence reframed: Multiple intelligences for the 21st century*. New York: Basic Books.

Haberman, M. (1995). *Star teachers of children in poverty*. West Lafayette, IN: Kappa Delta Pi.

Hale, J. E. (1982). *Black children: Their roots, culture, and learning style*. Provo, UT: Brigham Young University Press.

Hollins, E. R. (1996). *Culture in school learning: Revealing the deep meaning*. Mahwah, NJ: Erlbaum.

Levinsohn, K. R. (2007). Cultural differences and learning styles of Chinese and European trades students. *Institute for Learning Styles Research Journal, 1*. Retrieved December 30, 2007, from http://www.auburn.edu/~witteje/ilsrj/.

Moses, R. P., & Cobb, C. E. (2001). *Radical equations*. Boston: Beacon.

Pallapu, P. (2007). Effects of visual and verbal learning styles on learning. *Institute for Learning Styles Research Journal, 1*. Retrieved December 30, 2007, from http://www.auburn.edu/~witteje/ilsrj/.

Philips, S. U. (1983). *The invisible culture*. New York: Longman.

Reyes, P., Scribner, J. D., & Scribner, A. P. (Eds.). (1999). *Lessons from high-performing Hispanic schools*. New York: Teachers College Press.

Shade, B. J. R. (1989). *Culture, style and the educative process*. Springfield, IL: Charles Thomas.

Sleeter, C. E., & Grant, C. A. (2009). *Making choices for multicultural education: Five approaches to race, class, and gender* (5th ed.). Hobokon, NY: Wiley.

CHAPTER 3

Human Relations

Do any of the following incidents resemble situations you have encountered?

- A student who uses a wheelchair is mainstreamed into a fourth-grade class. She is excited and nervous on her first day. The student is introduced to the class and then wheels to her place in the front row. None of the other children speaks to her, but they stare and giggle when they think she is not looking. On the playground, several students gang up to tease her.

- This is the first day at Kennedy High School for two Muslim girls, Fatima and Akram. As they enter the science honor class wearing head scarves, several students snicker, some smile cordially, and others—three males—make flirtatious statements. Fatima and Akram are always together; some students, especially the boys who flirted and got nowhere, are starting to say they are lesbians, and other students see them as strange.

- A suburban high school in which the number of students of color is rapidly rising is the scene of a cold war. Although the European American, African American, and Asian American students inhabit the same classrooms and facilities, they rarely mix or talk to one another; when they do mix, their interactions are superficial. These three groups of students ignore one another most of the time, but occasionally fights and verbal insults occur. In the cafeteria, students sit with their own ethnic and gender groups, and a few food fights have erupted during the semester.

- Some of the Latino/a students refuse to acknowledge their ability to speak Spanish; they seem embarrassed by their parents and by their Spanish surnames, which suggest they know Spanish (and many of them do). They are eager to look and act like their White European American classmates. Other Latino students take pride in their culture and language and are put off by their Latino brothers and sisters who act like their White classmates; they are also put off by some of their White classmates who distance themselves from them.

- During recess, two girls ask a group of boys if they can play soccer with them. Some of the boys snicker, saying, "Girls can't play well enough to play with boys." A few boys point toward their less athletic male teammates, saying, "Those sissies are better soccer players than any girl."

If you have encountered similar situations, you may find yourself gravitating toward the human relations approach to teaching. Although this approach is not the only means by which to deal with the problems that exist among different groups of people, it is the only one that has as its primary concern the establishment of nondiscriminating interaction among different types of people.

▶ PRIMARY CONCERNS OF THE HUMAN RELATIONS APPROACH TO TEACHING

The human relations approach is directed toward developing respect among individuals of various races, genders, classes, religions, exceptionalities, and sexual orientations. It encourages students to see the beauty within people instead of looking only at the external surface. It teaches that differences in clothing, hairstyle, and language, accent, and birth location are either personal decisions or happenstance, and are not indicators of one's personal worth or kindness. Human relations also seeks to improve feelings and communication in the classroom and in the school as a whole. In addition, since the events of September 11, 2001, the human relations approach has become more global. It calls for greater cross-cultural communication across international borders and for international attention to nonmilitary efforts to erode terrorism, including international support for humanitarian assistance to war-torn nations and the formation of democratic governments. Specifically, it focuses on the following considerations:

- Respect for oneself and for others
- Positive student–student relationships
- Elimination of stereotypes students often hold about each other (which are often manifested in name calling)
- Improved self-concept, especially related to individual and cultural differences
- Positive cross-group communication
- Respect for those who live in a different country
- Respect for different religious affiliations

The term *human relations* generally encompasses any aspect of interpersonal relations, both nationally and internationally. The human relations—which is very similar to the intercultural approach in some countries—to multicultural education is directed primarily toward interpersonal and intergroup relations centering on race or ethnicity, gender, social class, sexual orientation, differences in ability, and religious differences. Also, it promotes and encourages respect among people of different nations, especially as more and more students use the Web and global chat rooms. In this approach, teachers work with students in a number of areas.

Cooperative Learning

Research over the past several decades suggests that cooperative learning improves student–student relationships across race, gender, and ability/disability lines as well as student achievement (Cohen & Lotan, 1997; Gillies & Ashman, 2000; Johnson, Johnson, & Maruyama, 1982; Slavin, 1995). However, to be effective, cooperative learning must satisfy several conditions for cross-group contact, as suggested by the pioneering work of Gordon Allport (1954) over fifty years ago. It must involve students both in cooperative activities across lines of difference and in roles of equal status, provide opportunities for students to learn about one another as individuals, and be strongly supported by the teacher. In addition, cooperative learning must be used consistently and frequently in the classroom.

Although there are different models for structuring cooperative learning, all models require students to interact in small groups to accomplish a common goal. They also require teachers to structure tasks so that each student is able to make a worthwhile contribution. Some of the lesson plans that appear later in this chapter illustrate the models for structuring cooperative learning. The group investigation model is presented in the lesson plan "Westward Ho!" (p. 91). This model requires students to contribute different talents, skills, interests, and roles to the creation of a group project or solution of a group problem. The team games model is used in the lesson "Factoring Polynomials and Making Friends at the Same Time" (p. 118). In this model, students practice academic skills while working together as a team. The jigsaw model is illustrated in "Solving Two Equations With Two Unknowns" (p. 115). In this model, students are grouped twice. First, each group masters different materials, and each student becomes an "expert" in his or her group's area. Students are then regrouped so that each new group has at least one "expert" from the first set of groups. The new groups solve a problem or complete an assignment that requires pooling their expertise and sharing what they learned in the first group. (See also "Cardiovascular Health," Chapter 2, p. 62.)

Cooperative learning involves much more than grouping students and asking them to work cooperatively. Rather, the group tasks need to be planned carefully so that each student has a significant role in the group, a contribution to make of which he or she is capable, and the incentive to work together with the group.

Attitudes, Prejudice, and Stereotyping

Teachers must be aware of what their students say and do to recognize stereotyping, which many students do without realizing it. They must be equally on guard for negative statements that students make consciously when they believe that their way of life is being threatened by those who are different. Negative attitudes, prejudices, and stereotyping develop through a complex range of factors; in our companion volume, *Making Choices for Multicultural Education* (Sleeter & Grant, 2009), we review research and theory on these concepts. Students need to be made aware that stereotyping goes against the principles they learned in both the natural and social sciences—that judgments should be formed only after a comprehensive analysis and evaluation of the data.

Eliminating stereotypes usually involves helping students to see how they are using stereotyping, for example, to provide privileges for themselves and those they like and respect. Also, it involves understanding that stereotyping involves making an oversimplified opinion or uncritical judgment. Neither of these is characteristic of students with inquiring minds and a sense of fairness. As preschoolers, students begin to notice differences among people (for example, sex, color of hair, color of skin) and begin to form attitudes and interpretations of those differences. Stereotypes represent peoples' attempts to understand what they see and experience and are formed on the basis of hearsay, narrow experiences, bad experiences, and interpretations of experiences that are a part of everyday discourse.

Stereotypes are also formed through bias and narrowly constructed methodology. For example, the "model minority" is a tag that non-Asians commonly apply to many, if not all, Asian American groups. Although some will argue that this is a positive stereotype, it is nevertheless an inaccurate generalization about all Asian Americans. Much of the research in the 1970s and 1980s that examined African American family life was conducted by White male researchers, who falsely interpreted African American family life, objectified the African American woman, and described her in stereotypical terms (Collins, 1998). Racial profiling relies on stereotypes, such as the stereotype of Middle Eastern men as terrorists, or of dark-skinned shoppers as shoplifters. Action Research Activity 3.1 is a useful tool to sensitize young people to their own tendencies to stereotype. Action Research Activity 3.4 is a questionnaire that looks at sex stereotyping.

Curricular interventions can help reduce prejudice and stereotyping. James Banks (1995) reviewed research on curricular interventions addressing racial and gender stereotyping. He concluded that research findings on the impact of curriculum on students' attitudes and stereotyping are inconsistent but optimistic. Some studies have found that interventions make no difference, whereas others have found that they make a positive change. Banks recommends that teachers use well-designed curricular interventions and materials and pay attention to the impact of their interventions on their own students so that they can make adjustments as needed. Young children seem to be particularly influenced by curricular interventions; elementary teachers have an especially important opportunity to develop open and democratic attitudes in children.

Lesson plans that help to correct the problem of stereotyping involve giving correct information to replace stereotypes and having students participate in activities that make them realize the inaccuracies of stereotypes. For example, a lesson seeking to counterargue the stereotype that males are not nurturing could have as guest speakers fathers who stay home and care for their children. Also, male students in the class who feed or babysit their younger brothers or sisters could be encouraged to share their attitudes and feelings. A lesson on the inaccuracy of stereotypes about females being unathletic could involve a discussion of the excellent performance by women in the Olympic Games of 2000 and 2004, the Women's National Basketball Association (WNBA), and college hockey In addition, some factual data are usually needed to replace stereotypes, as are activities that persuade students that factual data is preferable to stereotypes. The lesson plans "Toys" (p. 80) and "Bones and Muscles" (p. 88) are designed in this way. The plan "Luminescence or Incandescence?" (p. 96) counters stereotypes about non-Western and non-Anglo culture as being nonscientific by incorporating examples of science concepts developed by non-White scientists, and "Finding Symmetry" (p. 112) does the same with math.

Personal Feelings

As we all know, children can be cruel to one another and can hurt classmates' feelings without even realizing it. We hope that as students mature they learn that such cruel behavior is wrong. A school district familiar to one of us has implemented a "peace builders" program to teach students constructive ways of relating to people; this program is having a positive impact on how students treat each other. The teacher is an important influence on students' learning to eliminate cruel behavior and to replace it with peaceful and positive behavior. Lessons that focus on this behavior modification usually involve conflict resolution, role playing, and discussion of how name-calling and cruel actions hurt feelings. Action Research Activity 3.3 helps you investigate your students' experiences with name-calling, teachers' interventions, and students' ideas about how to handle it.

Students in grades 6 through 12 sometimes need lessons to help them understand how members of oppressed groups feel when they have little or no agency. Immediately after September 11, 2001, Arab Muslims in the United States were subject to racial profiling, threatened, ridiculed, and much more. They felt oppressed and powerless. Non-Arab Muslims who perpetrated threats and profiling were often unaware of the impact of their actions on innocent people. Experiencing the pangs of such discrimination and bias even in a role-playing situation can help students to better understand verbal and attitudinal hostility. Implement a lesson where students are segregated on the basis of characteristics such as right-handedness versus left-handedness. By encouraging students to experience personally how it feels to be neglected or ridiculed, teachers can have a more in-depth discussion of the significance of one's personal feeling and can foster greater respect and acceptance among students from different cultural groups. The plan "Class Meetings" (p. 103) is very helpful for establishing a climate of communication, constructive problem solving, and peace building.

Individual Uniqueness and Worth

Each student is unique, and if teachers fail to recognize this uniqueness, the students will often make it clear to the teacher in some way. The human relations approach highlights the difference and worth of each and every individual. Race, gender, and social class are important considerations, but the approach concentrates on the individual. Many teachers point out that it is also important to stress what we have in common rather than focusing entirely on differences. Teachers who demonstrate value for the worth of their diverse students usually connect this with the common value that all students share. Students bring different gifts to the classroom, but all of them bring a desire to feel worthy, successful, and accepted.

Included in this chapter are several lessons that help students develop pride in themselves and an appreciation of peers. The lessons attempt to sensitize students to the similarities and differences among people, helping them to see that people are more alike than different and that differences are valuable. A recent example of how valuable differences are occurred after September 11. Before the terrorist attack, comprehension and fluency in Arabic languages was not in demand, nor was it greatly appreciated. Since the attack, individuals who understand and are fluent in Arabic languages have been in great demand by the U.S. government and, increasingly, by school districts. The lessons can take on countless forms, but they often involve similar activities (e.g., students' identifying something unique and valuable about themselves, determining what would make another student happy and attempting to fulfill that wish, creating collages and classroom displays expressing personal interests, arranging fairs that highlight students' accomplishments). The lessons "Paper Flowers" (p. 78), "Billboards" (p. 94), and "Quintessentially Me" (p. 110) involve teaching about the contributions of ethnic and gender groups, especially those represented by students in the school. The main concern is to teach the idea that everyone has something worthwhile to contribute.

Cross-Group Communication

Communication, whether it occurs among groups or between two individuals living in the same household, should not be underestimated. Major organizations (e.g., the United Nations) have been formed solely to promote cross-group communication, and some school staff members (e.g., bilingual teachers and home–school coordinators) spend most of their workday striving to establish good cross-group communication. The people directly involved in establishing and promoting cross-group communication know that it takes dedication and hard work to accomplish.

Although it may be difficult to establish and maintain cross-group communication in the classroom, educators have some powerful advantages over those in other fields. The teacher is in charge, students ordinarily look up to the teacher, and parents want good home–school relations—these advantages help to create a classroom characteristic of open, civil, and honest interactions. We have observed teachers who are excellent at establishing cross-group communication in classes made up of several different kinds of groups. These teachers use a variety of techniques and strategies to achieve their success, including cooperative learning. They also teach communication skills (e.g., listening, sharing, and inviting) and have students practice these skills in structured lessons.

Another strategy is to teach students about cultural differences in communication style, allowing students of different cultural backgrounds to interpret correctly what others mean and to respond in a culturally appropriate manner. Lesson plans that seek to promote cross-group communication usually involve factual information about communication skills and styles, demonstrations of communication skills, role-playing, and contact with people whose communication styles differ from those of the students. Although these activities work well, cross-group communication must be a regular part of the daily curriculum to be successful.

In some of the lesson plans that follow, the "After" sections have different titles from those used in the "Before" sections. The change in title reflects a substantive change in the focus of the lesson to meet the needs of all students to "turn on" to learning.

▶ ACTION RESEARCH ACTIVITY 3.1

Stereotyping

This activity is a survey that investigates the extent to which your students or coworkers stereotype people on the basis of race, gender, and disability. Figure 3.1 contains photographs of people and their names, along with a list of personality characteristics and work roles. Photocopy the figure, making as many copies as you need.

Scoring

The best response is no response. People who say they cannot complete the survey are usually refusing to stereotype, as are those who put all the characteristics under every

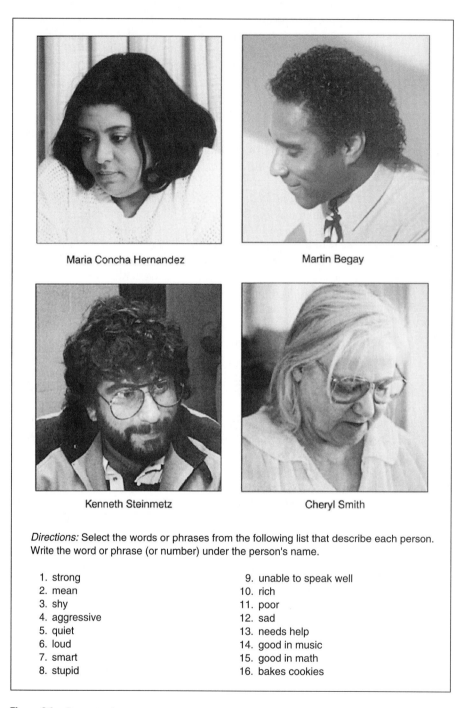

Maria Concha Hernandez

Martin Begay

Kenneth Steinmetz

Cheryl Smith

Directions: Select the words or phrases from the following list that describe each person. Write the word or phrase (or number) under the person's name.

1. strong
2. mean
3. shy
4. aggressive
5. quiet
6. loud
7. smart
8. stupid

9. unable to speak well
10. rich
11. poor
12. sad
13. needs help
14. good in music
15. good in math
16. bakes cookies

Figure 3.1 Stereotyping

Jane Fitzpartick

Pat Jackson

William Jones

Susan Noguchi

17. good at yard work
18. cleans house
18. teacher
20. principal
21. janitor
22. doctor
23. nurse
24. cares for children
25. car mechanic

26. owns a restaurant
27. president
28. secretary
29. police officer
30. thief
31. unemployed
32. stays home
33. goes skiing
34. plays basketball

Figure 3.1 *(continued)*

name. For those who do stereotype in their responses, you can analyze their responses through the following patterns:

1. Which persons received the success words and phrases (1, 4, 7, 10, 20, 22, 26, 27)?

2. Which persons received the failure or anonymity words and phrases (8, 9, 11, 12, 13, 30, 31, 32)?

3. Were sex-stereotypic personality traits and work roles chosen (e.g., for women, cleans house [18] and bakes cookies [16])?

4. Are there particular race stereotypes (e.g., for African Americans, good in music [14] and plays basketball [34]; for Asian Americans, owns a restaurant [26] and quiet [5])?

▶ ACTION RESEARCH ACTIVITY 3.2

Sociometric Survey

To find out how well your students know and like each other, use the survey shown in Figure 3.2. Fill in students' names in the left-hand column, and duplicate and distribute. Assure students that their responses will be kept confidential.

You can analyze the results of the survey in two ways. First, for each student, tally the total number of marks in each column. For example, which students are liked or known the most? the least? Are there identifiable characteristics of least-liked or least-known students? Second, look for segregation and grouping patterns, such as sex segregation and racial segregation. Use this information for group-building activities. You may also want to investigate potential stereotypes that accompany social segregation or dislike of peers.

▶ ACTION RESEARCH ACTIVITY 3.3

Name-Calling

These are interview questions about experiences with prejudice. They work best with older students (starting at 8 or 9 years of age).

1. Tell me about a time in which some students were making fun of another student.
   • What did the teacher(s) or supervisor(s) do about it?
   • How did students react to what the teacher(s) or supervisor(s) did or did not do?
   • Might the situation have been handled better, do you think? If so, how?
   • Did the teacher(s) or supervisor(s) do anything to teach students not to make fun of others like the one getting picked on? If so, what?

2. Can you think of times when girls/boys [opposite sex of the interviewee] have picked on other students on the basis of sex or have stereotyped your sex unfairly? Also, can you think of times when gay or lesbian students were verbally harassed?
   • Tell me about it; what did they do or say?
   • What, if anything, did the teacher(s) or supervisor(s) do about it?
   • How effective were their responses?
   • Would you have liked to see them do something different?

Student's Name	Very well___ a friend		Well, but not a friend		Not too well, would like to know better		Not too well, would not like to know better		Not at all	
1.										
2.										
3.										
4.										
5.										
6.										
7.										
8.										
9.										
10.										
11.										
12.										
13.										
14.										
15.										
16.										
17.										
18.										
19.										
20.										
21.										
22.										

Figure 3.2 How Well Do You Know Your Classmates?

3. Have you been aware of other students being prejudiced against other racial or ethnic groups?
   - How did you know they were?
   - What did the teacher(s) or supervisor(s) do about it?
   - How effective were their responses?
   - Would you have liked to see them do something different?

4. Can you think of times when students with disabilities have been picked on or called names?
   - What happened?
   - What did the teacher(s) or supervisor(s) do about it?

5. In addition to what we have just talked about, are there other ways that students make fun of each other? other names you have heard them call other kids?

6. Tell me about the most effective thing you have seen an adult do to help students who are different to get along better and appreciate each other more.
   - How do you know it worked?
   - Why do you think it worked? (In other words, what made it work?)

▶ ACTION RESEARCH ACTIVITY 3.4

Sex Stereotyping

Have sex stereotypes disappeared at long last? Find out! You can do this activity as either an interview or a questionnaire. If you do it as an interview, use questions such as the following:

1. Are there any occupations you consider (a) especially appropriate for a woman? Why? (b) especially appropriate for a man? Why? (c) inappropriate for a woman? Why? (d) inappropriate for a man? Why?

2. Around the house, which tasks do you think are more appropriate for the females to do? Why? for the males to do? Why?

3. In your household, which jobs do the females do? the males do?

4. If there are very young children in the household, who should have the main responsibility for them? Why? Should that person also hold a job?

Questionnaire

Name: _____

Directions: Choose the best word from the two given to complete each sentence. If neither choice is best, write any word you think is best.

1. Dr. Martin reads X rays. _____ helps people. (*He, She*)
2. We need milk, butter, and eggs. My _____ will go to the store. (*dad, mom*)
3. _____ is mowing the lawn. (*Ann, Tim*)
4. Dr. Meyer filled a cavity in one of Maria's teeth. _____ is a dentist. (*She, He*)
5. Steve's house is dirty. His _____ must clean it. (*dad, mom*)

6. _____ Johnson is our principal. (*Mrs., Mr., Ms., Miss*)

7. Jim's _____ is a firefighter. (*aunt, uncle*)

8. A police officer came to the door. _____ was wearing a blue uniform. (*She, He*)

9. An astronaut came to our school. _____ talked about rockets. (*She, He*)

10. _____ is a good baseball player. (*Tina, Steve*)

11. _____ enjoys playing on the computer at home. (*Judy, Willie*)

12. Carlos broke his watch. His _____ fixed it. (*mom, dad*)

13. The mechanic fixed our car. _____ knew what was wrong. (*She, He*)

14. Nurse Jackson took Rosa's temperature. _____ put Rosa to bed. (*She, He*)

15. _____ likes to bake cookies. (*Joey, Julie*)

16. _____ Kelley is our librarian. (*Mrs., Mr., Ms.*)

17. _____ is an artist. (*Todd, Gwen*)

18. _____ must take out the garbage. (*Joan, Jim*)

19. It is _____'s turn to do the dishes. (*Mike, Sue*)

20. _____ is going camping this weekend. (*Joy, Greg*)

Nombre: _____

1. _____ Martinez lee los rayos x. _____ ayuda a la gente. (*La doctora, El doctor*) (*Ella, El*)

2. Necesitamos leche, mantequilla, y huevos. Mi _____ irá a la tienda. (*madre, padre*)

3. _____ está cortando la (el) césped. (*Ana, Carlos*)

4. _____ Meyer llenó una carie en el diente de Maria. _____ es un(a) dentist(a). (*El doctor, La doctora*) (*El, Ella*)

5. El cuarto de Steve está sucio. Su _____ tiene que limpiarlo. (*madre, padre*)

6. _____ Rodriguez es nuestro(a) director(a). (*El Sr., La Srta., La Sra.*)

7. _____ de Luisa es un(a) bombero(a) (*El tío, La tía*)

8. Un(a) agente de la policia llegó a la puerta. _____ llevaba un uniforme azul. (*Ella, El*)

9. Un(a) astronauto(a) llegó a nuestra escuela. _____ habló sobre cohetes. (*Ella, El*)

10. _____ es un(a) buen(a) jugador(a) de béisbol. (*Rosa, Miquel*)

11. Las matemáticas son la matéria preferida de _____ en la escuela. (*Carmen, Mario*)

12. Carlos rompió su reloj. Su _____ se lo arregló. A Carlos Se le rompió el reloj. (*madre, padre*)

13. _____ arregló nuestro coche. _____ supo lo que estaba mal. (*El mecánico/La mecánica*) (*El, Ella*)

14. _____ Jackson le tomó la temperatura a Rosa. _____ puso a Rosa a dormir (*La enfermera/El enfermero*) (*El, Ella*)

15. A _____ le gusta cocer al horno las galletas. (*Jose, Diana*)

16. _____ Cruz es nuestro(a) bibliotecario(a). (*El Sr., La Srta., La Sra.*)

17. _____ es un(a) artist(a). (*El, Ella*)

18. _____ tiene qul sacar la basura. (*Ramon, Conchita*)

19. Le toca a _____ lavar los platos. (*Susana, Miguel*)

20. _____ va a acampar este fin de semana. (*Carlos, Maria*)

▶ LESSON PLAN

Paper Flowers

Subject Area: Art
Grade Level: 1–3
Time: One day

Objectives

1. Students will cut curves on paper accurately.
2. Students will create a colorful design.

Suggested Procedures

1. Pass out large pieces of construction paper, one to each student. Show them how to fold the paper in half to make a cover for their art work.
2. Demonstrate how to draw a flower shape using curves on colored paper. Show several different flower shapes; stress that they can be very different from one another. Show how to cut out a flower.
3. Make available colored paper, scissors, and paste. Tell students to draw several different flowers on different colors of paper, cut them out, and paste them to their covers.
4. When students are done, share covers.

Evaluation

Assess students' quality of design of covers, quality of cutting, and neatness.

Paper Flowers[1]

Subject Area: Art
Grade Level: 1–3
Time: One day

---

[1] Source: Dorothy Goines, Racine Unified Public Schools, Racine, Wisconsin.

Objectives

1. Students will cut curves on paper accurately.
2. Students will create a colorful design.
3. Students will appreciate their own uniqueness.

Suggested Procedures

1. Write the word unique on the board and pronounce it. Ask for a definition. Develop a common definition after having students share their thoughts.
2. Discuss the notion that people are all alike in some ways and unique in others; have students suggest ways we are alike and ways we are different.
3. Explain that we all have unique fingerprints. Have several ink pads available and ask each student to make a fingerprint on white paper. Compare fingerprints.

Commercial 1

Name of the toy _____

Who was in the commercial? (circle one)
     boys   girls   both boys and girls

How was the toy being used? _____

To whom do you think the company is trying to sell the toy? (circle one)
     boys   girls   both boys and girls

Commercial 2

Name of the toy _____

Who was in the commercial? (circle one)
     boys   girls   both boys and girls

How was the toy being used? _____

To whom do you think the company is trying to sell the toy? (circle one)
     boys   girls   both boys and girls

Commercial 3

Name of the toy _____

Who was in the commercial? (circle one)
     boys   girls   both boys and girls

How was the toy being used? _____

To whom do you think the company is trying to sell the toy? (circle one)
     boys   girls   both boys and girls

Figure 3.3 Toy Commercial Evaluation Sheet

4. Explain that students' uniqueness will be used to create art folders decorated with unique flowers. Pass out large pieces of construction paper, one to each student. Have them fold it in half to make a cover for their art work.

5. Pass out colored paper. Have each student decorate a piece with his or her fingerprints.

6. Demonstrate how to draw a flower shape using curves. Show several different flower shapes; stress that flowers are also unique in many ways. Show how to cut out a flower.

7. Tell students to decorate different colors of paper with fingerprints and to draw and cut out flowers from their decorated paper. Encourage them to share flowers and paste them on their covers.

8. Finally, have students share covers. Point out the beauty and interest contributed by their unique fingerprints, unique fingerprint designs, and unique flowers.

Evaluation

1. Assess students' quality of design of covers and quality of cutting.

2. Assess students' reactions to uniqueness in their covers and flowers.

Paper Flowers

Individual Uniqueness and Worth

In the "After" plan, the art lesson is now about the value and beauty of uniqueness. Note that the discussion of uniqueness is presented in a positive and nonthreatening context: Children usually find fingerprints fascinating, they usually enjoy art, and bright-colored paper flowers are visually pleasing. In this context, learning about individual differences is also a pleasant experience. A teacher with a class of students in which there is name-calling and stereotyping could start working on these problems with a nonthreatening individual difference, such as fingerprints, and in a relaxed and positive lesson, such as art. From there, one can move to more sensitive differences. Also, many young children watch the Disney channel and shows such as Sesame Street; many of the shows feature and stress the uniqueness of characters. Have students discuss the uniqueness and worth of the characters in their favorite show.

▶ LESSON PLAN

Toys

Subject Area: Mathematics
Grade Level: 1–3
Time: Two hours

Objectives

1. Students will subtract two-digit numbers.

2. Students will count change correctly.

Suggested Procedures

1. Give each student a store catalogue or advertisement featuring toys. Instruct them to cut out five pictures of toys they would like to own and to paste each picture on a sheet of tagboard. Instruct them to copy the listed price next to each toy and to round it to the nearest dollar.

2. Set up a mock toy store. Have three students act as cashiers (the role can be rotated). Give each student $50 in play money. Allow students to buy as many "toys" as they would like. Use this activity to practice subtraction and counting change.

Evaluation

Given story problems involving subtracting money and identifying change, assess students' ability to solve them correctly.

Toys[2]

Subject Areas: Social Studies, Mathematics
Grade Level: 1–3
Time: Four hours

Objectives

1. Students will recognize and describe sex stereotypes.
2. Students will understand how stereotypes are limiting and often inaccurate.
3. Students will identify sex stereotyping in toy commercials.
4. Students will subtract two-digit numbers.
5. Students will count change correctly.
6. Students will appreciate the interests and wishes of others.

Suggested Procedures

1. Seat students around tables. On each table, have several store catalogues or advertisements featuring toys. In selecting catalogues or advertisements, you should be sensitive to the price ranges that the students' families can afford; however, this should not mean censoring exposure to toys outside their price range. Instruct each student to cut out five pictures of toys he or she would like to own.

2. Have girls select toys they think boys would like and have boys select toys they think girls would like. Have them paste the pictures on one or two large sheets of tagboard. Compare the toys selected for girls with the toys selected for boys. Have children identify the characteristics of "girl" toys and "boy" toys; list them on the board.

---

[2]Source: Connie Olson, Kansasville, Wisconsin, and Sue Senzig, Racine Unified Public Schools, Rancine, Wisconsin.

Ask if girls and boys are really like the words on the board; draw out examples that show both sexes to be more complex. Point out that these words are stereotypes or show bias: They suggest that both sexes have limited interests and capabilities, that members of each sex are all alike, and that the sexes are very different from one another. Ask students to identify toys on the opposite sex's poster they would like.

3. Ask students about the people who help us decide which toys are right for us. One source that students will probably name is television commercials. Tell students that television commercials can teach them to limit their interests by showing a certain toy being used by only one sex. Another source may be some members of their family. Tell students that they will learn as they grow older that things change, and therefore some ideas, like that women cannot be soldiers or commercial airplane pilots, are no longer valid.

4. Instruct students to watch three toy commercials very carefully over the weekend. Give each student a copy of the "Toy Commercial Evaluation Sheet" shown in Figure 3.3 (on page 79). When the students have completed the form, help them to identify the following:
   • Toys shown with both sexes
   • Toys shown with one sex
   • Toys shown with one sex that could be enjoyed by both sexes

5. Have children cut tagboard to separate the toys. Instruct them to price the toys in whole-dollar amounts, using the catalogues as a guide. Set up a mock toy store. Have three students act as cashiers (this role can be rotated). Give each student $25 in play money.

6. Put two paper slips with each student's name in a hat. Have students draw two names. Instruct them to "buy" a toy for each name drawn; it should be something that the student would like, and students should not confine choices to sex stereotypes. Use this activity to practice subtraction and counting change. After buying and giving and receiving gifts, students may spend their remaining play money in the toy store as they wish.

Evaluation

1. Assess students' skill in identifying sex stereotypes through their toy commercial evaluations.

2. Assess students' attention to the interests of others and their willingness not to stereotype by observing what they buy in the mock toy store.

3. Assess students' skill in subtracting money and identifying change through some story problems.

Toys

WHY THE CHANGES?

Stereotypes and Stereotyping

The toys in the "Before" plan lend themselves excellently to lessons on sex stereotyping. Therefore, an examination of stereotypes was added to the math lesson. The discussion of "girl" toys and "boy" toys helps students become aware of what a stereotype is and of stereotypes they probably encounter every day. The teacher should not force students to accept toys with which they are uncomfortable but should encourage students not to limit themselves or their peers because of stereotypes. Students are taught to analyze toy television commercials because many of their ideas probably come partly from the media.

Feelings

In the "After" lesson plan, the teacher pays attention to what families can afford when selecting the toy catalogues and designing the store. An effort should be made not to put students from low-income families in a position of having to choose things their families cannot afford. Also, the "After" plan encourages students to pay attention to the interests and feelings of others by "buying" toys for each other. The teacher needs to monitor this activity to make sure students are actually trying to please those for whom they are buying toys.

Cooperating and Sharing

The "Before" plan reinforces individual consumption; each student has his or her own catalogue to cut and works at his or her own desk. However, in the "After" plan, students work at tables and share catalogues. This in itself is not cooperative learning, but it does encourage the sharing of materials and ideas.

▶ LESSON PLAN

Global Cooperation

Subject Area: Social Studies
Grade Level: 3–4
Time: Two days

Objectives

1. Students will learn that different countries specialize in products for world trade.
2. Students will value cooperation and interdependence.

Suggested Procedures

1. On a table, display items that come from different parts of the world, such as a bananna, a rubber ball, a radio, and a wool sweater. Ask students if they know where the items were made.

2. Explain that different countries produce different products and that countries trade products so that people can enjoy more than just what is produced in their own country. To illustrate this fact, select about six different countries that are located in different parts of the world and produce different products. Point them out on a map, and show pictures of their main trade products.

3. Distribute blank world maps. Have students locate each of the six countries and paste their own pictures or magazine cutouts of the countries' main products on the maps.

4. Instruct students to locate items at home that come from other countries and to bring a list of these items to class the following day.

5. The next day, share lists, writing items on a master list on the board. Ask students to consider the following questions:
   - What would happen if we stopped trading with a certain country?
   - Why is it important for countries to cooperate?
   - Do individuals in the family or local community need to cooperate and trade for similar reasons? Can you give examples?

Evaluation

Assess students' understanding of specialization, cooperation, and independence through class discussion.

Global Cooperation[3]

AFTER

Subject Area: Social Studies
Grade Level: 3–4
Time: Two days

Objectives

1. Students will appreciate the difficulties caused by maldistribution of products.
2. Students will learn that they must give up something to gain something else.
3. Students will value human life despite social and cultural differences.
4. Students will develop cooperation skills.

Suggested Procedures

1. Divide the class into four groups. Have each group pick a country's name, draw a flag for their country, and draw a picture or write a paragraph about its climate, land, and lifestyle.

2. Distribute trade cards for four products—blankets, bread, fruit, and medicine—as shown in Table 3.1.

3. The groups now must decide which products are important to them and then trade in the trade center in the middle of the classroom. Only one person

Table 3.1

	Group 1	Group 2	Group 3	Group 4	Total
Blankets	6	0	2	2	10
Bread	1	1	1	7	10
Fruit	2	7	0	1	10
Medicine	1	2	7	0	10

[3]Source: Chris Aamodt and Margaret Conway, Madison, Wisconsin.

from each group can be in the trade center, but all trades must be approved by the entire country.

4. Take away one country's bread (due to bad weather, that country's wheat crop failed), creating a famine there. The other countries must decide whether to help the starving country. If they refuse to cooperate, all except the starved country will experience a flood, which has the land with the highest elevation. The groups either cooperate or suffer from floods.

5. Discuss the following questions with the class:
   - How did you feel inside your group?
   - How did you feel toward the other groups?
   - What were differences and similarities between the groups?
   - What did the groups want from each other?
   - What were the differences between products?
   - How did you feel when the teacher took the bread?
   - How did the rest of you feel toward this group?
   - How did you solve the problem?
   - Have you ever wanted something you did not get? What?
   - How does that differ from wanting food or needing clothes?
   - Have you had to sacrifice or trade to get what you want?
   - Do your parents ever tell you to finish your food because there are starving children in other countries? Why do they say that?
   - How could we help people who do not have enough?

6. Have children sit in a circle. Put some candy in a bowl and pass it around the circle. No one can eat the candy until the bowl has made it all the way around the circle, but give this lenient rule: "You can take as many as you want." The bowl will probably not make it very far before it runs empty. At this point, give this problem to the students: "What are you going to do? Is it fair that a few have all the treats while others go away without any? Does cooperating mean you do not always get your way?" This should reinforce the idea of thinking of others.

Evaluation

Assess students' willingness to cooperate and share through discussion and through their behavior when the candy is passed around.

Global Cooperation

Cooperation

The "Before" lesson plan teaches about cooperation, but it does not teach students to cooperate themselves—students work individually rather than with each other. In contrast, the "After" lesson plan has students work together in groups that constitute a "country," and it requires the "countries" to work together to deal with product distribution and famine. The students themselves participate in cooperating.

Another problem with the "Before" plan is that it reinforces the idea that global specialization is beneficial to all, even though the economies of Third World countries are in many cases devastated by shifting production from diversified products for local consumption to specialized products for trade. Often the main beneficiaries of global specialization are wealthy countries that can afford to buy imported luxury items. The "After" plan does not criticize global specialization directly, but it also does not reinforce it. Rather, the lesson directs students' attention to the distribution of goods and asks them to consider how people can work together to distribute goods more fairly.

▶ LESSON PLAN

The Life Cycle

Subject Area: Science
Grade Level: 3–4
Time: One class period

Objectives

1. Students will define the term *life cycle* as the major stages of growth that all living things experience.
2. Students will describe the stages of the life cycle of humans and insects.

Suggested Procedures

1. Discuss each stage of the human life cycle (i.e., childhood, adolescence, and adulthood) in relation to students in kindergarten through college.
2. Ask students if they know what a butterfly is before it becomes a butterfly. Describe a butterfly's four-stage life cycle: egg, larva, pupa, adult. Point out that some insects (e.g., silverfish, grasshopper, and waterbug) have a three-stage life cycle: egg, nymph, adult.
3. Have students read pages in a textbook on the life cycle.
4. Ask students if they can identify the life-cycle stages of their family members (e.g., younger sister, teenage brother, parents).
5. Discuss the major changes in growth that are experienced during each stage of the human life cycle (e.g., voice change, balding).

Evaluation

On a test, ask students to define the life cycle and to describe the growth stages of insects and humans.

The Life Cycle

Subject Area: Science
Grade Level: 3–4
Time: Three or four class periods

Objectives

1. Students will define the term *life cycle* as the major stages of growth that all living things experience.
2. Students will describe the stages of the life cycle of humans and insects.

3. Students will state the developmental similarities, differences, and responsibilities associated with each life-cycle stage of humans.

4. Students will apply the appropriate meaning of respect to animals and humans of the different stages of the life cycle.

Suggested Procedures

1. Discuss each stage of the human life cycle (i.e., childhood, adolescence, adulthood) in relation to students in kindergarten through college.

2. Ask students if they know what a butterfly is before it becomes a butterfly. Describe a butterfly's four-stage life cycle: egg, larva, pupa, adult. Point out that some insects (e.g., silverfish, grasshopper, and waterbug) have a three-stage life cycle: egg, nymph, adult.

3. Have students read pages in a textbook on the life cycle.

4. Ask students what would happen to an insect if it tried to do something in one life stage that is normally done in another, as in the following examples:

   a butterfly trying to fly while in the larval stage
   a nymph grasshopper trying to lay eggs
   a mosquito trying to bite your arm while in the larval stage

   Students will learn that insects cannot perform activities of a life stage for which they are not equipped.

5. Group students heterogeneously, and have them discuss similarities in the experiences of all people—regardless of gender, class, disability, or race—at each human life stage. Also ask the groups to discuss the responsibilities associated with each life stage and if there are appropriate behaviors or attitudes that are normally expected across human life-cycle stages. For example, are there proper ways that humans in the childhood stage should treat humans in the adult stage? Do humans at the adult stage have certain responsibilities to humans at the childhood stage? Help students to understand that respect and responsibility are important attitudes for humans to have for each other regardless of the stage of development.

6. Have students discuss whether the amount of respect one gives to another person should differ according to that person's age, gender, race, or socioeconomic status. For example, should their respect be the same for a White European American male adolescent and an African American male adolescent? a working-class elderly Latina and an upper-class White European American elderly woman?

7. Lead a discussion that includes both sexes on the differences that occur in each stage between males and females, such as boys' developing a deeper voice and having to shave and girls' growing taller than boys during adolescence.

Evaluation

1. In a quiz, ask students to describe the life cycle of humans and insects.

2. During class discussion, assess students' ability to associate correctly the different meanings of respect with the stages of the life cycle.

The Life Cycle

Respect

The "Before" lesson plan asks students to describe the meaning of the life cycle for insects and humans. The "After" lesson plan also helps students to see a relationship between the stages and the meanings of respect. The "After" plan provides an opportunity for the teacher to discuss the two meanings of respect in relationship to life cycle, race, and gender. For example, will the definition of respect that students use be different for White European American teenage males than for African American teenage males?

Stereotyping

The "After" plan helps students to pay attention to stereotyping by encouraging them to examine the two meanings of respect in relation to race and gender.

Individual Uniqueness and Worth

The "After" plan has students examine appropriate behaviors and responsibilities at each stage of the life cycle to help them appreciate the inappropriateness of trying to "grow up" too fast or showing disrespect to members of other age groups. In other words, a third grader need not act like an eighth grader to be respectable, and adults should not act like adolescents. Furthermore, adults and children have responsibilities to each other.

Cross-Group Communication

The "After" plan encourages boys and girls to discuss sex differences with each other in order to develop comfort and honesty in communicating with the opposite sex.

▶ LESSON PLAN

Bones and Muscles

Subject Area: Health
Grade Level: 3–5
Time: Two class periods

Objectives

1. Students will describe the functions of bones and muscles.
2. Students will name and describe three kinds of joints and three kinds of muscles.
3. Students will identify the approximate number of bones and muscles in the body.

Suggested Procedures

1. Have students write their names. Then ask them to describe the characteristics that their hands need to do this. Make sure the discussion includes the following:

   Firmness, support (flesh cannot be like jelly)
   Flexibility (joints between firm parts)
   Voluntary movement of firm parts (something to move parts when you want to)

Have students do jumping jacks; ask if the same properties are necessary to do the jumping jacks as for writing their names.

2. Explain that bones and muscles are two body systems that perform these functions. Have students read pages in a textbook on this subject.

3. Review the text material orally in class. Stress the following points: functions of the skull, ribs, and pelvis to protect soft parts; different kinds of joints; different kinds of muscles; and voluntary versus involuntary muscles. Make it clear that everyone has over two hundred bones and over six hundred muscles.

4. Have students complete a crossword puzzle on bones and muscles.

Evaluation

Through oral review and the crossword puzzle, assess students' comprehension of the material.

Bones and Muscles

Subject Area: Health
Grade Level: 3–5
Time: Two to four class periods

Objectives

1. Students will describe the functions of bones and muscles.

2. Students will name and describe three kinds of joints and three kinds of muscles.

3. Students will describe alternative devices that perform similar functions to bones and muscles when these are impaired or absent.

4. Students will appreciate the similarities between people with orthopedic disabilities and people without such disabilities.

5. Students will feel comfortable discussing and handling devices used by people with orthopedic disabilities and older people.

Suggested Procedures

1. Have students write their names. Then ask them to describe the characteristics that their hands need to do this. Make sure the discussion includes the following:

> Firmness, support (flesh cannot be like jelly)
> Flexibility (joints between firm parts)
> Voluntary movement of firm parts (something to move parts when you want to)

Have students do jumping jacks; ask if the same properties are necessary to do the jumping jacks as are needed for writing their names.

2. Explain that bones and muscles are two body systems that perform these functions. Have students read pages in a textbook on this subject.

3. Ask students if they know of anyone who lacks working bones or muscles in their arms, hands, legs, or feet. Discuss why these disabilities occur (e.g., because of birth defects, amputations, skeletal or muscular diseases, injury, the aging

of the body). Ask if the people whom students have mentioned have the same needs and desires to accomplish activities as anyone else; lead students to the conclusion that most people strive to do for themselves, and in order to do so they may desire medical service or devices that will enable them to do so.

Ask students if they know someone who has had a knee or hip replacement. Invite a medical student or professional to talk to the students about bones and joints. Ask that person to bring an X-ray along so that students can see the difference between good and healthy bone and muscles and those that are feeling the effects of wear and tear. If the medical student or professional is a female or person of color, you may wish to connect their presence to Action Research Activities 3.1 and 3.4.

4. Show devices available for performing the same tasks as bones or muscles, such as prosthetic devices, braces, casts, and wheelchairs. Show how these devices work, enabling their users to perform much the same activities as other people. Show how they substitute for the bones and muscles that students read about in the text. Have someone who is using an artificial limb talk to students.

5. Have students keep a notebook on sports injuries and repairs. Assign a group of students (both boys and girls) to monitor the sports pages of newspapers and magazines to keep abreast of athletes who injure themselves. Have them discover how bone and muscle injuries are repaired (e.g., medical treatment, the length of rehabilitation time required, and the rehabilitation process). Have them note the amount of time that it takes for an athlete to recover and the amount of time it would take for a senior citizen to recover from the same or similar injury.

6. Ask students to read children's books such as the following, which teach about orthopedic disabilities while stressing the normalcy of people with disabilities.

Adams, B. (1979). *Like it is: Facts and feelings about handicaps from kids who know*. New York: Walker. (Chapter 3, on orthopedic disabilities)

Bennett, C. J. (1980). *Giant steps for Steven*. Mayfield Heights, OH: After School Exchange.

Heelan, J., & Simmonds, N. (Illustrator). (2000). *Rolling along: The story of Taylor and his wheelchair*. Atlanta, GA: Peachtree.

Osofsy, A. (1992). *My buddy*. New York: Henry Holt.

Powers, M. E. (1986). *Our teacher's in a wheelchair*. Niles, IL: A. Whitman.

Rogers, F. (2000). *Extraordinary friends*. Photographs by Jim Judkis. New York: Puffin.

Trueman, T. (2001). *Stuck in neutral*. New York: Avon Tempest.

Evaluation

1. Through class discussion of devices, assess students' comprehension of the material.

2. Through class discussion of people with physical disabilities whom students know and of the readings on orthopedic disabilities, assess students' appreciation of similarities among people.

Bones and Muscles

Stereotyping

The "Before" lesson plan implicitly teaches that all "normal" people have a specific set of bones and muscles. Although it does not explicitly state that people who are missing some working parts are not "normal," students often think this is the case. The "After" lesson plan dispels stereotypes while suggesting material that directly relates to those stereotypes. The "After" plan necessarily takes longer than the "Before" plan to provide information about the devices that people with disabilities use and to allow students to examine them.

Should the "After" lesson plan be taught when the class includes a student with a physical disability? Ideally, the lesson should be taught before the student enters the class, to prevent teasing and name-calling. If a student with a physical disability is already a part of the class, the teacher should make sure that he or she will feel comfortable with the lesson. This varies widely among individuals. In classrooms that include students with physical disabilities, often cordial and accepting relationships develop between the students with disabilities and those without. Furthermore, it may be tempting to assume that a lesson such as this is not needed. However, students without disabilities still may know little about the devices people use, and such a lesson may well answer questions they do not feel comfortable asking.

Grouping

The "After" plan calls for a group of male and female students to monitor the sports pages for muscle and bone injuries. This procedure will make certain that both boys and girls are acquiring sports health information.

Individual Uniqueness and Worth

The "After" plan helps students to develop respect and appreciation for senior citizens by observing the differences in healing time between young and old.

▶ LESSON PLAN

Westward Ho!

Subject Area: Social Studies
Grade Level: 4–6
Time: Two weeks

Objectives

1. Students will identify on a map the trails used by wagon trains traveling west and the geographic features of the land encountered.
2. Students will describe why pioneers went west, how their trips were organized, and how they handled obstacles and problems during their travels.
3. Students will appreciate the importance of the early pioneers.

Suggested Procedures

1. Using a large map, review the locations of the main settlements during the early 1800s. Point out the Oregon territory, and explain why the pioneers were drawn to the West. Have students study the map and suggest hazards or problems that pioneers in covered wagons might face while heading west.

2. Read a textbook about the westward movement of pioneers. As the class comes to each topic in the text, discuss the following questions:
   • Why would people leave their homes to head west?
   • What did they need to take with them?
   • How did they organize themselves for travel? Who played what roles?
   • What main routes did they take? Why? How did they know these routes?
   • What geographic hazards did they face? How did they deal with them?
   • What kinds of threats did the American Indians pose? How did the pioneers respond?
   • What health hazards did they face? How did they respond?

3. Show a film that portrays an account of the pioneers' trip west.

4. Have students construct a wall mural of wagon trains heading west. As a class, decide what should go on the mural; each student should draw and color at least one contribution.

Evaluation

1. Through a test, assess students' abilities to identify trails, describe geographic features, describe reasons for westward movement, and describe the process of westward movement.

2. Through their contributions to the mural, assess students' appreciation of the importance of the early pioneers.

Westward Ho![4]

Subject Area: Social Studies
Grade Level: 4–6
Time: Two weeks

Objectives

1. Students will identify on a map the trails used by wagon trains traveling west and the geographic features of the land encountered.

2. Students will develop attitudes and skills for cooperation.

3. Students will solve problems similar to those encountered by the pioneers going west.

4. Students will examine the stereotypes and negative attitudes associated with sex roles and American Indians.

5. Students will develop skill in writing paragraphs.

[4]Source: Kathro Taylor, Berlin Public Schools, Berlin, Wisconsin.

Suggested Procedures

1. Using a large map, review the locations of the main settlements of White European Americans, American Indians, and Mexican Americans during the early 1800s between the West Coast and the Mississippi River. Point out the Oregon territory, and explain why the pioneers were drawn to the West.

2. Divide the class into groups of five or six students so that each group contains students mixed on the basis of academic skill level, race, sex, and social class. Explain that each group is to act as a wagon train and that the following roles need to be filled each day:

   Wagon master (leader)
   Mule skinner or bullwacker (assistant leader)
   Journalist (keeps log of daily activities)
   Trail guide (plots routes on a map)

   Discuss that leaders and guides were usually men but that women can perform these roles as well. Have students rotate roles each day so that everyone gets a chance to play a major role. Explain that the log will be used to evaluate each group; thus, the journalist of the day has the main responsibility of seeing that day's log is completed, but all group members can pitch in. The log need not be straight narrative: Letters, pictures, and diaries may also be entered. If computers are available, ask students if they would like to keep their log on computers or if they would prefer to keep them with pen and paper, as they were kept when the pioneers moved west. This choice gives students another opportunity to be decision makers.

3. Have each group organize for the trip west. Each team is given money to spend; members must decide on the destination of the trip, the supplies needed, and how the roles are allocated.

4. The trip west begins. Show a video, show pictures, or have students read a description of a rainy day, wagons mired in mud. An axle is broken trying to free the wagon, and one team member injures a leg. Each team must decide what to do.

5. The next day's problem (on video, in pictures, or in story form) shows a raging river that the team must ford. The river frightens animals and could wash away supplies. Each team must decide what to do.

6. The next day, Plains Indians approach. Discuss with the class how the American Indians' perspectives of the westward movement may differ from the pioneers'. Suggest ways the two parties might respond to each other. Include the possibility of hostilities occurring and the likely consequences. Consider also the likely consequences of responding cooperatively. Have each team develop a respectful and constructive plan for interacting with the American Indians that would encourage cooperation and minimize hostilities.

7. The next day's problem is the desert, with water supplies low and temperatures high. The team must decide what to do.

8. The last problem is a steep mountain grade that must be scaled; the trail is partly blocked by rock slides, and light snow is falling. The team must decide what to do.

9. The teams all arrive at their destinations and must plan for settlement. They must decide how to organize each settlement in a way that fosters cooperation, good relationships with the American Indians, and minimal sex-role assignments.

10. Have students read textbook accounts of the westward movement and then relate them to their own "westward experience."

Evaluation

Evaluate each group's log in terms of cooperation, reasonableness of solutions, comprehension of geography, writing skills, and creativity.

Westward Ho!

WHY THE CHANGES?

Cooperative Learning

The "After" lesson plan uses the group investigation model; that is, students are presented with much of the same information as in the textbook. However, rather than being told how the pioneers coped, they must figure out what to do themselves collectively. Each group produces one product—the log—that is used to determine their grade. This provides motivation for all students to contribute to the production of a good log. Doing the log on a word processor facilitates cooperative writing. In the process, students develop better relationships with their peers and better problem-solving skills. Designating roles that must be filled helps keep the group on task, and it structures who will do what. Changing from individual textbook reading to cooperative learning not only builds classroom relationships and problem-solving ability but also encourages motivation.

Stereotyping

The "Before" lesson plan unintentionally reinforces several stereotypes: that the American Indians created problems for the settlers but not vice versa, that White European Americans were the only group of importance, that men were the leaders, and that students who cannot read well are unable to learn well. In contrast, the "After" plan deals with these stereotypes and does so without spending too much time. The "After" plan invites both sexes to share all roles. It also encourages the settlers to relate respectfully to the American Indians and to realize that hostility leads to hostile responses. The "After" plan points out that White European Americans were not the only racial group in the West.

▶ LESSON PLAN

Billboards

BEFORE

Subject Areas: Language Arts, Art
Grade Level: 4–9
Time: Two to three days

Objective

Students will appreciate and use visual devices as symbols for communication.

Suggested Procedures

1. Have available pictures of signs and billboards, or take the class on a walking tour of an area where students can view several of these.

2. Lead a discussion of how messages are conveyed through visual images, words, logos, colors, sizes, and shapes. Have students describe their responses to various signs and billboards and explain what features triggered their responses. Help students appreciate how visual devices can substitute for and often be more effective than verbal, discursive communication.

3. Each student should think of a message that he or she wishes to communicate and then design a sign or billboard to communicate that message. In art, students can produce their signs or billboards.

Evaluation

Assess the signs that students design for use as visual devices.

Billboards and T-Shirts[5]

Subject Areas: Language Arts, Art

Grade Level: 4–9

Time: Two to three days

Objectives

1. Students will appreciate and use visual devices as symbols for communication.

2. Students will appreciate the similarities and differences among themselves.

Suggested Procedures

1. The day before the lesson, ask students to wear their favorite T-shirt the next day.

2. Have students examine one another's T-shirts. Lead a discussion on how messages are conveyed on T-shirts through visual images, words, logos, colors, and the design of the shirt. As teacher, you may wish to wear a T-shirt, and also bring several others to class that you can hang around the room.

3. Organize students into groups of about five so that each member is wearing a different T-shirt. Have students discuss what their T-shirts are saying and why each person likes and wears his or her own T-shirt. You may wish to lend one of your T-shirts to students who forget to bring one to class.

4. Have students wearing similar T-shirts stand together. Ask them to what extent their T-shirts symbolize things they have in common with each other and things that make them different from their peers.

5. Discuss with the class that we all have similarities and differences and that we express them in how we dress. Point out that T-shirts are particularly popular and effective for doing this because of their low cost and versatility. Help students

[5]Source: Ozetta Kirby, Racine Unified Public Schools, Racine, Wisconsin.

appreciate how visual devices can substitute for and often be more effective than verbal, discursive communication.

6. Ask the class to help design a T-shirt that symbolizes the similarities among class members; if possible, the design should also reflect an appreciation of differences. The design should not impose some students' preferences on everyone else but should express ideas from the entire class.

7. As an art project, make these T-shirts for the entire class.

8. To extend the idea of this lesson, students may visit public places (such as a shopping mall) to list the messages on T-shirts and caps that people are wearing. Students may wish to record statements on the bumpers of cars and trucks. In addition, students may appreciate examining political and/or presidential slogans. Discuss with the class the messages conveyed through the symbols, logos, and words.

Evaluation

1. Assess students' understanding of visual devices for communication through the discussion of T-shirts.

2. Assess students' appreciation of the similarities and differences among people through the discussion of T-shirts and the quality of the T-shirt design produced by the class.

Billboards and T-Shirts

Individual Uniqueness and Worth

This language arts and art lesson was turned into a lesson about human similarities and differences, using a medium that students commonly use to express their self-identities: T-shirts. Most students have thought about visual devices and symbols when selecting T-shirts to wear, although they might not have thought about them in those terms. The "After" lesson plan uses this experiential knowledge that students already have and asks them to apply it to an analysis of their peers' T-shirts.

Cooperation

The "After" plan asks students to identify with each other as a class, to the extent that they can collectively design a logo symbolizing who they are. The creating and wearing of their own class T-shirts can be an excellent group-building device as well as a motivating activity.

▶ LESSON PLAN[6]

Luminescence or Incandescence?

Subject Area: Physical Science
Grade Level: 5–10
Time: Two days

[6]Source: Lawrence Escalada, University of Northern Iowa, Cedar Falls, Iowa.

Objectives

1. Students will explore the physical and light-emitting properties of various objects.

2. Students will classify these objects based on these properties and the type of energy used by the object to emit light.

3. Students will use accepted classifications to identify the type of light emission used by various objects, and compare their classifications with the accepted ones.

Suggested Procedures

1. Have students examine the following devices as they emit light:
   - Clear incandescent bulb connected to a lamp that is turned on. Caution students not to touch the bulb.
   - Lime Light® Night Light, any Indiglo® watch display, or any light-emitting diode (LED) being used as an on/off indicator in devices such as compact-disc players and computers.
   - Wint-o-green™ Lifesaver™ mint that is crushed in a darkened room with a pair of pliers. Caution students not to crush their fingers.
   - An activated light stick.
   - A glow-in-the-dark toy (but don't refer to the object as "glow-in-the-dark" with the students) in a darkened room that has been illuminated by light from an incandescent lamp or fluorescent lights.
   - A fluorescent mineral or object in a darkened room being illuminated with a low-energy ultraviolet light source (a "black light").

   Ask students to describe their observations of the physical features of each device and the resulting light being emitted. The students need to determine whether the device feels hot as it emits light and to identify the type(s) of energy used to emit light.

2. Have the students create a table that summarizes their data. Their table may include information such as name of the object being investigated, description of the light being emitted and other physical observations, the type(s) of energy used to emit light, and their observations of whether the objects feel hot when light is being emitted. Table 3.2 provides an example.

3. Have students group their objects into different categories based on whether the objects felt hot when light was emitted. Repeat, based on the type(s) of energy used to emit light.

Table 3.2

Object	Was Light Emitted?	Did the Object Feel Hot When Light Was Emitted?	Type of Energy Used to Emit Light	Describe the Light Emitted	Other Observations
Incandescent Lamp	Yes	Yes	Electrical energy	Yellowish-white light	Clear glass bulb and a metal wire inside

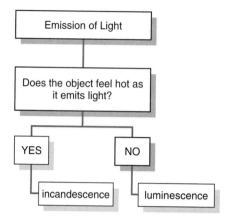

Figure 3.4   Processes of Light Emission

4. Have students compare their classifications with Figures 3.4 and 3.5. Ask students to use Figures 3.4 and 3.5 to identify the type of light emission used by each of the objects they investigated.

Note: Incandescence, or "hot light," is a process in which an object uses thermal energy as the primary mechanism to emit light. Luminescence, or "cool light," is a process in which light is emitted with very little change in the object's temperature; luminescent objects use forms of energy other than thermal energy to emit light. A living organism that emits light does so through bioluminescence—a special type of chemiluminescence. Phosphorescent, or glow-in-the-dark, objects require only visible light to emit their characteristic dim, yellowish-green light. Phosphorescent objects will continue to glow for a period of time after the light source is removed. A fluorescent object, however, will emit individual colors of light only in the presence of an ultraviolet light source, such as a "black light."

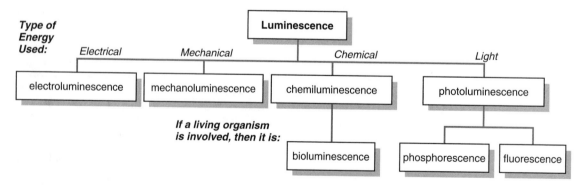

Figure 3.5   Types of Luminescence

Evaluation

1. Assess students' understanding of incandescence and luminescence and their ability to conduct a scientific investigation by providing students with the following objects: a lit birthday candle, a computer monitor with the on/off indicator light turned on, the logo of a credit card being illuminated by a black light; fireflies; and so on. Have students identify their physical and light-emitting properties.

   Have them use these properties and Figures 3.4 and 3.5 to identify the type(s) of light-emitting process(es) being used. Ask students to make predictions before they make observations. Students should provide evidence for their answers.

2. Since both light sticks and fireflies emit light through chemiluminescence, students in small groups could use light sticks as a model for fireflies to test their predictions on how temperature would affect the light emitted by fireflies. Students could also be asked to identify the limitations of using light sticks to model fireflies.

Luminescence or Incandescence?

AFTER

Subject Area: Physical Science
Grade Level: 5–10
Time: Three to four days

Objectives

1. Students will explore the physical and light-emitting properties of various objects.
2. Students will classify these objects based on these properties and the type of energy used by the object to emit light.
3. Students will use accepted classifications to identify the type of light emission used by objects and compare their classifications with the accepted ones.
4. Students will describe the contributions of various cultures to the development of materials used in various light sources.
5. Students will identify various examples of luminescence found in various cultures throughout history.
6. Students will examine their personal stereotypes of what a scientist looks like.

Suggested Procedures

1. Ask students to describe in words and a sketch what they think a scientist looks like; then discuss their descriptions. This exercise provides some insights into student perceptions of a scientist. Do they view a scientist as being male, White, and European, or do they view a scientist as one who could be female and of color? Do they view a scientist as having eyeglasses, facial hair, an unkempt appearance, or with pencils and pens in his or her chest pocket? Students could then be asked to explain their rationale for their descriptions. They could also be asked to explain whether they view themselves as future scientists.

2. Have students work in small groups to examine the following devices as they emit light:
   - Clear incandescent bulb connected to a lamp that is turned on. Caution students not to touch the bulb.
   - Lime Light® Night Light, any Indiglo® watch display, or any LED being used as an on/off indicator in devices such as compact-disc players and computers.
   - Wint-o-green™ Lifesaver™ mint that is crushed in a darkened room with a pair of pliers. Caution students not to crush their fingers.
   - An activated light stick.
   - A glow-in-the-dark toy (but don't refer to the object as "glow-in-the-dark" with the students) in a darkened room that has been illuminated by the light from an incandescent lamp or fluorescent lights.
   - A fluorescent mineral or object in a darkened room being illuminated with a low-energy ultraviolet light source (a "black light").

   Ask students to describe their observations of the physical features of each device and the resulting light being emitted. The students need to determine whether the device feels hot as it emits light and to identify the type(s) of energy used to emit light.

3. Have the students create a table that summarizes their data. Their table may include information such as name of the object being investigated, description of the light being emitted and other physical observations, type(s) of energy used to emit light, and their observations of whether the objects feel hot when light is being emitted. Table 3.2 provides an example.

4. Have students group their objects into different categories based on whether the objects felt hot when light was emitted. Repeat based on the type(s) of energy used to emit light.

5. Have students compare their classifications with Figures 3.4 and 3.5. Ask students to use Figures 3.4 and 3.5 to identify the type of light emission used by each of the objects they investigated. Engage the students in a class discussion of their results.

6. Have students conduct research on the contributions of various cultures to the development of the scientific study and technological application of incandescence and luminescence. Projects could include the following:
   - Students may already know that incandescent lightbulbs were invented in 1879 by Thomas Edison. They, however, will probably not be familiar with Lewis Latimer, an African American inventor who patented carbon filaments that lasted much longer than Edison's earlier filaments. Have students conduct research on Latimer. In the process, they will learn that he describes how an electric wire is heated to emit light through incandescence. They will also learn about his contribution toward providing electrical lighting to the streets of cities in the United States, England, and Canada. (Latimer connected electric street lights in parallel during a time when street lamps were initially connected in series.)
   - Introduce the students to the fact that on/off indicator lights (LEDs) are encased in very hard plastic resin that serves to focus light in a small cone and

to protect it from physical damage. Students could be introduced to the fact that the first plastic (called lacquer) was invented in China in the thirteenth century B.C.E., 3,200 years before the Europeans developed it.

- Introduce the students to the fact that the first written record of fluorescence was made in the sixteenth century in Mexico by Nicolas Monardes, a Spanish physician and botanist. He found that a certain wood, called *tlapazilla* by the Mexican natives, would emit an eerie blue light when made into cups, filled with water, and then held up to the sunlight. These cups were considered to be very fine gifts, fit for kings and queens.

7. Have students find luminescence mentioned in the literary and media works of various cultures. They can also search for examples of how luminescence has been and is currently being used in various cultures' customs and traditions. Here are some examples:
   - Shih Ching, writing in China about three thousand years ago, described the firefly's intermittent glow. A Chinese legend tells of a poor but resourceful student who lived almost two thousand years ago. Unable to afford lamp oil, Ch'e Yin collected fireflies and used their light to study at night.
   - Fireflies also appear in Japanese folklore. According to one legend, fireflies are ghosts of brave warriors who died fighting for their country.
   - In Japan, firefly festivals are celebrated every summer. People gather to catch fireflies, put them in cages, and row out to the middle of a lake or river. They then open their cages at the same time, sending out clouds of flickering fireflies into the night sky.
   - In Central and South America, Japan, and the West Indies, individuals make firefly lamps by catching fireflies and putting them in cages or net bags.
   - In South America and Mexico, women wear fireflies or glow worms (*cucujos*) on their clothing or in their hair as "glowing" jewelry.
   - In the West Indies, people who hunt or fish at night wear netted fireflies on their wrists and ankles to keep track of each other in the dark.

8. Students could also research examples of luminescent objects and organisms found in various countries. For example, the click beetle from Venezuela uses bioluminescence in the same way as the firefly. Puerto Rico's Phosphorescent Bay contains sparkling shell-shaped marine organisms that glimmer during the night. Many countries, including the United States, use fluorescent markings on paper currency as an anticounterfeiting measure.

9. Ask students to speculate what stereotypes a scientist of color, such as Lewis Latimar, would likely have encountered during the late 1800s and how it would compare to today's cultural climate.

Evaluation

1. Assess students' understanding of incandescence and luminescence and their ability to conduct a scientific investigation by providing students with objects such as the following: a lit birthday candle; a computer monitor with the on/off indicator light turned on, the logo of a credit card being illuminated with light from a black light, fireflies, and so on. Have students identify their physical

and light-emitting properties. Have them use these properties and Figures 3.4 and 3.5 to identify the type(s) of light-emitting process(es) being used. Ask students to make predictions before they make observations. Students should provide evidence for their answers.

2. You could pose the following question to your students, "How would temperature affect the light emitted by fireflies? In other words, how would the light emitted by fireflies on a cold summer evening compare with the light emitted by fireflies on a hot summer evening?" Ask students how they could test their predictions. Some students may want to conduct a scientific investigation on real fireflies. However, this may be difficult; fireflies may not be available. In scientific investigations, experimenting with biological organisms is not always feasible, practical, or ethical. Instead, scientists often use a model to represent the subject under investigation. Since both light sticks and fireflies emit light through chemiluminescence, students could use light sticks as a model for fireflies. Depending on the grade level, students could construct a light-stick firefly by using a light stick, two large plastic cups (one clear and the other opaque), a bottle cap, pipe cleaners, construction paper, and other materials. Students could also identify limitations of using light sticks as model fireflies.

3. Assess students' ability to provide examples of various cultures' contributions to the development of the scientific study and technological application of incandescence and luminescence.

4. Assess students' ability to identify literary and media works, customs and traditions, and examples of biological diversity related to luminescent phenomena. Have students catalogue their results, with each country represented being identified on a world map.

Luminescence or Incandescence?

WHY THE CHANGES?

Stereotyping

The objectives of both the "Before" and "After" plans are to introduce science concepts related to light-emitting processes (science content) and to develop student scientific inquiry skills (science process). Although the "After" plan is longer and would take more teaching time than the "Before" plan, the "After" plan provides more opportunities for students to act as scientists and to learn about the nature of science and who does science.

The "After" plan begins by investigating students' perceptions of what a scientist looks like. It encourages students to speculate on the stereotypes that existed in the 1800s as compared to those that exist today, and to gain an appreciation for the diversity of science. It also provides some insights into why students do or don't see themselves as scientists. Furthermore, it provides opportunities for students of color to feel empowered that they can contribute to the learning process by providing culturally relevant examples of luminescent phenomena and applications as well as individuals who contributed to the development of their study. Although the "After" plan is longer, it utilizes those aspects of teaching and learning science that are recommended by current science education initiatives.

Cooperative Learning

Although both plans can use cooperative learning, the "After" plan specifically recommends the use of small groups. Different groups could be assigned to investigate different objects that emit light and then share their results with other groups.

► LESSON PLAN[7]

Class Meetings

BEFORE

Subject Area: Social Studies
Grade Level: 1–8
Time: Weekly and Ongoing

Objectives

1. Students will participate in discussions relating to classroom rules, procedures, and curricular guidelines.
2. Students will learn to listen and communicate in a group setting.
3. Students will gain a better understanding of the teacher's expectations.
4. Students will have a specific time and place in which to learn about upcoming events or teacher concerns.

Suggested Procedures

Class meetings offer an opportunity for gathering students in a structured setting to discuss the rules of the classroom and as an informational tool to be used at the teacher's discretion.

- The students can be gathered together in a general meeting space on a weekly or as-needed basis to inform them of daily happenings, introduce or clarify classroom rules, or brief them on upcoming events.
- A regular time can be set aside and a common meeting place identified to allow for ease in setup.
- The teacher should present classroom rules to the students in a fair and friendly manner, allowing students to ask questions regarding policies and expectations.
- The teacher can plan to share daily schedules and curricular instructions, as well as offer positive feedback to deserving students.

Evaluation

The teacher uses the class meeting as a classroom management tool and can assess its effectiveness throughout the meeting and in daily interactions with the students.

[7]Source: Margaret Whiting, Madison, Wisconsin.

Class Meetings

Management issues that require further resolution can be addressed in subsequent meetings.

Subject Area: Social Studies

Grade Level: 1–8

Time: Weekly and Ongoing

Objectives

1. Students will participate meaningfully in decisions relating to classroom management and curriculum.
2. Students will gain experience in collaborative problem solving.
3. Students will develop community-building skills through dialogue.
4. Students will identify, explore, and appreciate various approaches to resolving conflicts.
5. Students will learn that differing ideas and opinions are an asset in developing workable resolutions.
6. Students will develop their individual and collective voice as citizens of a classroom community.

Suggested Procedures

Class meetings can be a powerful tool for resolving interpersonal conflicts and for addressing management and curricular issues in the classroom. Beyond these immediate goals, class meetings allow practice in the kind of skills and attitudes necessary for membership in a healthy democratic citizenry. Many issues arise in the classroom involving race, gender, and social inequities that can also be found in the larger community. A class meeting is an excellent forum for much-needed discussion on these subjects, which, though ever present, are often invisible or inadequately addressed in the official curriculum.

The focus of a given meeting can vary widely, from a student's seeking broader input on a personal issue to decisions regarding classroom policies or even input on curriculum planning. Although the use to which these discussions are put may vary, it is important to remember that class meetings are truly effective only when they are genuine. If the students are to take the process seriously, their voices should be at the heart of problem identification, discussion, and evaluation.

Class meetings are most effective when they occur frequently enough to be effectively used as a negotiation tool, yet not so often that the process becomes trivialized. They function best as one component of a democratic classroom, one in which opportunities for student input and idea sharing are continually sought and valued. The time taken to facilitate such ongoing discussion is repaid in student engagement and empowerment, and in a healthy and collaborative classroom environment.

Because it is expected that students will participate in the formation of the meeting structure, the exact plan of action can (and should) vary, but the following components are essential:

- A means through which students can identify and submit meaningful problems for group discussion.

- A regular time set aside for the meeting process, and arrangement of classroom space to accommodate face-to-face discussion (a group circle is ideal).

- Collaboratively identified guidelines for effective communication. For example, group members might refrain from using other students' names in problem description and also might establish a means for equitable turn taking, such as the passing of an object to indicate the opportunity to speak (as well as the right not to). In order for the students to develop active voices in the process, it is important that they take part in determining these guidelines.

- An effective means of evaluation. This should include the individual or group that brought the problem deciding whether they feel the solutions and advice offered are helpful. A brief followup discussion at the beginning of the next weekly meeting might allow students to assess the quality of help given over time.

Evaluation

In addition to the ongoing student evaluation of the process, a teacher can assess the quality of problems brought over time and the level of reflection the students demonstrate in response. Likewise, the number and kind of classroom management issues that emerge between meetings, the level of student engagement during meetings, and the degree to which students take an active role in classroom decision making can all serve as indicators of the effectiveness of class meetings.

Class Meetings

WHY THE CHANGES?

A Shift in Focus Toward Democratic Participation

In the "Before" plan, the role of the classroom meeting centers on teacher needs and expectations. In this model, the meeting functions primarily as a conduit to communicate rules, curricular expectations, and other items of the teacher's choice to a relatively passive audience. Topics for discussion reflect the teacher's agenda, while maintaining a hierarchical relationship between teacher and students.

In this "After" plan, the fundamental purpose of the meeting changes. The emphasis shifts to genuine dialogue and includes students' concerns, ideas, and voices. Where previously the teacher maintained ownership over the content and proceedings of the meeting, the "After" plan provides for more meaningful interaction by creating a community space where all perspectives are valued and encouraged. Through open dialogue, students' ideas and feelings about curriculum, classroom relationships, and their own development can emerge. As participants come to understand one another through collaborative exploration of a variety of issues, group ties are strengthened, while new understandings are generated that can then be incorporated into future planning. By seeking inclusive and in-depth participation by all classroom members, issues of race, gender, and social inequities can be examined in the context where they have the most meaning to students. Furthermore, these meetings can provide opportunities to develop students' voices and serve as essential practice for meaningful participation in democratic society.

▶ LESSON PLAN

Introductions[8]

Subject Areas: Social Studies/Humanities

Grade Level: 7–12

Date: The first day of the school year, or the first day of the second semester in schools in which students change classes each semester

Objective

Students will become acquainted with the teacher and with other students.

Suggested Procedures

1. The teacher introduces herself or himself, telling students a little bit about her or his own personal background and what the course will be like.
2. Students take turns introducing themselves to the rest of the class, telling their name, hobbies, or interests and something of interest they did during vacation.
3. The teacher passes out textbooks and gives students a brief overview of the text and its organizational structure. The teacher then introduces the first assignment or concept for the semester.

Evaluation

Although this is simply an introductory activity, teachers may wish to pay attention to students' ease and skill of participation.

Stereotypes[9]

Subject Areas: Social Studies/Humanities

Grade Level: 7–12

Date: The first day of the school year, or the first day of the second semester in schools in which students change classes each semester

Objectives

1. Students will define the word *stereotype*.
2. Students will examine historical events that often served as the basis for stereotypes.
3. Students will become aware of their own stereotypes.
4. Students will think critically about positive and negative connotations associated with stereotypes, the people/organizations who promote stereotypes, and the political implications behind using stereotypes.

---

[8]This "Before" lesson is followed by two different "After" plans that illustrate two different ways of transforming it: "Stereotypes" and "Quintessentially Me."

[9]Source: Kimberly Woo, California State University–San Marcos.

5. Students will sharpen powers of observation.

6. The teacher will establish a classroom atmosphere that encourages sharing and risk taking.

Suggested Procedures

1. Before class, place the chart in Figure 3.6 on the blackboard.

2. Hold up a stack of eight different photographs of the teacher, taken at different times and in different settings. Introduce the activity by saying, "I've got amnesia and I can't remember anything about my past. The only clues that I have are these photographs. Please get into groups of three or four, and take one photograph and one worksheet for each group. As a group, try to help me regain my memory by completing the worksheet [Figure 3.7]. Some of the questions on the worksheet cannot be easily answered and require careful observation and hypothesizing. You will have approximately twenty minutes to reach consensus about your answers. After you have completed your worksheets, please select a representative to write your conclusions on the chart on the blackboard."

3. While students are working in groups, the teacher should circulate and spend approximately two to three minutes with each group to answer questions, encourage teamwork, and remind students to write their answers on the chart on the blackboard.

4. After all groups have written their answers on the chart, review the categories that seem to have the strongest agreement or contradictions across groups. Ask students to explain how they formulated their answers using evidence from the photographs or other information. If pictures were well selected, they will elicit students' using stereotypes in their attempt to interpret them.

5. Point out that some conclusions were founded on assumptions and that, when people use stereotypes, they often rely on past experiences and information.

Evaluation

Ask students to make a list of ten situations in which they observed or experienced stereotyping. Have students focus on one stereotype and research the origins of the stereotype. Ask students to present written documentation (i.e., essay or other creative format, the length to be determined according to students' ability and grade) that does the following:

1. Briefly describes how the stereotype was used in the situation

2. Discusses the historical basis for this stereotype

3. Analyzes the political implications of the stereotype to the situation stereotypes

Stereotypes

WHY THE CHANGES?

This "After" plan invites students to attempt to draw some hypotheses based on visual photographs of the teacher. In the process, students will get to know the teacher but will also become aware of some of their own stereotypes. The author of this lesson has used it very successfully on several occasions for this purpose. The photos she has used of herself show her in different settings during a five-year period, wearing clothing

	Ques. #1	Ques. #2	Ques. #3	Ques. #4	Ques. #5	Ques. #6	Ques. #7	Ques. #8	Ques. #9	Ques. #10
Group 1										
Group 2										
Group 3										
Group 4										
Group 5										
Group 6										

Figure 3.6   Chart for Blackboard

| (name) | (name) |

| (name) | (name) |

1. What is the setting of the photo? (city, state, country) _____

_____

2. What is taking place? _____

_____

3. What is the teacher's economic status and occupation? _____

_____

4. What is the teacher's social status and age? _____

_____

5. What is the teacher's gender orientation and marital/dating status? _____

_____

6. What is the highest educational level the teacher has achieved? _____

_____

7. How long has the teacher been in the United States? (What generation is he or she?)

_____

_____

8. What messages from body language is the teacher giving? _____

_____

9. What are the teacher's personal values? _____

_____

10. What are your overall conclusions or impressions? _____

_____

Figure 3.7 Who Am I?

ranging from traditional Chinese dress to outdoor sportswear. The activities in which she is engaged range from petting the dog to socializing with friends, to serving appetizers. From the photos, students have suggested a variety of assumptions about things, such as what country she is from, how well she speaks English, and even whether all the photos represent the same person. The discussion of how students answered the questions about the photos and the evidence they used has always been lively and revealing.

Quintessentially Me[10]

Subject Area: Language Arts
Grade Level: 4–8
Date: Beginning of school year, just prior to back-to-school night
Time: Two to three days

Objectives

1. Students will identify commonalities they share with fellow students and the teacher, as well as ways in which they are unique.
2. Students will get to know each other better.
3. Students will compare how their parents see them, how their friends see them, and how they see themselves.
4. Students will actively use synonyms that are more descriptive than hackneyed expressions.

Suggested Procedures

1. Break down the word *quintessentially* and explain how it relates to the project.
2. Brainstorm vivid synonyms of commonly used words, and explain how some words are "dead" through overuse, for example, *nice, cool,* and *good.*
3. Have students write three adjectives they think best describe them.
4. Have students interview parents to obtain quotes about what the student was like when she or he was little, as well as three words the parents would use to describe her or him now.
5. Next have students interview their friends to elicit three words they would use to describe them.
6. Now have students discuss ways in which their parents' and peers' perceptions of them differ or are alike from each other and from their perceptions of themselves. Invite students to examine why this could be so.
7. Give student the "Quintessentially Me" worksheet to fill out (Figure 3.8).
8. Have students share their writing with numerous peers. Peer editors scan for vivid adjectives, as well as proofread for errors. Students also look for commonalities to their own descriptors.
9. Students then staple their sheet to the wall, in an accessible corner of the room.
10. When all the papers are on the wall, students make literal connections between themselves and other students by stapling rainbow-colored yarn from their paper to others'. For example, two students who share the same middle name or whose favorite music is the Beatles would affix the yarn between their papers at those points. Each student makes at least two different connections to other papers.

---

[10] Source: Natalie Bernasconi, Buena Vista Middle School, Spreckles, California.

My name is _____.

I was born on _____.

When I was little, I was _____.

One of the best memories of my life was _____

_____.

Now, here I am, _____ years old.

Three words my parents would use to describe me are:

_____   _____   _____

Three words my friends would use to describe me are:

_____   _____   _____

Three words I would use to describe myself are:

_____   _____   _____

Here are some of my favorites:

Favorite hobby _____   Favorite movie _____

Favorite sport _____   Favorite book _____

Favorite music _____   Favorite color _____

Favorite subject _____   Favorite place _____

One particular thing I'm really good at is _____

_____.

One thing I'd like to improve in is _____

_____.

Twenty years from now, I expect I will be _____

_____.

All in all, I'm a _____ person!

Figure 3.8   Quintessentially Me

This results in more than one hundred connections in a three-dimensional, rainbow-colored-string art exhibit (see Figure 3.9).

11. Any child who has some characteristic or preference that is not shared by anyone else in the room (e.g., a special hobby or career goal) can add a neon-colored mini Post-it labeled UNIQUE to their paper at that point.

12. Invite parents and siblings to enjoy "A Celebration of Our Similarities as Well as Our Differences" at back-to-school night.

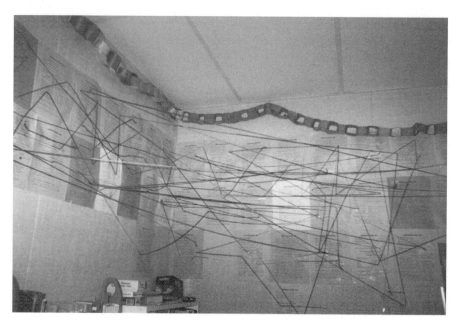

Figure 3.9 Quintessentially Me Connections

Evaluation

Evaluate the level of self-reflection in the worksheet, the vividness of the descriptors, and connections that were correctly made in tandem with fellow students.

Quintessentially Me

Individual Uniqueness and Worth

This "After" plan prods students to consider their own personal value, and how they are perceived as worthwhile by others. It does not simply focus on the individual, however; students also seek out commonalities they have with each other. The rainbow-colored-string art exhibit is great fun for students to create and helps them to get to know more about their peers. In the process, they discover interesting things they have in common with each other.

Finding Symmetry[11]

Subject Area: Math
Grade Level: 9–11
Time: One to two days

[11] Source: Linda Luiz-Rodrigues, James Logan High School, Union City, California.

Objective

Students will work with geometric shapes to reinforce their understanding of transitional, reflectional, rotational, and line symmetry.

Suggested Procedures

1. Define *symmetry*: Figures that are symmetrical can be folded so that each half matches the other half exactly. Parabolas are symmetrical. The fold line is called the line of symmetry or axis of symmetry. Graph a parabola on grid paper. Hold it to the light, and fold the parabola in half so that the two sides match exactly. Unfold the paper. Notice that each point on the parabola on one side of the axis of symmetry has a corresponding point on the parabola on the other side of the axis.

2. Define *translation*: If a figure is moved to a new location by sliding it a fixed distance in a fixed direction, the movement is called a transition or slide. Graph a triangle on grid paper. Move it to the right three units, draw it. Move it again three units, draw it. The figures are said to be translational.

3. Define *rotational*: If we move a figure to a new location by turning it through a fixed angle about a fixed point, the motion is called a rotation or turn. The point about which the figure is rotated is referred to as the center of rotation. The angle through which the figure turns is called the angle of rotation. Examples include a ferris wheel and a tire rotating around a wheel. Graph a triangle on polar graph paper. Rotate it 30 degrees counterclockwise.

4. Define *reflectional*: If we move a figure to a new location by flipping it about a fixed line, the motion is called a reflection or flip. The fixed line about which the figure is flipped is called the line of reflection. Examples include a reflection of a tree into a still lake and a face in front of a mirror.

Note: Dale Seymour Publications is a good resource for visual examples of various transformations.

Evaluation

Assess students' understanding of these concepts on chapter test.

Finding Symmetry

Subject Area: Math
Grade Level: 9–11
Time: One to two days

Objective

Students will work with geometric shapes and designs from various cultures to reinforce their understanding of transitional, reflectional, and line symmetry.

Suggested Procedures

1. Define transformations (transitional, reflectional, rotational, and line symmetry) as in the "Before" plan, and have students explore the concepts by drawing

simple figures on grid paper and polar graph paper. Ask students if they know of any real-life examples of transformations. (Hopefully, students will talk about things like wrapping paper, fabric, art designs, etc.)

2. Begin the connection with culture by asking students to think of various examples from their own cultures. Show a slide show or a video of examples of Native American, Asian, and African art that reflect these concepts as you lecture about how the various peoples use symmetry and transformations to create designs in weaving, beadwork, and art.

3. Give a brief lecture on, and show students examples of, how weavers from African tribes and Native American tribes use symmetry to create patterns in weaving and beadwork. Example include the following:

   • Men are the weavers in many African tribes, and they use long, narrow looms. In Africa, the pinwheel design represents the Circle of Life. This design is an example of rotational symmetry. The type of clothing and quantity of designs in the fabric determine power, status, and wealth.

   • The Ashante people of Ghana make a cloth called Adinkra (good-bye). Long ago it was worn at funerals to honor the memory of the dead. The Adinkra cloth is large and has many rectangles sewed together.

   • The Navajo burntwater rug designs show line symmetry. Many tribes use beadwork and a variety of materials to create their designs.

   • People in the Great Lakes area made flower designs. (For a multitude of cross-cultural sources on symmetry, go to www.math.binghamton; on Native American geometry, www.earthmeasure.com; and on Asian carpets, www.mathforum.org/geometry/rugs.)

4. Hand out several sheets of grid paper. Ask the students to build at least one African–inspired and one Native American–inspired design using the grid paper and color pencils.

Evaluation

1. Give worksheet questions on the type of symmetry of their designs.

2. Expand the lesson by having students bring in cultural examples of symmetry and report on the type of symmetry in the design.

Finding Symmetry

WHY THE CHANGES?

Stereotypes and Cultural Contributions

Symmetry is a basic concept that a math teacher will teach. Teachers use geometric patterns to show concepts of symmetry. In the "Before" plan, the teacher uses traditional examples of the transformations. What the "After" plan shows is that we can alter the examples we use to illustrate symmetry. Instead of generic objects, we can incorporate designs of different ethnic cultures. Students find these examples much more interesting.

Students usually connect better when they relate the math concepts to their own life. Students feel empowered when they are able to bring items in from home that reflect their culture. It helps show students that math is not a European concept but is shared by all peoples throughout the world.

▶ LESSON PLAN

Solving Two Equations With Two Unknowns

Subject Area: Algebra
Grade Level: 9–12
Time: Four class periods

Objective

Students will solve two equations with two unknowns using four methods: graphing, substitution, addition, and determinants.

Suggested Procedures

1. Explain to students that they will learn how to solve two equations with two unknowns using four different methods: graphing, substitution, addition, and determinants.

2. Demonstrate a detailed example of how the graphing method is used. Be sure to encourage students to ask questions if they do not understand an aspect of the method. Work through one or two more examples, allowing students to give input as to how the problem should be solved using the method. When you feel that students can apply the method, assign homework from the textbook.

3. Teach the other three methods using the process outlined in step 2.

4. Prepare a worksheet with problems involving all four methods. Distribute the worksheet for students to use as a review for the quiz.

Evaluation

1. Listen to students' input when demonstrating the examples on the board to determine if they are grasping the methods.

2. Assess students' understanding of the methods by grading their homework assignments, worksheets, and exams.

Solving Two Equations With Two Unknowns[12]

Subject Area: Algebra
Grade Level: 9–12
Time: Four class periods

Objectives

1. Students will solve two equations with two unknowns using four methods: graphing, substitution, addition, and determinants.

2. Students will teach the methods they have studied to another student.

---

[12]Source: Robin White, Racine, Wisconsin.

3. Students will interact with peers of the same and opposite sex.

4. Students will develop attitudes and skills for cooperation.

5. Students will develop planning skills.

6. Students will realize that both sexes are equally capable of learning and teaching math.

Suggested Procedures

1. Divide students into four groups with equal numbers of girls and boys in each group. Separate the girls and the boys who associate with each other often. Separate students at the same skill levels.

2. Assign to each group one of the four methods for solving two equations with two unknowns.

3. Tell students to use their textbooks and the supplementary books to learn how to use this method. They should work together to apply the method to various problems in the books and to make sure that everyone in the group can solve the equations using the given method.

4. Once students feel confident about using the method being learned by their group, the teacher should check their problems to be sure they understand it. (Some sample problems are given in Figure 3.10.)

5. If the teacher feels that the students understand the method, the group can begin to design its mini-lesson, which they will use to teach the method to other students. The mini-lesson should have four parts—objectives, materials, procedure, and evaluation—to allow each student in the group to make some contribution to the plan. The mini-lessons can be as long or short as the group feels is necessary to teach the concept. The students may choose to explain the method and ask the other students to do problems, or they may assign homework and a quiz—the decision is to be made by the group. The students should make sure that each group member can teach the mini-lesson they have created.

6. The teacher should check each group's lesson plan to see how the methods will be taught and then make copies of the plan for each student in the group.

7. Divide students into four new groups with equal numbers of girls and boys in each group. Each group should have one or two students who can do one of each of the four methods. Separate the girls and boys who associate with each other often. Separate students at the same skill level.

8. Each student in the group should teach his or her method for solving equations to the other group members. The students should follow their lesson plans.

9. The students should make sure that all of the members of the group can perform the four methods. When the groups feel they are confident about the methods, the game begins.

10. Each student in the group should choose a number from 1 to 4 (or up to the number of students in the group), which will serve to identify the student from each group who will be competing.

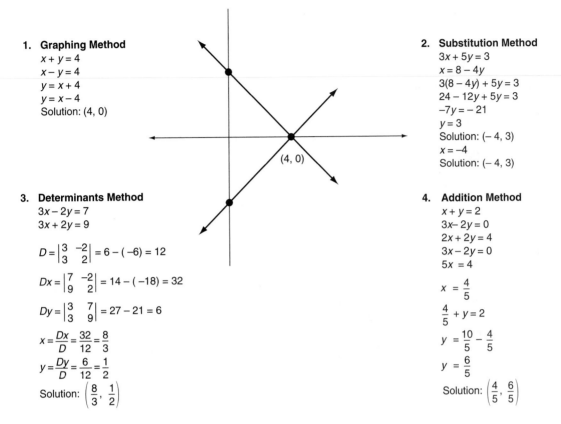

1. Graphing Method

$x + y = 4$
$x - y = 4$
$y = x + 4$
$y = x - 4$
Solution: $(4, 0)$

2. Substitution Method

$3x + 5y = 3$
$x = 8 - 4y$
$3(8 - 4y) + 5y = 3$
$24 - 12y + 5y = 3$
$-7y = -21$
$y = 3$
Solution: $(-4, 3)$
$x = -4$
Solution: $(-4, 3)$

3. Determinants Method

$3x - 2y = 7$
$3x + 2y = 9$

$D = \begin{vmatrix} 3 & -2 \\ 3 & 2 \end{vmatrix} = 6 - (-6) = 12$

$Dx = \begin{vmatrix} 7 & -2 \\ 9 & 2 \end{vmatrix} = 14 - (-18) = 32$

$Dy = \begin{vmatrix} 3 & 7 \\ 3 & 9 \end{vmatrix} = 27 - 21 = 6$

$x = \dfrac{Dx}{D} = \dfrac{32}{12} = \dfrac{8}{3}$

$y = \dfrac{Dy}{D} = \dfrac{6}{12} = \dfrac{1}{2}$

Solution: $\left(\dfrac{8}{3}, \dfrac{1}{2}\right)$

4. Addition Method

$x + y = 2$
$3x - 2y = 0$
$2x + 2y = 4$
$3x - 2y = 0$
$5x = 4$

$x = \dfrac{4}{5}$

$\dfrac{4}{5} + y = 2$

$y = \dfrac{10}{5} - \dfrac{4}{5}$

$y = \dfrac{6}{5}$

Solution: $\left(\dfrac{4}{5}, \dfrac{6}{5}\right)$

Figure 3.10 Sample Problems

11. Choose a number, and the student from each group with that number should come to the board. Read the problem, and the students must write and solve the problem. The problem must be solved by the method specified by the teacher.

12. The groups earn four, three, two, or one point for solving the problem first, second, third, or fourth, respectively. No points are given to a group that solves the problem incorrectly. All groups are required to keep score. The winning team may be given some reward, although the reward should not be overemphasized.

13. On the day after the game is played, give the students a quiz on which they must demonstrate their abilities to solve the equations.

Evaluation

1. Assess students' ability to solve the equations by correcting sample problems submitted by the initial groups and by observing their performance during the game and on the quiz.

2. Assess students' ability to teach the lessons by observing the second groupings.

3. Observe the groups to determine if interaction and cooperation are occurring.

4. Listen to group conversations to determine if boys are treating girls equally and if girls are treating boys equally.

Solving Two Equations With Two Unknowns

Cooperation

The "After" lesson plan uses the jigsaw model of cooperative learning to teach the same math concepts taught in the "Before" plan. The jigsaw model involves students interacting with a variety of peers to figure out a method of solving equations, to make sure all group members understand it, and to teach a method to other peers. Since every class member has an area of expertise in the second grouping, all students appear valuable and capable to their peers, which helps improve students' perceptions of and interactions with each other. The "After" plan also helps students learn the content better than if the teacher simply delivers it to them, in that cooperative learning actively involves them in figuring it out themselves and in helping each other to learn.

Stereotyping

At the secondary grade level, students often begin to view math more as a male subject rather than as gender neutral, and many begin to doubt the competence of females in math. The "Before" lesson does not address this issue, whereas the "After" lesson does. First, all students, including females, tend to learn math better when taught using cooperative rather than competitive methods. And second, by grouping males and females equally, and by preparing each student to be an "expert" who can teach math to his or her peers, the lesson encourages both sexes to view math knowledge as something that everyone can learn equally well.

▷ LESSON PLAN

Factoring Polynomials

Subject Area: Mathematics
Grade Level: 11–12
Time: One class period

Objective

Students will factor polynomials completely and accurately.

Suggested Procedures

1. Demonstrate on the board how to factor a polynomial, and ask for student input while doing so. (Students should have already studied factoring and should be familiar with polynomials.) Do two or three more examples at the board, continuing to ask for student input.

2. Assign problems in the math textbook to be done in class or as homework.

3. Review the problems with the class. Rework on the board those problems that students solved incorrectly.

Evaluation

Evaluate students' homework, or give each student three to five polynomials to factor independently.

Factoring Polynomials and Making Friends at the Same Time

AFTER

Subject Area: Mathematics
Grade Level: 11–12
Time: One or two class periods

Objectives

1. Students will factor polynomials completely and accurately.
2. Students will enjoy abstract math problems.
3. Students will get along with their peers of different races and of the opposite sex.

Suggested Procedures

1. Divide students into groups of about five members each. The groups should be as race- and gender-mixed as possible, and should also mix good algebra students with those who have more difficulty in this area. Have each group select a name.

2. Demonstrate on the board how to factor a polynomial. If students do not understand, demonstrate additional examples until they do understand.

3. Write a polynomial on the board similar to those that were demonstrated. One group is to figure out how to factor it and to do so on the board. The other groups are to demonstrate whether it was done correctly and, if it wasn't, what the correct solution would be. Scoring is done as follows:

   Two points are given when the group solves the problem correctly (but the points are not awarded until after the other groups have evaluated the solution).

   One point is given to the evaluating groups when they correctly evaluate the solution of the group doing the problem.

   No points are given to any group for incorrect solutions or evaluations.

4. Proceed to another problem: Rotate the group at the board, but repeat the procedure in step 3. Encourage group members to work together to figure out a solution.

5. Once students have mastered problems similar to those demonstrated by the teacher, and each group has had the same number of turns at the board, demonstrate a more complex problem, and repeat the procedures in steps 3 and 4.

Evaluation

1. Give students three to five polynomials to factor independently; they should score 100 percent if the concept has been mastered.

2. Observe student–student interactions during the game and during other class activities to assess their improvement in social relationships.

Factoring Polynomials and Making Friends at the Same Time

Cooperative Learning

The "After" lesson plan uses the same problems used in the "Before" plan but presents them in a team-games cooperative lesson. If used frequently, three outcomes of this change can be expected: (1) Students will make friends with teammates they might previously have ignored, (2) students will like math more, and (3) students will learn the concepts better. One of the authors used this procedure to teach grammar to high school students with learning disabilities. It worked so well that students not only learned the concepts and made new friends but also requested that the author continue teaching them more grammar than the author had planned, because the process of learning it "turned them on"!

▶ LESSON PLAN

State History: Wisconsin
Subject Area: Social Studies
Grade Level: Kindergarten
Time: One week

Objectives[13]

1. Children will develop an understanding of Wisconsin's history through the use of the Wisconsin State flag and its symbols.

2. Children will become familiar with the Revolutionary War and the role it played in the United States' becoming a country.

3. Children will be able to identify land and water on a globe. They will also become familiar with the names and locations of the seven continents and four oceans.

4. Children will learn about the different components of maps and what they mean. They will develop an understanding of maps being to scale and what the cardinal directions are by referring to compass roses.

5. Children will cooperatively engage in the activities by listening attentively, communicating clearly, taking turns, and including all students.

Suggested Procedures

1. Display the Wisconsin state flag (or a picture of one) in the classroom so that all students can see it clearly. Have all the students listen as the teacher discusses the meaning of the symbols on the flag and how it relates to Wisconsin history. Allow the students to ask questions at this time and encourage them to make connections between the symbols and attributes of Wisconsin with which they are familiar. For example, there is a badger on the flag, and it is also the state animal and the University of Wisconsin–Madison's mascot. Students should then create flags of their own that represent aspects of themselves, such as drawing a tree to represent enjoying nature or pasting on a picture of an airplane if they

---

[13]Source: Abigail Rose Reuler, University of Wisconsin–Madison.

like to travel. Encourage students to put symbols or pictures on their flags which have meaning and relate to them.

2. Refer to the American flag (or a picture of one) displayed in the classroom and explain to the students what the stripes, stars, and colors stand for. At the same time, include basic and relevant information about the Revolutionary War, such as why it started and what the outcome was. Next have the students work as a whole group to re-create the American flag using a large white piece of paper, a blue square, white star stamps, and seven red stripes (prepared by the teacher).

3. Gather the class in a large circle and toss an inflated globe to one another. The teacher will start the activity by tossing the globe to a student. As each student catches it, the teacher will ask if a specified finger is touching water or land. The student is expected to identify correctly if his or her finger is touching water or land. The teacher will keep a tally of correct responses. This activity is intended to show the students that Earth is made up of more water than land. Next, the students will be given an activity sheet and asked to color the water blue and the land green, and glue labels of the seven continents and four oceans in their appropriate places.

4. Initiate teacher–student discussion of what they know about maps. The teacher will explain the idea of maps being to scale and what the compass rose symbol means. The students will get into small groups and create a map of the classroom to practice making maps to scale. They will also play a game involving the cardinal directions. Signs of the directions will be posted appropriately in the classroom: N, S, E, W, SE, SW, NW, NE. The teacher will close his or her eyes and have the students stand underneath the signs with the directions on them. The teacher will then call out a direction while still closing his or her eyes, and the students standing under the called sign are eliminated. For example, if a student is standing under NW and that direction is called, she is eliminated. The students switch the direction they are standing under each time people are eliminated by walking to another one, with the intention of becoming more familiar with the directions. The game continues until there is only one person left.

Evaluation

The children will produce different projects, like their own flag and maps showing water and land, that will allow the teacher to evaluate the students' understanding. Observing the students in the social contexts and paying attention to their participation and cooperative behavior will also be a form of evaluation.

AFTER

State History: Wisconsin
Subject Area: Social Studies
Grade Level: 3–5
Time: One week

Objectives

1. The children will develop an understanding of Wisconsin's history and the roles that different ethnic groups have played, while looking at the symbols on the Wisconsin State flag and comparing them to present-day conditions.

2. Children will research a country that relates to their heritage and share the country's flag and history with their classmates.

3. Children will be able to identify land and water on a globe. They will also become familiar with the names, locations, and important information regarding each of the seven continents.

4. Children will learn about the different components of maps and what they mean. They will develop an understanding of maps being to scale and what the cardinal directions are by referring to compass roses.

5. Children will cooperatively engage in the activities by listening attentively, communicating clearly, taking turns, and including all students.

6. Children will gain knowledge about a variety of cultures that relate to their classmates. They will also gain knowledge about places and cultures that are unfamiliar or new to them.

Suggested Procedures

1. Display the Wisconsin State flag so that all students can see it clearly. Discuss the symbols on the flag and what they mean by analyzing the colors on the flag, what the significance of the thirteen stripes are, and the meaning of the fifty stars. Compare the representation to today's society in Wisconsin, and talk about the types of people and symbols that might be on the flag if they updated it. The teacher can then discuss the different ethnic groups that live in Wisconsin and the impact they had (and have) on Wisconsin's history. Students may then create flags of their own that represent aspects of themselves. Students should be encouraged to place symbols or pictures on their flags that have meaning and relate to them.

2. Have each student do library research on the country of origin of his or her family's ancestors. Every student will be responsible for collecting information about that country's history and drawing that country's flag using various art supplies.

   Next have the students present their information to the class and explain the meaning of the flag and how it relates to that country's history.

3. Gather the class in a large circle, and have them toss an inflated globe to one another. The teacher will start the activity by tossing the globe to a student. As he or she catches it, the teacher will ask if a specified finger is touching water or land. The student is expected to identify if his or her finger is touching water or land correctly. The teacher will keep a tally of correct responses. This activity is intended to show the students that Earth is made up of water more than land. Next, glue labels of the seven continents and four oceans in their appropriate places. After that, students will gather into seven groups, and each group will be assigned a different continent. As a group they will do research on the continent, collecting information about the people who live there, languages spoken, the climate, the geography, and any interesting traditions that they find. They will present this information by displaying it on a large cut-out of that continent. When all the groups have finished, they will put all the continents on a large world map and can share what they have found.

4. Initiate teacher–student discussion of what students know about maps. The teacher will explain the idea of maps being to scale, how to read map keys, and what the compass-rose symbol means. Each student will be asked to think of a place that is important to him or her and make a map of it. They will practice making maps to scale and using a key to label items. At the conclusion of the activity, the students will break into small groups of three or four and present their maps to their classmates by explaining why they chose to draw a map of that place and the items they included on it.

Evaluation

The children will produce different projects that will allow the teacher to evaluate the students' understanding. Observing the students in the social contexts and paying attention to their participation and cooperative behavior will also be a form of evaluation.

The "Before" lesson focuses on the general history of people from Wisconsin and United States of America. The "After" lesson narrows in on the children who make up the classroom by incorporating their own histories into the curriculum. It makes the material more interesting and more relevant to students, and is a great way to educate students about different ethnicities and histories other than America's. The "After" lesson also combines the learning of our planet's environments with the cultures that are embedded within them. The students continue to learn about basic geography while learning richer characteristics of the different places. The "After" lesson offers students a way to explore their own heritage and learn about their classmates' heritage as well. It challenges the students by presenting them with information that is unfamiliar to them, working to break down any language, racial, or cultural barriers that may be affecting the development of classroom community.

References

Allport, G. (1954). *The nature of prejudice*. Cambridge, MA: Addison-Wesley.

Banks, J. A. (1995). Multicultural education: Its effects on students' racial and gender role attitudes. In J. A. Banks & C. M. Banks (Eds.), *Handbook of research on multicultural education* (pp. 617–627). New York: Macmillan.

Cohen, E. G., & Lotan, R. A. (Eds.). (1997). *Working for equity in heterogeneous classrooms*. New York: Teachers College Press.

Collins, P. H. (1998). *Fighting words: Black women and the search for justice*. Minneapolis: University of Minnesota Press.

Gillies, R. M., & Ashman, A. F. (2000). The effects of cooperative learning on students with learning difficulties in the lower elementary school. *Journal of Special Education, 34*(1), 19.

Johnson, D. W., Johnson, R., & Maruyama, G. (1982). Interdependence and interpersonal attraction among heterogeneous and homogeneous individuals: A theoretical formulation and meta-analysis of the research. *Review of Educational Research, 53,* 5–54.

Slavin, R. E. (1995). Cooperative learning and intergroup relations. In J. A. Banks & C. M. Banks (Eds.), *Handbook of research on multicultural education* (pp. 628–634). New York: Macmillan.

Sleeter, C. E., & Grant, C. A. (2009). *Making choices for multicultural education: Five approaches to race, class, and gender* (5th ed.). Hobokon, NY: Wiley.

CHAPTER 4

Single-Group Studies

How much do you know about the history and contemporary culture of African American women? Latinos? Asian Americans? working-class Americans? people with disabilities? If you are like most U.S. citizens, you probably were taught very little about these groups of people in school, and you may be able to cite only a few names and historic events.

One way to enhance your knowledge about a group is to study it in some depth, and from the group's perspective. This is what the single-group studies approach is about.

Before proceeding, you may want to analyze your own curriculum, using Action Research Activity 4.1. At first glance, your current textbooks may seem to teach about a wide variety of groups. Prior to 1970, most school curricula concentrated on White, European American, male studies; today, most curricula represent an improvement. When you examine the results of your analysis, however, you will probably discover that some groups are barely included in the curriculum and still others are excluded altogether. For example, in an examination of some current textbooks, one of our classes discovered that Latinos were sparsely represented, even though most of the class's students were Latino/a. Native Americans are still represented as historical figures, and Arab Americans are almost completely excluded. People with disabilities are sprinkled lightly here and there. Single-group studies try to counterbalance these patterns by providing an entire unit or course about Latinos, indigenous Americans, Arab Americans, or people with disabilities.

You may not be aware of omissions and distortions, even when you are looking right at them, if you have not studied the history, literature, and culture of diverse groups. Your own knowledge base may reflect only what is in mainstream textbooks, if they have been the prime source of your own education. An eye-opening book we recommend is *Lies My Teacher Told Me* (Loewen, 1995), which critiques twelve U.S. history textbooks popular at the time and still contains valuable information on this topic for today.

Single-group studies courses are usually designed for all students. However, often only women enroll in women's studies courses, only Asian Americans in Asian American studies courses, and so forth. This occurs because such courses are usually electives, and students who are not members of the group being studied view the course as unimportant or even as threatening. A teacher of African American studies in a predominantly White high school told us how, to counter such perspectives, he works extra hard to make certain that all the students in the class feel comfortable about what he is teaching, and he encourages (through notices and displays) members of different ethnic groups to take the course.

Single-group studies can be done well, or they can be done superficially and poorly. Too often we have seen superficial attempts to teach about groups. For example, a fifth-grade teacher who normally teaches mostly about White European Americans decides to have a one-week African American studies unit during February. Knowing little about African American history and culture himself, he teaches about a smattering of famous people and events, selecting those African Americans who are best known by White European Americans. When the unit is completed, the teacher returns to his regular, European American–dominated curriculum. In contrast, at Dr. Martin Luther King African American Immersion Elementary School in Milwaukee, most of the curriculum is oriented around African American culture. Even math and science are taught through an African American cultural lens. So that they have a background to teach this curriculum, teachers are expected to attain eighteen graduate credits in African or African American studies (for more information, visit www.ncrel.org/sdrs/areas/issues/students/atrisk/at6lk112.htm).

If the single-group studies approach interests you, we encourage you to take the time to do it well. This means first spending time learning about the group yourself. A good single-group studies curriculum includes the following elements: perspective, history, culture, current social agenda, and other issues of particular concern.

► PERSPECTIVE

A single-group study takes a group's perspective about itself. This does not mean, for example, that a teacher needs to be Chicano to teach Chicano studies, but it does mean that the teacher needs to have studied Chicano history and culture from Chicano perspectives. The teacher should be able to present the points of view that are generated by and are receiving attention among members of the group being studied. While the teacher is not prevented from presenting his or her own point of view, the teacher should let students know that it is just another point of view. For years most groups were studied and written about by White European American male scholars. Although in recent decades this has changed, teachers still need to check source material to make sure the perspectives being presented are acceptable to members of the group (recognizing, of course, that no group shares a unanimous perspective on anything). A Chicana teacher we know recently expressed great frustration with the resistance of several White European American colleagues to the idea that their colleagues' perspectives, when teaching about people of color, might not be the same as the perspectives of people of color themselves. She used an analogy that helped get the point across: If a man were to teach women's studies, unless he was attentive to his own perspective and to those of women, most women would be upset and argue that he lacked the sensitivity and probably the knowledge to teach that topic.

Let's take an example. Logan High School in Union City, California, is developing the only high school Filipino studies program in the United States. Logan's students are about 20 percent Filipino. The effort was spearheaded by Oscar Peñaranda, who had been an immigrant himself. He started teaching Filipino studies courses because traditional curricula simply do not challenge colonial images of Filipinos and Filipino

Americans. In the Philippines, colonial schooling taught Filipinos to regard themselves as backward or not equal to European Americans; in the United States, a similar mentality pervades. And students buy it. Peñaranda's mission is "to teach Filipino history from the Filipino perspective" in an effort to challenge "degrading colonial mentalities that captured people's minds." Peñaranda begins by having students push their family tree as far back as they can, in order to uncover indigenous ancestry from which they can begin to learn. As students uncover wisdom within their own ancestry, and ways of understanding the sociopolitical context in which Filipinos find themselves today, students' sense of self becomes much richer and deeper.

It can take some work to see a topic from the perspectives of historically marginalized groups. For example, when studying immigration, one might see immigrants themselves as the historically marginalized group. But which immigrants? It is relevant to study immigration, but one might still do this from a European perspective and ignore immigrants from diverse parts of the world. Furthermore, voluntary immigrants and refugees have had rather different experiences: From which perspective is immigration studied? These questions are illustrated in the lesson plan "Immigrants and Refugees" (p. 136).

▶ HISTORY

History is usually included in single-group studies and often has two foci. The first focus examines the group's historical experience and may include reference to other groups. The group's past and recent experiences are told "fairly" but from the perspectives of the group. The purpose is to document the group's history and contributions to society, in order to equip young people to shape the future more justly. For example, Gary Glassman teaches tenth-grade history and was concerned that over 90 percent of the people in the text he used were male. To address this imbalance, he and his students created a "herstory" website. There, students posted original research papers and original historical fiction about very diverse women, including European medieval women, an Afghan woman, a Jewish girl in Spain during the Inquisition, women in the French Revolution, and politically active Tibetan women. You can visit their website at www.asis.com/sfhs/women/index2.html. Examples of lessons that focus on history include "Wheelchair Sports" (p. 144) and "Women and the Westward Movement" (p. 147).

The second focus traces and explains how the dominant group has oppressed the group being studied and how the oppressed group has responded to or resisted oppression. For example, Chicano studies begins historically, with indigenous people of Mexico, then Spanish colonization, and next liberation from Spain. Conquest by the United States is examined, as are strategies to resist conquest. Students learn about the claiming of a Chicano activist identity and about its connection with Chicano political movements, both historically and currently. Sometimes, teachers shy away from this second focus, believing it to be controversial and detrimental to students' cross-group relationships. We believe that unequal power relations between groups need to be studied, but in a way that opens up discussion about how the future can be constructed more fairly and how everyone can participate. Young people are often aware of various forms of inequalities between groups and wonder why things are the way they are; they are generally open to asking how they can make the world better for everyone. Examples of lessons that address oppression include "Mexican American Labor in the United States" (p. 173), "Culture in Native American Literature" (p. 168), "The Legacies of the African American Civil Rights Movement" (p. 158), and "Japanese Americans—U.S. Citizens" (p. 154).

▶ CULTURE

The culture of a group encompasses its whole way of life, including the group's literature, language, music, art, philosophy, and technology. Cultural contributions, which teachers often feel most comfortable emphasizing, show the group's creativity, the way the group has given meaning to its existence, and the way it has maintained and expressed its selfhood. Most students find cross-cultural sharing to be very interesting. The community can be an excellent resource for sharing culture: By exploring religious institutions, neighborhood stores, community centers, and neighborhood restaurants and by inviting students' family members to participate, teachers can design an interesting curriculum that is rooted in the perspectives and lives of real people.

For example, students at Ella B. Vernetti School in Koyukuk School District, Alaska, collaborated with the University of Alaska–Fairbanks and the Koyukuk community to develop a community cultural portrait. The main sections of this portrait include place (maps, native place names, houses), stories by elders, mushing and other means of transportation, subsistence living, and computer art. You can visit this project on the Web at www.vernetti.koyukuk.k12.ak.us/vernittihome.htm. Notice how culture connects historic ways of life (such as subsistence living) with the present (computers)!

Lessons that discuss and illustrate cultural contributions include "Story Quilt" (p. 133), "Wheelchair Sports" (p. 144), "Poster Design and the Voice of People with Disabilities" (p. 150), and "Japanese Americans—U.S. Citizens" (p. 154). The lesson "Culture in Native American Literature" (p. 168) was designed to get students to consider what culture means and to begin to identify their own family and community culture.

▶ CURRENT SOCIAL AGENDA

Advocates of the single-group studies approach hope to use education as a means of bettering a group's current social condition. Therefore, considerable emphasis is placed on the group's current needs and experiences, the issues facing the group, and the movements involving the group. The purpose of discussing the current social agenda is to help students view themselves as active citizens who can make a positive difference in society. Sometimes teachers do not include this component of single-group studies, believing that knowledge of the group's history and contributions is sufficient. Most advocates of single-group studies view the exclusion of this component as a potential suggestion to students that the group is no longer oppressed or victimized. Teachers who are unsure of the issues that are currently on a group's social action agenda should investigate them (being aware that different subgroups may emphasize different issues). The lessons "American Indians and Institutional Racism" (p. 140), "Gay, Lesbian, Bisexual, and Transgender Youth" (p. 161), and "Mexican American Labor in the United States" (p. 173) deal specifically with these groups' current social agendas.

▶ ISSUES OF PARTICULAR CONCERN

Most groups have particular issues that are especially important to them. For example, the study of Puerto Ricans, Central Americans, and Mexican Americans must include the issue of language. The study of Jewish Americans must examine the Holocaust. Arab American studies should examine the occupation of Palestine as well as the response of Arab and non-Arab communities to the 9/11 attack on the World Trade Center. Gay and lesbian studies must examine different family structures. Women's studies must deal with the extent to which males and females differ biologically. Disability studies must unpack conceptions of ability, who creates and maintains these conceptions, and how they locate disability in people rather than in social institutions. Two lesson plans, "Wheelchair Sports" (p. 144) and "Poster Design and the Voice of People with Disabilities" (p. 150), address these issues.

▶ ACTION RESEARCH ACTIVITY 4.1

Textbook Analysis

Select one textbook and record the following information:

Title:

Author(s):

Publisher:

Copyright date:

Grade level (if known):

Following are guides for six kinds of analysis. Some may be appropriate to your text, some may not. Select all the analyses that can be done with your text. Go through the text page by page, completing each analysis you select. Take your time and do this carefully. Then compile your findings using the guidelines that follow and the charts shown in Figures 4.1–4.3.

Indicate here the types of analysis you completed:

	Yes	No
1. Picture	_____	_____
2. People to study	_____	_____
3. Anthology	_____	_____
4. Language	_____	_____
5. Storyline	_____	_____
6. Other	_____	_____

Picture Analysis

Picture analysis is used for texts that picture American people in the United States.

1. Using the chart in Figure 4.1, tally the types of people in each picture by race, sex, and disability. The pictures may depict either individuals or groups. You will need to use your judgment on some pictures, but if a picture features one or a few individuals, tally each individual separately; if the picture features a group,

		Male	Female	Both Sexes
Asian American	Individual			
	Group			
African American	Individual			
	Group			
Hispanic American	Individual			
	Group			
American Indian	Individual			
	Group			
White American	Individual			
	Group			
Race Ambiguous	Individual			
	Group			
Mixed Race Group				
Disabled American	Individual			
	Group			

Total number of individuals depicted: _____

Total number of group scenes depicted: _____

Figure 4.1 Picture Tally

tally it in the "group" row. Code each tally according to whether the individual(s) is (are) named or unnamed in a caption or in the surrounding text (N = named, U = unnamed).

2. Make note of any race stereotypes.

3. Make note of any sex stereotypes/sex roles.

4. In group scenes, does any race or sex group consistently occupy the foreground? the background? Provide examples.

5. Can you tell the social class or setting of any of the depicted people? If so, make a note of them.

"People to Study" Analysis

This type of analysis is used primarily for science and history texts. In Figure 4.2, tally the race and sex of each person mentioned in the text. Distinguish between "important famous people," whose contributions are discussed in the main part of the content, and "extra people," who are added in boxes or supplementary pages at the beginning or end of the chapter.

Anthology Analysis

This type of analysis is used for elementary readers, literature texts, music books containing works by different composers, and the like. Across the top of the chart shown

	Main Part of Text		Supplementary	
	Male	Female	Male	Female
Asian American				
African American				
Hispanic American				
American Indian				
White American				
Race Unknown				
Disabled American				

Figure 4.2 People to Study

in Figure 4.3, write the name of each story, poem, essay, and song in the text (the figure has space for five titles; photocopy additional copies as needed). Complete all items that you can, using the following codes:

AM	= Asian American male	AF	= Asian American female
AAM	= African American male	AAF	= African American female
LM	= Latino male	LF	= Latina female
AIM	= American Indian male	AIF	= American Indian female
EAM	= European American male	EAF	= European American female
FM	= Foreign male	FF	= Foreign female
?M	= Male, race unknown?	?F	= Female, race unknown
DM	= Male with disabilities	DF	= Female with disabilities
GM	= Gay male	LF	= Lesbian female

Language Analysis

This analysis should be recorded on a separate sheet of paper.

1. Does the textbook deliberately use nonsexist language? If not, list the male words that are used to refer to both sexes.

2. Examine the adjectives used to describe people or the contributions of people who are not White European American: List any stereotypic words, along with the group with which these words are linked.

3. Examine the adjectives used to describe males and females; list any that contain sex stereotypes.

4. When the word *women* is used, does it refer primarily to European American middle-class women or to all women? Look carefully, especially if you are analyzing a social studies book. Provide examples.

5. Look for words or phrases that give the actions of some groups (often European American wealthy males) an image of goodness or legitimacy in situations in

Titles						
1. Race and sex of author						
2. Race, sex, and disability of main character						
3. Race, sex, and disability of supporting characters						
4. Are the characters all of one race? (Yes/No)						
5. Does the theme or storyline reflect the experiences of one particular group? If so, which group?						
6. Does the theme or storyline make one group look better or seem to have done more than another group? If so, which group?						
7. Is the setting rural (R), urban (U), suburban (S), or indeterminable (I)?						
8. Are there race stereotypes? If so, what are they?						
9. Can you identify the social class setting?						
10. Are there social-class stereo-types? If so, what are they?						
11. Are there sex stereotypes or sex roles? If so, what are they?						
12. Are there disability stereotypes? If so, what are they?						

Figure 4.3   Anthology Analysis

which their actions might be questionable. Do this especially if you are analyzing a social studies book. Words such as *progress, improved,* and *successful* are commonly used in this way.

6. Look for words or phrases that give the actions of some groups (often those that live at or below the poverty level or those from parts of the world the United States is in conflict with) an image of badness or trouble in situations in which there could well be another side that is not being told. Words such as *problems, unrest,* and *hostile* are examples.

7. Are dialects or accents portrayed? If so, what image is presented of the speaker(s)?

Storyline Analysis

This type of analysis is used for history texts, long stories in literature books, and novels. Record your answers on a separate sheet of paper.

1. What race/class/gender group receives the most sustained attention from beginning to end in the text?

2. What race/class/gender group resolves most of the problems that develop or accomplishes most of the achievements described? List the major problems and the people who resolve them. List the major accomplishments and the people who achieve them.

3. What other race/class/gender groups appear? How sustained is the attention given to each? What kinds of situations or accomplishments are associated with each?

4. How successfully and how often do the groups in item 3 resolve problems that develop? To what extent are the groups presented as causing problems? Give examples.

5. To what extent is the group in items 1 and 2 presented as a significant problem to someone else? How realistically or completely is this portrayed? Give examples.

6. What group(s) does the author intend the reader to sympathize with or to respect the most?

7. What group's experience does the reader learn most about?

8. Was the author, as nearly as you can tell, a member of the most featured group? If not, is there anything to suggest the author is qualified to write about that group?

Miscellaneous Analyses

If race, class, gender, disability, and sexual orientation can be examined in any additional ways in your text, do so. For example,

1. If the text includes story problems or story examples (e.g., a math text), list by race, sex, and disability who is doing what for each problem. Then search for any race or sex stereotypes and roles.

2. Determine if the text shows an awareness of and sensitivity to the experiences of U.S. Americans of color, women, or the poor in ways not captured by previous analyses. For example, how does a health text treat pregnancy or sickle-cell anemia?

Compiling the Findings

Compile your findings on a separate sheet of paper.

1. Compile all your data depicting the way each of the following groups is portrayed. Include how much space or attention (e.g., percentage of pictures) the text devotes to each group and to the roles and characteristics of the group.

> Asian Americans, of both sexes
> African Americans, of both sexes
> Latino Americans, of both sexes
> American Indians, of both sexes
> White European Americans, of both sexes
> Women, of various racial backgrounds
> Men, of various racial backgrounds
> The upper class
> The middle class
> People who live at or below the poverty level
> People who are gay, lesbian, or bisexual
> U.S. Americans with disabilities, of both sexes and various racial backgrounds

2. For each group in item 1, compile data on how the text depicts the concerns or experiences of the group and the group's ability to deal effectively with its concerns.

3. For each group, ask the following questions:
   a. Does the text give a student who is a member of that group much with which to identify?
   b. What kinds of roles and characteristics does the text suggest are appropriate for that student to develop or aspire to?

▶ LESSON PLAN

Story Writing

BEFORE

Subject Area: Language Arts
Grade Level: 3–5
Time: One week

Objectives

1. Students will demonstrate story comprehension.
2. Students will sequence events correctly.

Suggested Procedures

1. Read the story *Tar Beach* by Faith Ringgold. Faith Ringgold is both an artist and a children's author, and she is noted for her quilt making. *Tar Beach* tells a story of inner-city children creating a beach on a rooftop.

2. Have students complete a writing assignment summarizing the main idea of the story.

3. Before going to the computer lab, divide the class into groups of four students. Have each group think of a fun activity they would like to do but cannot where they live. Have them pretend to be magicians and imagine a way of creating that activity in their own neighborhood. Tell them that good story writers have good ideas and are able to convey them in an order that makes sense to other people.

4. In the computer lab, have each group create a short story that tells about their imaginary activity. After writing the story, they should save each sentence on a separate sheet of paper.

5. Have each group exchange stories, with the sentences scrambled. Each group should attempt to sequence the sentences into an order that makes sense. When all groups have finished, have them pass their sequenced sentences to another group, who will read the sequencing to see if the story makes sense. Then discuss the stories and the sequencing exercise.

Evaluation

1. Through the writing assignment, assess students' comprehension of the story *Tar Beach*.

2. Through their participation in the sequencing exercise, assess students' sequencing ability.

Resource

Ringgold, F. (1991). *Tar beach*. New York: Crown.

Story Quilt[1]

Subject Areas: Language Arts, Art, History

Grade Level: 3–5

Time: Three weeks

Objectives

1. Students will research a historical event or period of a cultural group.

2. Students will sequence events encapsulating the information acquired.

3. Students will connect literature with the group's history.

Suggested Procedures

1. Read the story *Tar Beach* by Faith Ringgold. Faith Ringgold is both an artist and a children's author, and she is noted for her quilt making. *Tar Beach* tells a story of inner-city children creating a beach on a rooftop.

2. Tell students about Faith Ringgold's quilt making. Two suggested resources are *Portfolios: African American Artists* (a book of prints of artists' works that includes a picture of Ringgold's quilt "Tar Beach") and *Talking to Faith Ringgold*.

[1] *Source:* Jacquelyn King, Kenosha Unified School District, Kenosha, Wisconsin.

3. Tell students that they will make a quilt depicting the Civil Rights movement. Help them during the period of a week or so to find information on the movement. Four useful children's books are *Tell All the Children Our Story: Memories and Mementos About Being Young and Black in America*, by Tonya Bolden; *Free at Last: A History of the Civil Rights Movement and Those Who Died in the Struggle*, by Sara Bullard; *Oh, Freedom! Kids Talk About the Civil Rights Movement With the People Who Made It Happen*, by Casey King, Linda Barrett Osborne, and Joe Brooks; and *The Civil Rights Movement for Kids: A History*, by Mary Turck.

   If possible, use the Internet to search for information. Have students make notes of the event.

4. Give each student two squares of scratch paper on which to write information about the event. Have students share one fact and tack it to a piece of butcher paper taped on a wallboard. If someone has a duplicate, use the second fact. After everyone has contributed information, the class will organize the facts in chronological order. Number the papers.

5. In journals, have students describe the event.

6. Before going to the computer lab, pass out one fact to each student. Have students type the facts, changing margins if necessary so that the text fits within a square. Back in the classroom, on cut-out squares of paper, have students center and glue their typed information. (The size of the font and quilt squares will be dependent on the number of students and desired size of the finished quilt. Cut a center square for the title of the piece and signature of each student participant and whatever other information you may desire.) Students should decorate the border of their square with paper scraps, glitter, cloth scraps, beans, buttons, markers, or other items. Their decorations should depict events or ideas related to the Civil Rights movement.

7. To assemble the quilt, glue finished squares to large pieces of butcher paper or poster board.

Evaluation

1. Assess students' research through observation and discussion as they are working and by the square each contributes to the quilt.

2. Assess students' ability to develop a sequence of events by the accuracy of their journal entry.

Resources

Bolden, T. (2001). *Tell all the children our story: Memories and mementos about being young and Black in America*. New York: Abrams.

Bullard, S. (1993). *Free at last: A history of the Civil Rights movement and those who died in the struggle*. New York: Oxford University Press.

King, C., Osborne, L. B., & Brooks, J. (1997). *Oh, freedom! Kids talk about the Civil Rights movement with the people who made it happen*. New York: Knopf.

Portfolios: African American Artists. (1994). Palo Alto, CA: Dale Seymour.

Ringgold, F. (1991). *Tar beach*. New York: Crown.

Ringgold, F. (1996). *Talking to Faith Ringgold*. New York: Crown.

Turck, M. (2000). *The Civil Rights movement for kids: A history*. Chicago: Chicago Review Press.

Story Quilt

WHY THE CHANGES?

History and Culture

The "Before" lesson disconnects Faith Ringgold's work from its cultural context. Although the story is written by a noted African American artist, little is done with the story to develop an understanding of African American history and culture. The "After" plan develops this understanding.

The "After" plan is much more involved than the "Before" plan, but it also incorporates three different disciplines rather than one. With careful planning, this can become a thematic interdisciplinary unit that works for three different disciplines simultaneously. This interdisciplinary teaching then lends itself very well to connecting literature, art, and history to delve into a significant event in African American history.

The structure of the "After" plan lends itself well to studying different groups. For example, one could study an event in Latino history by focusing on a Latina muralist such as Judith Baca. Students could then create a mural depicting an event such as the development of the United Farm Workers or immigration experiences.

▶ LESSON PLAN

Immigrants

BEFORE

Subject Area: Social Studies

Grade Level: 4–6

Time: One week, 45 minutes to 1 hour per day

Objectives

1. Students will identify some of the difficulties immigrants encounter.
2. Students will identify geographic locations where immigrants have come from and the reasons they came.
3. Students will appreciate the struggles and contributions of immigrants to the United States.

Suggested Procedures

1. Have students sit on the floor to introduce the unit. Ask students what they know about immigrants. It is very possible that some of your students or family members have immigrated to the United States. Invite students to share any personal first-hand information they might have about immigrants.
2. Read a section in a social studies text about immigration during the late 1800s and early 1900s. Have students locate Ellis Island on a map.
3. The next day, have students read the book *Immigrant Kids*, by Russell Freedman, which tells about the experience of being a young urban immigrant around 1900. Using a map of Europe, show the various countries that immigrants came from during that time. Pair students, and ask each pair to create a short set of interview questions they would want to ask someone who immigrated to the United States during that time.

4. The following day, read the book *If Your Name Was Changed at Ellis Island*, by Ellen Levine. This book is arranged in a question-and-answer format. Discuss how many of the students' questions were answered in the book; identify questions that are still unanswered.

5. Use the Internet to search for answers to questions students may still have.

6. Have each student write a short story in which the student imagines him- or herself as an immigrant to the United States around 1900. Invite students to read their stories to the rest of the class.

Evaluation

Assess students' understanding of the reasons immigrants came to the United States, and the difficulties and struggles they faced as these are reflected in the interview questions and stories students write.

Resources

Freedman, R. (1995). *Immigrant kids*. Glenview, IL: Scott, Foresman.

Levine, E., & Parmenter, W. (Illustrator). (1994). *If your name was changed at Ellis Island*. New York: Scholastic.

Immigrants and Refugees[2]

AFTER

Subject Area: Social Studies

Grade Level: 4–6

Time: One week, 45 minutes to 1 hour per day

Objectives

1. Students will describe differences between immigrants and refugees.

2. Students will identify some of the difficulties refugees encounter.

3. Students will identify geographic locations around the world where refugees have come from.

4. Students will describe family resettlement history in the United States.

5. Students will appreciate the struggles of family members who journeyed to the United States.

6. Students will identify the location on the East and West coasts of the United States where the majority of the newcomers arrives.

Suggested Procedures

1. Have students sit on the floor to introduce the unit. Ask students what they know about refugees. Typically, students confuse the concept of immigrants with refugees and will describe both without realizing there is a difference.

2. Draw two overlapping Venn diagram circles on butcher paper, with the headings "Immigrants" and "Refugees." Pair students. Have pairs list on index cards differences they think exist between refugees and immigrants. Bring the students

[2]*Source: Yer Thao, Claremont Graduate School, Claremont, California.*

back together, and have each pair read their list to the whole group. While each student is reading, jot down the pair's ideas in the Venn diagram, writing common ideas for both groups where the circles overlap.

3. Introduce books, magazines, newspapers, and pictures or posters about refugees to students. Have the students do an independent reading, exploring and discovering these materials for twenty-five minutes. Bring the class back together on the floor; have the class try to create a definition for refugees using the Venn diagram. It is import to help students understand some of the reasons people become refugees, the barriers and disruptions refugees face, and how they adjust.

4. The next day, read the book *A Bosnian Family* by Robin Landew Silverman out loud to the class. This story takes about twenty minutes to read. After reading, have an open-class discussion on the story about some of the issues that the main characters encountered.

5. Have the class brainstorm questions that they would like to ask refugees or immigrants to find out about their experiences. Have students pick ten questions from the list to ask a family member who immigrated; they will then bring back the responses to share with the class. Students who do not have a family member who was a refugee or an immigrant may interview a neighbor or friend.

6. When interviews are completed, have each student draw a picture of the person he or she interviewed and write a short paragraph describing that person's transition to the United States. On a large world map, post each interviewer's picture over his or her homeland. Have students use yarn to mark the route those interviewed took during their journey to the United States.

7. Make available to students a variety of books from the resource list included here. (Students who have some problem with grade-level reading must pick easier books so that they can understand the story.) Have each student prepare both an oral and written report on his or her book.

8. Invite community leaders or parents who were refugees to come share their personal experiences with the class. Allow the students to ask questions and to dialogue with the guest panel. Have students write an open letter expressing thanks to the panel about what they learned from the special guests.

9. Write a letter asking students' parents to help the students bring a food traditional to their home culture to share with the whole class for the unit's closing potluck. The teacher should also bring a dish and provide the drinks, plates, and napkins. (Allow students to briefly talk about their traditional dish.)

10. Have students identify and research the history of two locations in the United States where most newcomers arrive.

Evaluation

1. On the basis of class discussion and their book report, assess students' ability to differentiate between immigrants and refugees.

2. On the basis of their book report and their thank-you letter, assess students' appreciation of difficulties refugees encounter.

3. On the basis of their interview and their book report, assess students' understanding of family resettlement history.

Resources

Aliski, M. (1998). *Painted words/spoken memories: Marianthe's story*. New York: Greenwillow/Harper-Collins.

The Asian American Coalition. (1995). *Children of Asian America*. Chicago: Polychrome.

Bode, J. (1989). *New kids on the block: Oral histories of immigrant teens*. New York: Franklin Watts.

Cha, D. (1996). *Dia's story cloth: The Hmong people's journey of freedom*. New York: Lee & Low Books.

Shea, P. Deitz. (1995). *The whispering cloth*. Honesdale, PA: Author.

Faderman, L. (1998). *I begin my life all over*. Boston: Beacon.

Marchant, B., & Marchant H., (1992). *A boy named Chong*. Green Bay, WI: Project Chong.

Shea, Pegi Deitz. (2003). *Tangled threads: A Hmong girl's story*. New York: Clarion.

Sheth, K. (2004). *Blue Jamine*. New York: Hyperion.

Silverman, R. L. (1997). *A Bosnian family*. Minneapolis, MN: Lerner.

Strazzabosco, G. (1995). *Teenage refugees from Iran speak out*. New York: Rosen.

Surat, M. M. (1983). *Angel child, dragon child*. Milwaukee, WI: Raintree.

Tekavec, V. (1995). *Teenage refugees from Haiti speak out*. New York: Rosen Publishing Group.

Tran, K.-T. (1987). *The little weaver of Thai-Yen village*. San Francisco: Children's Book Press.

Walgren, J. (1998). *The lost boys of Natinga: A school for Sudan's young refugees*. New York: Houghton Mifflin.

Warren, A. (2004). *Escape from Saigon: A Vietnam war orphan becomes an American boy*. New York: Farrar, Straus & Giroux.

Immigrants and Refugees

WHY THE CHANGES?

Perspective

Typically during fifth grade, students study U.S. history, and they may encounter a unit like the "Before" plan. The "Before" plan is written from a European American perspective. It ignores immigrants who came from Asia during the same time period. Furthermore, it ignores differences between immigrants and refugees and assumes that students in the class are all descendants of voluntary immigrants.

The "Before" plan could be improved by including immigrants from Asia who came through Angel Island, as well as immigrants from Europe who came through Ellis Island. It could also be improved by having students ask their questions to immigrants in their families or communities, in addition to seeking answers from books or the Internet.

Issues of Concern

Students are typically confused about differences between immigrants and refugees. I [Yer Thao] interviewed five fifth graders to look at their understanding of refugees. According to the definitions by all five students, refugees suffered through wars. They were pushed out of their country when soldiers attacked them and took their belongings. They had no home, food, or good clothing, and they lived temporarily in refugee camps. Most of the students learned about refugees by watching TV. The students said that the refugees looked sad, poor, and homeless, and that their lives looked miserable. As they continued to talk, they gave examples of refugees from Japan, China, and England; some of their examples were of family members, some from TV, and some from what they learned in school.

The students knew the term *refugee* and the term *immigrant*, but were not clear on the differences between the two. Because the United States is home to both, it is helpful for students to know about the specific concerns and needs of both. Furthermore, in a classroom that has children who were refugees or descendants of refugees, presenting only immigrant experiences trivializes and misrepresents traumatic experiences they or their close relatives may have had.

▶ LESSON PLAN

American Indians in Our State

Subject Areas: Interdisciplinary (Social Studies, Art, Language Arts)

Grade Level: 5–8

Time: Three or four class periods

Objectives

1. Students will identify American Indian reservations on a state map and name tribes in the state.

2. Students will list towns, cities, rivers, and other geographic features in the states that have American Indian names.

3. Students will appreciate local American Indian art and literature.

Suggested Procedures

1. Ask students if they know what American Indian tribes live in the state. List the tribes on the board and teach students how to pronounce each one correctly.

2. On a large wall map, show where American Indian reservations are located in the state and where the majority of each tribe lives. (If a tribe lives on more than one reservation, or if more than one tribe lives on a reservation, clarify this; also point out where most American Indians live who are not on a reservation.) Pass out individual maps of the state; have students label and color the reservations and other places where the tribes live.

3. Ask students if they are aware of any American Indian names for places in the state. Start a list on the board. Supply American Indian names that students do not offer. Help students to see that one cultural legacy of the American Indians is names. Point out which tribes contributed which names. Discuss any history behind the names of places.

4. Bring to class samples and pictures of American Indian artwork. Point out the particular skills involved in creating them and any symbols in the designs. Also point out the uses that artifacts have in American Indian culture.

5. Select a few folktales, poems, or songs produced by local American Indian tribes. Have students read them and discuss their meaning and significance.

Evaluation

1. Evaluate students' appreciation of American Indian art and literature through their reactions to them.

2. Through a quiz, evaluate students' knowledge of American Indian reservations, tribe names, and American Indian names for geographic locations.

American Indians and Institutional Racism[3]

AFTER

Subject Areas: Interdisciplinary (Social Studies, Math, Composition)
Grade Level: 5–8
Time: Three or four class periods

Objectives

1. Students will identify areas of good and poor agricultural land on a map.
2. Students will analyze the distribution of agricultural land to European Americans and American Indians and the consequences of land distribution.
3. Students will construct bar graphs from numerical data.
4. Students will distinguish between institutional racism and individual prejudice.
5. Students will appreciate the potential of their own actions for changing institutional racism.

Suggested Procedures

1. Ask students what racism means. They will probably define the term or give examples in terms of individual prejudice; accept their definitions for the time being. Ask how they would describe racism toward American Indians today.
   Note: Students often think of racism only as the individual prejudice that one person displays toward another (e.g., calling someone by a racist name). The concept of institutional racism is usually more difficult to grasp because it involves questioning institutional practices that many of us take for granted. This lesson plan uses examples from one state to help students understand institutional racism. Similar lessons can be developed in other states, drawing on the particulars of how oppression of a group is maintained.
2. Pass out a soil map and a growing season map (see Figure 4.4). Discuss with students which land they would like to own if they were farmers and why.
3. Pass out the Wisconsin reservations map (see Figure 4.4) or a similar map of your own state. Ask students to compare the locations of American Indian reservations with the most and least desirable farmland.
4. Provide information on Wisconsin's and the federal government's treatment of American Indians, including the following:
   a. The six distinct tribes, each with its own language and culture (Chippewa, Menominee, Oneida, Potawatomi, Stockbridge, and Winnebago [later, the Hochunk Nation])
   b. The "hands-off" policy, which forced Indians onto reservations and made them fend for themselves
   c. The "Americanize" policy, in which tribal governments were undermined, religions suppressed, native arts discouraged, and family life hurt by government boarding schools
   d. The year 1924, when American Indians became full U.S. citizens.

[3] *Source:* Lynette Selkurt Zimmer, Kenosha, Wisconsin.

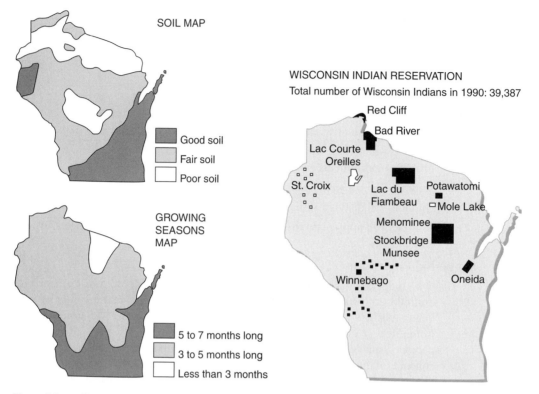

Figure 4.4 Indian Reservations and Land Quality
Source: Adapted from *Tiller's Guide to Indian Country* by Veronica E. Tiller & Velarde Tiller, 1996, Albuquerque, NM: BowArrow.

e. The Indian Restoration Act of 1934, which did away with severe Americanization programs

5. Divide the class into small groups and distribute a sheet like the one shown in Table 4.1. Have each group locate data using the Internet; suggested URLs include the following:

Associations and Discussion Groups www.h-net.msu.edu/~amind/
Ethnic Heritage: American Indian: www.cr.nps.gov/history/catsig/ethind.htm
National Congress of American Indians: ncai@ncai.org
U.S. Census Bureau: www.census.gov
National Museum of the American Indian: www.si.edu/resource/faq/nmai/start.htm
Native American Women Bibliography: www.radcliffe.edu/schles/libcolls/bks per/bibs/native.htm
Native Health History Database: http://hsc.unm.edu/nhhd/
Society for the Study of the Indigenous Languages of the Americas(SSILA): http://trc2.ucdavis.edu/ssila/default.asp

Table 4.1   Worksheet for Gathering Information About Wisconsin Indians' Access to Resources

	Wisconsin Indians	All Races
Resource: Housing		
Number of year-round housing units		
Percentage lacking some or all plumbing facilities		
Median number of rooms per unit		
Number of occupied units		
Median number of persons per unit		
Resource: Education		
Median number of school years completed		
Resource: Income, jobs		
Percentage of families living in poverty		
Percentage of families living in poverty headed by a female		
Percentage of total persons living in poverty		
Percentage of unemployed persons		
Percentage of civilian labor force employed in manufacturing		

Suggestions for Native American Research (Cherokee): www.state.tn.us/sos/statelib/pubsvs/cherokee.htm

Then have them construct a bar graph using data they located. For example, one group could construct a bar graph for American Indians and all races depicting the following data:

Percentage of families living in poverty
Percentage of families living in poverty headed by a female
Percentage of total persons living in poverty

6. Have students present their bar graphs and explain them to the class.

7. Discuss the relationship between the information on students' bar graphs and the arability of soil on the reservations. Explain that this is an example of institutional racism, in which American Indians today suffer the adverse effects of disadvantageous land distribution compounded by past government policies.

8. Ask students to suggest ways that Wisconsin citizens and the federal government could help solve these unequal conditions. From students' suggestions, select targets for a letter-writing campaign. Have students write letters (e.g., to members of Congress) expressing their feelings and proposing their suggestions.

Evaluation

1. Through class discussion, assess students' understanding of land distribution.

2. Through their presentations and discussion of small-group bar graphs, assess students' understanding of the consequences of land distribution.

3. Through class discussion and their suggestions for helping undo racism, assess students' understanding of institutional racism.

4. Through the content and quality of their letters, assess students' appreciation of themselves as social actors.

American Indians and Institutional Racism

WHY THE CHANGES?

Perspective and Current Social Agenda

The "Before" lesson probably seems more familiar than the "After" lesson. The "Before" lesson teaches mainly about the contributions that American Indians have made to European Americans, which often is the main perspective used by teachers. The "Before" lesson teaches the names that American Indians contributed for geographic locations and their artistic and literary contributions. When selecting these, we often choose historic rather than contemporary contributions. Although it is acceptable to teach this information, focusing on it gives more prominence to American Indians' cultural contributions than to the people themselves. In addition, it makes the contributions used and appreciated by White European Americans seem more valuable than those used and appreciated mainly by American Indians, and it makes historic American Indian culture seem more worthy of study than the status of the American Indian people today.

The "After" lesson shifts the perspective, and in so doing it shifts the focus of the entire lesson. It is oriented around the perspective that institutional racism is a major problem continuing to thwart the chances of American Indian people today, and that this is at least as important for students to understand as is American Indian culture.

Cultural Contributions

Students can and should learn more about American Indian culture. But they should learn what American Indians today are saying about themselves and about their lives through such media as literature and art. Contemporary art and literary forms can certainly be linked with historic art forms, but contemporary culture should focus on itself.

▶ LESSON PLAN

Wheelchair Basketball

BEFORE

Subject Area: Physical Education
Grade Level: 5–8
Time: Thirty minutes

Objectives

1. Students will learn how basketball can be modified to accommodate wheelchair athletes.
2. Students will become aware that there is a local wheelchair basketball league.

Suggested Procedures

1. In the context of teaching a unit on basketball, ask students if they have ever watched wheelchair basketball. Explain how the game is modified for

wheelchairs. Have available some wheelchairs and demonstrate or walk students through some of the moves and plays used in wheelchair basketball.

2. Tell students about any local wheelchair basketball leagues that exist. Provide students with a schedule in case they wish to attend any games.

Evaluation

Include two or three questions on wheelchair basketball on a quiz at the end of the basketball unit.

Wheelchair Sports

AFTER

Subject Areas: Interdisciplinary (Physical Education, Social Studies, Reading)

Grade Level: 5–8

Time: One week

Objectives

1. Students will appreciate the struggle that people with physical disabilities have had in developing programs and options in athletics.

2. Students will name several athletes with physical disabilities and appreciate their strength, determination, and skill.

3. Students will attend or participate in local wheelchair athletics.

4. Students will actively support the work of people with disabilities today directed toward taking control of their own lives.

Suggested Procedures

1. Have students read the trade book *Wheel Wizards*, by Matt Christopher and Robert Hirschfeld (2000), a story about an athletic adolescent boy who is injured in a car accident and will never walk again and who then discovers wheelchair basketball and is once more a dedicated and enthusiastic athlete. Have students discuss what they know about future life options for such a person and how they could deal with life if such an accident happened to them. Two other stories for students in grades 5 through 8 are Marty Kaminsky's *Uncommon Champions: Fifteen Athletes Who Battled Back* and Eric Walter's *Rebound*.

2. Have students study the history and development of wheelchair sports by reading *Wheelchair Basketball*, by Brad Hedrick (1994); *Wheelchair Basketball*, by Stan Labanowich (1998); or *Wheelchair Champions*, by May Savitz (1978); or by viewing the videotape *The Wheelchair Basketball Video*. This study also can be done through lectures and supplemented by guest speakers who have helped develop wheelchair sports locally. Wheelchair sports began in the United States during the 1940s, as soldiers with permanent disabilities returned from the war. Since then, athletes with disabilities have developed organized sports in many different areas of athletics and have made great achievements. Spend time providing information on the developments in different sports and on the achievements of athletes—there is a rich history to be told.

3. Attend a local athletic competition for people with physical disabilities. If possible, arrange for one of the athletes or coaches to visit the class first and explain to students what they will be seeing, including how the sport has been modified, how people train for it, and how local competitions are organized.

4. In physical education, teach students the rudiments of a sport such as wheelchair basketball or wheelchair floor hockey. Allow students to practice until they begin to gain some degree of competence; their biggest first challenge will be learning to drive a wheelchair. The students may not develop much skill, but the experience will help them appreciate the skill that a wheelchair athlete must develop.

5. Invite a speaker from a local organization for people with physical disabilities to describe current problems and issues that these people are addressing in athletics and other areas of life.

6. Start a bulletin board on which students may place newspaper and magazine articles about the current issues and needs that people with physical disabilities face. As articles are added, have students discuss how they as citizens, whether or not they have physical disabilities, can actively support work by people with disabilities to control their own lives and to open up options for productive living. (An excellent resource is The Ragged Edge, Box 145, Louisville, KY 40201.)

Evaluation

1. Through a quiz, assess students' knowledge of the history of wheelchair sports and of athletes with disabilities.

2. Through their reactions to attending a wheelchair athletic competition and to practicing a wheelchair sport, assess students' appreciation of wheelchair sports.

3. Through the articles they choose and their discussion of them, assess students' support of the current struggles of people with physical disabilities.

Resources

Christopher, M., & Hirschfeld, R. (2000). *Wheel wizards*. Boston: Little, Brown.
Hedrick, B. (1994). *Wheelchair basketball* (2nd ed.). Washington, DC: Paralyzed Veterans of America.
Kaminsky, M. (2003). *Uncommon champions: Fifteen athletes who battled back*. Honesdale, PA: Boyds Mills.
Labanowich, S. (1998). *Wheelchair basketball*. Mankato, MN: Capstone Press.
Savitz, M. (1978). *Wheelchair champions*. New York: Thomas Y. Crowell.
Walter, E. (2000) *Rebound*. Toronto: Stoddart Kids.
Hedrick, B., Byrnes, D. & Shaver, L. (producers). *The wheelchair basketball video*. (1989). Washington, DC: Paralyzed Veterans of America, Sports and Recreation Department.

Wheelchair Sports

WHY THE CHANGES?

History and Culture

The "Before" plan incorporates as much or more attention to wheelchair sports than one would normally find in lessons for students who are not physically impaired, simply by acknowledging that wheelchair basketball exists. The "After" plan draws on materials written for students in different subject areas to develop an interdisciplinary unit on wheelchair sports. The books can be read by students in the fifth- to eighth-grade range. The teacher can also use them as resources in the event that the school cannot acquire multiple copies. The "After" plan teaches students about an area most people know very little about and sensitizes them to the needs and abilities of people with physical disabilities. It also alerts students to the fact that all of us could one day have a physical disability and that concern for the quality of life of people with disabilities can be selfishly motivated as well as humanitarian.

Studying the history of wheelchair sports can reinforce students' understanding of political and social history. For example, wheelchair sports did not start by accident in the 1940s; rather, it was directly related to the war experience, as well as to the medical and technological developments of the time.

Students tend to find this area of study quite interesting, partly because it is new to them and partly because they usually know individuals who have disabilities. The topic can, in many cases, be motivating to students.

▶ **LESSON PLAN**

Pioneers

BEFORE

Subject Area: Social Studies

Grade Level: 6–8

Time: Five days

Objectives

1. Students will describe the problems that the pioneers faced as they moved westward.
2. Students will describe why the early settlers moved westward.
3. Students will identify the supplies the pioneers took west and explain why they needed them.
4. Students will name the time period when the westward movement took place.
5. Students will identify the routes that most wagon trains took west.

Suggested Procedures

1. Have students read about the westward movement in their textbook.
2. Ask the school librarian to provide students with a list of books on the westward movement. Encourage each student to read a book and to do a short oral report in class.
3. Provide students with a "supply record" guide sheet that they can complete as they read. An example is shown in Table 4.2.

Evaluation

1. Quiz the major points of the lesson.
2. Assess students' successful completion of the wagon train checklist.

Table 4.2   Wagon Train Supply Record: What Supplies Did Pioneers Carry on Wagon Trains?

Supplies	Amount	Date Opened	Date Used
Coffee	Ten 2-lb. bags	May 16, 1839, bag 1	May 31, 1839, bag 1

Women and the Westward Movement

Subject Area: Social Studies

Grade Level: 6–8

Time: Five to eight days

Objectives

1. Students will describe the important role that women of different races played in the movement west.

2. Students will describe and analyze why many European American and African American women wanted to move west and why many Native American women and Mexican women tried to resist their movement.

3. Students will describe and evaluate differences in the life changes and opportunities for pioneer men and women.

4. Students will identify evidence of gender inequity during the time of the westward movement and compare it with evidence of sexism in society today.

5. Students will identify, analyze, and discuss differences in the culture and roles of pioneer women and Plains Indian women.

Suggested Procedures

1. As a preliminary, discuss the life conditions of, and society's expectations for, African American and European American women in U.S. society during the time of the wagon trains.

2. Have students read and examine the chapter on the westward movement in their social studies textbook. They should ascertain how the textbook treats women. For example, how much is the pioneer women's role in the westward movement discussed? Are African American women included in the discussion? Are Native American women or Mexican women discussed and described as resistors to the movement?

3. If students discover that women—African Americans, Native Americans, Mexicans, and European Americans—are not sufficiently addressed in the chapter, have them write a letter to the publisher to ask why this is so.

4. Organize students into gender-mixed groups. Each group is to research a topic related to women and the westward movement (e.g., the reasons women moved west; the life and duties on the wagon train for men and women; family roles once the pioneers reached their destinations).

5. Ask the school librarian to provide students with a list of trade books about women and the westward movement. Suggested books include *Rodzina*, by Karen Cushman; *Great Women of the Old West*, by Judy Dewey; *Outrageous*

Women of Colonial America, by Mary Furbee; *Into a New Country: Eight Remarkable Women of the West: The Story of a Pioneer Girl*, by Marissa Moss; *The Stories of Juana Briones, Alta California Pioneer*, by Glenda Richter; and *Riding Freedom*, by Pam Munoz Ryan. Have the librarian point out which books include information about Native American, Mexican, and African American women. Tell each member of each group to read one book and to take notes on the treatment of women of all races in the book. The data students collect allow them to analyze and discuss with group members the treatment of women during the westward movement.

6. During class discussion, ask students to compare gender prejudices during the days of the wagon train with gender prejudices that exist today. Remind students that gender prejudice is directed toward both sexes (e.g., in the past, women were considered weak and timid, and men were considered unable to raise children and run a household). Encourage some students to prepare the information for the school newspaper.

7. Ask students to examine the customs, roles, and regulations of the school to determine if gender biases are present. Have some students develop the findings into an article for the school newspaper.

8. Have students view Western films to determine how they portray women: African American, European American, Mexican, and Native American.

Evaluation

1. Use students' written reports as a source of evaluation.

2. Observe students' attitudes and behavior toward sex bias.

3. Observe students' understanding and attitudes about the gender biases toward White European American women and women of color.

4. Give an essay examination of the main points in the activity.

Resources

Dewey, J. (2001). *Great women of the Old West*. Minneapolis, MN: Compass Point Books.
Furbee, M. (2001). *Outrageous women of colonial America*. New York: John Wiley.
Moss, M. (2001). *The Story of a Pioneer Girl*. New York: Harcourt Children's Books.
Richter, G. (2002). *The stories of Juana Briones, alta California pioneer*. Bonita, CA: Bookhandler.
Cushman, K. (2003). *Rodzina*. New York: Clarion Books.
Ryan, P.M. (1998). *Riding Freedom*. New York: Scholastic Press.

Women and the Westward Movement

WHY THE CHANGES?

Perspective on History

Many social studies textbooks do not give equal treatment to the roles of men and women in U.S. history. The "Before" lesson plan accepts the lesser treatment that women usually receive. In contrast, the "After" lesson plan provides an opportunity to examine how women worked side by side with men during the movement west and points out the hidden biases that often appear in instructional materials. The "After" plan explicitly asks students to learn about African American, Mexican, and Native American women in addition to European American women (often when lessons focus on women, they focus on European American women). In attending to Native American and Mexican women, students are asked to consider the perspective not only of the pioneers moving west but also that of the people whose land was being invaded by the pioneers. The "After" plan allows students to work in mixed-sex groups that encourage them to eliminate sex-role stereotyping as they examine the ideas, attitudes, and behaviors in the instructional materials.

Current Social Agenda

The "Before" plan deals only with historic events. In contrast, the "After" plan asks students to compare the roles of women in the 1850s with the roles of women today, encouraging them to think about contemporary issues of gender inequity. The lesson also promotes students' own analysis and evaluation of curriculum materials, whereas the "Before" plan asks students merely to describe events and to accept what they have read.

▶ LESSON PLAN

Poster Design and Disability Awareness

Subject Area: Art
Grade Level: 8–12
Time: One week

Objectives

1. Students will identify elements of poster design that catch an audience's attention.
2. Students will create works of art that are abstract.
3. Students will use visual art to communicate a message.
4. Students will identify stereotypes of people with disabilities in works of art.

Suggested Procedures

1. Have students examine several posters and identify those that best catch their attention. Discuss with them what elements of the posters drew their attention. Make a list of those elements on the board. Look at the posters that did not catch their attention, and discuss how they could be redesigned to make use of the attention-getting elements students identified.

2. Remind students that increasingly, though slowly, people with disabilities are being included in advertisements. Have them identify ads and other media where people with disabilities are featured.

3. Discuss with students the use of visual art to communicate a public message. Help students to see that art is not only for the enjoyment of the person who makes it but also to communicate to an audience. For example, art could communicate that it is wrong to stereotype people with disabilities.

4. Have students brainstorm messages they would like to communicate to an audience. Then divide them into groups of four. Each group should select a message and an audience with which they wish to communicate.

5. Demonstrate how to simplify figures in order to create symbols to help express a theme.

6. Have each group plan the design for their poster using pencil. After you have checked their work, they should go over all main lines with a wide, black, permanent marker.

7. Next, have students plan the colors. Using tempera paint, have them paint in all shapes. They can fill in with additional paint or lines when the paint has dried.

8. Use desktop publishing software to design words for the poster. Trace the layout of the words onto the poster, then either paint or fill in with black markers.

9. Place completed posters in a public spot where they will be seen by the intended audiences. If possible, gather feedback from the audience in order to evaluate how well the posters actually communicated their message.

Evaluation

1. Evaluate each poster on its design and its use of attention-getting elements.

2. Evaluate each poster on its effective use of abstractions to communicate a message.

Poster Design and the Voice of People with Disabilities

Subject Area: Art

Grade Level: 8–12

Time: One Week

Objectives

1. Students will identify stereotypes of people with disabilities in works of art.

2. Students will discover that people with disabilities wish to have a voice about how they are represented in all media, including advertisements.

3. Students will create works of art that are abstract.

4. Students will work with members of the disability community to use visual art to communicate a message that is meaningful to that community.

Suggested Procedures

1. If possible, take students to a museum and look for representations of disability. If this is not possible, use the website for Education for Disability and Gender Equity (EDGE) (www.disabledwomen.net/edge/curriculum/indexnetscape .htm), following the "Culture" link. There, you will find representations of disability in various forms of art.

2. Discuss portrayals of people with disabilities. Stereotypes of various kinds are common, such as people portrayed as being mad or lovable or simple. One can also find portrayals of more complex people. An excellent Internet resource for showing art produced by people with disabilities is the website of the National Arts and Disability Center (NADC) (http://nadc.ucla.edu).

3. Have students examine several posters and identify those that best catch their attention. Discuss with them what elements of the posters drew their attention. Make a list on the board of those elements. Look at the posters that did not catch their attention, and discuss how they could be redesigned to make use of the attention-getting elements students identified.

4. Discuss with students the use of visual art to communicate a public message. Help students to see that art is not only for the enjoyment of the person who makes it but also to communicate to an audience. Tell students that they will be working with members of the local disability community to educate the public about issues of concern to people with disabilities. Discuss why it is important that the people with the disability identify their own needs, instead of the nondisabled doing so.

5. Invite as a guest speaker a disability rights activist from the community to discuss problems and issues people with disabilities experience. Also ask that person to discuss barriers in the school and local community (or any other issue that is relevant to the local disability community). Ask the guest to discuss how stereotypes keep us from seeing barriers as barriers and locate the problem in the person rather than in the environment. Discuss images that would help the public see barriers that can be removed or addressed proactively.

6. Divide students into groups of four. Each group should select a message based on what the guest speaker said.

7. Demonstrate how to simplify figures in order to create symbols to help express a theme.

8. Have each group plan the design for their poster using pencil. Each student should then get feedback from a member of the local disability community before completing his or her group's poster. Help students identify with whom to work on this.

9. After their work has been checked, have students go over all main lines with a wide, black, permanent marker.

10. Next have students plan the colors. Using tempera paint, have them paint in all shapes. They can fill in with additional paint or lines when the paint has dried.

11. Use desktop publishing software to design words for the poster. Trace the layout of the words onto the poster, then either paint or fill in with black markers.

12. People who are blind cannot see posters, but posters can be made accessible through other means. Blindfold students before unveiling the posters, and discuss what would help them "see" the images or messages their peers are attempting to communicate: For example, audio and tactile messages are accessible to blind people. Have students add audio or tactile features. If, for example, the posters were to be posted on the Web, one would include "alt tags" for each graphic, describing what is represented in the graphic. Students could come up with a brief narrative for each symbol or graphic. In other words, how would their poster about people with disabilities "sound" to a blind person? Would the poster designers leave it up to any "reader" to interpret their poster for a blind person? Or would the poster designers proactively offer narrative for each

symbol and allow the blind person to interpret it? Narrative could describe that "in the upper-left corner there is a picture or drawing of an adult who appears to be of African heritage, who is smiling toward a smaller person and using sign language."

13. Place completed posters in a public spot where they will be seen by the intended audiences. If possible, gather feedback from the audience in order to evaluate how well the posters actually communicated their message.

Evaluation

1. Evaluate each poster on its design and on its use of attention-getting elements.

2. Evaluate each poster on its effective use of abstractions to communicate a message.

3. Evaluate each poster on the significance of its message to the disability community and on its portrayal of disability in a constructive and nonstereotypic manner.

Poster Design and the Voice of People with Disabilities

WHY THE CHANGES?

Culture

In the "Before" lesson, students learn how to create a visual image, but they don't necessarily explore in any depth community issues or social messages in public art. Since disability studies are usually absent from or on the margins of school curricula, the teacher in the "After" lesson decided to connect learning art technique and design with social learning. The teacher began by having students learn to identify stereotypes of disability in works of art. Some works of art are very well known, such as The Hunchback of Notre Dame. To teach nonstereotypic representations, the teacher draws on art created by people with disabilities (some of which deals with disability and some of which does not). After beginning with stereotypes, the teacher moves the discussion and activities to recognizing that people with disabilities have a voice and are as capable as any others of articulating their ideas and what is best for them.

In the "Before" plan, the teacher is the one who approves students' posters before they complete them. In the "After" plan, students ask someone from the disability community to review their work. (The teacher will most likely review it as well!) This is so that students communicate directly with that community about their representation of disability, rather than imagine how their work might be viewed.

Issues of Concern

In the "Before" plan, students come up with their own ideas about what they would want to communicate through art. This is worthwhile. However, the teacher in the "After" plan wants students also to learn to work with a community to use art for a purpose, so the teacher asks someone from the local disability community to work with the class. A common issue for disability communities is identifying and working to eliminate barriers; this may or may not be a key concern in specific communities. It should be up to the local disability community to decide what is relevant. However, the point of poster making in the "After" plan is to raise public awareness about real issues rather than simply to learn techniques of poster making.

In addition, the teacher in the "After" plan considers how to make the work accessible to people with various forms of disabilities. For information about how to make webpages accessible, go to the Web Accessibility Initiative Guidelines at www.w3 .org/WAI/GL/.

Note: Our thanks to Margaret Keith, California State University–Monterey Bay, for her helpful suggestions on how to make this project more accessible to people who are blind.

▶ LESSON PLAN

Back Home During World War II

Subject Area: Social Studies

Grade Level: 7–12

Time: Two class periods

Objectives

1. Students will describe the mobilization efforts of the U.S. government and the experiences of citizens on the home front during World War II.

2. Students will describe the national security efforts of the U.S. government and of its citizens on the home front during World War II.

Suggested Procedures

1. Ask students to read in their text about victory gardens, rationing, and the way war bond sales and taxation helped finance World War II.

2. Have students ask their grandparents or elders in their community about salvage collections of rubber, metal, and grease for the war effort.

3. Ask students to read in their text about the relocation of Japanese Americans. Have them discuss why the relocation occurred and whether the government had a right to relocate Japanese Americans.

Evaluation

On the next quiz, ask students to describe the mobilization and national security efforts on the home front during World War II.

Japanese Americans—U.S. Citizens

Subject Area: Social Studies

Grade Level: 7–12

Time: Two weeks

Objectives

1. Students will identify many Japanese people as long-time American citizens born in this country.

2. Students will appreciate the loyalty and contributions of Japanese Americans to their homeland, the United States.

3. Students will describe the immigration story of the Japanese to the United States.

4. Students will learn how prejudice, racism, and ethnocentrism can lead people to act unfairly and unjustly toward other people.

Suggested Procedures

1. Ask students to describe what they know about Japanese American history and contemporary life. Pay attention to the extent to which students associate Japanese Americans with the Japanese from Japan (e.g., do they associate televisions and automobiles made in Japan with Japanese Americans?).

2. Divide students into groups of four or five, and ask each group to prepare a report on the Japanese immigration to the United States. Provide some groups with information written by Japanese American authors and other groups in school textbooks from different publishing companies. Have students compare the quality of information as each group presents its report to the class.

3. Ask students to compare why the Japanese and the British settled in this country. Have them examine why the Japanese Exclusion Act of 1924 was passed and enforced.

4. Ask students to read about Hikozo Hamada (who later changed his name to Joseph Heco), the first Japanese person to become a U.S. citizen.

5. In groups, have students prepare a report on Japanese American loyalty to this country during their forced confinement in internment camps during World War II. If possible, invite Japanese American guests to speak on these topics. Also, have students examine the role of the Nisei soldiers during World War II.

6. Discuss with the class how racism and ethnocentrism can lead to unjust treatment of a group of people. Ask students to describe other examples of mistreatment caused by racism, prejudice, and ethnocentrism.

7. Invite to class a Japanese American speaker to discuss the problems and issues facing Japanese Americans today. Ask students to compare and contrast these problems and issues with those that occurred during World War II. Have them determine whether racism still exists and, if so, why.

8. Discuss the major similarities and differences between contemporary Japanese and Japanese Americans. Make sure students appreciate that the two groups are not the same.

Evaluation

1. Through small-group reports, assess students' appreciation of Japanese Americans' loyalty and contributions.

2. Through oral discussion and a quiz, assess students' knowledge of the Japanese immigration story and of prejudice, racism, and ethnocentrism.

Japanese Americans—U.S. Citizens

History

The "Before" plan covers a number of events and activities related to World War II but in a somewhat more limited manner than the "After" plan. Also, the "Before" plan is not directly connected to present-day events and experiences. In contrast, the "After" lesson plan focuses on and examines the past and present treatment of Japanese Americans. It also helps students to identify and describe how racism, prejudice, and ethnocentrism can lead to the unjust treatment of groups of people. The "After" plan makes clear the distinction between Japanese Americans and the Japanese: that is, the former are U.S. citizens.

Cultural Contributions

The "After" plan discusses the loyalty of and the contributions by Japanese Americans to the United States. Furthermore, by using different sources of information, the lesson provides students with an opportunity to discover how Japanese Americans overcame racism and prejudice in a nonviolent manner, demonstrated patriotism during World War II, and continue to fight racial prejudices today.

Current Social Agenda

The guest speaker and discussion of current issues of racism help focus students' attention on problems that still exist today, problems directly connected with the history being studied.

▶ UNIT PLAN: GAY, LESBIAN, AND BISEXUAL ISSUES[4]

Schools and teachers can do a great deal to develop a school culture that says that any type of discrimination and invisibility of any student are not acceptable. It is safe to say that most of us believe that all students have a right to an education that meets their needs and is reflective of themselves and their families. This means that teachers cannot ignore issues of importance to gays, lesbians, and bisexuals if we advocate being inclusive of difference in our classrooms. When we exclude these issues in our schools and classrooms, we are saying a great deal about what is legitimate and what is not.

Yet, when discussing this issue with heterosexual teachers, we are often met with fear and apprehension. However, it is vital that heterosexually identified teachers be among the first to eradicate homophobia (i.e., the irrational fear of gays, lesbians, and bisexuals and those perceived to be gay, lesbian, or bisexual) and heterosexism (i.e., the individual and institutional belief that all people are heterosexual). If they address these issues, it will do much to erase the notion that the only people who care to talk about heterosexism and homophobia are gays, lesbians, and bisexuals.

[4]*Source:* Lisa W. Loutzenheiser, University of Wisconsin–Madison.

Heterosexual educators must also speak out because their very heterosexuality gives them a measure of privacy and protection that gay, lesbian, and bisexual teachers do not have.

Educators can begin with small steps. First and foremost, as with an area of cultural difference, teachers must educate themselves about diverse gay, lesbian, and bisexual communities and explore their own attitudes and feelings before attempting to teach. There are many excellent resources available, among them Ann Heron (editor), *Two Teenagers in Twenty: Writings by Gay and Lesbian Youth* (Boston: Alyson Publications, 1994); Lea Due, *Joining the Tribe* (New York: Anchor Books, 1995); Kurt Chandler, *Passages of Pride* (New York: Times Books, 1995); and Dan Woog, *School's Out* (Boston: Alyson Publications, 1995). Teachers can do things as simple as acknowledging that homophobic comments, just as racist or sexist comments, are not acceptable in the classroom and defining homophobia if students do not understand it. Each and every time a student calls another student a name, or remarks that something is "gay" (meaning bad), address the issue, reminding students that all discriminatory remarks are unacceptable. This will begin to ingrain in students the concept that this is an issue of equality and human rights.

Another small step that can be made by instructors is not assuming their own students' heterosexuality. One exercise to try is to place yourself in your gay, lesbian, or bisexual student's chair and imagine a typical class in your room. How might he or she feel invisible, or less-than? Then rewrite the lesson or the lecture with this student in mind. By making gays, lesbians, and bisexuals an everyday part of the classroom curriculum and pedagogy, the discomfort and apprehension about discussing homosexuality begin to fade into the rest of classroom culture. For example, when assigning research topics, include issues of interest and importance to gay, lesbian, and bisexual youth. In biology class, for example, challenge students to explore the myths surrounding the transmission of AIDS or to explore the genetic theories about homosexuality. Mixing these examples in with all the other topics demonstrates to students that gay, lesbian, and bisexual issues are not special, only to be brought up during particular (and often uncomfortable) classes, but that they are everyday issues and can be discussed alongside any other.

Teachers can also alter the curriculum so that the contributions of gays, lesbians, and bisexuals can be acknowledged. For example, when discussing James Baldwin's contribution to literature, also consider that he was gay and the way his sexual orientation might have influenced his writings. The same can be done with the art of Michelangelo, the music of Tchaikovsky, and the scientific method of Francis Bacon. In these ways gay, lesbian, and bisexual students begin to see and hear themselves in the classroom not as odd or bad but as part of the discussion.

The lessons that follow can be used as a mini-unit for introducing students to gay, lesbian, and bisexual issues, or they can be used individually. They offer preliminary examples of how to approach discussing these issues by beginning with the abstract historical experiences of gays, lesbians, and bisexuals; moving the discussion to the more immediate by viewing a video about gay youth; and last, making it more personal by asking students to explore their own views, reactions, and opinions.

► LESSON PLAN

The Legacies of the African American Civil Rights Movement

Subject Area: U.S. History

Grade Level: 9–12

Time: Three to four class periods, as part of a larger unit on civil rights

Objectives

1. Students will identify how the women's, American Indian, Chicano/Latino, and disability rights movements were influenced by the push for civil rights among African Americans in the South.

2. Students will compare and contrast the social, political, and economic issues and development of the women's, American Indian, Chicano/Latino, and disability rights movements.

3. Students will appreciate the importance of the early African American Civil Rights movement for other subordinated groups such as women, people of color, and people with disabilities.

4. Students will gain experience in analyzing primary documents.

Suggested Procedures

1. Read the appropriate sections of the textbook for information about how the social, political, and economic issues of the times affected these civil rights movements.

2. Over the course of several days, students will read, analyze, and discuss a number of first-person accounts and other primary documents on each particular movement. This work is to be accomplished in small groups and full-class discussions.

3. Small groups will be formed and asked to develop a short classroom presentation on a different aspect of one of the movements and compare it with the early African American Civil Rights movement.

4. Keep a daily response journal.

Evaluation

1. Assess students' ability to compare and contrast the women's, American Indian, Chicano/Latino, and disability rights movements with each other and with the earlier civil rights movements through classroom and small-group discussion.

2. Through discussion, group presentation, and written exam or essay, evaluate the students' understanding of the legacies of the African American Civil Rights movement.

3. Assess students' ability to analyze primary documents through small-group discussion and daily response journals.

The Legacies of the African American Civil Rights Movement
(Women/LGBT/American Indian/Chicano/a)

AFTER

Subject Area: Social Studies

Grade Level: 7–12

Time: Four to five class periods as part of a larger civil rights unit; one to one-and-a-half class periods if this lesson is presented by itself, without unit

Objectives

1. Students will appreciate the influence of the African American Civil Rights movement on other human rights struggles, including gay liberation, women's, Chicano/Latino, Native American, and disability rights.

2. Students will explain why Stonewall was seen as the beginning of the modern gay, lesbian, and bisexual rights movement and why it should be included in studying the struggles of the sixties.

3. Students will appreciate the impact of the early African American Civil Rights movement on other subordinated groups such as women, people of color, people with disabilities, and gays, lesbians, and bisexuals.

4. Students will gain experience in analyzing primary documents.

Suggested Procedures

1. Ask students to brainstorm about the conditions for gays, lesbians, and bisexuals in the late 1950s and early 1960s. Point out that there were gays, lesbians, and bisexuals who were of color or had disabilities, if students don't raise this issue.

   Ask students what kind of public establishments they like to hang out in and with whom. Point out that they spend time with people who are like them in some way. Tell students of the laws that made it illegal to run bars or restaurants that catered to homosexuals. Draw comparisons with Jim Crow laws.

   Ask students to look at the clothes they are wearing and count how many articles they have on that could be labeled as unisex (like boxers and jeans). How many (like a bra) are considered for one sex only? Inform the students that gay men and lesbians could be and were arrested if they did not have at least three articles of clothing on that the police department deemed "male" or "female" as appropriate for their sex. Ask the students to compare this with the harassment of other subordinated groups they have studied.

2. Remind students of the changing urban culture in the late 1960s. Review the riots of 1968, the change in the war movements, and so on. Read Chapter 13 of *Becoming Visible* by—Kevin Jennings (or something similar on the Stonewall riots) and the *New York Daily News* article of July 6, 1969 (see Resources).

3. As a class, discuss the content of the articles and compare and contrast the views of the authors. Ask the students, What do you learn from one and not the other? Is either objective? What do you think happened at Stonewall? Why would this have been a catalyst for the gay liberation movement? It is important to note that

some of those arrested were people of color and to discuss how gays and lesbians come from diverse racial, class, and ethnic backgrounds.

4. Ask the students to write journal entries on how and why the reasons for the gay rights movement were similar to and different from those of other movements. How have rights of gays, lesbians, and bisexuals come as far as or farther than other groups? Why?

5. On the following day, ask for a volunteer or two to read her or his entry out loud, and ask the class for responses.

Evaluation

1. Through classroom and small-group discussion, assess students' ability to compare and contrast the women's, American Indian, Chicano/Latino, and disability rights movements and the gay liberation movement with each other and the earlier civil rights movements.

2. Through discussion, group presentation, and written exam or essay, evaluate the students' understanding of the legacies of the African American Civil Rights movement.

3. Assess students' ability to analyze primary documents through small-group discussion and daily response journals.

Resources

Jennings, K. (Ed.). (1994). *Becoming visible: A reader in gay and lesbian history for high school and college students*. Boston: Alyson.

Lisker, J. (1969, July 6). Homo nest raided, queen bees are stinging mad. *New York Daily News*.

The Legacies of the African American Civil Rights Movement (Women/LGBT/American Indian/Chicano)

Content

While the structure and content of the "Before" plan is retained, the "After" plan includes the gay rights movement, presenting a positive model of gay liberation in the context of other civil rights movements. Modeling in this manner gives gay, lesbian, and bisexual students a sense of inclusion. It also encourages all students to realize how gays, lesbians, and bisexuals have faced oppression and how they have responded.

Perspective

Using primary documents and encouraging discussion that includes the perspectives of gays, lesbians, and bisexuals, along with those of people with disabilities and people of color, develop a broad spectrum of opinions and voices, reflecting the diversity of our schools and society.

Comparing and contrasting the civil rights movements, including the gay liberation movement, and encouraging debate about the gay movement's place there, push students to develop the ability to see issues from multiple points of view and multiple perspectives which movement had what impact on the others.

▶ LESSON PLAN

Gays, Lesbians, Bisexuals, and Transgenders

Subject Areas: Social Studies, Health, Human Sexuality
Grade Level: 9–12
Time: One-half class period

Objectives

1. Students will understand that homosexuality exists.
2. Students will explore the debates surrounding the causes of homosexuality.

Suggested Procedures

1. Read the relevant section in a textbook (for instance, a health book).
2. As part of discussing an introduction to sexuality, explain that homosexuality is part of the spectrum.
3. Explain the nature-versus-nurture debate as it relates to the cause of homosexuality. Ask the students to state their opinions.

Evaluation

Students will correctly answer multiple-choice test questions.

Lesson 1—Gay, Lesbian, Bisexual, and Transgender Youth[5]

Subject Areas: Social Studies, Health, Human Sexuality
Grade Level: 7–12
Time: Two class periods

Objectives

1. Students will identify and analyze stereotypes of gays, lesbians, bisexuals, and transgenders.
2. Students will discuss the experiences of gay and lesbian youth.
3. Students will consider viewpoints about gays, transgenders, lesbians, and bisexuals that may differ from their own.
4. Students will recognize the ways stereotypes can lay the foundation for intolerance.
5. Students will gain the opportunity to openly discuss issues surrounding gays, lesbians, transgenders, and bisexuals.
6. Students will draw comparisons between the experiences of gay and lesbian youth seen in the video *Gay Youth* and those of gay, lesbian, transgender, and bisexual students at school.

[5]These two lesson plans can be done in either order, or pieces of each can be used in a different order depending on the instructor's desires and comfort level. For example, instructors could do parts 1 through 4 of Lesson 2, then do Lesson 1, and then return to the last activities of Lesson 2.

Suggested Procedures

1. It is very important that ground rules about insults, interrupting, and the ability to speak are set up with students before the lesson begins. It is vital that students be reminded that comments can be honest without being disrespectful toward any group or individual.

2. Show the video *Gay Youth* (forty minutes).

3. Break the students up into preplanned groups of four to five. (When forming groups, keep in mind the nature of the discussion, and attempt to balance the amount of trust needed to have such a discussion with the need not to form groups around friendship groups.)

4. Give each group a discussion question, asking each to appoint a spokesperson and a scribe. Tell them they have fifteen minutes to discuss the question and will be asked to report to the class.

Examples of questions:

  a. Many of the teens in the video talk about their parents. Bobby Griffith's mother discusses his suicide, and Gina is seen with her parents. Why might parental reactions be important? Is it fair that Gina's parents might have different rules for her sister than for her?

  b. Based on what you heard in the video, why might it be difficult to be a gay, lesbian, transgender, or bisexual teen today? What kinds of issues do they face, and how might they be different from their heterosexual peers? Why do you believe teens are, as Gina says, insensitive to other teens?

  c. Why would Bobby Griffith's mother think it is important to speak out now? Many of the young people in the video spoke of self-destructive behavior: What drives them to the point of alcohol or drug abuse, depression, or self-mutilation? How might schools respond to help these students?

  d. One of the parents in the video stated that "being different is harder." Is this still true? What kind of a reception would a student like Chris be expected to get at this school? Why would Gina be able or not able to do her monologue or go to the prom at this school? Are these responses proper for the school? Should they be changed?

  e. What purposes do you think Pam Walton (the director) had in making this video? That is, why do you think she made it? Does the video fulfill its purposes? What makes this a "good" or "bad" video, and would you suggest it be used in other classes?

5. Have each group read the question and report its discussion. Invite other class members to respond also.

Evaluation

1. Assess students' ability to apply the abstract images to their own lives and those of their peers through small- and large-group discussion.

2. Through classroom discussion, assess students' understanding of their own perspectives of gay, lesbian, and bisexual youth.

3. Through their willingness to listen and engage in discussion, assess students' ability to reflect on others' points of view.

Resources

Walton, P. (1991). *Gay Youth*. Pam Walton Productions, Box 391025, Mtn. View. CA 94039.
Levithan, D. (2003). *Boy meets boy*. New York: Alfred A. Knopf.
Peters, J. (2003). *Keeping you a secret*. Boston: Little, Brown.
Peters, J. (2004). *Luna*. Boston: Little, Brown.
Sanchez, A. (2004). *So hard to say*. New York: Simon & Schuster.
Walton, P. (1991). Two teenagers in twenty: Writings by gay and lesbian youth (three-tape series). Wolfe Video, PO Box 64, New Almaden, CA 95042; (408) 268–6782; or BANGLE (Bay Area Network of Gay and Lesbian Educators), (415) 648–8488. A similar unit can be built around the articles in the book.

Lesson 2—The Experiences of Gays, Lesbians, Transgenders, and Bisexuals

Subject Areas: Social Studies, Health, Human Sexuality

Grade Level: 7–12

Time: Two class periods

Objectives

1. Students will name several gays, lesbians, transgenders, and bisexuals in history and current affairs.

2. Students will identify and analyze stereotypes of gays, lesbians, transgenders, and bisexuals.

3. Students will recognize and discuss their own perspectives about gays, lesbians, transgenders, and bisexuals.

4. Students will consider viewpoints about gays, lesbians, transgenders, and bisexuals that differ from their own.

5. Students will recognize the ways stereotypes can lay the foundation for intolerance.

6. Students will gain the opportunity to openly discuss issues surrounding gays, lesbians, transgenders, and bisexuals.

Suggested Procedures

1. It is very important that ground rules about insults, interrupting, and the ability to speak be set up with students before the lesson begins. It is vital that students be reminded that comments can be honest without being disrespectful toward any group or individual.

2. Prior to students' entry into the class, list on the board ten to fifteen gays, lesbians, and bisexuals (e.g., James Baldwin, Leonardo da Vinci, Janis Joplin, James Dean, J. Edgar Hoover, Angela Davis, Alexander the Great). Ask the students what these people have in common.

3. After someone has guessed that they were all gay or lesbian, make sure, if not addressed, that the issue of bisexuality is included. Remind the students that it is important to be respectful of differences as they discuss a topic that can evoke strong emotions. Ask students to add to the list. Use this as an opportunity to ask how they know that the person is gay, lesbian, or bisexual. Discuss gender-based stereotypes of masculinity and femininity. If students state, "Well, everyone knows that person is gay," again ask how they know or why they think it, but this

time ask why it might be a negative thing to be called gay, lesbian, transgender, or bisexual.

4. Erase the board, and ask the students to brainstorm all of the pejorative names for gays, lesbians, transgenders, and bisexuals. If they have difficulty getting started, write *faggot* and *dyke* on the board. Allow a limited amount of time for this activity. Ask the students how these words might affect gays, lesbians, or bisexuals who hear them. Ask them if they have heard these words around the school and how they might affect students. Make sure to include gay, lesbian, transgender, and bisexual students and heterosexual students with gay, lesbian, transgender, or bisexual family members.

5. Pass out index cards. Tell the students not to sign the cards, and let them know they will not read their own cards. Without further discussion, ask the students to write down the answer to the following question: "What would you say and how do you think you would react if your brother/sister or best friend told you that she or he were gay, lesbian, or bisexual?" Collect the cards, mix them up, and hand them back out to the students. Have students read each card in succession, saving discussion until all the cards are read.

6. Solicit student responses to what was written on the cards. During the discussion, encourage students to analyze their own reactions and suppositions about gays, lesbians, and bisexuals.

7. Ask students to complete a ten- to fifteen-minute free-writing period or journal entry, and give them a choice of expanding on what they said on the cards and in classroom discussion or how and why the classroom discussion might affect how they feel about gays, lesbians, and bisexuals.

Evaluation

1. Assess students' skills in analyzing stereotypes and their impact through classroom discussion.

2. Through classroom discussion and the followup journal entries/free-writing period, assess students' understanding of their own perspectives of gays, lesbians, and bisexuals.

3. Assess students' ability to reflect on others' points of view through their willingness to listen and engage in discussion.

Gay, Lesbian, Bisexual, and Transgender Youth

Perspective/Issues of Particular Concern

Issues concerning gays, lesbians, and bisexuals are rarely discussed in the classroom. In reality, even lessons as basic as those detailed in the "Before" plan rarely occur.

The "After" plans allow all youth, regardless of their sexual orientation, to see adults modeling positive discussions about homosexuality. Students are given visual representations of the experiences of a wide variety of gay, lesbian, transgender, and bisexual youth, which along with followup activities allow and encourage students to compare these experiences with their own in and outside of school.

History

By listing gay men, lesbians, transgenders, and bisexuals in history, students are able to realize that homosexuality is not a modern phenomenon, as well as gain a better understanding of the many contributions that gays, lesbians, transgenders, and bisexuals have made to a wide variety of areas.

Current Social Agenda

Since there are few forums to discuss issues surrounding gays, lesbians, transgenders, and bisexuals in school, students do not have the chance to deal with their questions and curiosities, as well as their own intolerance. Within these plans, gay, lesbian, transgender, and bisexual students, and students with gay, lesbian, transgender, or bisexual family members, have an opportunity to gain positive images of themselves in the school setting. Heterosexual students are able to gain an awareness and understanding of the discrimination faced by gays, lesbians, and bisexuals.

▶ LESSON PLAN

Lesson 1 (early in the school year)—Science and Animal Instincts

Subject Area: Biology
Grade Level: 9–12
Time: One of two separate days

Objectives

1. Students will describe the method(s) used by scientists to solve problems.
2. Students will apply a methed used by scientists to a hypothetical problem.

Suggested Procedures

1. Ask students to imagine that they want to discover why trees lose their leaves in the fall. Ask them to suggest ways to investigate this problem.
2. Have students read pages in a textbook on methods used by scientists to solve problems.
3. When they have completed the reading, return to the problem of why trees lose their leaves. Help the class to formulate a hypothesis, identify variables, and design a procedure for testing the hypothesis and formulating a conclusion.

Evaluation

On the next quiz, present a problem, and have students state a hypothesis and suggest a procedure for testing it.

Lesson 2 (later in the school year)—Science and Animal Instincts

Subject Area: Biology
Grade Level: 9–12
Time: One of two separate days

Objective

Students will distinguish between innate and learned behavior and provide examples of each.

Suggested Procedures

1. Have students read pages in a textbook on innate and learned behavior. Review the main ideas and vocabulary terms.

2. Show a film on instinctual behavior.

3. Ask students if humans have any instincts. Encourage students to base their beliefs on their observations of human behavior and to determine carefully if the examples they provide could have resulted from learning.

Evaluation

Assess students' understanding of innate and learned behavior through class discussion and a quiz.

Using Science to Investigate Maternal Instinct

Subject Area: Biology
Grade Level: 9–12
Time: Five to eight class periods

Objectives

1. Students will distinguish between innate and learned behavior.

2. Students will describe methods used by scientists to solve problems.

3. Students will use a method used by scientists to investigate a real problem.

4. Students will realize that both sexes are equally capable of learning to parent.

5. Students will critique text materials for relevance to a real-life concern.

Suggested Procedures

1. Ask students if they believe males and females to be equally capable of caring for babies. Encourage them to voice what they have heard about maternal instinct (the term may not yet be a part of their vocabulary, so watch for the idea).

2. Have students read pages in a textbook on innate and learned behavior. Ask them to describe the extent to which the reading helped illuminate human behavior commonly classified as instinctual (most likely, the text will provide only a brief passage).

3. Ask students how they might design a study to investigate whether human females, more than males, instinctively know how to care for infants. Lead them to design an investigation they can actually carry out. For example, students could interview new parents about their own behavior, knowledge, and prior learning about infant care; the class could visit a hospital maternity ward and interview a nurse who works with new parents about what is known instinctively

and what parents must be taught; or students who have siblings who are parents can interview their siblings. Help the class design any interview questions and arrange interviews. Questions that could be asked of both parents include the following:

    a. Did you know what to do when your baby cried during the first few days? If so, where did this knowledge come from?

    b. Did you know how to hold the baby when he or she was born? If so, how did you know?

    c. Did you know how to change the baby's diapers? How much practice did it take until you became proficient?

In selecting the parents to be interviewed, try to include those of various cultural and social-class backgrounds.

4. Monitor students' data collection. When the studies are completed, divide the class into small groups to compile and analyze their findings. One way to organize this is for one group to compile data for question *a*, another for question *b*, and so on. Have the class examine the data for any cultural patterns.

5. Assign students to gather data from research on the Internet on parenting roles in different species. Make sure you include in the list the bonobo (i.e., a primate in which parenting is shared by both sexes) and the sea horse (in which males bear and raise the young).

6. The class should come to the conclusion that parenting responsibilities are different in different species and that, in the case of the bonobo, which is closely related to humans, parenting is not divided by sex. Human parental behavior is learned. Students may also discover that infant care is learned fairly quickly by necessity, and if one parent practices it more than the other, the practiced parent often assumes much of the responsibility for child care. Although this may appear to be instinctive, it is a result of learning, and some variation in learning may occur among different cultural groups. Discuss with the class why the myth of maternal instinct exists, and who benefits in what ways from its existence. Lead students to realize that the myth tends to maintain that child care is a female rather than a shared parental responsibility.

7. Based on their investigation, have students write an addition to or revision of their textbook discussion of innate and learned behavior. Ask students to select the best description, which should be duplicated and used with future classes.

Evaluation

1. Through class discussion and through their textbook "additions" and "revisions," assess students' understanding of innate versus learned behavior.

2. By monitoring their activities and by observing how they analyze data in small-group situations, assess students' ability to design and conduct an experiment.

3. Through class discussion and their textbook "additions" and "revisions," assess students' understanding of the research on maternal instinct.

Using Science to Investigate Maternal Instinct

Issues of Particular Concern

In the "Before" plan, methods used by scientists to solve problems about animal instinct are studied with little or no relationship to human issues or to issues of particular interest to adolescents. The "After" lesson uses concepts normally studied in biology to examine a topic of particular concern to women's studies: whether one sex is naturally more predisposed than the other to parenting. The topic is likely to generate student interest, in that students are probably thinking about it as they consider their own futures, and they are likely to hold different opinions about it.

The research conducted in the "After" plan is more of a survey study than an experimental one. The teacher needs to decide how much emphasis to give to scientific research over the school year; many teachers will probably find neither plan adequate in this regard. It is quite possible to introduce methods used by science at the beginning of the year, as the "Before" plan does, but to involve students in using it only minimally throughout the year. On the other hand, if students are involved in using it to investigate a number of different issues throughout the year, they can be exposed to a variety of research strategies such as the survey research used here.

The "After" plan encourages students to think critically about what they read, which the single-group studies approach often encourages. The plan asks students to examine the extent to which their biology textbook teaches them about human instinctual behavior. At the conclusion of the lesson, students write a new passage to be used, along with the textbook, by future students. This places students in a role of questioning knowledge produced by others—not rejecting it, but seeing its limitations—and producing knowledge themselves. The teacher of the "After" plan supplements the textbook with research students do about different species on the Internet. There are variations students will find interesting, particularly investigating sea horse behavior!

The "After" plan can stand alone as an isolated single-group studies lesson, but it is richer if linked with other women's studies lessons either in science or in other subject areas. In science, for example, students can investigate other gender differences to determine whether they are real or imagined, innate or learned. In other subject areas, students can study, for example, the domestic division of labor and how this affects division of labor in the workforce or female mental health.

▶ LESSON PLAN[6]

Identifying Themes in Literature

Subject Area: English
Grade Level: 9–12
Time: Six to eight days

Objectives

1. Students will identify main themes in short stories.

[6] *Source:* Anne Fairbrother, Del Norte High School, Albuquerque, New Mexico.

2. Students will identify common themes shared by three different stories.

3. Students will write a formal essay that is organized, contains an introduction and conclusion, and uses evidence appropriately.

Suggested Procedures

1. Explain to the students what a theme is. Have them give you examples of themes from the core works they read the previous year in their English class.

2. Read "If I Forget Thee, Oh Earth," by Arthur C. Clarke. (This story contains many possible themes, including those of hope, remorse, and responsibility. As fantasy, it can also be seen as an analogy.) After reading, have students take a quiz or answer discussion questions. Then have students brainstorm possible themes, list them on the board, discuss them, and write notes. Students should keep their notes until they have read all three stories.

3. Read "The Enchanted Bluff," by Willa Cather. (This story contains analogy and addresses many themes, including those of dreams, hopes, and growing up.) After reading, give students a quiz or have them answer discussion questions. Then have students brainstorm possible themes, list them on the board, discuss them, and take notes.

4. Read "Uncle Einar," by Ray Bradbury. (This story addresses many themes, including those of dreams and fulfillment of dreams, being true to one's nature, and maturity. It also can be seen as an analogy.) After reading, give students a quiz or have them answer discussion questions. Next, have students brainstorm possible themes, list them on the board, and discuss them.

5. Have students meet again with their groups, brainstorming from their notes on each story and the themes the three stories have in common.

6. Each student may choose his or her own theme from the group's choices and should complete the following thesis statement for him- or herself: "The major theme that all three stories have in common is _____."

7. Help students start to write an essay with an introduction and thesis statement, one paragraph for each story showing that the theme is indeed in that story, supported with interpreted evidence, and a conclusion. Set a date when the first draft is due and will be shared in response groups, and set a date when the final draft is due.

Evaluation

1. Through participation in class and group discussions or through quizzes, evaluate students' ability to identify main themes in short stories.

2. Through participation in group discussions and development of a thesis statement, evaluate students' ability to identify common themes shared by three different stories.

3. Give students one grade for the first draft of their essay, one for the quality of their response to a partner's essay, and two for the final essay—one for content and one for form.

Resources

Bradbury, R. (1980). Uncle Einar. In R. Bradbury, *The stories of Ray Bradbury*. New York: Alfred A. Knopf.

Cather, W. (1956). The enchanted bluff. In W. Cather, *Five stories*. New York: Random House.

Clarke, A. C. (1985). If I forget thee, oh Earth. In W. M. Miller & M. H. Greenberg (Eds.), *Beyond Armageddon*. New York: D. I. Fine.

Culture in Native American Literature

Subject Area: English

Grade Level: 9–12

Time: Eight to ten days

Objectives

1. Students will identify main themes in short stories.

2. Students will identify common themes shared by three different short stories that reflect the boarding school experience of Native Americans over two generations.

3. Students will examine what constitutes culture, how education relates to culture, and the concept of assimilation.

4. Students will write a formal essay that contains an introduction and conclusion and uses evidence appropriately.

Suggested Procedures

1. Write on the board these questions as you ask them: What is culture? How is it transmitted? Can it be destroyed? Introduce the idea of cultural assimilation.

2. Show the video *In the White Man's Image*, an excellent documentary of the boarding school "experiment." After the video, have students look at all the things they identified as making up culture (probably including language, religion, customs, food, music, clothes, history, stories, and values) and ask them what was happening to the students at the boarding schools. Students will see that there was a conscious attempt to replace the children's American Indian culture with the European American culture.

3. Explain the historical events and political and religious rationale behind establishing the boarding school policy in the United States (starting with Richard Pratt establishing Carlisle in 1879).

4. Read "Canassatego Gives an Offer of Help" (in *The National Experience: Part One. A History of the United States to 1877*, by A. M. Schlesinger et al.) (Any statement of American Indian resistance to the forced attendance of boarding schools could be used, with appropriate questions.) In groups, have students answer these questions:

   a. Why doesn't the American Indian want the White man's education?

   b. Judging from this statement, how does education relate to culture?

   c. What is the tone of the passage? What is implied in the closing sentences?

   On the board, have students discuss how education relates to culture. Brainstorm what education is for and how education is a socializing agency—that is, a method of transmitting culture to each generation.

5. Have students read three stories by Native American authors that deal with the boarding school experience:

   a. "Charlie," by Lee Maracle (from *Voices Under One Sky*, edited by Trish Fox Roman). Read it aloud in class, and have students make notes on what happens in the story.

   b. An excerpt from Chapter 2 in *Lame Deer—Seeker of Visions*, by John Fire and Richard Erdoes (as excerpted in *Growing Up Native American*, edited by Patricia Riley). Read it aloud in class, and have students make notes on what happens in the story.

   c. "Civilize Them With a Stick" (Chapter 3 of *Lakota Woman*, by Mary Crow Dog). Read it aloud in class, omitting sections as needed, and have students make notes on what happens in the story.

6. After reading all three stories, let students work in groups. Using a Venn diagram with three intersecting circles, have students show what each piece has in common with one or both of the other pieces and what is peculiar to each story.

7. When students have filled up all the parts of the diagram, show them that in the center of the diagram they have identified what themes the pieces have in common. On the back of their papers, have them write out the three major themes they all share, as part of a thesis statement: "Three themes that these stories have in common are (1) _____, (2) _____, and (3) _____."

8. Help students start to write an essay with an introduction and thesis statement, one paragraph for each theme, supported with interpreted evidence to show that the theme does appear in each story, and a conclusion. Set a date when the first draft is due, and will be shared in response groups, and set a date when the final draft is due.

9. An appropriate movie at the end is the TNT production of the book *Lakota Woman*. It will facilitate discussions about the Battle of Wounded Knee in 1890, the Occupation of Wounded Knee in 1973, the American Indian movement, and the issue of the Black Hills for the Sioux Nations. You could also show *The Spirit of Crazy Horse* for an excellent overview of Sioux history, experience, and issues. To continue the theme of educational assimilation, you could show the movie *Where the Spirit Lives*, which is about a Canadian Indian girl taken to a boarding school, where she and her brother experience enforced cultural assimilation.

Evaluation

1. Through participation in class and group discussions, evaluate students' ability to identify main themes in short stories.

2. Through participation in group discussions and through the group work, evaluate students' ability to identify common themes shared by three different stories.

3. Through participation in class discussions and a written essay, evaluate students' understanding of the concepts of culture and cultural assimilation.

4. Students will receive one grade for the first draft of their essay, one for the quality of their response to a partner's essay, and two grades for the final essay—one for content and one for form.

Resources

Print

Crow Dog, M. (1990). *Lakota woman*. New York: Harper Perennial.

Fire, J., & Erdoes, R. (1972). *Lame Deer—Seeker of visions*. New York: Simon & Schuster.

Riley, P. (Ed.). (1993). *Growing up Native American*. New York: Morrow.

Roman, T. F. (Ed.). (1994). *Voices under one sky*. Freedom, CA: Crossing Press.

Schlesinger, A. M., & Blum, J. M.; McFeely, W. S.; Morgan, E. S.; Stampp, K. M. et al. (1993). *The national experience: Part one. A history of the United States to 1877* (8th ed.). Ft. Worth, TX: Harcourt Brace Jovanovich.

Audiovisual

Lesiak, C. [Producer]. (1992). *In the White man's image* [Motion Picture]. WGBH-TV, Boston; WNET-TV, New York; and KCET-TV, Los Angeles.

Pierson, Frank [Director]. (1994). *Lakota woman: Siege at Wounded Knee* [Motion Picture]. Turner Pictures, Inc., Turner Home Entertainment, One CNN Center, Atlanta, GA 30303.

The spirit of crazy horse. (1990). Pacific Arts Video Publishing, 50N. La Cienego Blvd., Beverly Hills, CA 90211.

Where the spirit lives. (1989). Studio Entertainment, 386 Park Avenue So., New York, NY 10016.

Additional Resources

Bruchac, J. (2003). *Our stories remember: American Indian history, culture and values through storytelling*. Golden, CO: Fulcrum.

Lesley, C. (1991). *Talking leaves: Contemporary Native American short stories*. New York: Laurel.

Ochoa, A., Franco, B., & Gourdine, T. (2003). *Night is gone, day is still coming: Stories and poems by American Indian teens and young adults*. Cambridge, MA: Candlewick.

Culture in Native American Literature

History and Culture

In both lessons, students learn how to find themes in a story and how to write a formal essay focused on themes. In the "After" lesson, students are also looking at the boarding school experience of Native Americans over at least two generations. While looking for themes and discussing the stories, students are also gaining an insight from Native American points of view into Native American history, culture, and issues. These stories bring up a lot of historical and cultural matters, and the teacher will need to be well prepared to address them and to answer students' questions. Students will be able to draw on the knowledge and understanding developed in this unit when they encounter Native American poems and stories later in the school year. As a result, they will better appreciate and understand them.

When reading books from other cultures and other historical periods, students need to develop contextual knowledge and understanding, whether they are reading *A Tale of Two Cities*, by Dickens, or *Ceremony*, by Silko. This approach, of course, lends itself well to interdisciplinary teaching in which students, in this case, could learn some of the history, ideally through original documents and from Native American historians as well as from Anglo American historians, while experiencing the literature. The literature illuminates the people's lives and provides an authentic interpretation of the event—this is the flesh to put on the bones of the historical time line of events; this is the life to bring to the analysis of events.

▶ LESSON PLAN

Lesson 1 (in November)—Mexican Americans

Subject Area: Social Studies
Grade Level: 10–12
Time: One of three separate days over the course of seven months

Objectives

1. Students will identify reasons why Texas and California declared independence from Mexico.
2. Students will describe how the United States acquired territory in the Southwest.

Suggested Procedures

1. Discuss the idea of Manifest Destiny. On a wall map, point out the territory owned by Mexico in the early 1800s and the territory claimed by both Mexico and the United States.
2. Have students read pages in their textbook about the war with Mexico.
3. Ask students to discuss whether the war was justified.

Evaluation

Include questions on a test regarding how and why the United States acquired territory from Mexico.

Lesson 2 (in January)—Mexican Americans

Subject Area: Social Studies
Grade Level: 10–12
Time: One of three separate days over the course of seven months

Objectives

1. Students will explain why immigrants came to the United States between 1880 and 1920.
2. Students will describe how U.S. citizens reacted to the influx of immigrants and why they reacted that way.

Suggested Procedures

1. Ask students to brainstorm, from previous lessons, a list of the various industries that expanded during the late 1800s. Have them suggest sources of workers, from the perspective of business owners, and discuss which sources might be best and why.
2. Ask students to read pages in a textbook about industrial expansion during this time period.

Evaluation

Prepare a test, which includes questions about what industrial expansion involved, where immigrants came from, and why they came to the United States.

Lesson 3 (in May)—Mexican Americans

Subject Area: Social Studies
Grade Level: 10–12
Time: One of three separate days over the course of seven months

Objectives

1. Students will describe issues of concern to Latinos from the 1960s to the twenty-first century.

2. Students will name and describe prominent Latino/a leaders from that time period.

Suggested Procedures

1. Have students read pages in the text about the Chicano/Latino movement.

2. Discuss the similarities and differences among issues of concern to Latinos, African Americans, and American Indians during the Civil Rights movement.

Evaluation

On a test, present a civil rights issue and ask students to describe the relevant concerns and actions of Latinos, African Americans, or American Indians.

Mexican American Labor in the United States

Subject Area: Social Studies
Grade Level: 10–12
Time: One week

Objectives

1. Students will describe how the United States historically has shifted its policies toward Mexican and Mexican American laborers to acquire cheap, temporary labor.

2. Students will appreciate different perspectives on the history of Mexican labor in the United States, particularly the perspective of Mexican and Mexican American laborers.

3. Students will locate information, particularly information about subordinate groups.

4. Students will develop a personal perspective on current debates about the United States–Mexico border and illegal Mexican immigrants.

Suggested Procedures

1. Ask students to describe what they know or have heard about the issue of illegal Mexican workers in the United States. Ask for their opinions, based on what they know, regarding whether Mexican immigration should be restricted and border controls tightened. Point out that the perspective the public most often hears is that of White European American business owners; other groups' perspectives may be downplayed, distorted, or omitted altogether.

2. Divide students into six groups. Explain that they will research the history of this issue from the perspectives of the following groups (make sure students distinguish between Mexicans—citizens of Mexico—and Mexican Americans—citizens of the United States):

   a. Mexican business owners
   b. Mexican Americans living at or below the poverty line
   c. European American business owners
   d. U.S. government
   e. Mexican American workers
   f. European working-class Americans
   g. Mexican people searching for work

   Explain that students are to locate the answers for their group to the following questions:

   a. What were your group's economic needs?
   b. How did your group view each of the other groups?
   c. What was your group doing during the time periods 1845–1850; 1850–1900; 1900–1924; 1924–1930; 1930–1947; 1947–1965; 1965–1980; 1980–1995; 1995–present? Discuss sources of information; you may wish to locate sources yourself and make them available to students.

3. Assist students as needed while they complete their research.

4. Construct a large wall mural from butcher paper across the top of which the time periods noted in item 2 appear at intervals of two to three feet. Down the left-hand side of the mural, each of the six groups should be listed. Starting with the first time period (1845–1850), each group should report to the whole class on and chart the history of the issue. Have one student (or yourself) write key points and events on the chart for each time period. Encourage students to discover and explain the relationships among the groups' needs and desires and how they responded to each other and to historical events.

5. Have the class debate the following question: Should the United States further restrict immigration of Mexican workers into the country? Students should debate the question first from the perspective of the group they represent and then from their own perspectives.

6. Ask students which groups' perspectives and experiences were most difficult to locate and least publicized and whose were easiest to locate and best publicized. Lead them to recognize that the control of information can influence public opinion and distort the average person's understanding of history.

Evaluation

1. Through his or her oral contributions to the mural, assess each student's understanding of the group that he or she represented.

2. Through a quiz, assess students' understanding of U.S. history and policy and of the actions and perspectives of different groups.

3. Through their oral contributions to the mural, assess students' skill at locating information.

4. Through the class debate, assess students' development of personal perspectives.

Mexican American Labor in the United States

Perspective on History

The "Before" plan presents only one racial group and does so in a fragmented way—it gives little information about the group and in disconnected pieces, making it difficult to get a coherent sense of the group's experience. Furthermore, the information presented is not connected to current issues related to the group's experiences. The story being told is European American, with the perspective that Mexican Americans have occasionally interacted with and contributed to European American history.

In contrast, the "After" plan shifts the perspectives of the lesson to those of Mexican Americans. This helps students to recognize the diversity within the Mexican American population and the multiple viewpoints that have existed, to connect a viewpoint they hear with a group who shares that viewpoint, and to appreciate debates and conflict that surround history and policy.

The "After" plan asks students to compile research on their own (although the teacher must make the materials available to them). This activity encourages students to construct the story of what happened, which enhances their understanding more than if they are told of the events. It also helps students to realize that some groups' viewpoints are better preserved and publicized than others, providing a basis for examining how control over knowledge can help a group control public opinion and social policy. For example, students will find that locating information about the needs and views of White European American business owners is easier than obtaining the same information about Mexicans and Mexican Americans who live at or below the poverty level. From this discovery, students learn that a lack of knowledge about Mexicans and Mexican Americans who live at or below the poverty level can cause the average student or person to misunderstand this group of people.

Current Social Agenda

The purpose of the "After" plan is to help students understand the problems faced by Mexican Americans today and to show that their success in this country is greatly influenced by others. That is, battles over the group's status are still being fought, and all citizens have a say in how their struggles are resolved. The plan does this by concentrating on a current issue—how open the United States–Mexico border should be. Students come to understand that studying history is valuable not only for its own sake but also because it helps us understand current issues.

Finally, the cooperative learning and role-playing devices used in the "After" lesson are more enjoyable and conducive to learning than the textbook reading and large-group discussion and recitation strategies employed in the "Before" plan.

Reference

Loewen, James. (1995). *Lies My Teacher Told Me*. New York: Touchstone Books.

CHAPTER 5

Multicultural Education

Some of you probably like most of the ideas in the three approaches discussed in this text so far (teaching the exceptional and culturally different approach, the human relations approach, and the single-group studies approach) and are wondering how they can be combined. You may be asking yourself questions such as the following:

- What is the teacher's role in classes where there is a wide range of cultural groups, socioeconomic groups, sexual orientations, and disabilities?

- What is the teacher's role in providing a curriculum that addresses both females and males?

- What is the teacher's role in helping students to discover and examine inequities in society, especially those that are influencing the students' life chances?

- To what extent should teachers try to capitalize on the learning styles and interests of their students?

- Should high-stakes testing and the demands for increased student achievement serve as justifiable reasons to label individuals and groups of students?

- How should teachers teach about the influences—both positive and negative—of globalization?

- Should school staffing patterns as well as the curriculum provide students with a variety of role models, including those with nontraditional roles, those of various cultural and economic backgrounds and sexual orientations, those of both sexes, and those with disabilities?

- How far should teachers go in building a classroom and school climate that celebrates diversity, equal opportunity, and equity?

The multicultural education approach addresses these kinds of questions. It calls for the reform of the entire classroom and the school itself, and it is for all students.

The approach rests on two ideals: equal opportunity and cultural pluralism. The ideal of equal opportunity holds that each student should be given equal opportunity to learn, succeed, and become what he or she would like, with full affirmation of his or her sex, race, social class background, sexual orientation, and disability, if any. But equal opportunity does not just happen by will or by declaring it "policy"—one must work deliberately and consistently to implement it. For example, a student who is behind his or her peers in reading does not have equal opportunity to learn science when science is taught through reading material beyond the student's reading level. A Latina does not have equal opportunity to succeed if the curriculum portrays Latinas as invisible, unimportant, or not "American." Equal opportunity does not mean ignoring differences or pretending that they do not exist. On the contrary, it means viewing differences as normal and desirable, and supporting them in such a way that they do not hinder a person's ability to dream and strive to reach his or her goals.

To achieve equal opportunity, it is also important to explore issues of power and privilege. Sometimes power and privilege are accepted as invisible norms (rights) of the dominant group (e.g., for males), and this marginalizes the opportunity of other groups.

Equal opportunity supports the second ideal of the multicultural education approach: cultural pluralism. Essentially, cultural pluralism means that there is no one best way to be a U.S. resident. An "all-American" child does not necessarily have blond hair and light skin and eat toast and cereal for breakfast; one who is dark, lives in an extended family, and eats rice or tortillas for breakfast is an American too. Cultural pluralism is not separatism. Rather, it includes a sharing and blending of different ethnic cultures and other forms of culture that constitute the shared mainstream U.S. culture, and it also supports ethnicity, gender, disability, and other groups as they enjoy and continue to develop distinctive group cultures. U.S. residents should not have to give up their families' identities, sense of group solidarity, or cultural beliefs and traditions to be accepted as American or to participate fully in U.S. society.

▶ MEETING THE GOALS OF THE MULTICULTURAL EDUCATION APPROACH

Based on its two ideals—equal opportunity and cultural pluralism—the multicultural education approach includes the following goals:

1. To promote an understanding, appreciation, and acceptance of cultural diversity in the United States.

2. To promote alternative choices for people, with full affirmation of their race, gender, disability, language, religion, sexual orientation, and social class background.

3. To help all children achieve academic success.

4. To promote awareness of social issues involving the unequal distribution of power and privilege that limits the opportunity of those not in the dominant group.

The multicultural approach advocates transformation of the school as a whole. Action Research Activity 5.2 helps you examine your school as a whole, as well as your own classroom. What can the classroom teacher do to accomplish these goals?

Curriculum Materials

Many teachers begin to use this approach with materials for the curriculum. Materials should portray the contributions and perspectives of a variety of U.S. cultural groups—gays, lesbians, transgenders, and bisexuals; people with disabilities; and people of both sexes—and they should do so in a manner that does not reinforce and promote stereotypes or exoticize cultural groups. This material should also include discussions about who has power and privilege and whose interest is being served and at what cost. Diverse groups should be included substantively; adding a few names or pictures of Asian Americans, Latinos, Native Americans, and people with disabilities is not sufficient. Groups should be presented relatively equally; White European American males should not dominate the roles or space in the text. Language should be gender inclusive. You may feel that your materials already do this because great improvements in curricular materials have been made over the past twenty-five years. You should examine them closely: Materials that seem balanced at first glance often, on closer examination, are not. The lesson plans "Folk and Fairy Tales" (p. 207) and "Perspectives" (p. 223) illustrate how you can use biased materials.

There is a rapidly growing body of multicultural curriculum materials, published by both regional and larger commercial presses. Teachers can create rich, exciting multicultural curricula by collecting and drawing on these materials. The plans for "Families" (p. 196), "Hypermedia History" (p. 235), and "Literature on Migrant Workers and Exploitation" (p. 239) illustrate ways of doing this.

Curriculum Content

Curriculum content is a broader term than *materials*, but the same considerations apply. Examine the curriculum content you plan to teach in a given area over a period of time to determine whether it reflects multiple and diverse perspectives, engages all students in learning the different subject areas, and considers gender issues. Also, look at your curriculum to see how well it connects with the social context of your students' interests and experiential backgrounds and with the types of information they would want to learn more of. A lesson such as "Our National Anthems" (p. 231) connects content with students' everyday interests and concerns. Similarly, lessons such as "Estimation" (p. 200) and "Self-Interest" (p. 252) connect with students' life circumstances and help students to deal with issues of bias, power, and privilege. The focus of these lessons involves tapping into students' interests and drawing on a culturally expanded pool of knowledge for selecting academic content. The lessons also extend students' knowledge about the experiences and contributions of both sexes and various cultural groups and inform them about how gender and other biases are manifested in society.

To determine your starting points, you may wish to investigate how much you and your students already know about various groups and the issues and concerns of these groups. Action Research Activity 5.3 is useful with younger students. Action Research Activity 5.1 is appropriate for students in grades six through twelve as well as for adults. Making your curriculum content multicultural requires work. You will be challenged. Most of us have not been educated multiculturally and do not know where to go for information. Following are some helpful places to start:

1. Curriculum specialists and resource centers in many school districts have materials to help teachers in this area; often these resources are not used simply because people don't know that they are available.

2. Librarians can be an excellent resource; for example, a reference librarian at a public library may be able to provide a wide range of literature or music in a short period of time to a teacher who is not sure what to look for.

3. Students, parents, and local community members can be excellent resources for content on locally represented cultures; most people are receptive to teachers who genuinely want to learn more about their culture and customs.

4. Discuss your ideas with one or two of your colleagues. You may find that they have excellent ideas and suggestions and are also interested in multicultural education.

5. Most cities and larger towns have bookstores that have multicultural materials. It is well worth spending time (and money) there.

6. Three magazines—*Multicultural Perspectives*, *Multicultural Education*, and *Critical Inquiry Into Curriculum and Instruction*—contain curriculum ideas and materials reviews in each issue.

7. Increasingly, one can find helpful resources on the Internet. The book *Multicultural Education and the Internet* (Gorski, 2005) is full of helpful websites and suggestions for how to use them.

There are also many commercially produced bibliographies. Once a teacher has gotten started, these can be helpful sources of materials.

Multiple Perspectives

On virtually every issue there are multiple points of view. Yet historically, schools have tended to teach children to seek "the right answer." One important way the multicultural education approach affirms cultural pluralism is by helping students appreciate multiple perspectives or interpretations. Whenever possible, try to help students recognize that there is more than one way to view an issue, more than one side to a story, more than one "right" cultural practice, and help them discern the standpoints from which other people's perspectives make sense. By doing this, you can help students develop fairness, flexible thinking, an expectation that other viewpoints exist, and an appreciation of the similarities and differences among people. The lesson plans "Perspectives" (p. 223) and "Hypermedia History" (p. 235) concentrate on these goals.

Instructional Strategies

Earlier in the book we noted the importance of adapting to students' learning styles and skill levels; these recommendations are especially valuable here as well. Essentially, to help your students achieve, you need to be willing to test the various approaches to teaching to identify those that result in achievement. This is important today, more so than in past decades, because classrooms are more heterogeneous according to race, class, religion, and disability than in past decades. Also, in order to meet the demands of high-stakes testing, students need to learn in ways that both pique their interest and challenge their abilities. A good deal of patience is often required when trying out new ideas. Students may need a period of adjustment. Usually, the more information students receive about an idea (including why they are studying it), the more they will work with you. For example, "Our National Anthems" (p. 232) is a lesson that uses various learning and teaching styles.

Language Diversity

The multicultural education approach values language diversity and language resources available in the United States, specifically the millions of students who use another language, including sign language, in addition to English. Ideally, all U.S. residents should be bilingual, mastering English and at least one other language. Some schools offer content instruction (such as history or mathematics) in languages other than English, a practice that dates back more than a century. For example, one of the authors teaches at a university in which some courses outside the Languages Institute are taught in Spanish.

The regular classroom teacher usually is not trained as a language teacher, but with the United States becoming more diverse, teachers (as well as students) need to develop an interest in second-language learning. Resource people can teach conversational phrases or songs in another language. The concept of multilingualism can be presented in a positive manner, and the limitations of knowing only one language can be discussed. This is illustrated in the lesson "Our National Anthems" (p. 232). The languages students bring with them to school should also be used as a teaching resource, as the lessons "Families" (p. 196) and "An Inspirational Glimpse of Aztec Mythology" (p. 211) illustrate.

Student Evaluation

The high-stakes testing climate that schools and teachers are facing often evaluates students, teachers, and schools in terms of "winners" and "losers." The standardized norm-referenced tests, designed to compare and rank-order students and schools, are based on a conception of normalcy that usually favors the European American middle- or upper-middle-class child. A more productive way to evaluate, from the perspective of the multicultural education approach, is to scale back on the accountability rhetoric, teach the student instead of teaching to the test, and use evaluation as a means of helping both teachers and students instead of determining reward or punishment. By using evaluation to guide instruction, it should be possible for all children to be successful.

Furthermore, multiple forms of assessment that are respectful of diversity should be used to evaluate mastery of multicultural content. The materials used should not penalize students who have low-skill levels in areas other than those the teacher has taught. For example, students should be given ample time and not be penalized if they work slowly; they should be encouraged to spell correctly but not be penalized for incorrect spelling on a test (unless it is a spelling test); and oral evaluation should be offered to those who do not write well. Although some of these suggestions may conflict with the teaching procedures of some readers of this book, it is important to remember that our primary goal as teachers is to "turn on" learning.

Grouping Students

Grouping students for instruction is a complex practice that often institutionalizes biases and stereotypes. We become so used to grouping patterns that we assume the groups reflect characteristics of students rather than our own beliefs and expectations. Grouping practices that permanently define some students as inferior (e.g., tracking and ability grouping) or superior (e.g., gifted programs) are strongly discouraged. In some classrooms we have discovered what we call "grouping by isolation." We are noticing one or two students assigned to the hallway or the back of the classroom. Whereas some may refer to this as a "time out," such is not the case when students remain in a separate area away from the rest of the class for one hour or more. Also, we have observed that such grouping often becomes a recurring way of dealing with certain students. Once students are labeled and tracked, their chances of moving up a group are fairly slim, and the groups become more and more different from one another each year students are in them. Similarly, grouping students in ways that reflect stereotypes, such as enrolling girls in sewing and boys in autoshop, is also discouraged.

The multicultural education approach values small-group activities that allow students to get to know each other and to express their individuality and abilities. Thus, heterogeneous groups (in terms of race, gender, social class, and academic skill level) in which students work cooperatively work well in many situations. Such groups are used in the lessons "Tie-Dyeing" (p. 203) and "Our National Anthems" (p. 231). Interest groups, such as one composed of students interested in animal stories, are another alternative, as are temporary skill-level groups for working on building specific skills. At the same time, homogeneous groups are useful in some circumstances. In bilingual or multilingual classrooms, it is often helpful for students to work with others who speak the same language; talking over material in their first language helps them to learn. Sometimes girls work better in single-sex groups, where they do not defer to the boys. Grouping practices should be flexible, and multiple groupings should be used, as illustrated in the plan "Giving Thanks" (p. 194). Students need to learn to relate to their peers and not to categorize people on the basis of a permanent instructional group. At the same time, they also need the most optimal opportunity for learning.

Visuals

What does your classroom look like when you enter it? What do the halls look like? Whose pictures are displayed, what do the visuals tell about the students, and do they say clearly that this is the school of all the students enrolled? A school using the multicultural education approach radiates human life and diversity in visual displays. Posters depict people of different races, both sexes, and with disabilities, as well as extended and gay and lesbian families. Languages used by students and the community are used. Student work is displayed. The school and classroom look warm, friendly, and inviting. Quotations and statements on posters that encourage critical thinking about problems and issues students are facing are displayed as well.

Some high school teachers tell us that less attention is given to visuals at the secondary level because the students are older, and a teacher may have to share the classroom with several other teachers on a rotating basis. Therefore, they argue, they should not be too concerned about visuals. Although we recognize these issues, we also think that every student in a school should believe that it is his or her school, and this should not be left to chance. To do nothing may suggest to students that "business as usual" is okay.

Role Models

A school using the multicultural education approach provides students with diverse role models filling both traditional and nontraditional roles. For example, the principal may be a female of color. Teachers may include both men and women of various ethnic backgrounds, including some who are gay, lesbian, or bisexual, and they are not confined to sex-stereotypic subjects. There may be male secretaries and cafeteria workers and female custodians, and there may be a teacher who is hearing impaired or in a wheelchair. Role models are also provided through guests and speakers, and a conscious effort is made to provide models with whom students can identify, having a variety of careers and interests. Role models are involved throughout the school year, and not just for special occasions. Role models should also encourage students to aspire to high goals, to think creatively about their own futures. Lessons that deal with role models include "Division" (p. 217) and "The Importance of Math to Everyday Life" (Chapter 2, p. 32).

Home and Community Relationships

Normally, parents and child care providers occupy a spectator role when it comes to their child's education, and parents and child care providers living at or below the poverty line or from minority backgrounds may be excluded and/or turned off by the school in a number of ways. The multicultural education approach builds a partnership among the home, school, and community. This partnership seeks to include parents and child care providers in school activities and on decision-making and policy-formation committees. Also, this approach encourages communication in the parents' and child care providers' home language. It argues for meetings to be scheduled at convenient times and held in nonthreatening locations. For example, one of our colleagues who is an urban administrator holds family dinners in a church to discuss school issues, and his approach has been highly successful.

Teachers using this approach learn about the community in a methodical manner. For example, they learn the community's history, become familiar with the housing patterns, introduce themselves to the community leaders, and visit organizations, associations, and religious institutions. They read the community newspapers or neighborhood bulletins. They communicate personally with parents, providing them with progress reports on their children. This approach sees the school as just one of the institutions of the community and seeks to build communication with the other institutions to maximize the effectiveness of each one. For example, schools work closely with social service agencies and youth clubs to see that students receive the best care possible both during and after school hours. Also, with the number of homeless children on the rise, teachers' knowledge about community services is more significant today than in the recent past. The lesson plans "Giving Thanks" (p. 194), "Families" (p. 196) and

"An Inspirational Glimpse of Aztec Mythology" (p. 211) include parents as teachers and foster home–school partnerships.

Extracurricular Activities

This approach encourages a wide variety of extracurricular activities. It sees these activities as a way to stimulate greater interest in school and to appeal to students' special and unique talents. By using clubs, sports, dramatics, and school events as a vehicle, students can be given increased opportunities to demonstrate leadership skills and deal with social problems and issues facing society on their own terms. These activities are designed to avoid the perpetuation of stereotypes and categorization of students into stereotypic roles (e.g., boys as athletes and girls as onlookers cheering the boys). Students can join the activities of their choice but are encouraged to cross boundaries and participate in activities that challenge the way they have previously thought about things (e.g., girls joining the mechanics club and boys joining the cooking club).

The names and logos used to identify extracurricular activities (e.g., sport teams) should avoid using terms that may be offensive, such as the name of a racial group (e.g., the Mohawks). We have been in situations in which teachers have debated the merits of school clubs that cater to one group, such as Movimiento Estudiantil Chicano de Aztlán (MEChA), which caters to Latino/a students. Our own view is that such clubs may be exactly what a school needs to make its students feel welcome and provide a time and place to be with "their own." We endorse mixing students as much as possible but also recognize value in being with others with whom one shares a special bond. Opportunities for both kinds of interaction should be plentiful.

The preceding recommendations of the Multicultural Education approach span the entire school environment. Use Action Research Activity 5.2 to examine your own school.

▶ ACTION RESEARCH ACTIVITY 5.1[1]

How Culturally Literate Are You?

True/False

_____ 1. The first clock in the United States was made by an African American mathematician.

_____ 2. Charles Drew was an African American surgeon who performed the first successful heart operation.

_____ 3. Just over one hundred years ago, during the decade of the 1890s, the U.S. government took over Puerto Rico and the Philippines through war, legalized

[1] *Sources:* Bob H. Suzuki, California Polytechnical University, and Christine E. Sleeter. ©1989 Merrill/Prentice Hall Publishing Company. Permission is granted for noncommercial reproduction.

racial segregation in the United States, overthrew the government of Hawaii, consolidated the subjugation of Native American nations, and opened its gates to European immigrants.

_____ **4.** The forced migration of the Sioux people from their homeland in Georgia to Oklahoma, during which one-fourth of them died of starvation, disease, and exposure, is known as the "Trail of Tears."

_____ **5.** During World War II, the United States placed many innocent citizens in concentration camps and confiscated their property.

_____ **6.** There was no federal ruling protecting U.S. citizens' rights to marry a person of another race until 1970.

_____ **7.** Mong people began to immigrate to the United States after their Southeast Asian country was destroyed in their defeat by the United States.

_____ **8.** During the Renaissance, the status of women (especially creative and independent women) in Europe rose fairly significantly.

_____ **9.** Mexican women have never been involved in political or labor struggles because traditionally their place has been in the home.

_____ **10.** During the fifteenth and sixteenth centuries, Timbuktu, in the African kingdom of Songhay, was one of the world's greatest cities, renowned as an intellectual and cultural center.

Multiple Choice

1. The song "Yellow Rose of Texas" was written to refer to
   a. a flower.
   b. a poor African American woman.
   c. a European American southern belle.
   d. a cow.

2. LULAC is a
   a. name of a song.
   b. type of American Indian poetry.
   c. Filipino club.
   d. Latino American political organization.

3. The League of Six Nations was
   a. a political alliance of African states established in the 1600s for mutual protection against European encroachment.
   b. an organization of European countries formed in the 1700s.
   c. a sophisticated network of political alliances among the Iroquois, who lived in the northeastern part of the United States.
   d. an organization of the six major world powers formed after World War I.

4. The National Women's Party first introduced the Equal Rights Amendment in Congress in
   a. 1923.   c. 1963.
   b. 1949.   d. 1972.

5. America was discovered by
   a. African explorers in CE 1252.
   b. Hwui Shan, a Chinese Buddhist priest, in CE 458.
   c. Christopher Columbus in CE 1492.
   d. Japanese fishermen around 3000 BCE
   e. Leif Ericson in the eleventh century.
   f. none of the above

6. This statement was made by which of the following?

   I am not, nor ever have been, in favor of bringing about in any way the social and political equality of the white and black races; I am not, nor ever have been, in favor of making voters or jurors of Negroes, nor qualifying them to hold office. . . . I will say in addition to this that there is a physical difference between the white and black races which I believe will ever forbid the two races living together on terms of social and political equality.
   a. Herbert Spencer, a leading exponent of Social Darwinism in the late 1800s
   b. Jefferson Davis, president of the Confederacy
   c. Abraham Lincoln, sixteenth president of the United States
   d. The Know-Nothing Party's presidential candidate in 1852
   e. none of the above

7. *Akwesanse Notes* is currently the national newspaper of
   a. the Mohawk Nation.
   b. Puerto Rico.
   c. Japanese Americans in California.
   d. Bolivia.

8. The eleven persons who were murdered in a mass lynching in New Orleans in 1891 were members of which of the following ethnic groups?
   a. Chinese
   b. African Americans
   c. Italians
   d. French Indians

9. A man and his son were involved in a car accident in which the father was killed instantly and the son seriously injured. The son was rushed to the hospital and taken immediately into surgery. The surgeon entered the operating room, looked at the patient, and exclaimed, "Oh my god! I can't operate. That's my son!" The explanation for this situation is that
   a. it was a case of mistaken identity.
   b. the surgeon was the boy's stepfather.
   c. the surgeon was the ghost of the boy's father.
   d. none of the above

10. If you are a *sansei*, you are
    a. a master in karate.
    b. a respected grandparent.
    c. a third-generation Japanese American.
    d. a foreigner in an Asian American community.

Matching

_____ 1. Richard Wright

_____ 2. Mary McLeod Bethune

_____ 3. Emma Tenayuca

_____ 4. Patsy Takemoto Mink

_____ 5. Marian Anderson

_____ 6. Judy Baca

_____ 7. Larry Itliong

_____ 8. Leslie Silko

_____ 9. Reies Lopez Tijerina

_____ 10. Lerone Bennett

_____ 11. Ada Deer

_____ 12. Alvin Pouissaint

_____ 13. Lucy Stone

_____ 14. Yoshiko Uchida

_____ 15. Zora Neale Hurston

_____ 16. Rudolfo Acuña

a. Mexican American labor leader

b. African American psychiatrist on Harvard faculty

c. opera singer

d. founder and former president of a college

e. first Native American woman to direct the Bureau of Indian Affairs

f. Mexican American historian

g. African American male novelist

h. Filipino American labor leader

i. internationally known Chicana muralist

j. Mexican American political leader

k. author of children's books

l. American Indian novelist

m. African American female novelist

n. former member of the U.S. Congress

o. African American historian

p. active abolitionist and for women's suffragist

▶ ANSWERS: HOW CULTURALLY LITERATE ARE YOU?

True or False

___T___ 1. His name was Benjamin Banneker.

___F___ 2. The surgeon was Daniel H. Williams; Charles Drew pioneered research on blood plasma. Both were African Americans.

___T___ 3. The revolutionary movements of Puerto Rico and the Philippines were betrayed by the United States when it forced both countries to become its protectorates and replaced Spanish rule with U.S. colonial rule. This was the period of "Manifest Destiny" and the beginning of U.S. imperialism. The last decade of the nineteenth century could be considered the most aggressively racist and imperialist of U.S. history. Effects of that decade are still very real: the United States still occupies Puerto Rico. Puerto Ricans and Filipinos live and work on the U.S. mainland but experience highly disproportionate poverty rates; segregation was not legally undermined in the United States until 1954, and its effects are still felt; American Indian nations and Hawaiian people are still attempting to reclaim land, treaty rights, and legal recognition; and the economic status of European Americans is considerably higher than that of other groups partly because of their legalized access to jobs over several decades.

___F___ 4. It was the Cherokee who were moved, not the Sioux. This action was actually taken against a U.S. Supreme Court ruling.

__T__ **5.** The victims of this action were Japanese American citizens; Italian Americans also experienced confiscation of property.

__T__ **6.** Many states protected this right, but some did not, and the federal government did not until 1970.

__F__ **7.** Mong people had migrated to Laos before the Vietnam War; they had no country of their own. They sided with the United States during the war and lost many people then. Because they were allied with the United States, thousands were driven out of Laos to refugee camps in Thailand, and they subsequently immigrated to the United States.

__F__ **8.** Paradoxically, although creativity flourished among European men during this time, women's status fell as women in large numbers were persecuted and burned as witches. Creative and independent women were especially vulnerable; women's power was suppressed and maligned to such an extent that today "witches" are laughed at and ridiculed, and the persecution of women is barely remembered.

__F__ **9.** Mexican and Mexican American women traditionally have occupied an important place in the home but also have been involved in political and labor struggles. (A good source of information on this subject is Adelaida R. Del Castillo [Ed.], *Between Borders: Essays on Mexicana/Chicana History* [Encino, CA: Floricanto Press, 1990].)

__T__ **10.** Songhay was one of a number of highly advanced empires in Africa, a fact rarely developed in textbooks. Some books still perpetuate the myth of Africa as the "dark continent," despite increasing archaeological evidence that it may have been the seat of civilization where the human species originated.

Multiple Choice

__b__ **1.** This is an example of how some European Americans have appropriated a song created by another racial group and passed it off as their own. This has happened over and over again, particularly with music created by African Americans.

__d__ **2.** The acronym stands for League of United Latin American Citizens.

__c__ **3.** In fact, Benjamin Franklin is said to have obtained many of his ideas for the Federation of States from this organization.

__a__ **4.** It has been introduced every year since then.

__f__ **5.** While there is evidence ranging from well established to speculative that all of the people mentioned in (a) through (e) arrived in the Americas on about the dates indicated, the best answer is probably (f), inasmuch as millions of Native Americans were present long before any of these others arrived. In fact, to speak of the "discovery of America" is an insult to Native Americans, as it seems to imply that the Americas had no significance until someone who was not Native American arrived and "discovered" them.

__c__ **6.** It is interesting that despite this attitude toward African Americans, Lincoln later became known as the "Great Emancipator." His position on slavery was probably dictated more by politics than by moral concerns.

___a___ **7.** As semisovereign nations, several Native American nations have their own newspapers. Some, such as the Menominee, produce their own license plates. Many maps of the United States still do not recognize American Indian reservations, which perpetuates the invisibility of these governmental units among the non–American Indian population.

___c___ **8.** There were also many other incidents of violence against Italians in the late 1800s.

___d___ **9.** A more plausible answer is, of course, that the surgeon was the boy's mother.

___c___ **10.** A first-generation Japanese American is called *issei*, and a second-generation Japanese American is called *nisei*. These are Japanese terms that Japanese Americans use to describe themselves in the United States.

Matching

___g___ **1.** His most well-known novel is *Native Son*.

___d___ **2.** The college was called the Daytona Educational and Industrial School; it was for African American girls.

___a___ **3.** She was jailed for her actions in the Pecan Shellers' strike in 1937.

___n___ **4.** She was a representative from Hawaii and the only Asian American woman to serve in Congress.

___c___ **5.** She was the first African American to sing at Carnegie Hall; African Americans had previously been prohibited from singing there (as well as many other places).

___i___ **6.** She is currently on the art department's faculty at the University of California–Los Angeles.

___h___ **7.** He helped organize the grape boycott with César Chavez.

___l___ **8.** She is best known for her novel *Ceremony*.

___j___ **9.** He fought state and federal authorities for land grants to Latinos that were legally protected by the Treaty of Guadalupe.

___o___ **10.** He is best known for his book *Before the Mayflower*.

___e___ **11.** A member of the Menominee Nation, she has also taught at the University of Wisconsin–Madison.

___b___ **12.** He publishes widely in scholarly publications, as well as in popular magazines such as *Ebony*.

___p___ **13.** She was one of several European American women who first became politically active fighting against slavery, and then channeled that activism into fighting for women's right to vote. Unlike many European American feminists, however, she was not troubled by the possibility that African American men might become enfranchised before women.

___k___ **14.** A former Japanese American internment camp prisoner, she has published numerous stories.

___m___ **15.** Her most well-known novel is *Their Eyes Were Watching God*.

___f___ **16.** His best-known book is *Occupied America*.

▶ ACTION RESEARCH ACTIVITY 5.2

Classroom and School Assessment

Activity 5.2 is designed for the teacher or administrator interested in assessing his or her own workplace. Student teachers can use this instrument as well, substituting a specific teacher's name for reference to "you" and "your classroom" where appropriate. Indicate in the blank: to a great extent; somewhat; very little; not at all.

Classroom Level

_____ 1. To what extent do you consider affirming human diversity a top priority for your teaching?

_____ 2. To what extent do visuals (charts, pictures, and so on) reflect race, gender, sexual orientation, and disability diversity in a nonstereotypic manner?

_____ 3. To what extent do your regular instructional materials include people who differ by race, sex, class, language, sexual orientation, and disability in a nonstereotypic manner?

_____ 4. To what extent do resource materials include people who differ by race, sex, class, language, sexual orientation, and disability in a nonstereotypic manner?

_____ 5. To what extent does your plan for selecting materials include multicultural education criteria?

_____ 6. To what extent do your daily lessons reflect human diversity?

_____ 7. To what extent do your long-range curriculum plans promote multiculturalism and multilingualism?

_____ 8. Other than on special occasions, to what extent do you use resource people with various racial and social class backgrounds, those of both sexes, those of different sexual orientations, and those with disabilities?

_____ 9. To what extent do you use different strategies to teach students with different learning styles and skill levels?

_____ 10. To what extent do your teaching strategies promote active learning and critical thinking?

_____ 11. To what extent do you set and maintain high expectations for all your students?

_____ 12. To what extent is nonsexist and nonheterosexist language used?

_____ 13. To what extent do grading and grouping practices encourage and reward success for all students equally?

_____ 14. To what extent do your tests reflect sensitivity to multicultural education?

_____ 15. To what extent do plans for "special event" celebrations reflect diversity based on race, ethnicity, religion, or gender?

_____ 16. To what extent do you try actively to communicate with parents, especially those who live at or below the poverty level, are minorities, or speak a language other than English?

_____ 17. To what extent are notices sent home in the parents' language?

School Level

_____ 1. To what extent does the school philosophy explicitly address multicultural education?

_____ 2. To what extent do visuals in the hall or office (e.g., pictures, bulletin boards, and so on) reflect race, gender, disability, sexual orientation, and language diversity in a nonstereotypic manner?

_____ 3. To what extent is there a plan to ensure that curriculum and classroom materials schoolwide reflect multicultural education?

_____ 4. To what extent does the plan for selecting materials include multicultural education criteria?

_____ 5. To what extent do library materials reflect cultural and language diversity, both sexes, gays, lesbians, bisexuals, and people with disabilities in a nonstereotypic manner?

_____ 6. To what extent are resources, in-service, and planning time made available to help the staff work with multicultural and bilingual education?

_____ 7. To what extent are cooperative working relationships between special education and regular education staff supported and encouraged?

_____ 8. To what extent do policies and practices for assigning students to instructional groups and courses facilitate equal opportunity and equal access to a strong education?

_____ 9. To what extent are boys and girls offered the same education?

_____ 10. To what extent does the school support and encourage bilingualism or multilingualism for all students?

_____ 11. To what extent are notices sent home in the parents' and caregivers' language?

_____ 12. To what extent does the school staffing pattern provide students with diverse role models in nonstereotypic roles?

_____ 13. To what extent do plans for "special event" celebrations reflect diversity based on race, ethnicity, religion, gender, or disability?

_____ 14. To what extent do discipline policies and procedures treat all students and student groups equally and equitably?

_____ 15. To what extent are testing procedures nonbiased and used to help teach rather than categorize students?

_____ 16. To what extent is there a plan to involve actively all parents and caregivers, especially those who live at or below the poverty level and those with minority backgrounds?

_____ 17. To what extent is instruction available in the language of linguistic minorities, including American Sign Language?

_____ 18. To what extent are facilities accessible to students and parents and caregivers with physical and visual disabilities?

_____ 19. To what extent do school lunch menus reflect the culturally diverse tastes of students?

_____ **20.** To what extent do extracurricular activities provide for the diverse interests, cultural backgrounds, and physical capabilities of students?

_____ **21.** To what extent are students actively invited to participate in extracurricular activities, regardless of race, sex, social class, sexual orientation, or disability?

▶ ACTION RESEARCH ACTIVITY 5.3

What Do Kids Already Know? (And Where Did They Learn It?)

This is an interview to find out what (possibly inaccurate) knowledge kids bring to school with them about different groups and where they got that knowledge. The idea is that multicultural education of a sort is already going on in kids' daily lives. The issue for teachers often is not whether kids should learn about other groups but what the school should do to develop or even correct what kids are learning elsewhere.

When interviewing, ask about several groups, such as the following, select any group(s) except the one(s) the student is a member of:

African American males	European American	Latino/a American
African American	females living at the	males
females	poverty level	Mexican American
American Indians	European American	females
Arab Americans	males living at the	Puerto Ricans
Chinese Americans	poverty level	Southeast Asians
Cuban Americans	Filipino Americans	People who are blind
European American	Japanese Americans	or deaf
middle-class females	Jewish Americans	People in wheelchairs

1. Have you had any personal contact with [group]? If not, have you heard the term or do you know who they are? (You may have to give some equivalent terms or an example; if the student still does not know, select another group.)

2. If I were a visitor from outer space trying to find out more about the United States, how would you describe [group] to me?
   a. What have you heard about them?
   b. What have you seen?
   c. What has your own personal experience taught you?

3. How certain do you feel the information you have is accurate?

4. Where did you learn most of your information? (After the student has responded, probe to find out what was learned from each of the sources below.)
   a. parents, family
   b. TV
   c. movies
   d. books
   e. magazines, comics
   f. school
   g. personal experience

    h. the computer

    i. music

    j. Internet

▶ **LESSON PLAN**[2]

Thanksgiving

Subject Area: Multiple areas

Grade Level: Preschool

Time: One week

Objectives

1. Children will appreciate and be thankful for themselves and their families.
2. Children will develop familiarity with Thanksgiving holiday traditions.
3. Children will acquire vocabulary associated with the Thanksgiving season.
4. Children will develop skills in a wide range of areas, at age-appropriate developmental levels.

Suggested Procedures

1. Serve breakfast for children on the free-breakfast program. Select food items that reflect Thanksgiving colors, and use Thanksgiving table decorations. Encourage children to role-play a family gathering. Encourage children to brush their teeth by singing the "Brush Your Teeth" song.
2. More food has been added to the kitchen area this week because the children are aware that Thanksgiving will happen soon. During play time, encourage children to play out the various roles and ceremonies they see at home.
3. Place art projects on two tables. At one table, children make images of Pilgrims and Indians enjoying the first Thanksgiving dinner. At the other table, children create a decoration for their family's Thanksgiving table.
4. Read *Pumpkin Circle: The Story of a Garden* by Levenson, George and Thaler, Shravel, and discuss how pumpkins can be used. Then give children pumpkin seeds to count and to use to represent various numbers from one to ten.
5. With adult support, the children prepare batter for pumpkin cupcakes. They scoop it into the cupcake pan for the teacher to bake.
6. Read to the class *Patty's Pumpkin Patch* by Sloat.

Evaluation

By observing children's responses to the various activities, evaluate their grasp of the Thanksgiving holiday.

Resources

Levenson, G., & Thaler, S. (1999). *Pumpkin circle: The story of a garden*. Berkeley, CA: Tricycle.

Sloat, T. (1999). *Patty's pumpkin patch*. New York: Putnam.

[2]*Source:* Joya Chavarin, Oakland, California.

Giving Thanks

Subject Area: Multiple areas
Grade Level: Preschool
Time: One week

Objectives

1. Children will appreciate and be thankful for themselves, their families, and nature.
2. Children will make appropriate decisions about use of time.
3. Children will demonstrate the ability to relate to people who are different from themselves.
4. Children will develop skills in a wide range of areas, at age-appropriate developmental levels.

Suggested Procedures

1. Serve breakfast for children on the free-breakfast program. Encourage children to take part in breakfast preparation and clean up. While the children are washing their hands they sing the "Germs Go Down the Drain" song. Encourage children to brush their teeth while singing the "Brush Your Teeth" song during transition time.

2. Begin each day with a morning routine of greeting each child and her or his caregivers or parents to set the mood for the child's day, conduct the health check, obtain necessary information from parents, and allow time for transition for the children.

3. Give the children free choice in where to play. More food has been added to the kitchen area this week because the children are aware that Thanksgiving will happen soon. Encourage children to play out the various roles and ceremonies they see at home.

4. Have the children water the pumpkins they planted earlier in the year as a way of taking care of the environment. Read *Pumpkin Circle: The Story of a Garden* by Levenson, George and Thaler, Shravel, and discuss the pumpkin seed planting earlier in the year. Initiate conversation by reflecting on the process of growing the pumpkins. Later in the week, children pick their pumpkins. Each child washes his or her pumpkin for use.

5. Offer new and unexplored materials on two tables. At one table, children are encouraged to make images of themselves using an abundance of materials in various ways. At the other table, children are able to manipulate sequential cards with adult support. Later in the week this activity is replaced with pumpkin seeds; children who are interested clean pumpkin seeds and count how many are in each pumpkin.

6. Have the children listen to one of their favorite songs, "We Are Family." The teacher then transitions into a story, "Being With You This Way," while the children clap to the beat of the story's rhythm.

7. With adult support, have the children prepare batter for pumpkin cupcakes and scoop it into the cupcake pan for the teacher to bake. At the other table, have a food-matching game available.

8. Encourage children's parents or caregivers to bring items to share with the class. (This week, a child's parent brought in ten pounds of grapes from his job, a produce company. The children became very interested, and the teachers changed their curriculum to meet their interest. The teachers asked, "What could we do with all these grapes?" The children decided to make grape jelly for their families. They began by washing the grapes.)

9. Give children seeds to plant to keep the cycle of life going. After picking the pumpkins, the children may now want to plant a grapevine—give them seeds to do so during outside time.

Evaluation

1. Observing children as they take care of each other and of their pumpkins, evaluate their developing appreciation themselves, their families, and nature.

2. Observe children's interactions with each other in order to evaluate their developing ability to relate to those who differ from themselves.

Giving Thanks

WHY THE CHANGES?

Curriculum Content

The "Before" lesson is a stereotypic approach to Thanksgiving. The focus of the unit is on learning about the holiday itself. The "After" offers an alternative. Rather than focusing on the Thanksgiving dinner, Pilgrims, and American Indians, the "After" plan focuses on appreciation for family, peers, and nature. The unit includes planting and care for plants. In addition, families are invited to join the class. Children are taught to respect and be thankful for other people and nature, rather than focusing on the trappings of the holiday *per se*.

Curriculum Materials

In the classroom of the author of the "After" plan, children were surrounded by multicultural children's literature. While the "Before" plan lists two children's books and the "After" plan lists only one, children in the "After" plan are offered more choices and can choose to read or look at multicultural children's books throughout the year.

Instructional Strategies

In the "Before" plan, the whole class does the same thing. In the "After" plan, children are offered choices. Furthermore, their choices allow them to explore and are constructed around learning.

Home and Community Relationships

In the "Before" plan, families are absent. In the "After" plan, the teacher has regular interaction with families. The teacher greets and talks briefly with parents as they drop off their children. Parents are invited to share with the class. When the teacher taught this particular class, a parent who works in agriculture brought in grapes, and the teacher then constructed a short lesson around the grapes. In that way, parent contributions became a part of the curriculum.

▶ LESSON PLAN

Families

Subject Area: Multiple areas

Grade Level: K–1

Time: One week

Students: English Language Learners

Objectives

1. Students will describe and identify the members of their own families and answer questions about their family.

2. Students will distinguish between an activity performed indoors and one performed outdoors.

3. Students will use symbolic and D'Nealian-style writing.

4. Students will compare and contrast nontraditional families using key English vocabulary, including *mother, father, son, daughter, sister* and *brother*.

Suggested Procedures

1. To introduce the week's theme, have the class as a whole use magazine cutouts to create a collage that shows various families. Follow this activity with a whole-class discussion that brings out the idea that families are made up of many different people. Encourage the children to introduce their own families. Tell them that they will learn about their classroom members' families in greater depth.

2. Show the children the illustrations on the cover and title page of the book *Who's in a Family?* (written by Robert Skutch, illustrated by Laura Nienhaus). Read the title. As they look at the title page, ask children to make predictions about the story. Read the story as you point under each word to help children connect speech to print.

3. Have the children construct family portraits as an art project. Have them decide who will be included in their family portrait (nuclear or extended), and how many adults and children there are. Help children label family members with their names. Ask children to describe their completed pictures with family member names, their relationship, and any other information they wish to give.

4. The next day, read *All Families Are Different* (written by Sol Gordon, illustrated by Vivien Cohen). As a writing activity, have students copy today's date onto the first line on the top right-hand side of the paper. Ask them, "What is special about your family?" Model appropriate conventions of writing and letter formation. Students then write symbolic and D'Nealian-style responses. Have students draw a picture to match their written response.

5. On the third day of the unit, read and discuss *Why Am I an Only Child?* (written by Jane Annunziata et al.). In this book, a girl very much wants a baby brother. Follow up by having students draw pictures of their families in their favorite family activity. Then have students sort the activities and place them according to indoor or outdoor activities on the classroom chart.

6. The next day, read and discuss *The Room in My Heart* (written by Beverly Evans, illustrated by Christopher Nick). This is a story about a child who wonders if Mommy will still love her other children after the new baby is born. Have available a basket of books about different family stories. During DEAR time (Drop Everything and Read), have students choose books from this basket. For English language development, ask students in English to recall and identify the different family members as the books are individually displayed. Have them describe different family structures by choosing people and displaying them on the felt board to represent each book.

7. If an option is needed, read Rosemarie Hausherr's *Celebrating Families*, which gives brief descriptions of many different kinds of families, both traditional and nontraditional.

8. For the last day of the unit, create a big book of families, using students' art and writing projects. Invite families to join the class, participating in various activities throughout their school day. Share this book with the class and their families.

Evaluation

1. Evaluate students' understanding of family members, family relationships, and family structures based on their writings and class discussion.

2. Evaluate students' use of D'Nealian-style writing based on their writing samples; identify letters they are having difficulty making for further instruction and practice.

3. Identify students' comprehension of "indoors" and "outdoors" based on sorting activity.

Resources

Annunziata, J., Nemiroff, M. (1998). *Why am I an only child?* Washington, DC: Magination.
Evans, B., & Nick, C. (Illustrator). (2000). *The room in my heart*. Sisters, OR: Loyal.
Gordon, S., & Cohen, V. (Illustrator). (2000). *All families are different*. Amherst, NY: Prometheus Books.
Hausherr, R. (1997). *Celebrating families*. New York: Scholastic.
Skutch, R., & Nienhaus, L. (Illustrator). (1998). *Who's in a family?* Berkeley, CA: Tricycle.

Families[3]

AFTER

Subject Area: Multiple areas

Grade Level: K–1

Time: One week

Students: English language learners

[3] *Source:* Diana Flores, R. O. Hardin School, Hollister, California.

Objectives

1. Students will describe and identify the members of their own families, and answer questions about their family using the high-frequency word *mi*.

2. Students will identify the makeup of a traditional family, a single-parent family, a gay- or lesbian-headed family, and a grandparent-headed family.

3. Students will distinguish between an activity performed indoors and one performed outdoors.

4. Students will use symbolic and D'Nealian-style writing.

5. Students will compare and contrast nontraditional families using key English vocabulary, including mother, father, son, daughter, sister, brother, stepmother, stepfather, and so on.

Suggested Procedures

1. To introduce the week's theme, have the class as a whole use magazine cutouts to create a collage that shows families from various countries, cultures, and types. The teacher contributes to the collage by including every family type on which the week focuses. Follow this activity with a whole-class discussion that brings out the idea that families are made up of many different people. Encourage the children to introduce their own families. Tell them that they will learn about their classroom members' families in greater depth.

2. Show and read *Antonio's Card/La tarjeta de Antonio*, by Rigsberto Gonzales, where a young boy learns that love defines a family, no matter what it looks like.

3. Show the children the illustrations on the cover and title page of the book *Con Mi Familia* (written by Olga Ramero, illustrated by Pauline Rodriquez Howard). In this story, a little girl introduces her family and what they do together. Read the title, then tell the children that they will get to know the family in the story. As they look at the title page, ask them to make predictions about the story. Read the story as you point under each word to help children connect speech to print.

4. Have the children construct family portraits as an art project. Have them decide who will be included in their family portrait (nuclear, extended, blended), and how many adults and children there are. Help children label family members with their names. Ask children to describe their completed pictures with family member names, their relationship, and any other information they wish to give. To practice the high-frequency word *mi*, ask students to tell their teacher "mi. . . es. . ." responding to the familial pictures they drew.

5. The next day, read *La Cama de Mamá/Mama's Bed* (written by Joi Carlen, illustrated by Morella Fuenmayor). This is a story about a family of three and what they can do in their mother's bed, such as playing, being held, and sleeping. As a writing activity, have students copy today's date onto the first line on the top right-hand side of the paper. Ask them, "What do you and your family members do at bedtime?" Model appropriate conventions of writing and letter formation.

Students then write symbolic and D'Nealian-style responses. Students draw a picture to match their written response.

6. On the third day of the unit, read and discuss *One Dad, Two Dads, Brown Dad, Blue Dads* (written by Johnny Valentine, illustrated by Melody Sarecky). In this book, a girl questions a boy about his two blue-skinned dads, who are gay. She discovers that despite their blueness, they do all the usual things that other dads do. Follow up by having students draw pictures of their families in their favorite family activity. Then have students sort the activities and place them according to indoor or outdoor activities on the classroom chart.

7. The next day, read and discuss *Heather Has Two Mommies* (written by Leslea Newman, illustrated by Diana Souza). This is a story about Heather, whose favorite number is two. She has two arms, two legs, and so on; she also has two mommies. Have available a basket of books about different family structures. During DEAR time (Drop Everything and Read), have students choose books from this basket. For English language development, ask students in English to recall and identify the different family members as the books are individually displayed. Have them describe different family structures by choosing people and displaying them on the felt board to represent each book. A second book for this activity is *Mom and Mum Are Getting Married*, by Ken Setterington. It is about love and happiness in a changing world.

8. For the last day of the unit, create a big book of families, using students' art and writing projects. Title it *Con Mi Familia (Our Version)*. Invite families to join the class, participating in various activities throughout their school day. Share this book with the class and their families.

Evaluation

1. Evaluate students' understanding and appreciation of family members, family relationships, and multiple family structures based on their writings and class discussion.

2. Evaluate students' use of D'Nealian-style writing based on their writing samples; identify letters they are having difficulty making for further instruction and practice.

3. Through their oral discussion of their families, evaluate students' ability to use high-frequency words in both English and Spanish.

4. Identify students' comprehension of "indoors" and "outdoors" based on sorting activity.

Resources

Carlen, J. (2000). *La cama de Mamá/Mama's bed*. Illustrated by M. Fuenmayor. Volcano, CA: Volcano.

Gonzales, R. (2005). *Antonio's card/La tarjeta de Antonio*. Illustrated by C. C. Alvarez. San Francisco: Children's Book Press.

Newman, L. (2000). *Heather has two mommies*. Illustrated by D. Souza. Boston: Alyson.

Romero, O., & Rodriguez Howard, P. (1998). *Con mi familia*. Carmel, CA: Hampton-Brown.

Setterington, K. (2004). *Mom and mum are getting married*. Illustrated by A. Priestly. Toronto: Second Story.

Valentine, J., & Sarecky, M. (Illustrator). (1994). *One dad, two dads, brown dad, blue dads*. Illustrated by M. Sarecky. Boston: Alyson.

Families

Curriculum Content

This family unit was adopted and modified from the current language arts and English language development programs that the author's district currently utilizes. This unit is designed for K–1 but may be adapted and modified to any grade level. The "Before" unit addresses diverse family structures, but only up to a point. In the "After" unit, each activity has been modified with the sensitivity that marginalized groups are not usually introduced into the classroom curriculum. Many of the author's students, when questioned about the family, answered with the "traditional family portrait": mom, dad, brothers, and sisters. When asked if they knew of other family types, those only experiencing the nontraditional family responded with examples of a single parent and being raised by grandparents.

Many may not feel that kindergartners are capable of this type of lesson, which includes gay and lesbian parents. The teacher who created the unit soon overcame this underestimation of the students' ability to learn. At the time of planning this unit, she pondered the ability of her students to discuss and gain knowledge from this learning experience. As it turned out, their oral histories were very explicit and colorful to listen to. Being an educator of color, she used her own life experiences. Her experiences often paralleled the children's lives, which made this learning experience even more enjoyable. Utilizing the book *Family Pictures* (Yahp), she would remind the students that she herself went through many of those experiences. Personalizing this book made the students want to draw more information from their teacher, who reminded them (but most of all herself) that her heritage and culture were very important.

This grade level should not be held back because of the teacher's fear of not being able to make this learning experience worth while. The educator must project her or his own enthusiasm onto the learning experience: "Grab them" with whatever it takes, and don't let go. This lesson, as any other, would not have been attempted if there were the risk of a negative learning outcome.

Resources

Yahp, Beth. (1994). *Family Pictures*. Pymble, NSW, Australia: Angos of Robertson.

Language

The "Before" plan is all in English. The books are in English, and the discussion is in English. The "After" plan is bilingual; some books are in English and others are in Spanish. In the "After" plan, the teacher works on students' ability to use words and sentences correctly in both languages, as well as to read meaningful literature in both.

▶ LESSON PLAN

Estimation

Subject Area: Mathematics

Grade Level: 2–4

Time: One or two days

Objectives

1. Students will explain what estimation is and how it differs from guessing.
2. Students will make reasonable estimates.
3. Students will check their estimates by comparing them with real measurements.

Suggested Procedures

1. Show students a glass jar full of jelly beans, which you have already counted. Ask how many jelly beans are in the jar. Someone will suggest that they count them. Ask students first to give their best guess as to how many jelly beans are in the bowl.
2. Ask students to estimate the number of boys or girls in the classroom; then have them count to check their estimates. Discuss with them questions such as the following:
   a. How did you go about selecting your estimate?
   b. What clues can you use to help make an estimate?
3. Ask students to estimate the distance between two objects. Compare true measurement (tm) and estimate measurement (em).
4. Ask students to observe and record estimates of different measuring units and to select appropriate measuring units to check estimates.
5. Have students discuss their experience with estimation in terms of the following questions:
   a. How accurate were your estimates?
   b. Which estimates seemed easier? more difficult? Why?
   c. What clues were you able to use?
   d. In what situations might you want to estimate?

Evaluation

Give students a quantity to estimate, and have them explain why they think the estimate is reasonable and then check it.

Estimation

Subject Area: Mathematics

Grade Level: 2–4

Time: Two days

Objectives

1. Students will explain what estimation is and how it differs from guessing.
2. Students will make reasonable estimates.
3. Students will check their estimates by comparing them with real measurements.
4. Students will recognize race and gender biases in various aspects of their lives.

Suggested Procedures

1. Show students a large picture or poster that portrays a great number of people. Ask students how many people are in the picture. Students will probably start to count; ask them first to give their best guess. Explain the word estimate and the difference between estimation and guessing. Then count the number of people in the picture; ask students how accurate their estimates were.

2. Have students estimate the number of males, females, Asian Americans, blond-haired people, and so on in the picture. Then have them count to check their estimates. Discuss with them questions such as the following:
   a. How did you go about selecting your estimate?
   b. What clues can you use to help make an estimate?

3. Ask students to estimate the number of male teachers and female teachers in the school (teachers should have this information available). Ask them also to estimate other staffing patterns, such as the number of custodians and teachers of color, female secretaries, and so on. Then use this to discuss the following questions:
   a. Which estimates were more accurate and why?
   b. Did stereotypes or expectations influence their estimates?
   c. Was the race or gender of different staff members relevant?

4. Have students estimate the number of each of the following groups represented in pictures in one of their textbooks: European American males, European American females, African American males, African American females, Latino males, Latina females, American Indian males, American Indian females, Asian American males, Asian American females, and persons with disabilities. Then have them count to check their estimates. Use this to discuss questions similar to those in procedure 3.

5. Ask students to estimate the number of female physicians in the local hospital versus the number of male physicians. Ask them to estimate the number of physicians of color versus the total number of physicians.
   Have this information available. Discuss with students questions similar to those in procedure 3.

Evaluation

1. Through class discussion, assess the reasonableness of the estimations that students make in class and their understanding of estimation.

2. Through class discussion, assess students' awareness of race and gender biases.

Estimation

WHY THE CHANGES?

Curriculum Content

This lesson applies the content of a subject area that is often viewed as impossible to make multicultural—math—to a social concern without sacrificing the mathematical operations being taught. In math, we often give more attention to the mathematical operations we are teaching than to the content of the problems we ask students to solve. The problems are treated as a vehicle for practicing the mathematical operation more than as worthwhile areas of investigation in themselves. The "After" plan applies the mathematical concept of estimation to a social issue involving race and gender bias. It then asks students to consider not only the accuracy of their estimates but also the significance of their findings.

▶ LESSON PLAN

Tie-Dyeing

BEFORE

Subject Area: Art
Grade Level: 4–6
Time: Two class periods

Objectives

1. Students will identify primary and secondary colors.
2. Students will produce patterns through tie-dyeing.

Suggested Procedures

1. Show the color chart. Explain the meaning of primary and secondary colors.
   a. Primary colors—red, yellow, blue—are so called because they cannot be made by mixing any other colors.
   b. Secondary colors—orange, green, violet—are colors that come about from mixing the primary colors:

   Red + Yellow = Orange

   Yellow + Blue = Green

   Blue + Red = Violet

2. Explain to the class that they will be mixing secondary colors from primary colors. Pass out bowls of dye (one red, one yellow, one blue) and three empty bowls to each student. Have each student mix each of the three secondary colors.

3. Pass out 12-by-12-inch cloth and several pieces of string to each student.

4. Explain the concept of pattern. Pattern is the repetition of lines or shapes. The chief purpose of pattern is to provide a decorative quality to enrich the surface of the cloth.

5. Explain the principles of tie-dyeing. Cloth is wrapped in various ways with the pieces of string to make a pattern. The cloth is then put in the dye bath. The cloth underneath the string resists the dye and stays white, while the rest of the cloth turns the color of the dye, thus making a pattern.

6. Have each student wrap his or her cloth in the pattern desired; then dip all of it or sections of it in the dye.

7. When the cloth is dry, have each student unwrap his or her own piece, compare it with others in the group, and discuss how the pattern was obtained.

Evaluation

Assess students' understanding of the concepts of color and pattern and of the process of tie-dyeing through the quality of their tie-dyed products.

Tie-Dyeing[4]

Subject Area: Art
Grade Level: 4–6
Time: Two or three class periods

Objectives

1. Students will identify primary and secondary colors.
2. Students will appreciate the traditional Native American use of natural dyes to obtain various primary and secondary colors.
3. Students will produce patterns through tie-dyeing.
4. Students will appreciate the traditional Black/African use of pattern in clothing.
5. Students will work with peers of different races and gender.

Suggested Procedures

1. Divide the class into groups of six students each. Groups should be as race and gender mixed as possible.
2. Show the color chart. Explain the meaning of primary and secondary colors.
   a. Primary colors—red, yellow, blue—are so called because they cannot be made by mixing any other colors.
   b. Secondary colors—orange, green, violet—are colors that come about from mixing the primary colors:

   Red + Yellow = Orange
   Yellow + Blue = Green
   Blue + Red + Violet
3. Explain that art for the Native American Indian was not separate from life; rather, it was a balance of tradition and spirituality. Color to the Native American Indian had energy and spiritual qualities. Read examples of American Indian poetry and traditional stories involving color, such as the following:

   Prayer After Singing Gahe Songs (Chiricahua)
   Big Blue Mountain Spirit,
   The home made of blue clouds,
   The cross made of the blue mirage,
   There, you have begun to live,
   There, is the life of goodness,
   I am grateful for that made of goodness there.
   Big Yellow Mountain Spirit in the south,
   Your spiritually hale body is made of yellow clouds;
   Leader of the Mountain Spirits, holy Mountain Spirit,
   You live by means of the good of this life.
   Big White Mountain Spirit in the west,
   Your spiritually hale body is made of the white mirage;
   Holy Mountain Spirit, leader of the Mountain Spirits,
   I am happy over your words,
   You are happy over my words.

[4]*Source:* P. Lloyd Kollman, Kenosha, Wisconsin, and Debra Owens, Racine, Wisconsin.

Big Black Mountain Spirit in the north,
Your spiritually hale body is made of black clouds;
In that way, Big Black Mountain Spirit,
Holy Mountain Spirit, leader of the Mountain Spirits,
I am happy over your words,
You are happy over my words,
Now it is good.

(Hoijer, 1938, p. 69)

Song of the Sky Loom (Tewa Indian Weaving Song)
Oh our Mother the Earth, oh our Father the Sky,
Your children are we, and with tired backs
We bring you the gifts that you love.
Then weave for us a garment of brightness;
May the warp be the white light of morning,
May the weft be the red light of evening,
May the fringes be the falling rain,
May the border be the standing rainbow.
Thus weave for us a garment of brightness
That we may walk fittingly where birds sing,
That we may walk fittingly where the grass is green,
Oh our Mother the Earth, oh our Father the Sky!

(Spinden, 1933, p. 94)

4. Explain that many Native American nations got the colors used in dyeing wool from natural plants. Give examples:

   Red—Juniper ash (tree), bark of the root Cercocarpus parvifolius
   Blue—Indigo (plant), blue corn, blue clay
   Yellow—Rabbit weed (flower), Chamizo blossoms and twigs

5. Explain to students that they will mix secondary colors from the primary colors. Pass out three buckets of dye (one red, one yellow, one blue) and three empty buckets to each group. Have each group of six pair up (two-two-two). Each pair of students will mix a secondary color for their group (orange, green, violet).

6. Pass out 12-by-12-inch cloth to each student and several pieces of string.

7. Explain the concept of pattern. Pattern is the repetition of lines or shapes. The chief purpose of pattern is to provide a decorative quality to enrich the surface of the cloth.

8. Explain the principles of tie-dyeing. Cloth is wrapped in various ways with the pieces of string to make a pattern. The cloth underneath the string resists the dye and stays white while the rest of the cloth turns the color of the dye, thus making a pattern.

9. Explain to the class that in many Black/African cultures pattern and tie-dyeing are a way to decorate clothing. Show a sample of the loose-fitting garment called the *dashiki*, which probably originated in West Africa. Show examples of African animals as well.

10. Have each student wrap his or her cloth in the pattern desired; then dip all or sections of it in the dyes in the group.

11. When the cloth is dry, have each student unwrap his or her own piece, compare it with others in the group, and discuss how the pattern was achieved.

Figure 5.1 Wall Hanging

12. Pass out one 48-by-32-inch burlap piece and some glue to each group. Explain that each student in the group will contribute his or her tie-dyed cloth to make a large wall hanging for the class. It is up to the group members to decide on the design for the wall hanging. Figure 5.1 shows an illustration of a wall hanging made by one group. While the students are working on their wall hanging, play West African music.

13. When the wall hangings are finished, display one on each wall.

Evaluation

1. Through the quality of their tie-dyed products, assess students' understanding of the concepts of color and pattern and the process of tie-dyeing.

2. Through class discussion, assess students' appreciation of other cultures (Native American, Black/African).

3. Assess students' ability to work cooperatively and to contribute to the class through observation.

References

Hoijer, H. (1938). *Chiricahua and Mescalero Apache texts*. Chicago: University of Chicago Publications in Anthropology, Linguistic Series.

Spinden, H.J. (1933). *Songs of the Tewa*. New York: Exposition of Indian Tribal Arts.

Tie-Dyeing

WHY THE CHANGES?

Curriculum Content

The "After" plan explores the cultural uses and origins of the concepts in the "Before" plan for the purpose of enhancing students' understanding of them and their knowledge and appreciation of other cultural groups. Content about how American Indians mixed color teaches students how colors can be achieved in ways other than using purchased dyes, as well as how color is derived from nature. The American Indian poetry teaches students to view color aesthetically and symbolically. Content about African use of tie-dyeing teaches students about the origins of this art form, as well as about the technique and thought behind one kind of African textile.

Grouping of Students

In the "Before" plan, each student works alone. The "After" plan encourages cooperation for reasons similar to those in the Human Relations approach: to encourage the appreciation of peers and the development of skills and attitudes for cooperating.

▶ LESSON PLAN

Folk and Fairy Tales

Subject Area: Language Arts
Grade Level: 4–6
Time: Three days

Objectives

1. Students will appreciate lesser-known fairy tales.
2. Students will explain the origins of fairy tales.
3. Students will develop dramatization skills.

Suggested Procedures

1. Ask students what fairy tales they are familiar with (such as "Cinderella" and "Snow White").
2. Introduce some lesser-known folk and fairy tales (such as "Stone Soup"). Explain to students what is known about the historical origin of these and the more popular fairy tales. Have students suggest reasons why the popularity of folk and fairy tales often persists.
3. Divide students into three groups. Have each group read one folk or fairy tale. Then have them work out a dramatization for it. Help students improvise costumes and props. Have students perform for each other.

Evaluation

1. Assess students' appreciation and dramatization skills through their group presentations.
2. Through a test at the end of the unit, assess students' understanding of the origins of fairy tales.

Folk and Fairy Tales[5]

Subject Area: Language Arts
Grade Level: 4–6
Time: Four days

[5] *Source:* Earlier version contributed by Linda Roberts, Salem, Wisconsin.

Objectives

1. Students will analyze folk and fairy tales for racism, ageism, sexism, ablism, heterosexism, and classism.

2. Students will recognize stereotypic representations in folk and fairy tales.

3. Students will understand that literature often reflects the times in which it was written.

4. Students will develop small-group interaction skills and group relations.

5. Students will avoid stereotypes and stereotypic language in their writing and thinking.

6. Students will write folk and fairy tales from multicultural points of view.

7. Students will appreciate viewpoints other than their own and other than those presented in folk and fairy tales.

8. Students will learn that they can search on their own for books with gender, sexuality, ethnic, class, disability, and age stereotypes.

Suggested Procedures

1. Introduce some popular folk and fairy tales (such as "Cinderella" and "Snow White"). Ask students if they are familiar with these tales and to name others. Select one story for analysis. Have students brainstorm how the story depicts the perfect prince, perfect princess, perfect witch, and so on; record the findings on the board. Then ask the class to brainstorm the imperfect Prince and so on for comparing and contrasting. The lists will probably show that the story depicts "perfect" women primarily in passive roles, working in the kitchen, or following rather than leading. Most often, they are concerned with beauty, clothes, jewelry, and finding Prince Charming. Other females are depicted as little old women and wicked witches, with an occasional fairy godmother. Men are depicted as young, virile, handsome, solving problems, going on quests, slaying dragons, and rescuing maidens. Infrequently, a little old man is shown.
   Men are most often portrayed as strong and forceful, rarely displaying unmanly emotions. European fairy tales rarely have main characters that are not White, except an occasional stereotyped member of a European minority group. However, the movie Shrek (2000) features a prince and princess who do not adhere to the typical idea of the perfect prince and perfect princess. Ask students why the prince and princess in Shrek are different, and what they think about these differences. Shrek is available in video format, so the teacher may use it to supplement the lesson.

2. For the next day's assignment, ask students to bring in their own copies of folk and fairy tales to analyze (or they may use copies you have provided). Since many students may have their fairy tales on video, the teacher may consider having a video workstation setup.

3. Form cooperative groups based on students' interest in particular books or videos to analyze. Have each group role-play their book or video as it is originally written.

4. Remind students of the discussion in procedure 1. Ask the groups to rewrite their fairy tales from a nonstereotypic point of view, including groups that are

often omitted. Ask them also to explore nontraditional roles for men as well as women.

5. Have students role-play (in groups) their new version of the fairy tales. Discuss ways that the new versions are more egalitarian than the old ones and the ways students feel about both versions.

6. Have the class produce a booklet of their new fairy tales. It may be handwritten or produced on a word processor and should be illustrated. The booklet can be put in the library (complete with its own call number and card in the card catalog) and reproduced for each class member. This assignment can also make use of video recording. Students may write a script, make costumes, and film their production.

7. Introduce folk and fairy tales from cultures other than White and European, such as African American, Native American, Latino American, and Asian American. Also read folk tales from other countries, including those in Asia and Africa, pointing out literary style and story structure.

8. At the end of the unit, ask students to discuss how stereotypes can affect people's feelings and lives. Students should have the awareness needed to analyze literature for stereotypes on their own.

Evaluation

1. Through class discussion and the groups' analyses of the folk tales, assess students' ability to analyze folk and fairy tales for racism, sexism, ageism, ablism, heterosexism, and classism.

2. Through observation, assess students' small-group interaction skills.

3. Through their rewritten or video-recorded fairy tales, assess students' skill in writing and thinking multiculturally.

4. Through observation of their interactions and through the presence or absence of diverse viewpoints in their rewritten or video-recorded fairy tales, assess students' appreciation of other viewpoints.

Folk and Fairy Tales

WHY THE CHANGES?

Curriculum Materials

Folk and fairy tales often contain sexist and racist stereotypes and negative images of people with disabilities. The "Before" plan uses them without examining for stereotypes. The teacher can deliberately select some to be stereotype free, but it is more useful to teach students to recognize the stereotypes present within traditional folk and fairy tales. The "After" plan encourages students to examine materials for biases and stereotypes and to rewrite literature to make it more fair to diverse groups.

Curriculum Content

The "Before" plan does not specify the culture from which folk and fairy tales are drawn; most often they are from northern and western Europe. The "After" plan directs the teacher to teach folk and fairy tales from a variety of cultural groups.

Multiple Perspectives

In the "Before" plan, students share perspectives only when they suggest reasons fairy tales are popular. In the "After" plan, students share their perspectives about the fairy tales and their views about stereotypes. Students are also exposed to perspectives from various cultural groups on what constitutes a folk or fairy tale.

Grouping of Students

Both plans use cooperative learning. However, in the "After" plan, students not only plan and present a skit but also analyze and rewrite or re-record fairy tales.

▶ LESSON PLAN

Hidden Mythologies[6]

BEFORE

Subject Area: Language Arts (English language development)

Grade Level: 4–8

Time: Three or four weeks

Note: This lesson plan is written for Latino students who are learning English as a second language.

Objectives

1. Students will read and write a summary of a creation myth by identifying and sequencing the main ideas in the story.

2. Students will increase acquisition of English through discussion and carefully organized comprehension of questions in English.

Suggested Procedures

1. Discuss with students the definition of the term *myth*, since they will be reading a myth. According to the *Macmillan Dictionary for Students*, edited by William D. Halsey, a myth is a "traditional story of unknown authorship that expresses a belief of a particular people usually involving gods and heroes. A myth is an attempt to explain a phenomenon of nature, an event in history, or the origin of a particular custom, practice, or religious belief."

   This discussion will be in English. Tell students that the myth they will be reading is an Aztec myth. In the discussion, the question will be raised on the validity of myths: Are myths true? Students may be told that myths are beliefs, and beliefs cannot be proven. Myths and beliefs must be distinguished from fact. Facts can be proven. The Aztecs used these myths to explain their beliefs. The Aztecs were a civilization that was still developing in the sixteenth century.

2. Tell students to follow along in their own copies of the bilingual myth while the teacher reads the English version of *How We Came to the Fifth World/Como vinimos al quinto mundo* by *Harriet* Rohmer and *Mary* Anchondo. As an

[6] *Source:* Gloria Najera, Alisal Union School District, Salinas, California.

introduction, tell students that the Aztecs believed the world was destroyed four times, each time by a natural element or gods because of the evil or the imbalance the people caused. After the destruction of each world, one good couple survived. According to this story and Aztec mythology, the fifth world is the present world.

3. Since this story is divided into five parts, or five worlds, discuss the story with students to identify each world and state verbally in English how each world was destroyed. This activity is necessary to give students a general sense of the sequence of events.

4. Ask students to take turns reading about the first world aloud, while the teacher asks questions that have been prepared in advance to elicit comprehension of the storyline and increase the acquisition of English.

5. Ask students to write a summary about the first world in English. Ask them to re-read and edit their own summaries. Next, ask students to copy their summaries neatly and turn these in for further editing and corrections.

6. The teacher will edit and correct students' versions of the first world and will return these to students. Ask students to rewrite stories neatly on binder paper with mistakes corrected. Also ask students to illustrate their stories, since each student will make his or her own book.

7. Ask students to repeat procedures 4–6 to write about each world; each student will then have a copy of his or her own book.

Evaluation

1. Assess students' understanding of the myth by giving them a quiz each time they write their own version of each world of the myth. The questions on this quiz will have been carefully written in English by the teacher to gain an accurate assessment of the students' comprehension of the story in English.

2. Assess students' understanding of sequence by giving students a quiz with statements out of the order in which they occur in the story. The students' task is to arrange these statements in the proper sequence as they occurred in the story.

Resource

Halsey, W.D. (1984). *Macmillan Dictionary for Students*. New York: Simon & Schuster.

An Inspirational Glimpse of Aztec Mythology

AFTER

Subject Area: Language Arts (English language development)

Grade Level: 4–8

Time: Three or four weeks

Note: This lesson plan is written for Latino students who are learning English as a second language.

Objectives

1. Students will read and write a creation myth by identifying and sequencing the main ideas in the story.

2. Students will increase acquisition of English through discussion and carefully organized comprehension questions in English.

3. Students' identities will be validated by interviewing/recording parents' mythologies.

4. Students' histories will be validated by researching mythologies of their own ethnic ancestry.

Suggested Procedures—Lesson 1

1. Discuss with students the definition of the term *myth*, since they will be reading a myth. According to the *Macmillan Dictionary for Students*, edited by William D. Halsey, a myth is a "traditional story of unknown authorship that expresses a belief of a particular people usually involving gods and heroes. A myth is an attempt to explain a phenomenon of nature, an event in history, or the origin of a particular custom, practice, or religious belief."

   This discussion will be in Spanish to make sure students acquire adequate knowledge of the topic, especially since this is academic information being presented for the first time. Tell students that the myth they will be reading is an Aztec creation myth taken and deciphered from the Aztec calendar. In the discussion, the question will be raised on the validity of myths: Are myths true? Do not take a position, but do give information on Western and Meso-American views on mythology. As a follow-up lesson, you may want to show students the Aztec calendar and present the creation myth as shown on the face of the calendar.

2. Tell students to follow along in their own copies of the bilingual myth, while you read the Spanish version of *How We Came to the Fifth World/Como vinimos al quinto mundo* by *Harriet* Rohmer and *Mary* Anchondo. The myth is read in Spanish to give students "comprehensible input." As an introduction to the story, tell students that the Aztecs believed the world was destroyed four times, each time by a natural element or gods because of the "evil" or the imbalance the people caused. After the destruction of each world, one good couple survived. According to this story and Aztec mythology, the "fifth" world is the present world.

3. Since this story is divided into five parts, or five worlds, discuss the story with students, in Spanish ("comprehensible input"), having them briefly identify each world and state how each world was destroyed. This activity is necessary to give students a general sense of the sequence of events.

4. Ask students to read about the first world silently in English. Give a reasonable amount of time for most students to finish reading. On an overhead projector or on the blackboard, do a "webbing" activity: Put the central character (in this case, a god) in the center of a circle, and write the main ideas in the form of sentences or phrases around the circle. Have the whole class participate with you on this activity. This is done in English. Ask students to copy this information in journals; as a next step, students will use this information with a partner to write summaries in English about the first world. Tell students that these summaries will be made into books after corrections are made.

5. In advance, identify students with advanced English acquisition and students with less advanced language acquisition. Divide students into two groups and let students select a partner. Let students know that in the future you will identify and divide students into groups according to Spanish dominance. Stress the idea of the equitable value of both languages and the value of working cooperatively. Tell students that they will help each other edit their stories. In addition, they will be expected to illustrate their stories.

6. The following steps are taken from Katherine Davies Samway's *Writers' Workshop and Children Acquiring English as a Non-Native Language*. Ask students to write a summary about the first world in English. Ask them to reread and edit their own summaries.

7. Ask students to pair off with their partners and edit each other's summaries based on a rubric the class has developed together. Have one student read his or her essay while the other gives positive feedback and points out errors. (The student rubric is based on the district rubric for language arts/writing.)

8. Ask students to combine both summaries to create one version of the first world. This needs to be recopied neatly after corrections have been made. While one partner is recopying the story, have the other partner draw the illustration for the first world. Ask partners to decide which task each of them will do. They must take turns when writing subsequent versions of the other four worlds. Ask students to turn in recopied and corrected versions.

9. Request a conference with both partners to give positive feedback and point out errors, usually for areas students need to work on. Ask the students to make corrections on their papers as you point out errors. Ask them to rewrite their story and redo a final draft of drawings for publication.

10. Request that students repeat procedures 4–9 to write about each world.

11. Ask students to write their own ending to this creation myth by analyzing what changes we would need to make to save our world and keep it from being destroyed.

12. Show students how to make Aztec codices (folded fanlike books made with grocery bag paper).

Evaluation—Lesson 1

1. By reading their written summaries of myths when conferencing with students, assess students' understanding of sequencing.

2. By comparing each student's written rough drafts of the first world and the fifth world and doing holistic scoring according to the student-written rubric, assess students' acquisition of English.

Suggested Procedures—Lesson 2

1. Review and discuss the definition of *myth* in Spanish (refer to objectives 1 and 2 for a rationale of this discussion in the students' primary language). According to the *Macmillan Dictionary for Students*, edited by William D. Halsey, a myth is a "traditional story of unknown authorship that expresses a belief of a

particular people usually involving gods and heroes. A myth is an attempt to explain a phenomenon of nature, an event in history, or the origin of a particular custom, practice, or religious belief." It is important that students truly have an understanding of this definition; therefore, discuss the following words that are a part of the definition: *heroes, natural phenomenon, event in history, custom, practice, belief, religious belief,* and other pertinent words that come up in the discussion.

2. Have students reread the Aztec myth *How We Came to the Fifth World/Como Vinimos al Quinto Mundo*, written by *Harriet* Rohmer and *Mary* Anchondo, and discuss and apply the particulars of this definition to this myth. This discussion is in Spanish (rationale stated in objectives 1 and 2).

3. Have students read other myths and apply the particulars or categories of the definition while doing a thorough analysis (critical, contextual, literary, historical, etc.) of myths. It is very important to select myths that are about the students' ethnic and cultural backgrounds and then include myths about other ethnic and cultural groups. This is crucial not only because it will validate students' identities but also because it will increase their understanding of the definition of myth, since you are building on the students' own previous background knowledge (cultural and possibly historical). It is also important to select powerful and meaningful myths (are these myths worthy of reading and writing about?).

4. Have students select myths from the school or city library to share with peers. This will ensure students' participation in and responsibility for their own learning. Tell students to choose myths from their own cultural backgrounds to share with the class. This will give students an opportunity to build background knowledge of their own culture and ensure that all ethnic groups have been included and respected. In addition, this activity will offer a demonstration and an informal assessment of students' understanding of myth through their respectively selected stories. This offers the class a learning opportunity to decide whether the student-selected stories are really myths or another literary genre. It is important to share stories in the students' primary language and some in English.

5. Teach students interviewing strategies and techniques, since they will be interviewing parents, grandparents, extended-family members, or respected elder friends of the family. Students should plan on interviewing at least three or four people—either one or both parents and grandparents and one or two extended-family members or friends, preferably elders. Together with students, brainstorm what information or questions should be included in the interview on myths, and then work on a draft. Students should also receive training in tape-recording techniques if this is to be part of the interviewing process.

6. Give students an opportunity to practice the interviewing process before they conduct their interviews. They can interview each other using the draft of the interview on myths. This may be followed by a discussion to decide what information or questions are necessary, what should be deleted, what areas need

clarification, and so on. A final draft of the interview may then be written and formulated to be used in the actual interviews. Make sure students also have practice time using a tape player when interviewing their peers. Borrow several tape players from other teachers, and do this activity in a cooperative center. Video-record students' interactions as they interview each other.

7. Draft a letter together with students that will be given to all interviewees explaining the interviewing process. Decide what information, steps, or procedures are necessary so that interviewees have an understanding of myths and the procedure students will follow to carry out the interview. Explain in the letter that students will do the following: explain the definition of the term *myth*, read one or two myths to interviewees (to promote an understanding of what a myth is), audio- or video-record a myth interviewees would like to share. In the letter, emphasize the preference for myths that are generational, but indicate that it is fine to share myths that have been heard outside the family or that have been read. Also stress the importance of sharing powerful myths worthy of learning, reading, and writing. Emphasize that the interviewees' participation is crucial for the students' fulfillment of the assignment and for the completion of this project.

8. Meet with the whole class to discuss any problems that surfaced when students were conducting their interviews. Make any necessary adjustments, and have students continue their interviews.

9. Have students work in pairs (one dominant English/bilingual proficient student with one student who has less English proficiency) so that they can verbally share their favorite myth bilingually. To do this, students will have to help each other translate their favorite myths. Students can also work in their "language" pairs to type their myths on the computer either in class or in the computer lab.

10. When all mythologies have been typed, compile them into a book and invite interviewees and students to a special program, preferably in the evening when most parents are not working. Have interviewees or students read their recorded myths bilingually. Video-record the program, keeping in mind the way students interact with each other and with interviewees.

Evaluation—Lesson 2

1. By listening to the myths that students selected from the library, assess students' understanding of myths.

2. By students' identification and labeling of actual myths from teacher-selected pieces of different types of literary genres, assess students' understanding of myths.

3. By conferencing with "language"-paired students and comparing myths recorded in the primary language and the same English translated myths, assess students' acquisition of English.

4. Assess students' interactions on video-recorded copies of student/peer interviews and compare them with video-recorded student/interviewee oral presentations.

Resources

Rohmer, H., & Anchondo, H. (1976). *How we came to the fifth world/Como vinimos al quinto mundo.* San Francisco: Children's Book Press.

Samway, K. D. (1992). *Writers' workshop and children acquiring English as a non-native language.* Washington, DC: National Clearinghouse for Bilingual Education. (www.LiteracyConnection.com)

An Inspirational Glimpse of Aztec Mythology

WHY THE CHANGES?

Curriculum Content

The "Before" lesson includes content from the cultural tradition of the students, but it is not well developed. The "After" lesson develops children's sense of cultural identity and personal history, which empowers students. If you teach them about their culture, their identity, and their personal histories, this strengthens their sense of who they are and their sense of their own importance. As a consequence, the teacher raises their motivation, self-confidence, rate of learning, and efficiency of learning. Students can take this experience and apply it to other learning situations, becoming more self-directed learners. The "Before" lesson simply lacks this grounding.

Furthermore, the "Before" lesson implies that Aztec mythology lacks truth. The "After" plan encourages students to seek truth in mythology and in the stories passed down through generations in their families.

Instructional Strategies

In the "Before" lesson, the teacher is more in control of learning than are the students. The teacher gives assignments and the students do them. In the "After" lesson, the students are more responsible for their own learning. The "After" lesson uses a writer's workshop, in which students read each other's writing and give feedback. The "After" lesson also has students gather information from their families and teach that to other students. The students act as teacher to other students, teaching something they learned through the interviewing process.

Many more instructional strategies are used in the "After" plan than in the "Before" plan. The "Before" plan doesn't use technology; the "After" plan uses both computers and video recorders.

Home and Community Relationships

In the "Before" lesson, the role of parent or caregiver is absent. In the "After" lesson, the parent or caregiver is a participant, involved in education, a teacher. Passing on information from parent or caregiver to child is a powerful learning experience for the child and the family as a whole. This reinforces self-empowerment, self-identity, and the value of knowledge.

Language Use

In the "After" plan there is a more equalized status of the Spanish language. Bilingualism is used: The students' language is used for instruction, and bilingual students' expertise in two languages is used to help those who are not as bilingually proficient.

▶ LESSON PLAN[7]

Division

Subject Area: Mathematics
Grade Level: 4–8
Time: One class period

Objective

Students will divide whole numbers using division.

Suggested Procedures

1. After having demonstrated long division with two-digit divisors the day before, distribute the worksheet shown in Figure 5.2. Have students practice computing long division.

2. Review students' answers in class. Work any problems on the board that students found difficult.

Evaluation

By evaluating their worksheets individually, assess students' mastery of division.

Division: You Too Can Be a Mathematician!

Subject Area: Mathematics
Grade Level: 4–8
Time: One class period

Work all of the following problems using long division. Show your work!

1. 14)784	2. 23)1702	3. 33)693
4. 56)2352	5. 21)1386	6. 10)320
7. 18)486	8. 30)1350	9. 17)1224
10. 61)1098	11. 25)1275	12. 42)2520

Figure 5.2   Division Worksheet

[7]This plan can be used to teach various math operations, with or without the aid of a calculator. For example, some teachers do not drill students in long division but instead teach the concept of division and how to compute it on a calculator. The worksheet can be redesigned to reflect this alternative approach.

Objectives

1. Students will divide whole numbers using division.
2. Students will appreciate the contributions made by mathematicians and scientists of various racial backgrounds and both sexes.
3. Students will enjoy practicing mathematics skills.

Suggested Procedures

1. After having demonstrated division with two-digit divisors the day before, distribute the worksheet shown in Figure 5.3. Explain that it contains a puzzle—a person's name—that they should solve by computing the division problems.
2. When students have completed the exercise, have them tell you the name on the worksheet; it is Kovalevskaya. Tell students who Sonya Kovalevskaya was, using resource material like that shown in Figure 5.4. Discuss the difficulties she faced because people did not believe a woman should be an excellent mathematician or a university professor.
3. Review the math problems in class. Work any problems on the board that students found difficult.

Evaluation

1. Assess students' mastery of division by evaluating their worksheets individually.
2. Through their participation in the activity, assess students' enjoyment and appreciation of math.

Work all of the following problems using long division. Show your work! Locate the alphabet letter that corresponds to the correct answer for each problem. Arrange the letters in the order in which problems are numbered to spell the mathematician's name.

1. 14)784   2. 23)1702   3. 33)693

4. 56)2352   5. 21)1386   6. 10)320

7. 18)486   8. 30)1350   9. 17)1224

10. 61)1098   11. 25)1275   12. 42)2520

A	B	K	S	L	M	A	Y	O	Q	C	B	T	V	U	K	D	G	O
18	12	56	45	28	37	60	51	43	52	19	39	40	21	54	72	47	45	74

P	Z	O	J	E	S	N	A	G	L	N	E	B	M	C	H	S	O	T
34	22	26	38	32	55	58	42	16	66	73	17	33	76	49	63	75	61	23

I	Y	V	R
44	51	27	29

She is: ___ ___ ___ ___ ___ ___ ___ ___ ___ ___ ___ ___
        1.   2.   3.   4.   5.   6.   7.   8.   9. 10. 11. 12.

Answer Key

1. 56 = K   7. 27 = V
2. 74 = O   8. 45 = S
3. 21 = V   9. 72 = K
4. 42 = A   10. 18 = A
5. 66 = L   11. 51 = Y
6. 32 = E   12. 60 = A

Figure 5.3 Who's the Mathematician?

Caroline V. Still Anderson, M.D. (1849–1919). An African American pioneer in medicine. She was refused internship at the Boston New England Hospital for Women and Children the first time she applied because she was black but was later accepted unanimously. She also helped organize the first Colored Young Women's Christian Association.

Benjamin Banneker (1731–1806). The first African American to publish scientific material. He taught himself math and astronomy and helped survey and draw plans for the site on which Washington, D.C., was built.

F. Chin Chu, Ph.D. (1919–) A professor of chemical engineering at Polytech Institute of Brooklyn and one of the foremost chemical engineers in the United States. He has represented the United States at NATO conferences on propulsion and specialized in research on various aspects of propulsion technology.

Charles Alexander Eastman, M.D. (1858–1939). A Sioux physician who received his M.D. from Boston University's School of Medicine in 1890. He practiced at Pine Ridge, South Dakota; St. Paul, Minnesota; and Crow Creek, South Dakota. He also represented the Sioux people in Washington, D.C.

Sir William Rowan Hamilton (1805–1865). One of the greatest mathematicians and scientists to have come from Ireland. He published extensively during the 1800s on optic rays and his theory of quaternions.

Sonya Kovalevskaya, Ph.D. (1850–1891). A Russian woman who became one of the most notable European mathematics researchers in the late 1800s, specializing in mathematical analysis and infinite series. She was unable to obtain a teaching position in a Russian university because of her sex but was hired as a lecturer at the University of Stockholm.

Seki Shinsuke Kowa (1642–1708). Considered the greatest mathematician in Japan during the seventeenth century. He was largely self-taught in math and mechanics. He developed theories in calculus and in solving higher equations and used determinants in solving simultaneous equations.

David Sanchez, Ph.D. (1933–). A professor of mathematics at the University of New Mexico. He conducts research on direct methods in the calculus of variations and nonlinear ordinary differential equations.

Chien Shiung Wu, Ph.D. (1929–). A Chinese American woman who is one of the world's leading physicists and a professor of physics at Columbia University. She conducted important research on particles of the nucleus of an atom.

Grace Chisholm Young, Ph.D. (1868–1944). An English mathematician and a productive researcher in number theory and geometry. She collaborated with her husband on several books, including books on how to teach math to children.

Figure 5.4   Resource Material: Mathematicians and Scientists
Sources: E. T. Bell *Men of mathematics* (New York: Simon & Schuster, 1965); L. M. Olson, *Women in mathematics* (Cambridge, MA: M.I.T. Press, 1974); T. Perl, *Math equals* (Menlo Park, CA: Addison-Wesley, 1978); and D. E. Smith, *History of mathematics, vols. I and II* (New York: Dover, 1958).

Resources

Albers, D., Alexanderson, G., & Reid, C. (Eds.) (1990). *More mathematical people: Contemporary conversations*. Boston: Harcourt Brace Jovanovich.

Bell, E. T. (1965). *Men of mathematics*. New York: Simon & Schuster.

McClure, J. (2000). *Theoreticians and builders: Mathematicians, physical scientists, inventors*. Austin, TX: Raintree/Steck Vaughn.

Morrow, C., & Perl, T. (1998). *Notable women in mathematics: A biographical dictionary*. Westport, CT: Greenwood.

Nasar, S. (2001). *A beautiful mind: The life of mathematical genius and Nobel Laureate John Nash*. New York: Simon & Schuster.

Reimer, L., & Reimer, W. (1990). *Mathematicians are people too: Stories from the lives of great mathematicians*. Palo Alto, CA: Dale Seymour.

Division: You Too Can Be a Mathematician!

Curriculum Content

The "Before" plan stresses only practice in a mathematical skill. The addition of the puzzle to the worksheet in the "After" plan does at least two things. First, it makes the drill worksheet more fun. Second, it allows the teacher to teach about people who have contributed to the fields of math and science, particularly women and men of color. Students often do not connect math with people, particularly with people who are not White men.

▶ LESSON PLAN

Wholesale and Retail

Subject Area: Math

Grade Level: 5–8

Time: Four days

Objectives

1. Students will define the terms *wholesale, retail, mark-up, mark-down,* and *supply and demand.*
2. Students will describe how these concepts influence shopping.

Suggested Procedures

1. Explain to students the meanings of the concepts of wholesale, retail, markup, markdown, and supply and demand.
2. Have students clip advertisements that are examples of these concepts.
3. Have students compute price changes, using percentages and decimals, based on story problems from newspaper advertisements about the pricing of various items.
4. Invite proprietors from local stores to the class, and have them give examples of how supply and demand of merchandise will influence the markup and markdown of the goods.

Evaluation

Through discussion and written exam, assess students' understanding of the meanings of *wholesale, retail, markup, markdown,* and *supply and demand.*

Carpets and Rugs from Asia

Subject Areas: Math, Economics, Social Studies, Art

Grade Level: 5–8

Time: Two weeks

Objectives

1. Students will discover how money and tradition often serve as excuses for those in power to argue against making constructive changes.

2. Students will identify the term *oriental rug* as one that many Asian Americans find offensive, although it is commonly used to refer to carpets made in Asia.

3. Students will define the terms *wholesale, retail, markup, markdown,* and *supply and demand.*

4. Students will examine carpets and rugs from Asia for different mathematical designs and artistic beauty.

5. Students will distinguish between hand-knotted Asian rugs and machine-made Asian rugs and between their prices and artistic value.

6. Students will identify countries where hand-knotted Asian rugs are made, the people who make them (e.g., race, class, gender), and the way they are made.

7. Students will discover who makes the most money from the sale of hand-knotted Asian rugs: the maker, the dealer, or the owner of the store where they are sold.

Suggested Procedures

1. Have students discuss why the use of some words and phrases that have been a part of U.S. folkways is considered insensitive to certain groups (e.g., *paddy wagon, oriental, noble savage, blacklisted, lame*). Remember, many of these terms were developed by European Americans at a time when the United States was not as aware of or concerned about racial and other issues regarding marginalized groups as we are now. Therefore, the origin and history of these taken-for-granted terms need to be discussed and challenged.

2. Ask students why some people are against changing or eliminating the use of certain words and phrases (e.g., *Cleveland Indians, Chicago Blackhawks, oriental rug*) to describe a team or a product. Have students conduct interviews to collect responses to the question. Next, have students analyze the responses to determine whether there are categories of reasons (e.g., tradition, financial market image).

3. Explain to students the meanings of the words *wholesale, retail, overhead,* and *supply and demand.*

4. Take the students on a field trip to a store that specializes in selling carpets made in Asia, or invite a dealer/seller of Asian rugs to visit the class. Have the dealer/seller bring along several examples of hand-knotted and machine-made Asian rugs so he or she can explain the difference between the two (e.g., how they are made, how the design and style of hand-knotted rugs give specific information on where they are made, how the colors of the rugs look different when examined from different angles).

5. Invite a home decorator from a department store and have him or her provide a cost comparison between the hand-knotted and the machine-made Asian rugs, and have him or her explain the difference between wholesale and retail cost.

6. Set up an Asian rugs center, including color pictures of different sizes of Asian rugs from different locations. Also have several picture books that provide historical information on Asian rugs.

7. Have students consult the Web for information on where Asian rugs are made and the people who make them and their way of life.

8. Explain that rugs, like other commodities, pass through several hands in the process of economic exchange: the laborers, the factory owners, wholesalers, and retailers, such as local store owners. Help students to conduct research on the amount of money from the sale of rugs that goes to each person or role group (i.e., from production to final sale). If possible, find out whether there is a gender distinction in this chain of work and profit. Invite students to question who profits most from the production and sale of Asian carpets and rugs.

9. Ask students to compare and contrast how various individuals they encountered during this unit talked about Asian rugs, and formulate hypotheses as to how one's relationship to the rug production and selling process affects one's viewpoint.

10. Using census data on annual income, have students identify which families can most likely afford to purchase hand-knotted Asian rugs.

Evaluation

1. Through class discussion, assess students' understanding of why the term *oriental* is seen by many people as a negative or inappropriate term.

2. Assess students' understanding of the terms *wholesale*, *retail*, *markup*, *markdown*, and *supply and demand* in a written essay or exam.

3. In small-group discussions, assess students' ability to tell the difference between machine-made rugs and hand-knotted rugs.

4. Assess students' creation of an art project in which they represent visually what they learned from this unit about Asian rugs and economics.

5. Through a written essay, assess students' understanding of where Asian carpets are made, who makes them, and how these people live.

Carpets and Rugs from Asia

WHY THE CHANGES?

Curriculum Content

The "After" plan helps students to see that materials that come out of non-Western areas can serve as a primary source to gain knowledge. In the "Before" plan, the concepts are presented almost in isolation of anything else, although they are connected to advertising that students might encounter. The "After" plan connects several disciplines to provide students with a richer experience and with a more in-depth examination of key concepts. It is longer than the "Before" lesson because it is interdisciplinary and connects several subject areas. This would require some planning across subject areas. The "After" plan prompts students to begin to think about social and economic inequities by examining who profits the most from the sale of the rugs. Often we romanticize imported commodities without questioning social class relationships and economic effects. Students are also encouraged to question traditions and commonly accepted terms that are not respectful of cultural groups of color and other marginalized groups and to consider the reasons for the maintenance of and allegiance to these traditions.

Multiple Perspectives

The "After" plan encourages students to examine the opinions of the home decorator and the dealer, and to compare and contrast the information they collect. Here students will have to analyze and critique the information they receive. Also, the "After" plan encourages students to examine the positions of the various people involved in the production and sale of the rugs. Here they judge whether they would rather be a rug maker, wholesaler, or retailer and how these positions influence the way people in these different roles live. Students examine the weight these different people assign to the artistic versus the economic value of the rugs.

Visuals

The "After" plan presents the students with curriculum material (rugs) that comes from different countries and regions in Asia.

▶ LESSON PLAN

Composition

BEFORE

Subject Areas: Reading, Literature, and Language Arts

Grade Level: 6–8

Time: Ongoing throughout the semester

Objectives

1. Students will identify the main idea of literature selections.
2. Students will write a business letter, a poem, and an essay using correct form.
3. Students will state a clear position or perspective in support of an argument, describe the points in support of the argument, and employ well-articulated evidence.
4. Students will improve their use of organization, word choice, grammar, and Standard English writing conventions to write newspaper articles and poetry.

Suggested Procedures

1. Read a poem from a literature textbook to the class. Ask students to identify the main idea of the poem. List their ideas on the board as they discuss, then have the class sort through the various interpretations students have suggested to determine the most accurate identification of the main idea.
2. Read a story from a literature textbook; select a story that has an adult and a young person as main characters. Use the same process as in procedure 1 to identify the main idea of the story.

3. Show students the proper form for a business letter. For homework, ask students to draft the body of a letter to the adult in the story regarding their views about the issue facing the young person in the story. Students will be shown examples of a business letter format and peer-edit their letters.

4. Introduce several different newspapers. In groups of four, have students analyze one newspaper article, identifying the main idea of the article and the structure in which it was written. Then have them identify an issue that is important to them, the school, or the community. Have students do research about the issue, if necessary, to learn more about it.

5. Model writing a newspaper article on the overhead projector using a newspaper as an example. Have students use this model to write a newspaper article using their group's issue. Then assemble their articles into a class newspaper.

6. After reading another selection from the literature book, have students practice analyzing the selection in terms of strengths and weaknesses. In class discussion, list strengths and weaknesses on the board. Get students to clarify what they mean and offer examples from the story. Emphasize that not everyone necessarily sees the story in the same way; they will each develop their own analysis.

7. Use student suggestions to model how to write about the story in a mini-essay. Then have each student write her or his own analysis of the story.

8. After reading another selection in the literature text and discussing it briefly, have each student write her or his own analysis, as they did above.

Evaluation

1. For a culminating assessment, have students read any story in their literature book and, in a mini-essay, analyze the story's strengths and weaknesses.

2. Evaluate the various writing assignments on the following criteria: states a clear position; uses correct conventions, spelling, and grammar; uses descriptive words; identifies and represents perspective clearly; uses supporting evidence where needed.

3. Determine whether the form of writing (newspaper article, business letter, five-paragraph essay) was used correctly as demonstrated.

Perspectives[8]

Subject Areas: Reading, Literature, and Language Arts
Grade Level: 6–8
Time: Ongoing throughout the semester

Objectives

1. Students will recognize perspectives in literature, newspapers, and expository writing, and distinguish between one perspective and another.

2. Students will recognize the difference between insider and outsider points of view.

[8] *Source:* Jennifer Clayton, Gambetta Middle School, Castroville, California.

3. Students will express their own perspectives through various forms of writing.

4. Students will evaluate cultural representations in textbooks and media.

5. Students will determine the importance of cultural authenticity in literature.

6. Students will consider the relationship between an author's perspective and the author's cultural and ethnic background.

7. Students will state a clear position or perspective in support of an argument, describe the points in support of the argument, and employ well-articulated evidence.

8. Students will improve their use of organization, word choice, grammar, and Standard English writing conventions to write newspaper articles and poetry.

Suggested Procedures

1. To introduce the concept of perspective, have students do quick journal writing, expressing their perspectives about an issue, such as school dress code, then have them listen to a reading of "Honeybees," a poem by Paul Fleischman, which contrasts the life of a drone and a queen bee.

2. Ask what students already know about perspectives. With your help, have students produce a collective definition of perspective to be posted on the wall. Ask them to examine what they wrote in their journals and try to describe their perspective on the issue. Discuss various factors that affect one's perspective, including one's background, race or ethnicity, gender, age, and so forth.

3. With one student, write a two-perspective poem on the board, similar to "Honeybees," getting ideas from the class. Then, in pairs, have students create a poem like "Honeybees" and present it to the class if they want to share. Their homework will be to interview a parent or adult family friend about an issue and write a perspective poem from two points of view.

4. Have students flip through their literature anthology and jot down what they notice about the authors and the literature in the book. Who is included? Who is not? Ask them to discuss what they think cultural representation means and why it is or isn't important.

5. In groups of four, have students tally the ethnicities of the authors in the anthology and count the ethnicities of the people in the pictures. When they are finished, have students share their data. (To connect with math, students may make graphs or pie charts using their data.) Discuss the way they think the ethnic groups in the textbook should be represented and why they feel that way. You will record the data and ideas on chart paper.

6. Explain the concept of insiders and outsiders. All of us are members of some groups and not others, such as families, grade levels, neighborhoods, and so forth. Using examples, help students see that insiders tend to view groups of which they are members differently from outsiders. Insiders tend to have a richer working knowledge of the group than do outsiders. Insiders are more likely than outsiders to be aware of strengths and assets, feelings, and intentions of other insiders. Outsiders are more likely to compare groups of which they are not members with groups of which they are members. Discuss students' findings from their

analysis of the literature anthology with respect to insider and outsider points of view, record students' responses to this idea on chart paper.

7. For homework, ask students to draft the body of a letter to the publisher explaining their own position regarding their findings from the analysis of ethnic representation. Students will be shown examples of a business letter format and peer-edit their letters.

8. Introduce several different newspapers and tell only where you bought them. In groups of four, have students analyze one of the newspapers, asking the following questions: "From whose perspective are the articles written? How can you tell? What are some biases or stereotypes in the articles? Who would read this paper? Why? What issues are discussed in the articles?"

9. Have students identify an issue that is important to them, the school, or the community. What are the various sides to the issue? How can they find out more about the issue from various perspectives? Have students do research about the issue, if necessary, and plan a presentation using cooperative learning strategies in which at least two sides of the issue are discussed. They may format this presentation like a debate, and they must have visuals such as transparencies, posters, or a PowerPoint presentation.

10. Model writing a newspaper article on the overhead projector using a newspaper as an example. Students will use the teacher's model to write a newspaper article using their group's issue. Then, students will assemble their articles into a class newspaper.

11. Ask a student to briefly tell the story of the Three Little Pigs as he or she remembers it. Then read *The True Story of the 3 Little Pigs*, by Scieszka, Wolf, and Smith. Have students discuss the different perspectives in the book and the student's version.

12. Students will use their understanding of perspective, bias, and stereotyping to compare and contrast Rumpelstiltskin, by *Paul* O. Zelinsky, and Rumpelstiltskin's Daughter, by *Diane* Stanley in a written response. This written response will also discuss the perspectives being shown in the two books.

13. Read a traditional Christopher Columbus book, such as *Meet Christopher Columbus* by *James* T. De Kay or *Columbus* by Edgar Parin D'Aulaire and Ingri D'Aulaire, with *Encounter*, by Jane Yolen and David Shannon. During reading, students will use a Venn diagram to compare and contrast the perspectives and "facts" in the two stories.

14. You will use student suggestions to model how to respond to these books in a mini-essay. The essay will discuss bias, stereotyping, perspectives of the characters, and story. A "Checklist for Cultural Authenticity" can be found at the website www.4children.org/news/9-97mlit.htm. It may help in analyzing the cultural authenticity of literature.

15. In a Socratic seminar, students will discuss what they have learned about perspective. Students will form two circles. A smaller circle of six to ten students will be on the inside, and the rest of the class will be on the outside. Students in the middle will discuss general questions about perspective that are posted

on chart paper or on the board. Students in the outside circle will take notes on what is discussed and what comments they might want to make later. If time permits, students will switch so that the students on the inside will move to the outside circle and listen. You may record ideas on chart paper for display.

Evaluation

1. For a culminating assessment, have students read *The Circuit* by *Francisco* Jiménez and, in a mini-essay, analyze the story's cultural authenticity, perspective, and author.

2. Evaluate the various writing assignments on the following criteria: states a clear position; uses correct conventions, spelling, and grammar; uses descriptive words; identifies and represents perspective clearly; uses supporting evidence where needed.

3. Determine whether the form of writing (i.e., poem, newspaper article, business letter, five-paragraph essay) was used correctly as demonstrated.

Resources

D'Aulaire, I., & D'Aulaire, E. P. (1983). *Columbus*. Sandwich Village, MA: Beautiful Feet Books.
De Kay, J. (2001). *Meet Christopher Columbus*. New York: Random House.
Fleischman, P., & Beddows, E. (1995). *Joyful noise: Poems for two voices*. New York: HarperTrophy.
Jiménez, F. (1999). *The circuit: Stories from the life of a migrant child*. Boston: Houghton Mifflin.
Scieszka, J., Wolf, A., & Smith, L. (1991). *The true story of the 3 little pigs*. London: Puffin.
Stanley, D. (1998). *Rumpelstiltskin's daughter*. New York: Scholastic.
Weisner D. (2001). *The three pigs*. New York: Clarion.
Yolen, J., & Shannon, D. (1996). *Encounter*. San Diego: Harcourt Brace Jovanovich.
Zelinsky, P. (1997). *Rumpelstiltskin*. New York: Puffin Books.

Perspectives

WHY THE CHANGES?

Curriculum Materials

Both plans use materials, but they select and use them differently. The "Before" plan simply uses materials that are available to teach students to recognize the main idea in a reading selection. In the "After" plan, students not only use materials, but they also examine them and critique the point of view they represent. Students also learn to analyze materials from a multicultural perspective, using the curriculum analysis instrument in this chapter. (Several teachers we have worked with over the years have taught students to do this, and it is quite "eye-opening" for both the students and the teacher!)

Multiple Perspectives

The "After" plan specifically uses the same kinds of teaching strategies that appear in the "Before" plan to teach students to recognize multiple perspectives. The "Before" plan does not attempt to do this, which does not make it an inferior plan. However, by teaching students to recognize the perspective from which an author writes, the "After" plan adds a significant dimension to student learning, and one that is a building block for multicultural education.

The "After" plan weaves the idea of perspectives throughout. Students write from their own perspectives. They use the dialogue poem "Honeybees," which contrasts two perspectives and makes the idea of perspective quite visible. From there, the teacher teaches students to identify perspectives in what they are reading, and to consider the relationship between an author's background and perspective. As a result of the kinds of analyses students in the "After" plan do, they engage in more critical thinking than do students in the "Before" plan.

Student Evaluation

The "After" plan modifies the evaluation process so that students have to apply what they learned about perspective and cultural authenticity by evaluating a book that is new to them.

▶ LESSON PLAN[9]

Techniques of Painting

Subject Area: Art
Grade Level: 7–9
Time: Two weeks

Objective

Students will express emotion through sketching and painting, using at least two of the techniques of color, contrast, perspective, form, line, subject matter, and texture to give meaning to an art form.

Suggested Procedures

1. Review with students the following techniques of painting, asking them to take notes during your review:

   Color
   Contrast
   Perspective or space
   Form or relationship of the shapes
   Line
   Meaning or subject matter
   Texture

2. Show slides of paintings by the U.S. artists John Copley, Gilbert Stuart, George Caleb Bingham, Thomas Cole, and James A. McNeill Whistler. Review each technique thoroughly as you discuss the paintings with the class, making sure that students write down important information related to technique (e.g., sharp lines, dull colors, smooth textures). Ask students how each painting makes them feel (e.g., happy, sad, bored, angry, mixed up) and record their answers. Point

---

[9]*Source:* David Castaneda, Waukesha Public Schools, Waukesha, Wisconsin.

out the elements in each painting that convey an emotional response and how these elements work together to convey the meaning of the work.

3. Over the remaining days of the unit, ask students to complete three sketches and one painting in which they use at least two of the techniques discussed to convey personal meaning. Have students share their final products with each other.

Evaluation

1. Through discussion of the slides, assess students' understanding of the concepts presented. With practice, students are better able to identify the important elements in the paintings.

2. Through their sketches and paintings, assess students' understanding of the concepts presented.

Techniques of Painting

Subject Area: Art

Grade Level: 7–9

Time: Two weeks

Objectives

1. Students will express emotion through sketching and painting, using at least two of the techniques of color, contrast, perspective, form, line, subject matter, and texture to give meaning to an art form.

2. Students will learn that different ethnic groups use art to convey meaning across cultural barriers, regardless of the time period in which the art work is completed.

Suggested Procedures

1. Tell students that they will examine six U.S. paintings from the 1930s. Also note that, during the next week, as they study U.S. cultural history of the 1930s in their U.S. history class, they will learn how these paintings portray the styles of the period.

2. Have prints or posters of works by the following U.S. artists displayed around the room (these artists are of diverse racial and ethnic backgrounds and sexual orientations and of both sexes): Consuelo Gonzalez Amezcua, Mary Cassatt, Helen Frankenthaler, H. N. Han, Keith Haring, Richard Hunt, Frida Kahlo, Jacob Lawrence, Piet Mondrian, Elie Nadelman, Louise Nevelson, Isamu Noguchi, Georgia O'Keeffe, Lucas Samaras, Grandma Moses, Raphael Soyer, Joseph Stella, Yves Tanguy, Andy Warhol, and Charles White.

3. Review with students the following techniques of painting, using the works by the preceding artists as examples:

> Color
> Contrast
> Perspective or space
> Form or relationship of the shapes

Line
Meaning or subject matter
Texture

4. Show the following pair of slides or pull up the pictures on the Web:

    Ben Shan, *Passion of Sacco and Vanzetti* (1931–1932)
    Raphael Soyer, *Under the Bridge* (1932)

    Explain that the artists were White immigrants from Russia, and tell why each came to the United States. Review each technique thoroughly as you compare and contrast the two paintings, making sure that students write down important information related to technique (sharp lines, dull colors, smooth textures, and so on). Ask students how each painting makes them feel (e.g., happy, sad, bored, angry, mixed up), and record their answers. Point out the elements in each painting that convey an emotional response and how these elements work together to convey the meaning of the work. If evident, emphasize how the artists reflect their cultural heritage.

5. Continue to the next pair of slides:

    Diego Rivera, *New Workers School* (mural, 1933)
    Antonio Garcia, *Woman Before a Mirror* (1935)

    Explain that both artists were born in Mexico and that Garcia became a U.S. citizen. Give the historical context of each painting. Repeat the process outlined in procedure 4.

6. Continue to the last pair of slides:

    Allan Crite, *Tyre Jumping* (1936)
    Charles White, *Fatigue* (1940)

    Explain that both artists were African Americans, and briefly summarize the historical context of each painting. Repeat the process in procedure 4.

7. Hang all six prints on the wall. Have students discuss how the different artists used the techniques discussed earlier to convey emotion and meaning and how this transcends culture. Help students to recognize the particular ways an artist's cultural background influences his or her work, as well as the universals in art itself that transcend culture.

8. Over the remaining days of the unit, ask students to complete three sketches and one painting in which they use at least two of the techniques discussed to convey personal meaning. Have students share their final products with each other.

Evaluation

1. Through discussion of each pair of slides, assess students' understanding of the concepts presented. With practice, students are better able to identify the important elements in the paintings.

2. Through their sketches and paintings, assess students' understanding of the concepts presented.

3. Through class discussion, assess students' understanding of the cultural diversity and universality of art.

Techniques of Painting

Curriculum Materials

The "Before" plan uses mainly paintings by white male artists, whereas the "After" plan presents the work of a variety of U.S. artists, including White European Americans, Latinos, and African Americans, among others.

Curriculum Content

The "Before" plan focuses solely on the techniques of painting. In contrast, the "After" plan extends this focus into broader concepts involving art. One such concept is how art reflects its historical period; by linking the art class with the history class, the plan helps students learn an interdisciplinary concept. Another concept presented by the "After" plan is how culture is reflected in art, which is achieved by drawing on artists whose cultural backgrounds differ. The concept of art as a universal, cross-cultural language also is taught through examples of artwork produced by members of diverse cultural groups.

Visuals

The "Before" plan does not specify the kinds of visuals to be displayed around the room. However, the "After" plan specifies that visuals should represent U.S. artists of diverse racial and ethnic backgrounds and both sexes.

▶ LESSON PLAN

Our National Anthem

Subject Area: Music
Grade Level: 6–10
Time: One class period

Objectives

1. Students will sing the national anthem.
2. Students will explain why the national anthem was written.

Suggested Procedures

1. Pass out the lyrics to "The Star-Spangled Banner" and ask students to read them. Review the song's history, and discuss the types of events at which the anthem is commonly sung.
2. Play a recording of "The Star-Spangled Banner" and have students sing along. Then ask them to sing it without the aid of the recording.

Evaluation

Assess how well the class learns and sings the national anthem.

Our National Anthems[10]

Subject Area: Music
Grade Level: 5–10
Time: Two class periods

Objectives

1. Students will recognize the national anthems written by several U.S. groups.
2. Students will describe the purpose of a national anthem.
3. Students will sing "The Star-Spangled Banner."

Suggested Procedures

1. Ask students to sing their school song. Have them discuss why they sing it and what their school song tells about the school. Use this discussion as a basis for examining anthems.
2. Pass out the lyrics to anthems such as the following (Figure 5.5A–C):

The Star-Spangled Banner

Lyrics by Francis Scott Key
Music by J. Stafford Smith

O say can you see, by the dawn's early light,
What so proudly we hail'd at the twilight's last gleaming,
Whose broad stripes and bright stars, thro' the perilous fight,
O'er the ramparts we watch'd were so gallantly streaming?
And the rockets' red glare, the bombs bursting in air,
Gave proof thro' the night that our flag was still there.
O, say, does that Star-Spangled Banner yet wave
O'er the land of the free and the home of the brave.

On the shore, dimly seen thro' the mists of the deep,
Where the foe's haughty host in dread silence reposes,
What is that which the breeze, o'er the towering steep,
As it fitfully blows, half conceals, half discloses?
Now it catches the gleam of the morning's first beam,
In full glory reflected now shines on the stream;
'Tis the Star-Spangled Banner, O long may it wave
O'er the land of the free and home of the brave.

O thus be it ever when free man shall stand
Between their loved homes and the war's desolation!
Blest with vict'ry and peace, may the heav'n-rescued land
Praise the Pow'r that hath made and preserved us a nation.
Then conquer we must, for our cause it is just,
And this be our motto: "In God is our trust."
And the Star-Spangled Banner in triumph shall wave
A. O'er the land of the free and the home of the brave.

Figure 5.5 National Anthems

[10]To listen to "Bread and Roses" by Judy Collins using Real Player on the Internet, go to www.maxwell.syr.edu/maxpages/faculty/gmbonham/collins.htm

Lift Every Voice and Sing

Lyrics by James Weldon Johnson

Lift every voice and sing,
'Till earth and heaven ring,
Ring with the harmonies of Liberty.
Let our rejoicing rise,
High as the list'ning skies
Let it resound loud as the rolling sea
Sing a song full of the faith that the dark past has taught us
Sing a song full of the hope that the present has brought us;
Facing the rising sun of our new day begun,
Let us march on till victory is won.

Stony the road we trod,
Bitter the chast'ng rod,
Felt in the days when hope unborn had died;
Yet with a steady beat,
Have not our weary feet
Come to the place for which our fathers signed?
We have come over a way that with tears has been watered
We have come, treading our path thro' the blood of the slaughtered,
Out from the gloomy past, till now we stand at last
Where the white gleam of our bright star is cast.

God of our weary years,
God of our silent tears,
Thou who hast brought us thus far on our way;
Thou who has by Thy might,
Let us into the light,
Keep us forever in the path, we pray
Lest our feet stray from the places, our God, where we met Thee;
Lest our hearts drunk with the wine of the world we forget Thee;
Shadowed beneath Thy hand, may we forever stand
True to our God, True to our Native land.

B.

Figure 5.5 (continued)

"The Star-Spangled Banner"
"Himno Nacional" (Mexican national anthem)
"Lift Every Voice and Sing" (Black National anthem)
"Bread and Roses" (women's anthem)[10]

Arrange students into small groups and assign an anthem to each group. Have students write down what they think each anthem says about the group that wrote it and why they think the group wrote the anthem.

3. Have each group report to the class, writing down key points on the board. After they report on each anthem, tell the history of the anthems.

4. Discuss the following question: If "The Star-Spangled Banner" is the anthem of all U.S. citizens, why have some groups written their own anthems?

5. Play recordings of the anthems, asking students to sing along. Choose some favorites to learn as a class.

Himno Nacional

Lyrics by Francisco Gonzalez Bocanegra
Music by Jaime Nuno

Mexicans when the trumpet is calling,
Grasp your sword and your harness assemble.
Let the guns with their thunder appalling
Make the Earth's deep foundations to tremble.
Let the guns with their thunder appalling
Make the Earth's deep foundations to tremble.

Mexicanos al grito de guerra
El acero aprestad yel bridón.
Y retiemble en sus centros la tierra
Al sonoro rugir del cañón,
Y retiemble en sus centros la tierra
Al sonoro rugir del cañón,

May the angel divine, O Dear Homeland,
Crown thy brow with the olive branch of peace;
For thy destiny, traced by God's own hand
In the heavens, shall ever increase.
But shall ever the proud foe assail thee,
And with insolent foot profane thy ground,
Know, dear Country, thy sons shall not fail thee,
Ev'ry one thy soldier shall be found, Thy soldier ev'ry one shall be found.

¡Ciñe ¡Oh patria! tus sienes de oliva
De la paz el arcángel divino
Que en el cielo tueterno destino
Por el dedo de Dios se escribió
Mas si osare un extraño enemigo
Profanar con su planta tu suelo
Piensa ¡Oh patria querida! queel cielo
Un soldado en cada hijo te dió, Un soldado en cada hijo te dió.

Blessed Homeland, thy children have vowed them
If the bugle to battle should call,
They will fight with the last breath allowed them
Till on thy loved altars they fall.
Let the garland of olive thine be;
Unto them be deathless fame;
Let the laurel of victory be assigned thee,
Enough for them the tomb's honored name.

En sangrientos combates los viste
Por tu amor palpitando sus senos,
Arrostrar la metralla serenos,
Y la muerte o la gloria buscar.
Si el recuerdo de antiguas hazañas,
De tus hijos inflama la mente,
Los laureles del triunfo, tu frente
Volverán inmortales a ornar.

C.

Figure 5.5 (continued)

Evaluation

1. Through class discussion, assess students' understanding of the purpose of a national anthem.

2. Assess students' ability to sing the anthems.

Our National Anthems

Curriculum Content

The "Before" plan assumes that there is only one national anthem sung by U.S. citizens and uses it as the sole example of an anthem. The "After" plan makes several changes. First, it adds an analogue to an anthem from students' experience: the school song. Second, it draws on anthems sung by several different U.S. groups to teach that there is more than one anthem sung by U.S. citizens, even though virtually all U.S. citizens also sing "The Star-Spangled Banner." Third, it teaches what an anthem is by offering several different examples and asking students to identify what they have in common.

Multiple Perspectives

The "After" plan includes multiple perspectives in two ways. First, students are provided with multiple anthems that were written from the perspectives of different groups for expressing group sentiment. Second, in small groups, students are encouraged to gain different perspectives from their peers on the purpose of an anthem.

Language Diversity

"Himno Nacional" is sung in Spanish; in our experience, it is useful in classes that contain Mexican American students. They appreciate hearing it. Other U.S. cultural groups also have anthems that may not be in English; these can be translated for study or learned in their original language.

Instructional Strategies

Students are in a passive role in the "Before" plan, whereas small-group work places students in an active role in the "After" plan, allowing them to think together and to create part of what they are learning. The modalities used in the "Before" plan consist of reading, listening, and singing. The "After" plan adds small-group discussion and cooperative student–student interaction, which are not present in the "Before" plan.

Visuals

Although visuals are not described, the "After" plan can be modified to include such visuals as pictures of different artists singing "The Star-Spangled Banner," flags or emblems associated with different anthems to be studied, or pictures taken at events during which anthems are sung.

▶ LESSON PLAN

U.S. History

Subject Area: Social Studies
Grade Level: 7–12
Time: Ongoing

Objectives

1. Students will identify the names associated with historic events.

2. Students will describe the causes of major historic events, such as the Mexican-American War.

3. Students will describe contributions that different sociocultural groups made to those historic events.

Suggested Procedures

1. Select a time period or event in history, such as the Mexican-American War of 1846. Ask students what they already know about that event, and brainstorm their responses on the board.

2. Have students read the textbook account of this war or other event being studied.

3. Supplement their reading with a lecture, film, or video that expands on significant parts of the material. For example, when studying the Mexican-American War, the story of the Alamo can be taught.

4. Identify four to six significant historical figures who played a part in the event being studied. For example, if the Mexican-American War is being studied, the historical figures could include James K. Polk, John C. Fremont, Kit Carson, Samuel Houston, Zachary Taylor, Mariano Vallejo, and Antonio Lopez de Santa Ana. Have each student select one figure and find out what kind of a person he or she was and what contribution he or she made to history. Students should write sketches of the person they select.

Evaluation

Evaluate students' ability to identify names and events and to explain causality through a written test as well as through oral class participation.

Hypermedia History

Subject Area: Social Studies

Grade Level: 7–12

Time: Ongoing

Objectives

1. Students will identify the names associated with historic events.

2. Students will recognize that often different sociocultural groups perceive and experience the same historic event or time period differently.

3. Students will compare and contrast perspectives of dominant and subordinate groups historically.

4. Students will collect research information from diverse sources.

5. Students will represent different perspectives and experiences using hypertext and/or hypermedia.

Suggested Procedures

1. Select a time period or event in history, such as the Mexican-American War of 1846. Have available a variety of history texts, including a standard U.S. history textbook such as *American Passages: A History of the United States* (Ayers, Gloud, Oshinsky, & Soderlund, 2005); and other books, such as *Indian Country* (Harvey & Harjo, 1994), *A People's History of the United States* (Zinn, 2003), *A Different Mirror* (Takaki, 1993), *Caribbean Connections* (Sananta, Callin., Colasser 2005), *Japanese American Journey* (Japanese American Curriculum Project, 1985), *Japanese American History* (O'Brien, 1991), *Journey to Topaz: A Story of the Japanese-American Evacuation* (Yoshiko Uchida, 1971), *Lies My Teacher Told Me* (Loewen, 1995), *The Legacy of Vicente Guerrero, Mexico's First Black Indian President* (Vincent, 2001); *African American Women Confront the West, 1600–2000*(Taylor & Moore Wilson, 2003).

2. Have students read the standard textbook account of this war (or any other event the class is studying), then have them brainstorm as many different sociocultural groups as they can who may have viewed or experienced this event or time period differently than, as well as similarly to, depicted in the textbook account (including anyone in the textbook account). If they are studying the Mexican-American War, their list should include, for example, James K. Polk, the Mexican government, Mexican people in territory that is now part of the United States, different Native American nations in that same territory, Anglo Americans in that territory, African American leaders during that time period, and so forth.

3. Assign each item on the list to a small group of students whose task is to find out as much as they can about how the person or sociocultural group that they are assigned experienced or perceived this war. In the process, students should note any significant differences within the group they are assigned (such as gender differences and tribal differences) that may emerge in their investigations.

4. Have the class create a Hyperstudio program about this historic event. Each small group is responsible for creating one or more cards that include text information (such as excerpts from speeches and summaries of textbook accounts or other books) and can also include pictures, maps, diagrams, and so on. When scrollable text inserts are used, text information can be fairly extensive.

5. When students have completed their Hyperstudio cards, have each group present their cards. Then as a class determine how to link them electronically. To do this, students will need to consider what events relate most directly, how events relate, and so forth. Students can then enter appropriate buttons or hypertext links into their cards to create links. Do not rush through this process, since determining how best to link cards will cause students to examine relationships between events and between groups.

6. Have each student view the linked package about this event and look for any significant patterns. Students may record and present their observations in a variety of ways, such as in a journal each student keeps to record her or his analysis of each historic event that is studied.

7. Hold a class discussion in which students present and discuss their own analyses of patterns they discovered. The class can then use insights from this discussion to finish its Hyperstudio package of this historic time frame or event.

Evaluation

1. Evaluate each group's card(s) for accuracy, comprehensiveness, and general success in locating and presenting appropriate information.

2. Evaluate each individual student's analysis of historic patterns, such as the student's ability to identify patterns of aggression or to connect nationalism and military power.

3. Evaluate the class's success in identifying and representing different perspectives and experiences, linking these in a meaningful way and abstracting historic insights from the process of doing this.

Resources

Ayers et al. (2005) *American Passages: A History of the United States*. Wadsworth Publishing.

Globe Fearon. (1995). *Multicultural milestones in United States history*. Globe Fearon book series. African Americans in U.S. History and Hispanics in U.S. History. Paramus, NJ: Globe. See http://www. pearsonlearning.com/globefearon/globefearon_default.cfm

Harvey, K. D., & Harjo, L. D. (1994). *Indian country*. Golden, CO: North American Press.

Japanese American Curriculum Project. (1985). *Japanese American journey*. Sacramento, CA: Spilman Printing.

Loewen, J. W. (1995). *Lies my teacher told me*. New York: New Press.

McWhorter, D. (2004). A dream of freedom: The Civil Rights movement from 1954 to 1968. New York: Scholastic.

O'Brien, D. J. (1991). *Japanese American History*. Bloomington: Indiana University Press.

Santana et al. (2005) *Caribbean Connections: The Dominican Republic*, Washington: Teaching for Change.

Sunshine, C. A., & Menkart, D. (1991). *Caribbean connections*. Washington, DC: Network of Educators on Central America.

Takaki, R. (1993). *A different mirror*. Boston: Little, Brown.

Zinn, H. (1995). *A people's history of the United States* (Rev. ed.). New York: Harper & Row.

Hypermedia History

WHY THE CHANGES?

Curriculum Materials and Multiple Perspectives

History textbooks today include a wider diversity of people than they did previously, and many educators assume that this is enough to make history multicultural. The "Before" plan makes the assumption that materials are already multicultural and that because a few Mexican names are included in studying an event (such as the Mexican-American War) that event is being taught fairly.

What is missing from any single text, however, are diverse perspectives not only presented in depth but used to organize the entire account of U.S. history. Increasingly, books are becoming available that provide teachers and students with diverse perspectives; however, each book presents mainly the perspective of the authors of that book. Some of these are included with the "After" lesson plan. No single book represents a plurality of perspectives, but the collection taken together does.

In addition, the "After" plan provides a way for students to examine and acknowledge diverse interpretations and perspectives without having to reduce them to one main "storyline" on history. Hypertext or hypermedia programs lend themselves well to representing different experiences, linking these where appropriate and leaving them unlinked where appropriate. Students can juxtapose three or four different experiences taking place at the same time in the same geographic area without having to reduce these to one story.

Instructional Strategies

The "Before" plan depends on the textbook, lecture, additional reading, and possibly a film or video for instruction. This presents students with a rather limited array of ways to learn. The "After" plan expands ways of learning considerably. Students find Hyper-Studio very engaging to use. As a multimedia program, it allows students to learn and create through text, pictures, maps, diagrams, and so forth. Students can work alone or cooperatively on their cards. The final product is a complex multimedia package that can be burned onto a CD-ROM disk. Completing this kind of project lends itself to different student talents and interests and is inherently motivating to many students today.

▶ LESSON PLAN[11]

John Steinbeck

BEFORE

Subject Area: English
Grade Level: 9–12
Time: Five to six days

Objectives

1. Students will appreciate John Steinbeck as an author who wrote about his concern for migrant workers and their exploitation.

2. Students will identify the main features of Steinbeck's writing style and subject matter.

Suggested Procedures

1. Introduce Steinbeck. Tell students about Steinbeck's work and his concern for migrant workers. He was concerned with social exploitation wherever he found it, and he chronicled the life of the poor and downtrodden. He was banned in Salinas, California, for many years because he wrote an exposé of the owners of the land where the migrant workers were treated badly, and also because it was a small town—people did not like to read about themselves in his accurate stories!

2. Let students group themselves into fours, and assign them a research project: to use the school library, the public library, computer resources, and textbook sources to prepare a multimedia presentation (with speeches, enactments, illustrations, video, audio, etc.) about Steinbeck's life and his major works. Set up a timeline for group work in class, for the declaration of each member's

[11] *Source:* Anne Fairbrother, Del Norte High School, Albuquerque, New Mexico.

research focus, and for presentations. Let students know that there will be two grades—one for the group presentation and one for the individual research handed in. Explain the criteria for a good presentation.

3. Read two pieces by Steinbeck: "The Leader of the People," from *The Red Pony*, and a selection from *Travels With Charley*. Prepare quizzes, discussion questions, and free-write topics as appropriate.

Evaluation

1. Through graded quizzes, individual free writes, and group discussions, assess students' comprehension of Steinbeck's writing style and subject matter.

2. Through their presentation, assess students' understanding of Steinbeck's life and concerns. Students will receive two grades for the presentation: one grade for the quality of presentation and one grade for the written research.

Resources

Steinbeck, J. (2000) *The Red Pony*. London: Penguin. "The leader" is Chapt 4 of the book. Use the previous citation.

Steinbeck, J. (1984) *Travels with Charley: In search of America*. New York: Penguin.

Literature on Migrant Workers and Exploitation

Subject Area: English

Grade Level: 9–12

Time: Seven to eight days

Objectives

1. Students will examine working and living conditions of migrant workers in rural California from different cultural perspectives.

2. Students will describe the main features of the writing styles of Carlos Bulosan, Raymund Barrio, and John Steinbeck.

3. Students will identify and understand rich metaphorical language.

Suggested Procedures

1. Find out what students know about the Philippines: its Independence Day, length of Spanish rule, length of U.S. occupation, and nature and extent of resistance. Tell of Filipino involvement with the United Farm Workers in Delano, California, before César Chavez was involved.

2. Tell students that they will be reading three chapters from the book *America Is in the Heart*, an autobiography by Carlos Bulosan. In the book, Bulosan recounts his life in the Philippines, his journey to the United States, and his experiences working in the canneries in Alaska and in California fields and orchards. (Carlos Bulosan was born in 1913, came to the United States in 1930, and died in 1956.)

3. Read the first chapter of *America Is in the Heart* aloud or silently. Afterward, students will take a quiz, part of which will involve a description of life in the Philippines as Bulosan was growing up there: "Describe—paint a picture with words—what you remember of the life of the peasant farmer and his family."

4. After the quiz, have students create a booklet for work to be done in response to this and two more chapters from *America Is in the Heart*. The booklet should have three to six lined pages, three blank pages, and a blank cover.

5. Have students write a double-entry journal response to three self-selected quotes from the chapter. Have them draw a picture illustrating one scene from the chapter and create a title for the chapter.

6. Read Chapter 13 of *America Is in the Heart*, which tells of Bulosan's journey to the United States in 1930, when he was 17 years old. Afterward, have students write a double-entry journal response to three quotes from the chapter. Have them draw a picture illustrating one scene from the chapter and create a title for the chapter.

7. Read Chapter 19 of the book, which is set in the California fields and orchards in 1941, when there was great anti-Asian sentiment in the United States. Afterward, have students write a double-entry journal response to three quotes from the chapter. Have them draw a picture illustrating one scene from the chapter create a title for the chapter.

8. Have students create a cover for their responses to the three chapters from the book.

9. Read Chapter 10 from *The Plum Plum Pickers*, by Raymund Barrio. After reading, have students work in groups to answer questions about what happens in the story and about some of the major images in the story. Another option is to read Chapters 1 and 2 from *The Circuit: Stories From the Life of a Migrant Child*, by Francisco Jimenez.

10. As a last assignment in the group, ask students to identify and explain images and metaphors in the story: "As the story was read aloud, you should have noted that throughout the story there is vivid imagery. Find one vivid image each and explain what the image is and how or why it is effective."

11. When you give students back their work, go over many of the images as a class, on the board, showing denotations and connotations of images, and assess power and vividness of the metaphors.

12. Introduce John Steinbeck. Discuss the realities of life for farm workers as seen in the pieces "The Leader of the People" and a selection from *Travels with Charley*. Tell students of Steinbeck's work and concern for migrant workers. He was concerned with social exploitation wherever he found it, and he chronicled the life of the poor and downtrodden. He was banned in Salinas, California, for many years because he wrote an exposé of the owners of the land where the migrant workers were treated so badly, and also because it was a small town—people did not like to read about themselves in his accurate stories!

13. Read one of Steinbeck's novels: *Grapes of Wrath*, *In Dubious Battle*, or *Of Mice and Men* are suggested. Specific suggestions for teaching his work are not developed here, as they will be familiar to most English teachers.

Evaluation

1. Through the quiz on Chapter 1 of *America Is in the Heart*, assess students' understanding of rural life in the Philippines in the early twentieth century.

2. Through their booklets containing their journal responses, drawings, and titles and their group work on The Plum Plum Pickers, assess students' comprehension of living and working conditions for migrant workers in rural California; these assignments should be graded.

3. Assess students' identification of the main features of the writing styles of Carlos Bulosan, Raymund Barrio, and John Steinbeck through their writing assignments and class discussion.

4. Assess students' understanding of rich metaphorical language through their group work on *The Plum Plum Pickers*.

Resources

Barrio, R. (1971). *The plum plum pickers* (2nd ed.). Binghamton, NY: Bilingual Press.
Bulosan, C. (1946). *America is in the heart: A personal history*. New York: Harcourt, Brace.
Jimenez, F. (1999). *The circuit: Stories from the life of a migrant child*. Boston: Houghton Mifflin.

Literature on Migrant Workers and Exploitation

WHY THE
CHANGES?

Curriculum Content and Materials

John Steinbeck is commonly taught in English classes. As in the "Before" lesson, students could prepare to read novels by Steinbeck by researching his life and reading some of his short stories. The "After" lesson retains Steinbeck's work but shifts the focus from the person of Steinbeck to the issues he and others wrote about. By widening the context to include the experiences of other California migrant workers, the students have a richer experience—often one that includes them more easily.

My Filipino students were enchanted by the chapters from Bulosan's book, since it was the first time they had ever seen themselves included in the curriculum! The students were a source of elucidation for some parts of the story and an inspiration to me to include more Filipino literature. I have learned in my studies that the Filipino American experience is a rich part of this country's history and hence should be addressed in any American literature class. My Mexican American students also need to see themselves reflected in the curriculum, and others need to encounter Mexican American experiences in a way that leads to empathy and understanding—with a respect for differences and an appreciation of commonalities. Latino literature allows for this if used by a teacher who is comfortable with the stories and sensitive to the culture. Students whose first language is Spanish are empowered when a story contains a few words in Spanish and they are then the expert in translation or pronunciation. It seems a little thing, but I cannot tell you how often an otherwise quiet boy comes alive when he sees his life mirrored in the story; a light comes into his eyes that ever is my inspiration to bring more Latino literature into my classroom, where 50 percent of my students are Mexican American.

Yes, this route "into" Steinbeck's work takes longer in the "After" plan but when you decide as a teacher to bring multicultural perspective into your curriculum, you are revisioning the whole curriculum. As you bring in more good, diverse literature, some other pieces, perhaps those that have become favorites over the years, will have to go.

That does not mean that an author like Steinbeck goes, but his work is recontextualized. Maybe it will take longer to teach a particular book because you have transformed your approach to focus on a theme, enriched by multiple perspectives! Clustering your curriculum around themes, dipping into the rich veins of literature that reflect many cultural experiences, will be such a rewarding experience for you and your students that you will not miss the way you used to teach. I promise!

▶ LESSON PLAN[12]

Clothing in Spanish

BEFORE

Subject Area: Elementary Spanish
Grade Level: 9–12
Time: One class period
Note: It is important that students learn colors in Spanish before this lesson.

Objectives

1. Students will use clothing vocabulary orally and the present indicative of the verb *to wear* in declarative, negative, and interrogative sentences.

2. Students will use this language in writing.

Suggested Procedures

1. Review colors by displaying crayons one at a time and asking students to identify them by color name in Spanish.

2. Describe what you are wearing in Spanish, using a story to make it interesting (e.g., "It's summer so I'm wearing shorts. But this is Seattle and—surprise—it's raining and I'm cold."). Continue describing your clothing, making sure everyone understands the vocabulary.

3. Choose a student to describe his or her clothing in Spanish. Continue with several students, letting them gradually take over the descriptions. Make sure everyone practices the declarative, negative, and interrogative forms. For example,

FIRST STUDENT:	Is Peter wearing blue jeans?
SECOND STUDENT:	No, Peter's not wearing blue jeans. He's wearing black pants.

Also make sure all forms of the verb *to wear* are learned. For example, "Jack is wearing blue jeans. You are wearing blue jeans. They are wearing blue jeans." If anyone has trouble understanding the idea of *to wear* in Spanish, remove your watch and say, "I'm not wearing a watch." Put the watch back on and say, "I'm wearing a watch." The students should catch on.

4. Tell the students to close their eyes. Choose one student to leave the room. Have the other students open their eyes and together try to remember what the

[12]*Source:* Claire Alldred, Seattle, Washington.

missing student is wearing. As the items are named in Spanish, one student can draw them with crayons on butcher paper tacked on the wall. This reinforces the vocabulary visually and helps everyone remember what items have been named. When students have listed all the items they can, the missing student returns and the remaining items are named. Repeat this procedure with several students.

5. Give half the students pictures of people from magazines and the other half descriptions written in Spanish that each match one picture. The students move around the room, matching pictures with descriptions. Displaying their picture, one of each pair reads the description to the class.

6. Distribute magazines. Each student cuts out a picture of a person and writes a description in Spanish. This can be done as homework.

Evaluation

1. Through their oral participation, evaluate students' comprehension and oral mastery of the language presented.

2. Through their written descriptions, evaluate students' ability to use the language in writing.

Clothing in the Spanish-Speaking World

Subject Area: Elementary Spanish

Grade Level: 9–12

Time: Two class periods

Objectives

1. Students will use clothing vocabulary orally and the present indicative of the verb *to wear* in declarative, negative, and interrogative sentences.

2. Students will use this language in writing.

3. Students will combine new language with previously learned language: colors, professions, and weather.

4. Students will appreciate the cultural diversity of the people who speak the target language.

5. Students will appreciate clothing different from their own.

Suggested Procedures

1. Preliminary activity: Have each student read a different article in Spanish, written or adapted by the teacher, about the way of life of a certain Spanish-speaking community. The communities should be in Spain, Central America, South America, the United States, and the Caribbean. The articles may or may not refer directly to clothing but should include information that allows students to form ideas of the clothing worn by the people. For example, an article about Galicia (the northwestern region of Spain) could inform students that farming is an important industry in Galicia and that the farmlands are divided into small plots so that many people own some land; that the climate is temperate, rainy,

and unpredictable; and that, in the larger towns, people are fashion conscious, and several of Spain's most famous fashion designers are from Galicia. Students can deduce that work clothes, rain gear, and high-fashion clothes are all likely to be worn by people living in Galicia.

2. Review colors by displaying crayons one at a time and asking students to identify them in Spanish by color name. Review professions and weather by displaying relevant pictures and asking students to describe them.

3. Describe your own clothing in Spanish, relating it to your gender, age, nationality, region, and occupation, as appropriate. After enumerating all items of clothing, return to each item and ask, "Why?" Elicit ideas from students, supplying them when necessary. For example,

TEACHER:	I'm wearing a skirt. Why?
STUDENT:	You're a woman, you work, you're a teacher.
TEACHER:	Why am I wearing boots?
STUDENT:	You're wearing boots because it's cold out. It's raining. You live in Seattle.

If anyone has trouble understanding the idea of *to wear*, remove your watch and say, "I'm not wearing a watch." Put the watch back on and say, "I'm wearing a watch." The students should catch on.

4. Choose a student and elicit from the class, in Spanish, what he or she is wearing and why. You may need to supply vocabulary. Note that, although each item of clothing should be described, there will not always be a clear reason why the student is wearing it. Continue with several students, making sure everyone practices the declarative, negative, and interrogative forms. For example,

FIRST STUDENT:	Is Peter wearing blue jeans?
SECOND STUDENT:	No, Peter's not wearing blue jeans. He's wearing black pants.

Also make sure all forms of the verb *to wear* are learned. For example, "Jack is wearing blue jeans. You are wearing blue jeans. They are wearing blue jeans."

5. Tell students to close their eyes. Choose one student to leave the room. Have the other students open their eyes and together try to remember what the missing student is wearing. As the items are named in Spanish, one student can draw them with crayons on butcher paper tacked to the wall. This reinforces the Spanish vocabulary visually and helps everyone remember what items have been named. When students have listed all the items they can, the missing student returns and the remaining items are named. Repeat this procedure with several students.

6. Give half the students pictures of people from magazines, representing Spanish speakers of different ages, sexes, and nationalities. Give the other half descriptions written in Spanish. Have students move around the room, matching pictures with descriptions. Displaying their picture, have one of each pair of students read the description to the class.

7. Divide students into groups of five, making sure each group contains both more able and less able students. Give each group a packet containing five photos of Spanish speakers, mounted on tagboard and labeled with name, age, country, region or town, and occupation. The packet should also contain cutout photos of articles of clothing, some of which are suitable for each person.

   The students' task is to decide which clothes each person wears. Assembling the packets requires careful planning. Each person pictured must correspond to the culture described in one of the students' articles in the preliminary activity (see procedure 1). One student in each group will be the expert on the clothing worn by one of the people pictured. However, while some connections may be direct and unquestionable (e.g., the traditional clothing of some American Indians), others will be more open to interpretation and discussion. Rain gear, for example, may be appropriate for several people in the same packet. The choice of pictures will determine how many different combinations are possible in each packet. Pictures can also be chosen to raise specific points about Spanish-speaking cultures. For example, Spanish-speaking communities within the United States have points in common with those in foreign countries. American Indians live in varying degrees of separation and integration within Latino cultures. While countries may differ widely, their large cities are often similar. (These ideas can be expanded in future lessons, perhaps in social studies lessons conducted in English.)

8. After each group has matched people and clothing, have the group present its choices with its reasons to the rest of the class. For example, "Mari Carmen is a university student in Granada. She is twenty years old. Granada is very hot. Mari Carmen wears a white T-shirt, a blue skirt, espadrilles, white earrings, and a wristwatch." This example challenges the stereotypic notion that everyone in the south of Spain is either a bullfighter or a flamenco dancer. A university student there may wear something traditional and particularly suited to the climate (espadrilles) but also clothing similar to that worn by students in the United States. Her occupation eliminates possible choices of clothing more than it demands a certain kind. This could be exploited to practice negative sentences. For example:

   TEACHER: Does Mari Carmen wear a business suit?

   STUDENT: No, she doesn't wear a business suit.

9. Have each student write a description of one of the people in their packet.

10. Distribute old magazines. Each student cuts out a picture of a person and writes a description. Procedures 9 and 10 can be done as homework.

Evaluation

1. Through their oral participation, evaluate students' comprehension and oral mastery of the language presented.

2. Evaluate students' ability to use the language through their written descriptions.

3. Through the choices they make in procedure 10, evaluate students' acceptance of different kinds of people as Spanish speakers.

Clothing in the Spanish-Speaking World

Curriculum Content

World language classes often do not teach enough about the culture of the people who speak the target language, especially people in countries other than where the language originated. For example, while many Spanish teachers teach some information about the culture of Spain, fewer teach about the cultures of Spanish-speaking people in the Americas or about Latino Americans. Neglecting to teach about culture, and especially the culture of speakers of the target language in the United States, encourages students to retain false stereotypes and may keep them from cultivating opportunities to practice the language close to home.

In the "Before" lesson, the teacher is concerned only with teaching vocabulary and grammar; no attempt is made to relate it to culture. In the "After" lesson, however, the teacher uses the vocabulary to teach about the cultural diversity of Spanish speakers. In the process, students are asked to think about why people wear what they wear and to do so in Spanish. Not only do students learn more about cultural diversity among Spanish speakers, but their language practice is richer than in the "Before" plan. Clothing is not the only area in which cultural diversity can be taught. Many areas of vocabulary, such as foods, transportation, and family, lend themselves to this teaching.

Instructional Strategies

Both plans use a variety of modalities and grouping patterns. The "After" plan uses heterogeneous grouping to solve problems in addition to practicing language, which fosters higher-level thinking skills.

▶ LESSON PLAN

The Vietnam War

Subject Area: U.S. History

Grade Level: 10–12

Time: One week

Objectives

1. Students will describe U.S. foreign policy in Southeast Asia during the Johnson presidency.
2. Students will appreciate the pros and cons of U.S. involvement in Southeast Asia.
3. Students will learn of the major political and military events that took place during the Vietnam War.

Suggested Procedures

1. Discuss how the United States first became involved with Vietnam.
2. Have students read about reasons for Johnson's policy of escalating the Vietnam War in their history textbook.

3. Have students debate the pros and cons of President Johnson's authorization of military forces in Vietnam without a declaration of war from Congress.

4. Have students prepare reports about one of the following topics: the Gulf of Tonkin Resolution, the Tet Offensive, the Ho Chi Minh Trail, congressional Hawks versus congressional Doves, the Green Berets, the Geneva Agreement of 1954, and Operation Plan 34A.

5. Discuss with students why the Vietnam War divided our nation.

6. Have students interview their parents about their role in and feelings about the Vietnam War. Have them share this with the rest of the class.

Evaluation

1. Through a quiz, assess students' understanding of U.S. foreign policy in Southeast Asia and the major events of the Vietnam War.

2. Through discussion, assess students' appreciation of the pros and cons of U.S. involvement in Southeast Asia.

3. Through their research reports, assess students' knowledge of a major event of the Vietnam War.

The Vietnam War, Desert Storm, and the Wars in Afghanistan and Iraq

AFTER

Subject Area: U.S. History

Grade Level: 10–12

Time: Two weeks

Objectives

1. Students will describe U.S. foreign policy in Southeast Asia, the Middle East, Afghanistan, and Iraq.

2. Students will compare and contrast how those policies affected domestic policy during the Johnson, Bush I, Clinton, and Bush II presidencies.

3. Students will appreciate the pros and cons of U.S. involvement in Southeast Asia, the Middle East, Afghanistan, and Iraq.

4. Students will describe the role of U.S. soldiers during the Vietnam War, during Desert Storm, in Afghanistan, and in Iraq, including female soldiers and soldiers of color.

5. Students will describe the reactions of U.S. citizens to the four wars; they will examine how the reactions to these military engagements differ from each other.

6. Students will appreciate how soldiers who served in the Vietnam, Afghanistan, and Iraq wars were and still are affected—medically, economically, socially, and politically.

7. Students will examine the impact of the Vietnam War on Southeast Asian people (e.g., becoming refugees, living in camps for extended periods of time, immigrating to other countries) and develop an appreciation of their friendship and loyalty to the United States. Similarly, they will examine the impact of the

recent wars in Afghanistan on the Afghan people and their country. In addition, they will examine the impact of the the war in Iraq on the citizens of Iraq and their country.

Suggested Procedures

1. Have students read in their history text about Johnson's policy of escalating the Vietnam War. Have them also read the comments of Senator J. William Fulbright concerning his opposition to the war. Ask students to examine the merits and weaknesses of both of these arguments. Have other students retrieve and examine the editorial page of several U.S. newspapers at the beginning of Desert Storm and the wars in Afghanistan and Iraq.

2. Have students research the number of soldiers and other military personnel involved in the four military engagements and organize these data along race, class, and gender lines. Have students compare the number of soldiers of color and the number of white soldiers involved in the war with their representation in the total U.S. population. Discuss reasons why so many people of color and poor rural Whites participated in these military actions.

3. Have students investigate the role of women in the wars, both in the combat region and at home. Discuss ways that women's involvement has increased in these military actions.

4. Have some students research the attitudes of civil rights advocates (e.g., Martin Luther King Jr.) and peace advocates about the Vietnam War, Desert Storm, and the wars in Afghanistan and Iraq. Have students find out the reasons they felt as they did. If possible, have students interview or invite as guest speakers some conscientious objectors, to find out their views and the reasons for their actions.

5. Have some students research Mohammed Ali's position on the Vietnam War and how his attitude affected his boxing career. Also, compare that time in his life with how he was received at the 1996 Olympic Games. In addition, evaluate how the movie *Ali* was received and how Ali's position on the Vietnam War was portrayed.

6. Have students explore, analyze, and compare the differences in news coverage of the four wars.

7. Have some students prepare reports about the following topics:
   - Interviews with some people from Southeast Asia about their feelings on the Vietnam War and the effect it had on the average citizen of Southeast Asia.
   - The experiences of Amerasians, Vietnamese children whose fathers are U.S. soldiers who served in Vietnam, particularly their current struggle to find their fathers here in the United States.
   - The Amerasian Homecoming Act of 1987; 1987 was the year that Amerasians and families began to arrive in the United States. There are more than 70,000 Amerasian family members now in the United States.
   - The effects of war on soldiers who were involved. For a helpful resource, contact Veterans Affairs Secretary, Department of Defense, Washington, DC.

Evaluation

Assess students' knowledge and understanding of the Vietnam War, Desert Storm, and the wars in Afghanistan and Iraq by having them (as individuals, in pairs, or in small groups) present oral reports on a project they prepared about the military actions.

The Vietnam War, Desert Storm, and the Wars in Afghanistan and Iraq

WHY THE CHANGES?

Curriculum Content

The "After" plan helps students to understand how race, class, and gender factors relate to war. Also, the "After" plan has students examine four recent military actions.

Multiple Perspectives

For many years, U.S. citizens have debated the outcome of the Vietnam War and the role of the United States during that war. The "After" plan provides students with both pro and con perspectives on the war from two policymakers' (President Johnson and Senator Fulbright) points of view. The plan also presents the perspectives of U.S. soldiers who served in the war, of objectors and peace activists, of ordinary citizens, and of Southeast Asian people on whose territory the war was fought. The plan encourages students to examine these multiple perspectives and to form their own opinions about the war as well as the U.S. attack on Iraq.

In addition, the "After" plan, by comparing the four military actions, allows students to examine how groups who usually have diverse and varying opinions come together to support the country when the people believe they are fighting for the right thing.

Instructional Strategies

The "After" plan provides greater sensitivity than the "Before" plan to the ways students learn by offering more avenues for students to collect information on the war. For example, interviewing recent arrivals from Southeast Asia and Middle Eastern coutries can serve as strong motivating factors, getting students turned on to learning.

Evaluation

The "Before" and "After" plans have similar forms of evaluation. The advantage of the "After" plan, however, is that students present their reports in small groups, which fosters cooperative learning.

▶ THE MANY FACES OF SELF-INTEREST: A MULTIDISCIPLINARY AND MULTIGRADE UNIT[13]

The concept of self-interest is associated with many behaviors exhibited by a person or a group of people. Self-interest can be associated with personal or collective gain (e.g., greed or generosity and kindness). In this unit, students examine economic, political, national, group, and personal self-interest.

[13] *Source:* Deborah Bicksler, Stoughton, Wisconsin, and Carl A. Grant, University of Wisconsin—Madison.

Subject Areas: Economics, Social Studies, Language Arts, Computer Literacy
Grade Level: 8–12
Time: Ongoing throughout the semester

Authors' note: Because this unit is so long, to conserve space, we include here only the "After" Plans.

Lesson Plan 1

Objectives

1. Students will understand that self-interest is a motivating force in people's economic behavior.
2. Students will identify a number of different human behaviors that indicate that people make choices based on self-interest.
3. Students will define the following concepts: self-interest, pure market, competition, bargaining power, substitutes, and wealth.
4. Students will examine the economic behavior of individuals.

Suggested Procedures

1. Have students use the text *Economics Today and Tomorrow* (McGraw-Hill/Glencoe) or a similar text to research and write about the meaning of these concepts: self-interest, pure market, competition, and bargaining power.
2. Divide the students into five groups. Have each group assume one of the five occupations listed in the chart in Figure 5.6. Each group should discuss the self-interest of the person in that occupation with regard to price and cost

	Cloth Mill Operator	Garment Worker	Clothing Manufacturer	Consumer	Retail Merchant
Price/Cost	Low Cost, High Price	High Wages	Low Cost, High Price	Low Price	Low Cost, High Price
Safety					
Durability					
Fashion					
Competition					

Figure 5.6 Self-Interest Chart

of the product being made, safety of the workplace and product, durability of the product, fashionability of the product, and competition of the market for the product. After the initial discussion, have each group do some research on the market behavior of the person they are representing. Resources for research information can include television talk shows and newspaper articles (e.g., talk shows about money; articles written during the debates over raising the minimum wage; articles on the manufacturing of celebrity-endorsed products in so-called Third World countries at extremely low wages; TV personality Kathie Lee Gifford's and others' testimonies before Congress on the low pay and use of child labor to make products).

3. After the groups have completed their research from procedure 2, have them fill in the self-interest chart.

4. After completing the chart, have each group describe in one or two paragraphs how self-interest helps or hinders society to function better.

Evaluation

1. Through their short essay assignment and discussions, assess students' understanding of the concepts.

2. Evaluate each group's completion of the self-interest chart to which they were assigned.

Resource

Miller, R. L. (2007). *Economics today and tomorrow* (14th ed.). New York: Glencoe/McGraw-Hill.

Lesson Plan 2: Personal Self-Interest

Objectives

1. Students will relate their own self-interest with their social attitude and behavior.

2. Students will discuss how their own self-interest can affect their economic, national, and political behavior and behavior toward other groups.

3. Students will relate the self-interest behavior of literary characters to their own behavior or that of friends.

Suggested Procedures

1. Have students report on two literary characters whose self-interest affected their circumstances or the circumstances of their family or friends. They should tell whether the self-interest was to achieve economic, political, or personal gain.

2. Have students discuss in their working groups the times in life when it is important to consider one's self-interest.

3. Have students write a short essay on a time in their life when self-interest served as a motivating force. Have them answer the following: Was the outcome gratifying? Why or why not?

4. Discuss the implications from procedure 3 in terms of whether their decision making was self-serving with or without a concern for the common good.

Evaluation

1. Evaluate students' reports on two literary characters whose self-interest affected the circumstances of their family or friends.

2. Through their short essay assignment on a time in their life when self-interest was a motivating force, assess students' understanding of self-interest.

Lesson Plan 3: National Interest

Objectives

1. Students will learn that national interest is a motivating force that affects a country's economic behavior.

2. Students will identify the ways in which a country may respond to protect its national (self-)interest.

3. Students will examine the economic (self-)interest of countries.

4. Students will learn that sometimes actions taken on behalf of the entire country may have differential effects on groups of people living in that country (e.g., farmers).

Suggested Procedures

1. Discuss with students U.S. policies on protectionism and free trade in terms of national interest.

2. Organize students into six groups, and have each group report the reason(s) given to a country by its leaders before the country dealt with a national or international crisis: for example, President Franklin D. Roosevelt's first inaugural address, in 1933, to a depression-weary nation, when he said, "Let me assert my firm belief that the only thing we have to fear is fear itself—nameless, unreasoning, unjustified terror," and President Abraham Lincoln's second inaugural address, in 1865, when he said, "With malice toward none, with charity for all, with firmness in the right as God gives us to see the right, let us strive on to finish the work we are in, to bind up the nation's wounds."

   Other examples could include the following

   • President George Herbert Walker Bush's comments on Desert Storm (http://bushlibrary.tamu.edu/research/papers/1991/)
   • Shawnee leader Tecumseh's addresses in 1809–1811 to other American Indian tribal leaders to prevent further encroachment of tribal land
   • Winston Churchill's address to the British people during World War II
   • Lincoln's Gettysburg Address (www.loc.gov/exhibits/gaddl)
   • Corazon Aquino's address to the Philippine people after her election as president
   • Roosevelt's address to the United States at the beginning of World War II
   • George W. Bush's comments at the beginning of the war with Iraq (http://162.140.64.234/cgi-bin/getdoc.cgi?dbname = 2003_presidential_documents&docid = pd24mr03_txt-9)

- Winston Churchill
  (www.winstonchurchill.org/i4a/pages/index.cfm?pageid = 389)
- Tecumseh's address to William Henry Harrison
  (www.americanrhetoric.com/speeches/nativeamericans/chieftecumseh.htm)
- Roosevelt asks Congress to declare war
  (www.fdrlibrary.marist.edu/tmirhdee.html)
- Nelson Mandela's address to the South African people upon being elected president
  (www.anc.org.za/ancdocs/history/mandela/1994/sp940502.html)
- Wilma P. Mankiller's initial inaugural address to the Cherokee Nation in 1987
- Mankiller, Wilma P. (1994) "Inaugural Address as Prinipal Chief of the Cherokee Nation," De Franciso, V & Jenser, M. (eds.) *Women's Voices in Our Time: Staments by American Leaders*. Prospect Heights, IL: Waveland.

3. Have students examine the reasons given by each of the leaders (e.g., military, economic, humanitarian; producer versus consumer welfare; the policy of free trade versus the policy of protectionism, or protection of national interest, which sets up a forced choice between the welfare of two groups). Free trade favors the welfare of consumers, whereas protectionism favors the welfare of producers. When one economic policy is employed by a government regarding a particular industry, the costs will vary. It matters greatly whether we favor policies that benefit almost everyone to some degree or policies that help or hurt a few people to a considerable degree. For example, there is a tradeoff when we weigh the gains from trade that accrue as lower prices for textiles or cars against the impact of protectionism on the jobs of textile workers or auto workers.

Another way to view the choice is the cost of inflation, which affects all, versus the cost of unemployment, borne by a few. The political voice of inflation drowns out the voice of unemployment. The injuries of those affected by foreign competition overshadow the whisper of consumers who would benefit from lower prices.

Have students work individually or in groups to complete the National Interest Chart in Figure 5.7. Remind them that newspapers and newsmagazines are excellent sources of information.

Evaluation

1. Through their written essay and oral presentation, assess students' understanding of national interest.

2. Assess students' group reports on a country's demonstration of national self-interest versus a broader interest.

Resources

Blanche, J. D. (1990). *Native American reader: Stories, speeches and poems*. Juneau, AK: Denali Press. (for Mankiller's address)

Constantino, Renato (1982) Civil liberties and the Aquino rhetoric: The new historic task. Quezon City, Philippines: Karre.

Josephy, A. M., Jr. (1969). *The patriot chiefs*. New York: Viking Press. (for Tecumseh's speech)

Country: _____

Problem/Issue	Action 1	Action 2	Action 3
1. Protectionism of domestic families (vegetable vs. free trade)	ban imports from Mexico Who does this policy help or hurt and why?	continue open import of vegetables Who does this policy help or hurt and why?	import tax placed on all vegetables Who does this policy help or hurt and why?
2.			
3.			
4.			

Figure 5.7   National Interest Chart

Lesson Plan 4: Political Interest

Objectives

1. Students will describe self-interest as a motivating force in a politician's behavior.
2. Students will examine the political behavior of politicians from different political parties.

Suggested Procedures

1. Organize students into pairs, and have them report on how political party leaders respond to national concern (e.g., social security reform; No Child Left Behind; the Republican leadership and the Democratic leadership's position on the minimum wage).
2. Have the pairs use computer research methods, such as NewsBank (www.newsbank.com), to retrieve from various newspapers across the country politicians' responses to different legislation.
3. Have students watch C-SPAN channels and take notes on the information given in speeches by members of Congress discussing their positions on issues.
4. Have student groups identify an interest group within their community and ascertain how and why it has taken a position on a certain problem or issue. Have the student group seek to discover the group motivation for its actions.
5. Have students complete the Political Interest Chart in Figure 5.8 with information collected from procedures 2, 3, and 4. (Students may wish to keep this chart active throughout the semester, adding information as it becomes available.)

Politician: _____

Political Position	Action 1	Action 2	Action 3
1.			
2.			
3.			

Figure 5.8 Political Interest Chart

Evaluation

1. Assess students' understanding of political interest in their written reports and oral discussion.

2. Assess students' research skills by the success they have locating information for their assignment.

3. In a short essay, assess whether students understand why and how politicians make decisions to satisfy their political interest.

Lesson Plan 5: Self-Interest and Self-Determination of Marginalized Groups

Objectives

1. Students will learn how the self-interest and self-determination of marginalized groups served as a sustaining factor in their determination to survive and become socially (i.e., economically and politically) successful.

2. Students will learn how some groups in this country have been marginalized.

Suggested Procedures

1. Discuss with students the sensitivity that needs to be exercised when students begin to examine issues that may be personal.

2. Organize students into five or six groups, and have each group select a historical or contemporary group that fought major obstacles to survive as a group (e.g., Amish; Pilgrims; Cherokee tribe's 1830s fight against relocation; Chinese who were recruited to the United States in the 1860s to work as contract laborers on the transcontinental railroad; German Jews who survived the Holocaust; African Americans who survived enslavement; women who fought to achieve voting rights; Cambodian and Laotian refugees who were displaced from their homes and country; Japanese Americans who survived internment).

3. Have students complete the chart in Figure 5.9 with information collected from procedures 1 and 2 (e.g., for women as the marginalized group, the problem could be listed as "suffrage" and the issue could be listed as "mobilizing and

Marginalized Group: _____

Problem/Issue	Action 1	Action 2	Action 3
1.			
2.			
3.			

Figure 5.9   Marginalized Group Self-Interest/Self-Determination Chart

heightening of awareness and activism" [overt demonstrations and political pressure on state and federal government]). Also, have students keep this chart active throughout the semester.

Evaluation

1. Assess students' sensitivity toward one another by the way they ask questions and interact with each other.
2. Assess student groups' success completing the Marginalized Group Self-Interest/Self-Determination Chart.
3. Assess each student group's written and oral reports.

Features of This Unit

Curriculum Materials

During this unit, students will be asked to use a variety of curriculum resources, including newspapers, the Web, television, magazines, and textbooks.

Curriculum Content

The curriculum materials will provide students with varying points of view, utilizing national and international perspectives from men and women. The material is designed to appeal to students' interests by suggesting the use of current topics and topics relevant to their life circumstances.

Multiple Perspectives

The unit is designed to engage students in an examination of how the self-interests of individuals and groups of people influence the perspectives that they hold.

Instructional Strategies

The unit is designed to appeal to the many different ways students like to learn. It makes use of the Web. (We know that all students may not have access to the Web, but we hope an increasing number will.) Students work in pairs and small groups to discuss and research topics to complete charts or prepare reports based on their findings. Oral and written reports are requested to strengthen both methods of presentation. Research using materials other than the encyclopedia or textbooks is included to introduce and strengthen students' research skills and avenues of investigation.

Student Evaluation

The unit allows for a comprehensive and continuous evaluation over an extended period of time. Students are afforded greater opportunity to learn concepts and to demonstrate their knowledge of these concepts. Students' knowledge and procedures for conducting research should show improvement throughout the unit; their critical thinking skills should be increasingly sophisticated as they learn how interest influences many human actions.

Home and Community Relationships

Often, home and community relationships are discussed in terms of "partnerships" and "working together," without exploring why members in a community feel and act as they do. This unit has students examining why community groups take the positions they assume on certain issues and how certain groups or workers within a community may be particularly affected by policy decisions made for national interest.

References

Gorski, P. C. (2005). *Multicultural education and the Internet*. Boston: McGraw-Hill.

Hoijer, H. (1938). *Chiricahav and Mescalero Apache Texts*. Chicago: University of Chicago Press.

Spinder, M. J. (1933). *Songs of the Tewa*. Santa Fe: Soustore Press.

CHAPTER 6

Multicultural and Social Justice Education

What can schools do to help bring about a fairer world, or can they do anything? In what ways do schools themselves help to produce patterns of institutional discrimination, and how can those processes be interrupted? In the twenty-first century, what does it mean to be a citizen in a large, democratic society, built on racism and the competitive pursuit of wealth? What does it mean to be a citizen in a new global economy in which conflicts over racism, escalating gaps between rich and poor, cultural imperialism, and environmental sustainability are fought behind conference doors and in the street?

These are among the concerns addressed by this educational approach. The term *social justice* refers to philosophical roots of the approach—the belief that schools in a democracy can and should prepare citizens to work actively and collectively on problems facing society. To have social justice and a multicultural education in most societies individuals will have to work together for change. Individuals often feel powerless to effect significant social changes, believing that their only source of major government and social participation is through voting, and even then they wonder whether their single votes will make a difference. But history—the histories of our country and other countries—teaches us that when people organize and coalesce with other existing advocacy groups, they can make a significant difference. However, to do so successfully requires the ability to identify manageable aspects of social problems, which takes practice and commitment. Consider, for example, the United Farm Workers, who collectively pressed for and in many cases achieved better working conditions and wages. Or consider community action groups such as renters' organizations who have won rent controls so that people will not be forced out of their homes. Also consider Mothers Against Testing, an action group of parents and caregivers who challenge all of the purposes for all the tests students have to take.

Multicultural social justice education is based on the premise that political participatory consciousness should be learned in school. We develop this argument more fully in our companion text, *Making Choices for Multicultural Education* (Sleeter & Grant, 2009). The school is the primary social institution, outside the immediate family and perhaps religious institutions, in which young people spend much of their time. As such, the school is an ideal place for young people to learn collectively how to make an impact on social institutions. To a limited extent, schools already do this when they develop a student government or teach conflict resolution skills, but multicultural social justice education develops participation further than schools usually take it. Generally, schools limit the range of issues students can address to those that are relatively noncontroversial. At the same time, schools generally teach the young to revere rather than critique the nation's political and economic institutions, and to view society as fair and just, even with its flaws. One can argue that much of schooling helps to foster acquiescence and political apathy. Most of us would agree that social participation should include more than voting and obeying, and that the passive obedience schools generally demand of students contradicts our belief in an active, democratic society. Thus, the multicultural social justice approach holds that the school should consciously and actively teach and model participatory democratic living and that the entire school experience should be reoriented to address difference and justice based on race, social class, language, disability, sexual orientation, religion, and gender, both locally and globally.

Some people argue, for example, that racism in the United States is slowly withering away and will disappear altogether with time, but this argument ignores the poverty and powerlessness that people of color continue to experience. It also ignores the increasing degree to which people of color, immigrants, poor people, people who are not Christian or Jews, gay men, lesbians, transgenders, and bisexuals have felt under assault during the last two decades. Furthermore, even though U.S. citizens recognize that racial and gender inequality are unjust, most accept our highly class-stratified society, in which both poverty and extreme wealth exist and gaps between rich and poor are growing exponentially. As a society, we remain perplexed about how to deal with homophobia, even though we know that the gay, lesbian, transgender, and bisexual population make up a significant portion of our society. Globally, U.S. citizens tend to view our own way of life and our economic and political institutions as best, but by incorporating the rest of the world into this way of life one can say that we are engaging in a new form of colonialism. These are highly significant issues worth serious examination.

The multicultural social justice education approach deals with multiple forms of oppression as they intersect. For example, the approach would not concentrate solely on sexism because sexism does not fully address the needs and concerns of women of color and women living at or below the poverty level. Sexism needs to be connected to racism and class oppression. Furthermore, connecting issues such as ecology to other social justice issues is not difficult. For example, environmental racism connects ecology with racism by critiquing the use of communities of color and American Indian reservations as waste dump sites for affluent European American communities. In other words, this approach to multicultural education places justice, democracy, and sustainability at the center.

▶ GOALS AND OBJECTIVES

The approach discussed in this chapter attempts to prepare students to be citizens able to actualize the social justice ideology that is the cornerstone of democracy. It teaches students about justice and power, encourages them to be aware that the "isms" (e.g., racism, sexism) are continually being redefined in order to continue existing as society changes, fosters an appreciation and acceptance of the diverse peoples around the globe, and teaches political action skills and a consciousness that affirms human worth. Although the approach builds on the multicultural education perspective, it is more action oriented.

Critical Questioning

Why is it that, in a very wealthy nation, large numbers of children and families go without anything even approaching adequate medical or dental care? This is not an unsolvable problem, but it is one that persists as if it were unsolvable. Paulo Freire (1970, 1973) wrote extensively about the development of critical questioning and critical consciousness among people who either have learned to accept the status quo or have accepted that they are powerless to do anything about it. He argued that the dominant class in any society will give answers to questions such as the one above, but that their answers will not disrupt fundamental existing relationships of power and resources. The dominant class has the power to promote its perspective as if it were the only legitimate perspective. Today, the media are a prominent venue through which the dominant ideology is given shape in people's everyday world. Because newspapers, TV, films, textbooks, and bookstores are today owned by a shrinking number of corporations, some voices dominate while others have to fight to be heard.

Empowerment begins by asking questions that arise out of the everyday living conditions of people, and by refusing to accept answers and explanations as true without investigation. Critical questioning involves asking not only "Is this true?" but also "Who says so?" "Who benefits most when people believe it is true?" "How are we taught to accept that it is true?" and "What alternative ways of looking at the problem can we see?" There is a real challenge here for teachers because generally curricula do not arise out of the everyday living conditions of ordinary people; curricula are increasingly defined by state standards, federal policy. and textbook companies. Thus, teaching critical questioning may begin by questioning "truths" and silences in textbooks. An example of a lesson plan that teaches critical questioning is "Story Time" (p. 269).

Practice Democracy

Most schools are not democratic places. The flow of decision making is generally top-down rather than rising up from below. State legislators tell educators what to do, principals tell teachers what to do, teachers tell students what to do, and educators tell parents what to do, particularly parents who are not well educated or who are economically poor. As a result, most school curricula do not relate directly to students' own lives, which may account for much of their boredom with and alienation from school. Students often ask why they must learn about things that are unrelated to their experiences.

In this approach, the teacher deals with issues in students' own lives and helps them to connect broader social issues with their own experiences. Although individual teachers cannot change a whole system of hierarchical decision making, teachers can reverse the flow of discussion and decision making around them and build relations of dialogue in their classrooms and with parents. What knowledge, viewpoints, and interests do students bring? What concerns do parents, caregivers, and community members have? How can the classroom and school be opened for dialogue?

To practice democracy in the classroom and school, students can collectively learn to make substantive decisions in matters they care about. This does not mean giving free rein to students; rather, it means opening up considerably more avenues for student decision making than are generally found in schools. Of course, structure and learning to respect authority are important, but real growth and maturity come from an understanding of why structure is needed and from participation in forming and establishing that structure.

Dialogue and democratic decision making are difficult because they involve opening up differences of opinion for discussion. It means learning to listen to other points of view, including points of view that one might have been taught "don't count" or are products of ignorance. It means learning to negotiate rather than simply accepting majority rule. Lesson plans that teach dialogue and democratic decision making include "Language Experience" (p. 266), "Ancient Egypt and Its Lens on Social Organization" (p. 281), "City Government" (p. 294), and "The U. S. Legal System: Justice for All (p. 314).

Analyze Systems of Oppression

In a study that we conducted (Grant & Sleeter, 1996), we noticed that many of the junior high girls who were from the lower middle class were not strongly interested in patterning their gender identity after their mothers and were more thoughtful about their futures than the boys. The girls argued that, although they admired and loved their mothers, they wanted a different kind of life. They were not mainly interested in raising kids, taking care of their husbands or significant others, and providing part of the family income. Instead, they wanted professional careers and more control of their lives. Many of the boys, on the other hand, held unrealistic dreams of playing professional sports and gave little consideration to other professional alternatives. Complicating the girls' pursuit of their goals, however, was their lack of consistent and careful analysis about their choice of boyfriends and their occasional downplaying of their intellectual side to appeal to the boys. For many girls, the selection of boyfriends was based more on the boy's popularity, coolness, or romantic pursuit than the boy's dedication to a realistic career-oriented future.

The school involved in this study missed a chance to engage students on these issues, which were of real concern to the students. Although it is very important to encourage young people to aspire to become anything they wish, it is also important to help them learn to think systemically about oppression and justice as it plays out in their own lives. Why is it that young men in communities of color and White low-income communities see relatively few options for a better life and tend to latch onto dreams such as becoming an athletic star? Why is it that young women from working-class backgrounds very often aspire to a career, but at the same time often subordinate themselves to the men in their lives? These questions beg for a systemic analysis of sexism, social class, and racism. A systemic analysis of sexism, for example, would examine why full-time working women still earn less than men. It would help students connect devaluation of women in the job market with devaluation of women's work in the home. A systemic analysis of social class would examine why working-class jobs are increasingly being replaced by very low-paying service work, and how worker efforts to organize are constantly being thwarted. It would also extend this line of analysis to the restructuring of the global economy, examining what kinds of jobs are going where, how large corporations are directing these changes, and what people can do to challenge the trends.

In the United States, people in general are not taught to think systemically. For you as a teacher, learning to analyze in terms of systems and institutions of oppression may require work. Generally, people in the United States think in terms of individual opportunity. Also, when considering culture and human differences, generally, people disconnect these from social structures. For example, one of the authors came across a curriculum guide that presented different kinds of housing around the world as a way of examining cultural diversity. Africa was represented by a Zulu hut. The author of the curriculum guide appeared to be unaware that most Africans today live in houses and apartments, but also that a very large proportion of dwellings in Africa lack access to electricity, running water, and so forth. Housing as a manifestation of culture needs to be situated within relations of racism, colonialism, and economic exploitation. Without connecting everyday culture to access, and access to systems that may be just or unjust, teachers can inadvertently end up teaching stereotypes and reinforcing ignorance.

To teach about systems of oppression, the teacher can begin with students' own experiences with issues of race and class or with unequal opportunities and resources available to dominant (versus minority) groups. We know of a teacher in a farm community who encouraged students to find out about pesticides that were being used in the fields and causing health problems to farm workers (including students' family members). On the basis of their investigation, students began to speak out about pesticides and farm-worker health. As another example, as young people become curious about sex, they also become concerned about diseases such as AIDS/HIV. This curiosity (and fear) provides an excellent opportunity for examining people's feelings about AIDS and about gay and lesbian people, and the way those feelings have translated into inadequate funding of research on cures. In addition, discussion of AIDS and HIV and the use of condoms in relation to traditional male behavior and inequities toward females in Africa provide an excellent opportunity to discuss gender equity.

Social issues become more real and meaningful to students when they are encouraged to examine them from a personal viewpoint, and students are more likely to act on issues that have meaning than on distant, abstract issues. For example, that European Americans in general have greater access to jobs than African Americans or Latinos is a significant social issue but one that is difficult to resolve in the abstract. However, that European American teenagers are being more actively recruited by employers than African American or Latino teenagers may be an issue students are actually experiencing. Also, another issue may involve the fact that male teenagers are being more actively recruited for employment or for positions that provide some managerial training than female teenagers. As students experience systems of oppression in their own lives, they usually want to dig more deeply into them. They can often sense when adults are sidestepping issues or glossing over real concerns. As students learn to use education as a tool for addressing issues they face, schooling can become much more relevant and empowering.

Lessons in which students analyze issues in their own life experiences include "Language Experience" (p. 266), "Rate and Line Graph" (p. 290), "Advertising for an Audience" (p. 301), and "Biological Determinism" (p. 318). Action Research Activity 6.2

is designed to help teachers identify the social issues of most concern within the local community.

Encourage Social Action

The approach we discuss here encourages social action by having students actually work on social issues. Student involvement can take many forms, including writing letters, engaging in community service, and producing and distributing information about a community problem. The teacher must investigate the suitability of various forms of action in the local community (see Action Research Activity 6.2). In addition, the teacher must be careful not to pressure students into doing or saying anything that is contrary to their beliefs. Rather, the teacher should show students how they can act constructively on issues and needs that exist within the community. The lesson "Taking Action Against Discrimination" (p. 322) illustrates social action.

Many schools teach students the skills of conflict resolution. By itself, conflict resolution is not necessarily the same as social action, but when it is combined with political awareness it can lead to social action skills. Let us give an example. A school experiences student fighting and implements a conflict resolution program. In that program, students are taught to express their feelings using "I" statements, to actively listen to feelings that other students express, and to cooperatively develop solutions for conflicts in which no student loses. Peer mediators may be trained to assist in this process.

When examined politically, we can see that many of the conflicts erupting within the school stem from community conflicts or issues related to powerlessness in the community. For example, students who lack access to jobs and meaningful recreational opportunities often hang out on the streets and become involved in gang activities. Conflict resolution may mean examining issues in the community that affect students' lives and figuring out how to do something constructive to meet students' needs. If recreational activities are lacking, students can organize to get their community to provide more recreational opportunities.

One of our former colleagues spent years organizing urban gang youth to produce murals articulating their concerns publicly. In so doing, she helped students work through conflicts they had with each other, learn to identify larger social origins of their frustrations and conflicts, and begin to collaborate to voice their needs and concerns to larger audiences. In so doing, she was able to channel the energy of conflict into social advocacy and action. Another colleague told us about teaching her first-grade class the use of conflict resolution to settle their disputes. She described how these first graders taught older students (third and fourth grade) to use conflict resolution to resolve disagreements on the playground as well as arguments with older brothers and sisters.

▶ ACTION RESEARCH ACTIVITY 6.1

Student Decision Making

Use Table 6.1 to help you analyze your classroom or school in terms of the extent to which students are involved in decision making, as well as to identify the areas in which decision making can be broadened and for which students. Pay attention to

Table 6.1   Analyzing Students' Opportunities to Make Decisions

Situations Requiring Decision Making	Decisions Are Made by		Which Students Are Involved?			How Often?		
	Individual	Group	All	Some	A Few	Often	Sometimes	Never
1. Where to sit								
2. Whom to work with; whether to work alone or with someone								
3. What order to accomplish or to work on tasks								
4. Due dates								
5. What materials or procedures to use in accomplishing assignments								
6. Classroom rules								
7. What assignments must be completed								
8. Grading policies and procedures								
9. Supplementary or "extra" content to learn or study								
10. Main content to study								
11. Schoolwide behavior rules								
12. School policies								

which students are hindered in decision making and why. Also determine the extent to which students are invited to make decisions on an individual versus a group basis.

▶ ACTION RESEARCH ACTIVITY 6.2

Discovering Issues of Concern to the Community

The multicultural social justice approach to education contends that teachers become familiar with issues that are of concern to the communities their school serves. Student demographic changes, school boundary changes, and the growth of specialized schools (such as charter and magnet schools) make it increasingly difficult to determine a school's community and to familiarize oneself or keep up with the concerns of the different groups of people the school serves.

To learn more about the community, first find out who, if anyone, local residents of the community see as their leaders/spokespeople. Find out with what religious institutions and local organizations the people in the neighborhood are affiliated. Also learn what media (newsletters, local and ethnic newspapers, religious institution bulletins) serve the neighborhood.

To identify the main issues currently facing the community, interview two or three community leaders or parents and pay attention to media that represent the community, or organize teams of teachers to visit different neighborhood centers and community organizations and report back to the entire staff what they learned. Some questions that can help your investigation include the following:

1. What problems or issues are currently facing the community?
2. What main improvements would community members like to see?
3. What kinds of additional resources could the community best use, and for what?
4. What resources does the community currently have for addressing these issues, and what is the community currently trying to do about them?
5. What are the community's greatest strengths?
6. What should future citizens be learning to contribute best to the local community's growth, development, and improvement?

▶ LESSON PLAN

Language Experience

BEFORE

Subject Area: Reading

Grade Level: 1–6

Time: Ongoing

Objectives

1. Students will express themselves orally.
2. Students will read orally with accuracy and expression.
3. Students will distinguish between fact and fiction.

Suggested Procedures

1. Discuss with students the difference between fiction and nonfiction, emphasizing that fictional characters are made up, even though they may seem like real people.
2. Tell students to create a fictional story about children their own age in a fictional school. They should begin the story with an opener such as, "Once upon a time, a fourth-grade class was working on spelling, when suddenly something happened." Ask students to dictate the story while you write it on the board or type it into a computer with a display screen large enough for all students to view. Students can contribute lines to the story in round-robin fashion so that everyone is included.
3. Distribute a copy of the story to each student. Discuss elements of the story that make it fiction rather than fact.

4. Have students practice reading their completed story. Ask each student to add new words from the story to his or her own collection of flashcards of new words to practice.

5. When students have mastered the story to the best of their ability, repeat the procedure. (This activity may be integrated with other approaches to teaching reading.)

Evaluation

1. Assess students' reading skills by listening to them read the class's story.

2. Assess students' oral skills through their contributions to the stories.

3. Through the content of their stories and through class discussion, assess students' ability to distinguish between fact and fiction.

Language Experience

Subject Area: Reading
Grade Level: 3–6
Time: Three or four days

Objectives

1. Students will express themselves orally.

2. Students will read orally with accuracy and expression.

3. Students will distinguish between fact and fiction.

4. Students will analyze how student groups oppress each other.

Suggested Procedures

1. Discuss with students the difference between fiction and nonfiction, emphasizing that fictional characters are made up even though they may seem like real people.

2. Tell students to create a fictional story about children their own age in a fictional school; the story should be about a real event that occurs in the classroom or on the playground. Ask them to discuss and to choose collectively from the following list of events (the teacher can offer other choices, but all choices should relate to students' experiences):

   a. At recess, some students try to join an activity or use equipment that other students usually dominate; however, they are unwelcome.

   b. When teachers are not present, some students tease others, putting them down and trying to hurt or anger them.

   c. During a classroom activity, some students manage to hog the most and best resources.

   d. When choosing teams for an activity, some students are always chosen first and others are always chosen last.

   e. At recess, some large students pick on some of the smaller students.

   f. At recess, boys do not allow girls to play; they tell them that girls are not strong enough or skilled enough to play.

Tell students that the story should portray fictional characters who act like real children.

3. Ask students to dictate the story while you write it on the board or type it into a computer with a display screen large enough for all students to view. Students can contribute lines to the story in round-robin fashion so that everyone is included.

4. Have students practice reading their completed story. Ask each student to add new words from the story to his or her own collection of flashcards of new words to practice.

5. Through class discussion, analyze the students' story using the following questions (reword them as needed so that students comprehend):
   a. Which children lose in the story? Is there anything about them that may lead to their losing? (Probe for descriptors, not evaluative judgments.)
   b. Which students gain something? (Probe in the same way.)
   c. Is there anything about the students that may lead to their winning?
   d. Of the children that gain, who are the leaders and who just go along for what they can gain from the situation?
   e. How do the students who gain something work things so that they can keep controlling situations like this?

6. Ask students whether it might be possible to resolve this situation so that everyone is treated fairly and equally. After discussing some possibilities, using the language experience approach again, have students make up a story about the same fictional characters in which the losers resolve the problem fairly and successfully.

7. Have students practice reading the new story.

8. Ask students if similar problems happen at their school. If so, discuss ways of resolving them and of establishing rules or procedures for students that promote fairness.

9. Pay attention to race, class, gender, and disability dynamics in what students talk about, and use this as a basis for helping them understand more about these areas. For example, if the "losers" tend to include special education students, regular education students probably know and appreciate little about their peers' needs and characteristics; the school may also unintentionally reinforce the low status of special students and the relatively higher status and "normalcy" of regular education students.

Evaluation

1. Assess students' reading skills by listening to them read the class's stories.

2. Assess students' oral skills through their contributions to the stories and to class discussion.

3. Through class discussion, assess students' understanding of oppression among peer groups.

4. Through class discussion and through the action they take on real conflicts in the school, assess students' skills at resolving group conflicts.

Language Experience

Practice Democracy

Democracy plays no role in the "Before" plan. In the "After" plan, students democratically select the topic for the story, and the teacher encourages students to consider and use democratic means to resolve group conflicts.

Analyze Systems of Oppression

In the "Before" plan, the content of the story is practically irrelevant; rather, students are encouraged to talk for the purpose of developing oral skill and to produce something to practice reading. In the "After" plan, however, content is important. The teacher uses a story based on students' own experiences to examine how groups of students oppress one another. The story itself is fictional, so students may analyze a problem from an objective perspective. Thus, the teacher specifies that the characters and the school be fictional but that the story revolve around how one group controls or puts down another group and that the characters behave like real people.

Class discussion of the story is also important in that the teacher helps students to identify the oppressors and the oppressed as groups (as opposed to a few individual bullies or victims with no shared characteristics), as well as to determine how the oppressors use a situation to their own benefit. The teacher must decide the extent to which race, class, gender, and disability dynamics are reflected in the story and discussion. At the same time, care should be taken not to force the students' experience into these categories; careful thought should be given to what the students' story tells about how these are operating in the school. As students become aware of race, class, gender, and disability dynamics in their own relationships with each other, this can be extended to lessons about diversity and oppression in the neighborhood, the community, and the wider society.

Encourage Social Action

The "After" plan encourages social action in two related ways. First, the second story that students dictate is one in which the oppressed group acts successfully in its own interest. The teacher should encourage students to make this story reflect some of the real problems, obstacles, and strategies that people use to defend themselves. Second, the discussion moves to real problems in the school and what can be done about them. Democratic processes should be encouraged here, and students should be actively supported in their attempts to resolve group conflicts fairly.

▶ LESSON PLAN[1]

Story Time

Subject Area: Reading
Grade Level: 1–8
Time: Ongoing

[1] *Source:* Maureen Gillette, William Patterson University, Wayne, New Jersey.

Objectives

1. Students will become interested in reading highly acclaimed books.
2. Students will gain an appreciation for and an enjoyment of reading through being read to. Students will enjoy books that are at or above their instructional levels.

Suggested Procedures

1. Select trade books that are considered classics to read to students throughout the year (e.g., *Charlotte's Web*, by E. B. White; *Tales of a Fourth Grade Nothing*, by Judy Blume; and *Curious George*, by H. A. Rey).
2. As time permits, read a portion of the chosen book to the class each day.

Evaluation

Assess students' enthusiasm for the books through their attentiveness to the teacher as books are read and through their own selection of books at a later date.

Resources

Blume, J. (1986). *Tales of a fourth grade nothing*. New York: Dell.
Rey, H. A. (1973). *Curious George*. Boston: Houghton Mifflin.
White, E. B. (1952). *Charlotte's web*. New York: Harper & Row.

Story Time

Subject Area: Reading
Grade Level: 3–8
Time: Ongoing

Objectives

1. Students will become interested in reading highly acclaimed books that represent diverse peoples in both text and illustrations.
2. Students will enjoy a variety of books both above and below their instructional levels.
3. Students will learn that some groups of people are oppressed and that oppression can manifest itself in many forms.
4. Students will analyze and synthesize ideas in stories.
5. Students will understand that reading is a prerequisite to the acquisition of certain types of knowledge, as well as a necessity for taking advantage of certain types of opportunities.
6. Students will generate alternatives to social conditions that restrict opportunities for oppressed groups of people and develop strategies for their accomplishment.

Suggested Procedures

1. Select trade books, especially those dealing with issues pertaining to race, class, gender, or disability, to read to students throughout the school year, for example:

   Baseball Saved Us, by K. Mochizuki
   Family Pictures/Cuadros de Familia, by Carmen Lomas Garza
   Felita and its sequel, *Going Home*, by Nicholasa Mohr

The Hot and Cold Summer, by J. Hurwitz
The Hundred Penny Box, by Sharon Bell Mathis
My Friend Jacob, by L. Clifton
Silent Lotus, by Jeanne M. Lee
Slake's Limbo, by Felice Holman
Smoky Night, by E. Bunting
Tar Beach, by F. Ringgold
The Well, by M. D. Taylor.

2. Develop a set of discussion questions related to the issues presented in the book. If the book is lengthy and will span two or three weeks, develop a series of questions to follow sections of the book.

3. As time permits, read a book (or a portion of a book) to students each day. Following the reading, have the class discuss issues raised in the reading, guided by the teacher's planned questions. This can be done in small groups or with the whole class. Focus specifically on issues related to race, class, gender, or disability in the story, probing for their relationship to story events. For example, probe the causes that led the boys in *The Hot and Cold Summer* to have preconceived stereotypic ideas about what the girl who was coming to visit would be like. It is often necessary to role-play parts of the story to give students a feeling for events from the viewpoint of the characters, especially when using stories outside children's experiential background, such as having a disability or living in an urban area when they do not. It may be helpful for the teacher to keep a journal of students' reactions to the books and to the discussions generated in class, as well as of ongoing evidence of improvement in their reading ability. The journal will help the teacher to see visible evidence of change in the students as individuals, in the class as a whole, and in the teacher's own practice.

4. Encourage students to generate alternative courses of action for the story characters based on earlier discussions of story events and to consider all applicable consequences to these alternatives. The teacher may want to ask for volunteers to state the alternative they prefer and to explain their rationale.

Discussion follows as other volunteers agree and disagree and offer alternative rationales. The teacher will be able to assess the extent to which students are critically analyzing and synthesizing issues related to race, class, gender, and disability. The teacher needs to provide a nonthreatening environment for doing this. Since much of what one believes comes from one's experiential background, the teacher must be aware of students' ability to understand the issues and should guide the discussion so that students experience a wide variety of ideas and rationales. The teacher also should help students to analyze their own backgrounds for experiences with oppression, either as oppressors or as the oppressed, which is best done in a nonthreatening way using examples from the story.

5. On completion of a book, give students a choice of projects related to the story. The class, either as a whole or in small groups, should decide in a democratic fashion on a follow-up activity that they believe is suitable for that particular book. The teacher should provide a short list of alternative projects and explore with the class the pros and cons of each one. The list of activities may vary but should end with one that allows students to design their own project. The following are some examples:

a. After reading *The Hot and Cold Summer*, students will have discussed the origins of sex-role stereotypes and how those stereotypes are broken down, and they will have speculated about the ability of the boys in the story to apply what they have learned about one female to all females. A small group of students then interviews younger students about their nontraditional roles (e.g., boys who enjoy playing with dolls or girls who enjoy playing with cars and trucks). The older students work with their younger partners to create a language experience book about that child. The finished product may be bound or laminated and shared with the younger student's peers. The younger child reads the book to a small group of his or her classmates, and the older child leads a discussion of nontraditional roles in an effort to break down stereotypes held by those children and to reinforce issues of equity. This activity not only gives older students an opportunity to become actively involved in promoting change, but can open the door for ongoing cooperative partnerships between older and younger students as well.

b. A small group of students reads another book dealing with the same or a related issue as the book discussed in class and then prepares a comparison between the two books. They may choose to read the book to the class and lead a discussion, or they may meet with the teacher to discuss their analysis. For example, following *The Hot and Cold Summer*, the class could read *Amazing Grace* by Mary Hoffman and discuss preconceived notions of ethnicity as it relates to theatrical role assignments. Since both books deal with strong, positive female protagonists, the theme can become explicit as the teacher addresses gender and ethnicity stereotypes.

c. In small groups, students rewrite the story (or part of the story) in play form, incorporating one or more of the alternatives and their consequences as discussed in class. As students rewrite the story, they should role-play the scenes to get a feel for the dialogue and the feasibility of the chosen alternative. The finished play can be produced with costumes and scenery and performed for the rest of the class.

d. The class can research the author(s) of text read in class. They can then compile a list of issue-related questions that they would like to ask the author. The list can be sent to the author or publisher with a cover letter written by the group that explains their discussion of the issue and their interest in the book. If feasible, they can invite the author to the school. When a high school class in California did this, the popular author Terry McMillan came to the school for a visit! She discussed her ideas and rationale for character development, plot, and the image of African American women that her works portray.

e. Two or three students can prepare the story and a plan for discussion with the students in the role of book leader. The story is then read and discussed in another class with the students as readers and discussion leaders.

f. Students rewrite the story (or part of it) from another person's perspective (e.g., having a disability versus not having a disability), with a different ending (perhaps more realistic), with a different protagonist (e.g., Latino instead of European American), or in a different setting (e.g., suburban rather than inner city).

    g. Older students rewrite difficult or longer stories for younger students. Pages may be illustrated, laminated, and bound. The books are read to and discussed with younger children by older children.

    h. The teacher should maintain a reading center in the class so that the students have available to them a wide variety of books that address the themes being discussed in class. Once they understand the format, students should be encouraged to develop their own literature circles whenever possible.

6. If the projects are done in small groups rather than as a class, students should meet as a whole class and share their projects. They should tell their classmates what they did, explain how and why they chose their project, and detail their analysis of the results.

Evaluation

1. Assess students' enthusiasm for the books being read to them through their attentiveness and their own selection of books at later dates.

2. Assess students' levels of discussion following the readings.

3. Assess the quality of students' project activities and the sharing of projects.

4. Determine the extent of students' carryover discussion of issues related to oppressed groups and social inequality into other content areas.

5. Assess students' improvement in reading ability as evidenced in all subject areas.

Resources

Bell Mathis, S. (1975). *The hundred penny box*. New York: Viking Press.
Bunting, E. (1994). *Smoky night*. San Diego: Harcourt Brace.
Clifton, L. (1980). *My friend Jacob*. New York: E. P. Dutton.
Garza, C. L. (1990). *Family pictures/Cuadros de Familia*. San Francisco: Children's Book Press.
Hoffman, M. (1998). *Amazing grace*. New York: Penguin.
Holman, F. (1977). *Slake's limbo*. New York: Schribner.
Hurwitz, J. (1985). *The hot and cold summer*. New York: Scholastic.
Lee, J. M. (1991). *Silent Lotus*. New York: Farrar, Straus & Giroux.
Mochizuki, K. (1993). *Baseball saved us*. New York: Lee & Low Books.
Mohr, N. (1996). *Felita*. New York: Penguin Books.
Mohr, N. (1999). *Going home*. New York: Penguin Books.
Ringgold, F. (1991). *Tar beach*. New York: Crown.
Taylor, M. D. (1995). *The well*. New York: Dial Books for Young Readers.

Story Time

WHY THE CHANGES?

Modeling and Celebrating Diversity and Equal Opportunity

Students who enter school with what has been termed "school knowledge" often do well from the start, especially in reading. Students who enter school without this knowledge are often members of an oppressed group, and many times they are of the "low-reading group" or characterized as "corrective readers." Once behind, they tend to fall farther below their grade levels. We all know how strongly a teacher's words and actions can influence students. Furthermore, reading to students of all ages has a positive impact on how they view reading. It is imperative that all students reach their full reading potential, because reading is such an essential life skill, a prerequisite for taking advantage of existing opportunities and for engaging in work to change societal inequalities. By setting up a reading center in the classroom and encouraging students to take charge of literature circle discussions as soon as they are able, the teacher fosters independent reading as a lifelong practice.

In both plans, the teacher models reading. The "After" plan, however, avoids what Smith, Greenlaw, and Scott (1987) found in their study of books most often read in elementary classrooms—that they maintain stereotypic sex roles and are void of people of color and those with mental or physical disabilities. Bishop (1993) confirms this view and comments on the detrimental effects on children of a monocultural and biased view of the world. More recently, in 2004 the Gender stereotypes@Everything2.com reported that "Traditional gender roles and stereotypes are so deeply ingrained in many societies that it is difficult to eliminate them in any arena of expression. Textbooks are now prevented by law from expressing any overtly sexist themes, and publishers work to avoid any sexist images or statements, but not everything you learn in school comes from textbooks. Children's literature often expresses women and men in traditional gender roles and helps to reinforce socialization that is recieved at home." The "After" plan uses books that offer a more equitable view of society while tapping the experiential background of a wide range of students. Critical teachers will want to obtain a copy of *Beyond Heroes and Holiday* edited by Lee, Menkart, and Okazawa-Rey (2002), a publication that contains numerous articles on how to help students detect bias in books, videos, software, and the media.

Critical Questioning

The use of books is a nonthreatening way for students to ask questions related to oppression. By using the story plot and the characters, the teacher can develop issues of social inequity outside students' own lives. As students feel comfortable with the issues, the teacher can gradually lead the discussion to the lives of the students. As children begin to recognize incidents involving oppression in their own lives, they can see them in context rather than as a personal statement about themselves.

Practice Democracy

The "After" plan allows for both collective decision making and student choice in the design of follow-up projects. Through a collective process of choosing a follow-up project, either as a class or in small groups with the teacher as guide, students learn to choose from among alternatives in a manner that is fair to all participants. By sharing projects, students become aware of alternative methods for goal accomplishment and gain an appreciation of the learning styles of their peers.

Encourage Social Action

Each followup activity, whether suggested by the teacher or students, should require students to apply what they have discussed to another situation. For many students, the ideas will be new and may need to be further thought out and assimilated; these students may benefit from a project that opens avenues for discussion with others. The "After" plan places students in the active roles of critical thinkers and problem solvers as they consider conditions that structure inequality. Thus, the reading becomes not only exciting and enjoyable to students but a communicative process as well. Only when reading reaches this level can students use it to take advantage of opportunities and to generate workable alternatives for action based on choice.

▶ **LESSON PLAN**

Environmental Studies

BEFORE

Subject Area: Science
Grade Level: 5–10
Time: One to two weeks, and throughout the semester

Objectives

1. Students will research the environmental/ecological problems in their area.

2. Students will list things they can do to become more involved in eliminating environmental/ecological problems.

Suggested Procedures

1. After prior investigation, initiate this lesson by taking the students on a walk to two teacher-selected contrasting areas in the community that illustrate a polluted area and a carefully monitored environment that shows good ecological management. After returning to the classroom, the students will discuss, compare, and contrast what they have seen and brainstorm the causes of the polluted area and why pollution is a detriment to the community and society.

2. Have the teacher and students set up an ecological interest center complete with research material (e.g., newspaper and magazine articles, books, films, videotapes). The center can also house the computer. Students working alone or in study pairs should examine the material in the center. At this time, the teacher will introduce the environmental/ecological unit.

3. Organize students into cooperative groups, and have each group choose an environmental/ecological problem they wish to research in the Computer Instruction Material Center (CIMC).

4. Lead a group discussion pertaining to the three Rs of environmental care: reduce, reuse, and recycle. Ask students to think of ways that they can work toward solving environmental problems in their community via the three Rs.

5. Have students prepare a written report in which they outline their suggestions for environmental improvement in their community.

Evaluation

1. Through a written test or short essay, evaluate the students' knowledge of the environmental/ecological problems in their community.

2. Evaluate the reports that students present to the class.

Environmental/Ecological Studies: A Local, National, and Global Concern[2]

Subject Area: Science
Grade Level: 5–10
Time: Three weeks and throughout the semester

Objectives

1. Students will define the terms *environment* and *ecology* and discuss the importance of each to the welfare of an area.

2. Students will describe interrelationships between organisms and their environments.

3. Students will research their immediate environment and another environmental area outside the United States.

4. Students will value conservation and describe what they can do to promote good conservation.

5. Using computers, students will research what students throughout the world are doing to solve the environmental/ecological problems in their communities.

6. Students will show respect for how people deal with environmental issues in other countries that have different ethnic, socioeconomic, religious, and political views from theirs.

Suggested Procedures

1. Brainstorm and record what students know about the terms *environment* and *ecology*.

2. Look up the words in a dictionary, then review what the students have brainstormed and make whatever changes they determine are necessary. Discuss why the terms have been confused in the past, and suggest that the students devise a method that will help them use the terms correctly.

3. Take a walk to two contrasting areas in the community that illustrate an area that is polluted and an area that exhibits good ecological management. (Note: Observe the areas throughout the school year periodically and discuss and record the changes.) Back in the classroom, students brainstorm the causes of the polluted area and why pollution is a detriment to the community and society. Develop a K-W-L chart (What We Know, What We Want to Know, and What We Have Learned) on which the students record their responses as they progress in the unit.

4. Set up an ecological interest center complete with research material (e.g., newspaper and magazine articles, science and reference books, trade books, bulletin boards, posters, films, and video recordings). The center can also house computers. Students working alone or in study pairs will examine and study the

---

[2] *Source:* Carl Grant, Lola Ferguson, and Jo Richards, University of Wisconsin — Madison.

material in the center through individual or group projects and during their free time.

5. Organize students into cooperative groups, each of which will choose an environmental/ecological problem (determined from their field trips or from class assignments and study) that they wish to research in the CIMC.

6. Write and illustrate a guidebook to local plants and animals and their dependency on one another.

7. Study local pollution problems; have speakers from a nature reserve, a greenhouse, a local park, or the local or state EPA agency address the class.

8. Color-key a state or local map according to the major water resources and indicate waterfalls, lakes, rivers, streams, and reservoirs. Determine which resources are for commercial use and which are for human consumption. Note the effects on the water source(s) by commercial use.

9. Study the depletion of resources in the community: Brainstorm why it is happening, what the economic impact is, how to contain it, what the students can do about it, and how they can encourage or lead the community to participate. Plant a tree, tend to it, advise other classes how the tree will improve the school's aesthetic and physical environment, keep a log of its care and growth, and write or produce an Arbor Day celebration to present to all the classes (through poems, stories, songs, etc.).

10. Write a letter to the community newspaper presenting an environmental/ ecological problem and offer solutions to the problem; write a federal representative (in the House or the Senate) about environmental/ecological concerns and possible solutions.

11. Bring in supermarket products and discuss their environmental impact (e.g., many claim to be from recycled materials but are not biodegradable). Research 100-percent-recycled materials, make a list to send to students' families, and encourage their use as often as possible.

12. Discuss, research, and prepare informative addresses to school assemblies or other classrooms about the depletion of the ozone layer, its causes, and measures that can be taken to prevent more damage.

13. Tour a local factory to learn what steps the owners had to take to reduce emissions for pollution control, how it affects the local community, what the financial price tag for such action will be for the owners and what the social and financial price tag will be for the community.

14. Study garbage, and discuss what happens when garbage is burned in incinerators or is dumped into landfills. Conduct experiments to determine what conditions are necessary to break down garbage into reusable nutrients. Work in groups to predict, then observe and compare, what happens to apple slices that are sealed in plastic bags and those that are buried in loose, damp soil that is periodically turned (i.e., compost). Survey the class about how their families dispose of garbage and discuss the pros and cons of alternative methods (paper bags, no bags, recycling pails, and composting). Test how quickly a variety of materials

decompose (paper, aluminum foil, cotton cloth, and a piece of banana and hot dog) after the students have predicted the outcomes and observe and record changes over a two-week period. Write conclusions that members of the class have made from the experiments.

15. Write environmentally conscious mottoes for displays around the school (e.g., Don't Feed the Trash—Feed the Hungry: Students concentrate on diminishing school lunch waste and ways the wasted food can be put to better use).

16. Demonstrate the balance of life with an aquarium in the room. Note the effects of water temperature, balance of plants, lack or overabundance of food, balance of fish and other animals and plants, and availability of food, plants, and oxygen. Note the role of snails, plants, and supply of oxygen pumped into the aquarium. Graph the number of fish-gill movements at different temperature readings and discover when and why there are more or less.

17. Use a variety of resources that report on current, prevalent worldwide environmental/ecological problems (e.g., global warming, pollution of lakes and streams, depletion of the rain forest and other resources, and soil erosion).

18. Divide the class into seven teams and assign each a continent. Each team will choose a country on their continent to research the environmental/ecological problems. Each group will present their research to the total class on the nature of the environmental/ecological problem(s) and the strategies that the country is employing to prevent or eliminate the problem. Probe for connections between environmental problems in Third World nations and actions of western nations that may have caused or aggravated these problems.

19. With the assistance of the Web, have students learn about environmental problems in different parts of the world (especially the country they are studying) and ways they are being resolved.

20. Have students make a curriculum web on environmental concerns, including ways to address these concerns.

21. Have students read former vice president Al Gore's 2007 Nobel Peace Prize lecture on climate change.

Evaluation

1. Based on students' suggestions, develop and implement a class or all-school plan to improve the local environment.

2. Through group presentations or written essays, assess students' understanding of worldwide environmental problems.

3. Evaluate students' curriculum web on environmental concerns, causes, and possible solutions.

4. During small- and large-group discussions, assess students' understanding of and appreciation for cultural values and the steps a country might take to deal with the concerns (e.g., excess use of fuel consumption that may cause smog and other environmental problems).

5. Assess the value of the unit by the students' changed attitudes and behaviors that demonstrate concern and respect for their environment and the students' efforts to monitor themselves and others in protecting and conserving it.

Environmental/Ecological Studies

WHY THE CHANGES?

Critical Questioning

The "After" plan has students examining environmental/ecological problems in their community, as well as in another country. The challenge of discovering environmental problems in their country and relating and comparing these problems to environmental problems in other countries will foster an *esprit de corps* among the students. Also, the way the "After" plan is structured (i.e., student groups presenting reports on environmental/ecological problems in different countries) will lead students to understand that the issue is important to all people. In addition, the "After" plan teaches respect for how environmental/ecological problems are dealt with in other countries, and asks students to identify U.S. policies and practices that may be creating or aggravating problems elsewhere.

Practice Democracy

An important tenet of democracy is listening to multiple points of view. The "After" plan teaches students to show respect for the way different countries deal with their environmental and ecological problems. Also, as students retrieve information on environmental problems from a webpage that has been prepared by someone in another country, they may have the opportunity to learn how decisions are made in different countries to deal with environmental/ecological problems.

Encourage Social Action

The "After" plan has students investigating and attempting to eliminate environmental problems and issues in their own community.

Instructional Strategies and Grouping Students

Although the "Before" plan uses student groups and several instructional strategies, the "After" plan uses student groups with a wealth of different student activities. Students are provided numerous opportunities and multiple ways to acquire interest in this topic.

▶ LESSON PLAN[3]

Ancient Egypt

BEFORE

Subject Area: Social Studies
Grade Level: 6
Time: Nine weeks and throughout the semester

[3]*Source:* Teresa Pipes, Colton Middle School, Monterey, California.

Objectives

1. Students will describe how the geography of Egypt related to the growth of civilization.

2. Students will describe the basic social structure of Ancient Egypt.

3. Students will describe the cultural achievements of Ancient Egypt, particularly during the period of the New Kingdom.

4. Students will connect beliefs about the afterlife in Ancient Egypt with artifacts that have been discovered there.

Suggested Procedures

1. Using a textbook such as *A Message of Ancient Days*, by Beverly Armento or the Web, have students study a map of Ancient Egypt and predict what we might know about the development of civilization from its geographic features. Then read and discuss the section of the text that discusses these ideas. Particularly stress the importance of the Nile River in sustaining early civilizations.

2. Moving from early humans to early civilization, read and analyze social class structure in Ancient Egypt using the textbook or website that highlights this issue. Include role and status of pharaoh, vizier, priest, officials, scribes, artisans, and farmers. To help students visualize what life might have been like, read excerpts from *The Golden Goblet*, by Eloise Jarvis McGraw.

3. Explain that the Ancient Egyptians loved life so much that they wanted to have the same life after they died and believed that this was possible if they were buried with all the things they loved in this life. Thus, archaeologists have found in Egypt pyramids that served as tombs and bodies mummified through an elaborate embalming process. Show a video about King Tut's tomb, preparation for the afterlife, and pyramid construction.

4. If possible, take students on a field trip to a museum with Egyptian artifacts.

5. Using the textbook, distinguish between the Old, Middle, and New Kingdoms. During the New Kingdom particularly, there were cultural and artistic advances and trade throughout the region. Emphasize achievements such as the lunar calendar, the embalming process, development of medicine, exquisite artifacts, tomb paintings, and pyramid building.

6. Assign students a research paper on some aspect of Ancient Egyptian civilization. Alternatively, students might complete a project such as creating a model of a pyramid.

Evaluation

1. Through a quiz, evaluate students' understanding of the geography, basic social structure, and cultural achievements of Ancient Egypt.

2. Through their research papers, evaluate students' deeper comprehension of the cultural achievements of Ancient Egypt.

Resources

Armento, B. J. (1999). *A message of ancient days*. Boston: Houghton Mifflin.

McGraw, E. J. (1990). *The golden goblet*. New York: Viking.

Ancient Egypt and Its Lens on Social Organization

Subject Area: Language Arts and Social Studies

Grade Level: 6

Time: Nine weeks and throughout the semester

Objectives

1. Students will distinguish between the characteristics of a hierarchical society and those of an egalitarian society.

2. Students will identify the social classes in Ancient Egypt, their roles, and power relations among the classes.

3. Students will compare and contrast the power structure in Ancient Egypt with the Neolithic social models: hierarchy and egalitarianism.

4. Students will identify different social groups in the United States, as represented in literature, and their roles, and their power relations, comparing and contrasting these with the social structure in Ancient Egypt.

5. Students will identify insiders' perspectives from different marginalized cultural groups.

6. Students will apply their understanding of egalitarian and hierarchical societies to identify the social groups at their school, their roles, and their power relations.

7. Students will develop an egalitarian strategy that will challenge the present social structure at their school, giving marginalized students a chance to compete more fairly in student government.

Suggested Procedures

1. Choose multicultural selections from the literature text *Elements of Literature* edited by (Anderson) that highlight issues of social class and power in the United States: for example, *Ta-Na-E-Ka*, by Mary Whitebird; *The All-American Slurp*, by Lensey Namioka; *Field Work*, by Rose Del Castillo Guibault; *Yes, It Was My Grandmother*, by Ludi Tapahonso; *Los Petalos*, by Pat Mora; *A Glory Over Everything*, by Harriet Tubman; *Conductor on the Underground Railroad*, by Ann Petry; *All Summer in a Day*, by Ray Bradbury; *Eleven/Once*, by Liliana Valenzula; *The Gold Cadillac*, by Mildred D. Taylor; *The Bracelet*, by Yoshiko Uchida; *The Sneetches*, by Theodor Geisel; and *The Southpaw*, by Judith Viorst. Each week throughout the quarter, the students will read, discuss, and explore these stories using the textbook's critical reading questions and exercises that highlight marginalized peoples' experiences with injustice.

   For possible extension, students could research the history of a marginalized culture, such as the Kaw Indians, introduced in the story *Ta-Na-E-Ka*, by Mary Whitebird.

2. Choose a class novel that highlights issues of social organization and justice for a marginalized culture, such as *Roll of Thunder, Hear My Cry*, by Mildred Taylor. This story helps to connect students with the great disparities in the education of Blacks and Whites in the 1930s. After reading and discussing, students should

write about a scene from the story and present it from the characters' points of view in a readers' theater play. Putting themselves in the characters' shoes will begin to help students to identify with the characters' feelings.

3. After studying about early people in a textbook such as *A Message of Ancient Days*, by Armento, have students connect the sixth-grade social studies curriculum (Ancient Civilizations) with the sixth-grade literature curriculum. They will study and experience the difference between two Neolithic forms of social organization: hierarchy and egalitarianism.

   a. Students are organized into cooperative learning groups.

   b. Each student creates a picture of an ancient artifact and cuts it into ten puzzle pieces.

   c. The cooperative groups mix their pieces together and put them in separate small boxes. Each group exchanges their box with that of another group.

   d. Announce a contest to see who can be the first person in each group to put together a puzzle of one of the artifacts.

   e. Assign the winner in each group the role of leader, and give a reward. Tell the leaders to change the seating in the classroom and decide where everyone sits. Debrief the activity, asking students how it felt to win and get to be in charge and how it felt to lose and be told where to sit.

   f. Next, gather each group's puzzle pieces in boxes again and distribute them to a new group. Tell them they are going to have a new contest in which everyone in the group works together to make the puzzles. When a group finishes their puzzle, they can help other groups. When the whole class finishes, everyone is rewarded.

   g. Debrief this experience, asking how it felt to work together and win. Discuss advantages and disadvantages of this system. Students write in their journals about which model they prefer.

   h. Make comparisons to the two social systems of hierarchy and egalitarianism. Provide students with information about Catal Hoyuk, an early egalitarian society described in *A Message of Ancient Days*. There is an excellent selection that can be found in Unit 1, Activity 3.2, "Early Humans" from *World History Program*, by High School Modern World History Development Team. Teachers can also find information about this society on the Internet. See, for example, www.focusmm.com/civcty/cathyk00.htm.

4. Moving from early humans to early civilization, read and analyze social class structure in Ancient Egypt using *A Message of Ancient Days* or other sixth-grade social studies textbook that highlights this issue, as well as excerpts from *The Golden Goblet* by Eloise Jarvis McGraw.

5. Have students design a social pyramid for Ancient Egypt, share and discuss its ramifications, and explore the concepts of power, privilege, and hierarchy.

6. Have students participate in an activity designed to help them explore the concepts of power, privilege, and hierarchy.

    a. The roles of the various social classes in Ancient Egypt—pharaoh, vizier, priest, official, scribe, artisan, and farmer—are distributed, with only one card made for the first four roles. After students receive their roles, the Vizier is placed in charge of distributing wealth.

    b. Each group receives seven paper cups and about fifty M&Ms. Students separate the candies by color into the paper cups.

    c. The Pharaoh, Priest, and Official go up to the front of the room and sit in a place of importance with the Vizier.

    d. The Vizier explains to the Scribes, Artisans, and Farmers that Pharaoh is demanding their labors and they must bring all their tan and brown candies to Pharaoh to deposit them in her cup.

    e. The Vizier tells them to give her their yellow candies so that she can do her job.

    f. The Priest comes forward and demands all the orange and green M&Ms for the gods.

    g. The Official tells the people to give a part of their labor to him and requires the red candies.

    h. Students return to their seats, and everyone enjoys the fruits of their labors. Then debrief this experience, allowing students to express their feelings and evaluate how the different classes in Egypt might have felt about this hierarchical arrangement. Journal writing is encouraged.

7. Have students participate in an economic activity that shows how economic privilege affects what they can buy.

    a. After studying the Egyptian beliefs in the afterlife, ask students to list what items they would want in their pyramids.

    b. Ask them to rank their lists from what is most important to what is least important. They should discuss their lists in their groups.

    c. Use raisins to represent wealth. Have each student start with twenty raisins and then roll a die to determine how many more he or she gets. One dot equals ten, two equals twenty, and so on. Those who roll a seven get an extra roll of the die to represent inheritance.

    d. Make a general list on the board of the major items students want to take with them to the afterlife.

    e. Have an auction with these items and let the students bid. Write down the names of the highest bidders for each item. Assign one student to be the wealth collector.

    f. After everything has been auctioned off, students discuss their feelings and give special attention to how money or resources affect people's ability to get the things they value most. Make comparisons to life today.

8. After reading all the literature selections, have the students identify the main characters they've read about and compare and contrast their issues of social justice in Venn diagrams. They will analyze their conflicts in terms of resources available to them and social position and power.

9. Have students create a social pyramid for the main characters in their stories and discuss their rationales for the pyramids they created.

10. Ask students to identify the various social groups at their middle school and create a pyramid of power. Debrief in journals, identifying their positions and feelings about the advantages and disadvantages (resources and power) each group may or may not have. Then evaluate the social system (hierarchy or egalitarian). Note: Caution and care need to be given to the issues of stereotyping, labeling, or overgeneralizing about the student groups at the school site.

11. Instruct students to analyze their school's student government election results and evaluate why certain people won, which groups they represented, and why students voted the way they did.

12. Have students create an egalitarian action plan that will empower students from marginalized groups to have equal access to student government positions.

Evaluation

1. Through their journal writings and class discussions, assess students' understanding of hierarchical society versus egalitarian.

2. By evaluating their social pyramids and rationales, assess students' understanding of social class structure and power in Ancient Egypt, in the United States, based on literature in reading texts, and in their school.

3. Through discussions and journal reflections, assess students' understanding of marginalized cultures.

4. Through evaluating their student elections action plan and reading reflections in journals, assess students' understanding of fair competition.

5. Assess effectiveness of the lesson to create change through examining the election process and results at the end of the year.

Resources

Anderson, R. A. (2005). *Elements of literature*. Austin, TX: Holt, Rinehart & Winston.

Armento, B. J. (1999). *A message of ancient days*. Boston: Houghton Mifflin.

High School Modern World History Development Team. (1996). *World history program*. Palo Alto, CA: Teachers' Curriculum Institute.

McGraw, E. J. (1990). *The golden goblet*. New York: Viking.

Taylor, M. (1997). *Roll of thunder, hear my cry*. New York: Puffin Books.

Ancient Egypt and Its Lens on Social Organization

Analyzing Social Inequality

WHY THE CHANGES?

Schools need to prepare students to be socially active and responsible citizens of a democratic society. In order to do so, we must help them understand the history of the world from many different perspectives and give them the tools necessary to create a more just society. If students are experiencing an education where they find that others are given privileges because of social class, perceived ability, race, gender, language, culture, or other stereotypical dividers, they need to know that they can challenge the oppression and work to create a more egalitarian school community.

The "Before" lesson describes a hierarchical social system, but does not examine it from the perspectives of those on the bottom. For example, only high officials and pharaohs had tombs and an elaborate embalming process. There is no mention of how the rest of the population would have felt about spending most of their lives making sure that the upper class achieved a good afterlife when their own was probably in doubt. The "After" plan analyzes this structure critically and connects this analysis with critical analysis of hierarchical social structures in other contexts, including the students' own peer culture. It should be emphasized that the "After" lesson can be taught along with portions of the "Before" lesson. We are not suggesting, for example, throwing out an analysis of geography.

Practicing Democracy

It is our job as educators to construct lessons that both help students to acquire the necessary skills they need to compete in today's society and are culturally relevant. Also, it is important for students to understand how power relations are constructed and operate. Good multicultural education addresses standards and social consciousness; it doesn't just pretend to be democratic in its goals, but demonstrates democracy in its presentation of knowledge that is accessible to everyone. It is democratic in that it truly tries to give equal opportunity to each and every student (regardless of race, learning style, social class, disability, gender, belief system, etc.) to learn and acquire the skills necessary to live a successful life. The lessons students learn in school should relate to their lives and deal with current issues that are important to them. The "After" plan incorporates democracy in both the content and process of the lesson, whereas the "Before" plan does not.

Multiple Perspectives

Education should help students think critically about history and present-day problems. The "After" plan on social class structure allows students to see not only the dominant culture's interpretation, but also the different perspectives of historically marginalized cultures, to learn about the different classes in Ancient Egypt, to experience two different forms of social organization (i.e., hierarchy and egalitarianism), and to connect history with their lives today. The students are involved in a variety of ways that tap into learning styles and demonstrate educational equity. When students are taught to see issues from different groups' points of view, they begin to be aware that change is possible. Things don't have to stay the same just because that's the way it's always been. This is why the "After" plan connects social studies with literature. Literature selections can help students see multiple viewpoints quite effectively and can become powerful teaching tools when connected with a sociological and historical analysis.

Encouraging Social Action

The "After" plan attempts to motivate students to become aware that what they are learning can make a difference in their lives. The social structure of the school is a very significant problem in the school of the author of this plan, as it is in many schools. Following teaching this unit, the author was hopeful that students might challenge the social system in their school that reflects the dominant culture of our society. In the future, this kind of education will produce citizens that are actively involved in creating a more just society.

▶ LESSON PLAN[4]

Writing Business Letters

Subject Area: Language Arts

Grade Level: 6–8

Time: One week

Objectives

1. Students will write letters that meet state standards.

2. Students will use the components of a business letter, including rubrics for content and mechanics.

3. Students will learn to identify a topic and to incorporate that information into their own letters.

Suggested Procedures

1. Have students read sample business letters written for varied purposes.

2. Ask students to analyze the letters for form and content and identify the portions that include Introduction, Definition of the Issue or Problem, Addressing the Issue or Solving the Problem, and Conclusion.

3. Have each student write a business letter that addresses something that he or she believes is important.

4. Create a "Communication Circle" where students can share their letters with the rest of the class and discuss the issues or problems that were identified.

5. Have students mail their letters to an organization, agency, or individual that might address their issue.

Evaluation

1. Assess the completion, content, and form of student letters in relationship to state standards.

2. Assess the students' quality of analysis and discussion.

3. Determine the percentage of responses received to their letters as one indicator of the effectiveness of students' letter-writing skills.

Writing Business Letters to Assist Homeless Children and Youth

Subject Area: Language Arts

Grade Level: 6–8

Time: One week

---

[4]*Source:* Jill Moss Greenberg, National Association for Multicultural Education, Washington, DC.

Objectives

1. Students will write letters that meet state standards.
2. Students will use the components of a business letter, including rubrics for content and mechanics.
3. Students will research a topic and incorporate their findings into a business letter.
4. Students will apply analytical skills to assess inequities and act on a current social issue.

Suggested Procedures

1. Have students review the content and mechanics of an effective business letter by analyzing sample letters and critiquing the form and content.
2. Have students summarize the content components (heading, inside address, salutation, body, and closing necessary for a complete letter) and review the mechanics (form, sentence structure, sentence variation, punctuation and capitalization, spelling and grammar, and transitional word usage).
3. Introduce the topic of homelessness and provide the list of Resources given (on page 289).
4. Divide students into small groups to research the history and current status of homelessness. Provide Worksheet #1 to half of the groups and Worksheet #2 (Figures 6.1 and 6.2) to the other half of the groups.

Definition of Homelessness:

_____

_____

_____

_____

_____

_____

How It Affects Homeless Students:

_____

_____

_____

_____

_____

Extent of Problem:

_____

_____

_____

_____

_____

Causes and History:

_____

_____

_____

_____

_____

Figure 6.1   Student Worksheet #1: What's the Problem?

Laws and Policies:	Attitudes and Practices:
_____	_____
_____	_____
_____	_____
_____	_____
_____	_____
Role(s) of Government Agencies and Other Organizations/Individuals:	**My Suggestions for Legislators or Other Community Leaders:**
_____	_____
_____	_____
_____	_____
_____	_____
_____	_____

Figure 6.2   Student Worksheet #2: What's Being Done?

5. Allow time for students to research their topics, including use of the Internet if possible. Arrange for time to visit a homeless shelter during or after school.

6. Form a "Communication Circle" for each group to report back to on their findings.

7. Have each group draft and send a letter to a legislator, other policy maker, community leader, or organization. The letter should include information from their textual and on-site research and make recommendations for programs, services, or other changes that the group has determined would assist children and youth in homeless situations.

8. After letters of response have been received, or after a two-week period if all letters have not received responses, reconvene the "Communication Circle." Engage the students in a discussion of the process and the responses to their letters and determine what, if any, further action they deem necessary. If possible, allow time for students to visit the legislators or agencies to deliver their follow-up perspectives and information in person.

9. Involve the students in assessing the learning that was acquired and the effectiveness of the process.

Evaluation

1. Assess the completion, content, and form of letters and worksheets in relationship to state standards.

2. Engage students in the evaluation process. Discuss with students their perspectives on the effectiveness of this process and their feelings and knowledge about homelessness.

3. Determine, with students, potential follow-up application of what was learned.

Resources

National Alliance to End Homelessness
1518 K Street NW, Suite 206
Washington, DC 20005
Website: www.endhomelessness.org

National Center for Homeless Education at SERVE
915 Northridge Street, 2nd Floor
Greensboro, NC 27403
Website: www.serve.org/nche

National Coalition for the Homeless
1012 14th Street NW, Suite 600
Washington, DC 20005
Website: www.nationalhomeless.org

The National Law Center on Homelessness and Poverty
1411 K Street NW, Suite 1400
Washington, DC 20005
Website: www.nlchp.org

Writing Business Letters to Assist Homeless Children and Youth

WHY THE
CHANGES?

Perspective

Homelessness is a growing social and educational issue in the United States, with women and children comprising the fastest growing segment of the homeless population. This is a dramatic demographic change and is found in urban, suburban, and rural areas. Despite this prevalence, many schools, policy makers, and communities are unaware of the experiences of homeless people and how this situation may affect their readiness for academic achievement. Children and young adults experiencing homelessness not only lose their homes but their stability, belongings, privacy—and their friends. Many homeless students are with one or both of their parents or guardians, but a growing number of adolescents and teens are homeless and unaccompanied or legally emancipated from their parents or guardians.

The McKinney-Vento Homeless Assistance Act guarantees that homeless students are provided with an education comparable to that afforded to permanently housed students. It also requires schools to ensure that homeless students are admitted to school immediately, even without proof of residency, immunization, or previous school records.

Despite this legal mandate, many homeless students remain unidentified or inappropriately served within our schools and other agencies. They experience teasing and inappropriate placement in school programs. By learning about homelessness in the "After" lesson, students will become knowledgeable about and sensitive to the stigma experienced by homeless students in their classrooms, creating the potential for their involvement in decreasing bias and increasing advocacy for these students.

Analyzing Social Inequities

In the "After" lesson plan, students research the legal rights and real-life experiences of their homeless peers. It enables them to explore the conditions experienced by homeless students and the ways that gender, race, language, and poverty may affect homelessness. The lesson engages the students in identifying needs and resources, in developing recommendations for people in decision-making positions, and in creating strategies for their own involvement in advocacy and social change.

Practicing Democracy

The "Before" plan enables students to learn skills, but not to apply them to an issue where they could practice taking an active role within our legislative process. Writing and sending letters to community leaders or elected officials, and potentially receiving responses, provides students with a sense of efficacy about their capacity to affect critical issues within our society. Learning about the homeless also permits students to apply their knowledge to reducing the bias against homeless students in their schools and to take action, including obtaining student service-learning credits for assisting people who are homeless.

Curriculum Content

Students are required to learn letter-writing skills, including those for business letters. The changed context of the "After" plan enables them to develop and apply their research skills to an emerging social issue for children and youth and to incorporate these skills in their letters. Writing and sending letters to community leaders or elected officials, and potentially receiving responses, may demonstrate that curricular content has real meaning and can be applied to make a difference. In the "After" lesson plan, students are extensively involved in a collaborative process to identify accurate information, including the history and causes, and in the process of assessment/evaluation of the lessons themselves. With these procedures, students experience being an active, integral, and valued part of the teaching-learning-advocating process.

▶ LESSON PLAN

Rate and Line Graph

Subject Area: Mathematics
Grade Level: 6–8
Time: One class period

Objectives

1. Students will complete a rate table that expresses rate as a percentage.
2. Students will construct a segmented line graph showing relationships among rates.

Table 6.2 **Rate: 35% Discount (0.35 × M = D**

Marked price (M), in dollars	$100.00	$150.00	?	$75.80	?
Discount (D)	?	?	$425.00	?	$113.65

Table 6.3 $R_m = M - D$

	Store A	Store B	Store C	Store D	Store E
Marked price (M), in dollars	$450.00	$450.00	$450.00	$450.00	$450.00
Discount price (D), in dollars	$431.00	$382.50	$414.00	$261.00	$279.00
Discount rate (R)	?	?	?	?	?

Suggested Procedures

1. Review the concept of rate and the rate table from your previous lessons.
2. Explain that rate can be expressed as a percentage. On the board, complete the rate table shown in Table 6.2, with student input.
3. Ask students to name some discount stores in the area. Ask them whether all the stores charge the same price for the same item; point out that prices usually vary somewhat among stores.
4. Explain that the discount rates on television sets in different stores will be compared. In the rate table shown in Table 6.3, each column refers to a different store, and the marked and discounted prices of each store's television set are given. With student input, compute the discount rate for each store on the board.
5. Distribute graph paper. Explain that rates can be graphed and compared visually. Have each student construct a segmented line graph of the discount rates in Table 6.3.

Evaluation

1. From class discussion, assess students' understanding of the concept of rate.
2. Check students' line graphs for accuracy.

Rate and Line Graph

Subject Area: Mathematics
Grade Level: 6–8
Time: Two class periods

Objectives

1. Students will complete a rate table that expresses rate as a percentage.
2. Students will construct a segmented line graph showing relationships among rates.
3. Students will compare poverty rates among different racial groups.

Suggested Procedures

1. Ask students whether they know if poverty in the United States has increased, decreased, or remained the same in the last two decades. Ask whether people are more likely to be poor if they are White or of color. Ask also how well students believe U.S. society has reduced economic racism over the past two decades. The concepts of rate and line graph can help students examine these issues.

2. Review the concept of rate and the rate table from your previous lessons. Explain that rate can be expressed as a percentage. On the board and with student input, complete the rate table shown in Table 6.4. Population data are expressed in thousands in the table; have students convert the statistics to thousands.

3. Give each student a copy of a table such as the one shown in Table 6.5. Explain that each column refers to a different racial group within the United States and that the numbers refer to 2000 census population data. Ask students to describe population concepts that might be expressed as rate (e.g., unemployment rate, high school dropout rate, poverty rate).

4. Explain that the rate of any population concept can vary among different racial groups. Using Table 6.5, have students compute the subgroup when the following rates apply to each racial group: Asian American, 13 percent; African American, 36 percent; Latino, 30 percent; Native American, 28 percent; European American, 11 percent. Explain that these rates refer to the poverty rate of each racial group during 1983 and discuss this in terms of how many people lived in poverty during that year.

5. Distribute a table such as Table 6.6. Explain that the figures in the table refer to poverty rates; make sure students understand that the figures do not refer to numbers of people. You can access census data on the Web (www.census.gov) to keep this kind of table current.

   Distribute graph paper. Review how a segmented line graph is constructed. Have students work in pairs to construct segmented line graphs of poverty rates over time, using different colors to represent different racial groups.

6. Discuss the persistence of poverty over time and the reasons poverty rates seem to be higher among African Americans and Latinos than among European Americans and Asian Americans.

Table 6.4   Rate: 22% of a Population (0.22 × P = s)

Population (P), in thousands	100	?	820	5,550	?	?	30,800
Subgroup (s), in thousands	?	44	?	?	128	1,262	?

Table 6.5   Rate: 15%

	Asian American	African American	Latino	Native American	European American
Population (P), in thousands	3,726	27,263	14,609	1,534	196,036
Subgroup (s), in thousands	?	?	?	?	?

Table 6.6   Poverty Rates in the United States, 1975–2000 (in percentages)

Year	All Races	White[a]	Black	Hispanic	Asian/Pacific Islander
1975	12.3	8.6	31.3	23.0	—
1976	11.8	8.1	31.1	26.9	—
1977	11.6	8.0	31.3	24.7	—
1978	11.4	7.9	30.6	22.4	—
1979	11.7	8.1	31.0	21.6	—
1980	13.0	9.1	32.5	21.8	—
1981	14.0	9.9	34.2	25.7	—
1982	15.0	10.6	35.6	26.5	—
1983	15.2	10.8	35.7	29.9	—
1984	14.4	10.0	33.8	28.0	—
1985	14.0	9.7	31.3	28.4	—
1986	14.6	9.4	31.1	29.0	—
1987	13.4	8.7	32.4	27.3	—
1988	13.0	8.4	31.3	28.0	17.3
1989	12.8	8.3	30.7	26.7	14.1
1990	13.5	8.8	31.9	26.2	12.2
1991	14.2	9.4	32.7	28.1	13.8
1992	14.8	9.6	33.4	29.6	12.7
1993	15.1	9.9	33.1	30.6	15.3
1994	14.5	9.4	30.6	30.7	14.6
1995	13.8	8.5	29.3	30.3	14.6
1996	13.7	8.6	28.4	29.4	14.5
1997	13.3	8.6	26.5	27.1	14.0
1998	12.7	8.2	26.1	25.6	12.5
1999	11.8	7.7	23.6	22.8	10.7
2000	11.3	7.5	22.1	21.2	10.8

Source: http://www.census.gov/hhes/poverty/histpov/hstpov2.html
[a] Non-Hispanic origin

7. Collect state or city data on the same type of poverty rates. Have students compute local poverty rates over time and construct segmented line graphs. As part of another class, students should investigate the specific policies and practices that have contributed to poverty and racism locally. Students can then prepare a report for a local newspaper that includes rate tables, line graphs, and results of their investigation, along with suggestions for how to deal with poverty and racism more constructively.

Evaluation

1. Check students' rate tables and line graphs for accuracy.
2. From class discussion, assess students' understanding of the concept of rate and of rate changes over time.
3. From class discussion, assess students' awareness of poverty and inequality in the United States.

Rate and Line Graph

Critical Questioning

Rate tables and line graphs can be constructed using any set of quantities that express rates. The "Before" plan is concerned only with teaching these mathematical concepts and uses discount rate as a meaningful set of quantities that students would understand. However, it is not truly concerned with teaching about discounts. The "After" plan, however, teaches a social issue and mathematical concepts simultaneously. Poverty rate lends itself well to the concepts of rate and line graphs. The lesson encourages students to consider whether society actually values racial diversity and equal opportunity when it continues to allow a sizable percentage of citizens to live in poverty and to sustain particularly high rates of poverty among Americans of color. The lesson demonstrates how a central purpose of math is to better understand problems and issues taking place in society.

Before teaching this lesson, the teacher should be ready to deal with the "blame the victim" reasoning that students may use to explain poverty. The teacher is encouraged to coordinate with other teachers on efforts to help students understand institutional racism and classism. This lesson alone will not do that, but it can be a valuable one when taught in conjunction with other lessons on these issues.

Analyzing Systems of Oppression

Data on national poverty rates give a global picture of racism and classism in our society over time, but may appear abstract and removed from students' own lives. Therefore, the teacher is encouraged to locate similar data from the state and local levels. Often, such data are available through state and city governments or local social service agencies. The teacher may find that these local data have not been prepared into rate tables and line graphs, which may depict local trends over time.

Encouraging Social Action

Although the math teacher may not feel comfortable with having students investigate reasons for institutionalized poverty in their city, working with teachers in other disciplines is important for helping students link math with other areas of living. In this case, math and social studies could be linked well, and these could be linked with English in the preparation of a written research report. Such interdisciplinary teaching helps subjects gain relevance and meaning for students and makes social action projects such as the one illustrated in this lesson possible.

▶ LESSON PLAN

City Government

Subject Area: Social Studies

Grade Level: 7–9

Time: One week

Objectives

1. Students will identify important city services and explain their functions.
2. Students will identify the typical problems of a given city.
3. Students will recognize that various decisions are necessary to run a city.
4. Students will recognize that the quality of urban life can vary.

Suggested Procedures

1. Discuss with students how government plays an important role in a city and determines the types of city services that are available.
2. Determine as a group the types of services available in most major cities. Read about city services in a textbook or on the Internet.
3. Have guest speakers from two or three different city services visit and speak to the class.
4. In groups of four, have students develop a paragraph that outlines the problems of a city. They should also identify what city services they consider important and how those services could offer a solution to the problems. A final summary statement should express how city services affect the quality of urban life.

Evaluation

Assess students' mastery of the objectives through a quiz.

City Government[5]

Subject Area: Social Studies
Grade Level: 7–9
Time: One or two weeks

Objectives

1. Students will describe an urban area in terms of a variety of ethnic, racial, age, and religious groups, each with its own needs.
2. Students will demonstrate sensitivity to these diverse needs.
3. Students will identify necessary city services.
4. Students will recognize that cities should make city services equally available to a diverse city population.
5. Students will view making decisions as a necessary part of running a city.
6. Students will learn that mutual cooperation is one method of solving common urban problems.
7. Students will recognize that city services have an impact on the quality of urban life.
8. Students will appreciate that cultural diversity makes a city a "better place."

[5]*Source:* Virginia Kester, Madison Public Schools, Madison, Wisconsin.

Suggested Procedures

1. In groups of three or four, have students discuss who lives in any given city (e.g., those with physical disabilities; the aged; racial, ethnic, and religious groups). Have the groups present their findings to the class and record their responses for the class to see.

2. As a class, discuss how the needs of a diverse population vary from group to group (e.g., neighborhoods with large numbers of children need more schools; limited-English-speaking communities need services in their own languages; a neighborhood center could serve the young after school and the elderly during the day).

3. As a group, have students determine what city services could meet these diverse needs.

4. Present the following scenario to the class: "You are all members of a city council. It is your job to determine what city services will be funded in the neighborhood described in the accompanying packet. You may not go over budget, and you will have to make decisions. There is not enough money for everything this area needs. As a group, you should give attention to how you solve this problem (through bullying, cooperation, and so on) as well as to solving the problem itself. Be prepared to describe to the class how you resolved this issue and what you actually decided."

5. Give each group a packet that includes the following items:
   a. Map of the area
   b. List of needs for the area
   c. Population (who lives there?)
   d. Possible city services that could meet needs. Each city service should be given a fixed dollar amount that it would cost to implement.
   e. Amount of money the council has to spend (must be less than what is needed for all services, so decisions have to be made)

6. Have students in small groups discuss and decide which city services they feel should be implemented in "their neighborhood." Remind them that they should decide how they want to make these decisions and present their findings. Their presentations should include the city services that should be implemented in the area, an explanation of how each service will meet the needs of the area, reasons the service was chosen over other services, and the way the group arrived at its decision (i.e., the group decision-making process).

7. Once all group projects have been presented, guide the class in drawing some conclusions. Discuss the following questions and ideas:
   a. How does the availability of city services affect the quality of your life (e.g., How good would your education be if it was in a language you did not understand? Is a new bus line good for you if the bus stops six or seven blocks from your house or if it is impossible for you to get on?) and the quality of city

life as a whole (e.g., health clinics that reduce the spread of communicable diseases)?

b. How do the city services available to you make your life better in the long term versus the short term (e.g., If the school is two blocks from your house, how does its close proximity affect your feelings about it)?

c. City governments always have to make some kind of decision about which service to supply and how it will be implemented in a city. This has the potential to be a heated, emotional decision in real life, and students need to discuss the kinds of behaviors that help ensure a fair decision-making process. They should refer back to their own discussions and identify behaviors that allowed for an open discussion (discuss also why an open discussion is in the best interest of all people).

8. Have students collect newspaper articles about current city service issues. They should present in written or oral form what they consider the issue to be and how it relates to quality of life within their city.

Evaluation

1. Through initial class discussion and their participation in the mock city council, assess students' appreciation of the diversity of an urban population.

2. Through their solutions to the groups' problems, assess students' understanding of city services.

3. Assess students' decision-making skills through their small-group work.

City Government

Modeling Diversity

The "Before" plan does not mention the diversity that characterizes a city's population, whereas the "After" plan makes this its focal topic. In the "After" plan, students examine what diverse groups compose a city and then analyze competing claims that different groups have on city service resources.

Practicing Democracy

In the "After" plan, students role-play a city council and must collectively decide how to allocate resources. The "Before" plan does not provide this type of active democratic simulation.

Analyzing Systems of Oppression

By examining the allocation of a city's resources and by role-playing a city council, students in the "After" plan learn that resources are often distributed unequally and that the decision-making process can produce that result. Then, by collecting and discussing newspaper articles on city services in their own city, students can begin to apply this analysis to where they live. The lesson is usually successful with middle school students, who enjoy issue-oriented activities in which they can express values that are important to them. It is extremely important to follow through on the final discussion, in that students more readily internalize concepts that are applied to their daily lives.

▶ LESSON PLAN

Settling the West

Subject Area: Social Studies
Grade Level: 8–9
Time: One week

Objectives

1. Students will identify and describe the goals of the Western settlers during the 1800s.
2. Students will analyze the effect of the increased presence of settlers on Native American culture.
3. Students will describe what settlers found on arriving in the West.

Suggested Procedures

1. Outline for students the reasons why people went west (e.g., economic reasons).
2. Read the selected U.S. history textbook for a description of the trip west and the things people found on arriving there.
3. Use study sheets to reinforce key concepts.
4. Through class discussion and appropriate films or texts, discuss the effect of the increase of settlers on the Native American lifestyle.

Evaluation

Assess students' mastery of the concepts through a quiz.

Conflict Over Western Land[6]

Subject Area: Social Studies
Grade Level: 8–9
Time: Two weeks

Objectives

1. Students will recognize that the settlers who went west were from a variety of ethnic, religious, and racial backgrounds.
2. Students will identify that the settlers went west for many reasons.
3. Students will describe the hardships of those who moved west.
4. Students will recognize that the land and its use formed a major source of conflict among different cultural groups.
5. Students will identify and describe the various Native American nations indigenous to the American West.

[6] *Source:* Virginia Kester, Madison Public Schools, Madison, Wisconsin.

6. Students will appreciate that the Western lands were already home to many Mexican and native peoples.

7. Students will identify a variety of approaches to solving a conflict and recognize that individuals always have a choice.

Suggested Procedures

1. Read available materials on Native American nations west of the Mississippi River. Films or guest speakers can also give students the necessary historical background. Have students take notes on the mainstream native economy and culture as well as various Native American viewpoints toward their land.

2. Discuss as a group how members of Native American nations felt about their land and lifestyles. Have students infer the responses of these groups to others with varied purposes moving into their area. Have students role-play what might be said at a meeting of Native Americans discussing rumors of settlers (or invaders) moving in and possible responses to them.

3. View videos on the Mexican lifestyle of the Southwest as well as Mexican viewpoints of new settlers. (A video available through La Raza or other Latino organizations will give a Mexican point of view, which is essential.) Have students note, as they did with Native American people, what the mainstay of the Southwestern economy would be, as well as Mexican attitudes toward the land.

4. Have students role-play what might be discussed at a meeting of Mexicans concerning the incoming settlers. They should note possible settler responses.

5. Students should read or view available material on the people who went west. (The material should cover the various ethnic groups who traveled west.)

6. Discuss with the class how these different groups would view the Western land and what needs they would hope to meet by moving there.

7. Divide the class into small groups. Have each group choose two viewpoints toward the land and develop each viewpoint as well as the methods they plan to use if others challenge this viewpoint.

8. Have each group present its viewpoints and methods.

9. Summarize with the class the idea that conflict occurred in the West because different people wanted a limited amount of land for different uses and they had different cultural views about land ownership. The class should also read and discuss selections on the conflicts that occurred between the various groups in the 1800s (e.g., Mexican-American War, Indian War) and should identify the causes of these conflicts.

10. Locate and share with students current examples of conflict over land. These can be arguments over land use, urban renewal versus renovation, "gentrification" of a city, landlord or tenant rights, expansion of White-owned recreation facilities on indigenous sacred sites, or other examples from their own neighborhoods. Discuss how land and its distribution has remained a focus of conflict in our society.

Students can also discuss other current conflicts caused by varied interest groups desiring a limited resource such as employment or housing (e.g., recent immigration laws and their impact on the local economies). Students should try to draw parallels between these current examples and the conflicts of the past.

11. Refer back to students' discussion of the methods of coping with conflict. Rank the methods that worked toward ending the conflict. Discuss how the methods of resolving conflict can be applied to today's issues.

Evaluation

1. Assess students' mastery of the main ideas through a quiz or essay.

2. Have students choose one of the current conflicts and develop a plan for resolving it.

Conflict Over Western Land

Critical Questioning

The "Before" plan represents the perspective usually taken in studying the West, in that it focuses on White European American settlers and mentions other groups only within their context—mainly Native Americans. In contrast, the "After" plan gives equal attention to Native Americans, Mexicans, and European Americans. That is, the lesson's focus is not on only one group's story but on the ways various groups interacted in conflict over control of the land and on their diverse viewpoints about land use. The "After" plan tries to help students raise questions about who has a right to land, cultural perspectives on land, and uses of power.

Practicing Democracy

The "After" plan provides more opportunity for students to practice democracy than the "Before" plan. Students role-play meetings of Native Americans and Mexicans, discussing the advancing settlers. These meetings can and should be run democratically. The "After" plan also uses a wider variety of teaching strategies than the "Before" plan. In the "Before" plan, students mainly read, listen, and watch, whereas they also role-play and discuss in the "After" plan.

Analyzing Systems of Oppression

After studying conflict over Western land, in the "After" plan students examine conflict over other limited resources, including land, in their own community. They are encouraged to discover who has how much of the best land and to examine how this came to be and how current struggles for land and other resources take place.

▶ LESSON PLAN

Writing for an Audience

Subject Area: Language Arts
Grade Level: 6–9
Time: Three class periods

Objectives

1. Students will identify the audience for whom a short story or persuasive essay was written.
2. Students will identify writing techniques the author used to appeal to that audience.
3. Students will write an essay or story specifically for an audience.

Suggested Procedures

1. Pass out a short story or persuasive essay, or use one in the literature text. Give students time to read it.
2. Divide the class into groups. Have them answer the following questions:
   - Who was this story or essay written for? What clues can you locate to substantiate your thinking?
   - What does the writer want the audience to do, feel, or experience?
   - What techniques does the writer use to do this? For example, does the story or essay portray someone the target audience might identify with? Does the author use language that provokes feelings? Does the author draw on examples that might be familiar to that audience?
3. Discuss each group's analysis, and on the board make a list of techniques writers use to move target audiences. Students should see that experienced writers do not simply write in the abstract; they write to an audience and often have a purpose of trying to inform or persuade.
4. Ask students to think of an audience they would like to inform or persuade. Brainstorm ideas for what would appeal to or catch the attention of that audience.
5. Have students design and write a story or persuasive essay directed to that target audience. If possible, students should try out their writing on the audience, and find out the extent to which it communicated what and had the effect that they intended.

Evaluation

1. Through small group reports and class discussion, evaluate the extent to which students are able to identify audiences, and techniques writers use to appeal to audiences.
2. Through their written products, evaluate the extent to which students are able to use these techniques themselves to speak to a specific audience.

Advertising for an Audience

Subject Area: Language Arts
Grade Level: 6–9
Time: Four class periods

Objectives

1. Students will identify the audience to whom an advertisement was directed and what that advertisement wants the audience to do.

2. Students will identify techniques the advertiser used to appeal to that audience.

3. Students will identify who profits by their spending money in response to the advertisement.

4. Students will create a message for that audience, raising their awareness about advertising and its connection to money.

5. Students will observe the race, gender, and social class demographic of the people used in the advertisement.

6. Students will observe that people from some groups are often not included in certain advertisements or are shown in a minor role.

Suggested Procedures

1. Instruct each student to bring an advertisement to class. It can be from a magazine, a newspaper, the Internet, or a description of an ad on TV.

2. Briefly discuss how easy it was to locate advertisements and the degree to which advertisements permeate our surroundings. Make sure that everyone can distinguish commercial advertisements from the program or story itself, since young people sometimes may not see these as different. Discuss ways in which advertising blends with magazine stories or TV shows, such as products featured in TV shows, movies, or infomercials.

3. Select four to six advertisements students brought, and divide the class into groups. Each group should take one advertisement. Have the students answer the following questions:
   • What demographic group does the ad target? Look at the race/ethnicity, age, gender, and socioeconomic status of the people featured in the ad and in the magazine, TV show, or other source in which the ad was placed.
   • What does the advertisement want to get this audience to do?
   • What techniques does it use to do this? For example, does the ad use someone the target audience might identify with? Does it try to make the target audience feel deficient without the advertised product?

4. Discuss each group's analysis. Students should see that advertisements generally try to get people to spend money and are targeted at specific audiences. Some demographic groups are rarely targeted at all, whereas others are targeted repeatedly. Help students to identify which groups are commonly targeted by advertisers and for which kinds of products. For example, students might identify ads for alcohol as common in Black and Latino neighborhoods; ads for cleaning products as commonly targeted at women; many ads targeted at young, White, upwardly mobile people; and few targeted at people who are poor.

5. Have students examine the advertisements in *Ebony* and *Latina* and on television channels that carry African American and Latino programming. Have students compare them with the advertisement in mainstream media discussed above.

6. Have students analyze what proportion of a medium (such as TV, magazines) consists of advertising. For example, how many minutes of a half-hour TV show or how many pages of a magazine consist of advertisements? Investigate ways in

which advertisers influence the content of media. Some helpful sources on the Internet:

FAIR (Fairness and Accuracy in Reporting): www.fair.org
Global Issues That Affect Everyone: www.globalissues.org

7. Select a company that advertises extensively to young people. Have students find out as much as they can: for example,
   • Who owns the company
   • Racial and gender composition of their board of directors
   • What kind of affirmative action hiring and promotion policy they have
   • Their environmental record
   • Their fair labor policies
   • Political and community organizations they contribute to
   A watchdog group that monitors fair labor practices is the National Labor Committee (www.nlcnet.org). Have a discussion about where students' money goes when they purchase products and who benefits most from that flow of money (and influence).

8. Have students design and produce an advertisement that raises awareness about advertising, money flow, and corporate profit and target that advertisement to an audience of their peers.

Evaluation

1. Through small group reports and class discussion, evaluate the extent to which students are able to identify audiences, and techniques advertisers use to appeal to audiences.

2. Through their discussion of research into companies, evaluate the extent to which students are able to connect advertising with corporate profit.

3. Through the awareness-raising advertisement they develop, evaluate the extent to which students are able to use these techniques themselves to speak to a specific audience.

Resources

Graydon, S. (2003). *Made you look: How advertising works and why you should know*. Toronto: Anmick Press.
Nye, N. S. (2005). *Going, going*. New York: Greenwillow Books.

Advertising for an Audience

WHY THE CHANGES?

Analyze Systems of Oppression

The "After" lesson extends the "Before" lesson by applying it to media literacy—specifically, a critical analysis of advertising. Although media literacy is becoming more common in schools, it is still not a part of the curriculum in most U.S. schools, and yet people are bombarded with media messages daily. Many of these messages, and particularly advertising, are carefully designed to get people to act in a particular way, with most advertising trying to get people to spend money on a certain product.

The "After" lesson teaches students not only to identify audiences and techniques used to persuade those audiences, but also how buying power is connected to what we see in the media. In other words, increasingly the mass media is designed to appeal to segments of the public that companies see as having good cash flow. In addition, corporations are often able to influence what kinds of messages and people do and do not appear in the media in which they advertise.

The "After" plan further extends this analysis to examine who benefits from the profits of specific companies. In other words, when students spend their money, where is it going and what kinds of employment and social relations is it supporting? Companies vary widely; some are quite socially responsible, and others are not.

Encourage Social Action

Both "Before" and "After" plans encourage students to use what they learned about audiences to create something. By creating, students both learn better how others write or create for audiences and learn to use their own voices more effectively. The "After" plan has them use their skills about writing to an audience to inform their peers, and possibly move their peers to act.

▶ LESSON PLAN

Creating a Newspaper

BEFORE

Subject Areas: English, Journalism
Grade Level: 8–12
Time: Four weeks

Objectives

1. Students will describe the purposes and forms of various parts of the newspaper.
2. Students will describe the roles and responsibilities of news professionals.
3. Students will communicate effectively, using correct writing conventions.
4. Students will examine the implications of audiences for newspaper content.
5. Students will create a school newspaper.

Suggested Procedures

1. Find out the extent to which students use the newspaper and, if they do, which section(s) they read. Then distribute several community newspapers and, if possible, school newspapers from several schools. Have students skim these, and then discuss why people use newspapers and what the common sections are in a newspaper. Tell them that they will be creating a newspaper for their own school.

2. Invite a panel of guest speakers who work for local newspapers, magazines, and TV stations. Have them talk about the purpose of the newspaper, magazine, or TV station they work for, what they do in their own jobs, what a typical day for them is like, how knowledge of the audience influences stories and coverage to the audience, and what trends they foresee in their work.

3. Gather information about the interests of students in the school. Have students each interview one or two people in the school to find out (a) what they would like to see in a newspaper, (b) what they don't like in a newspaper (or on TV), and (c) what would make them want to pick up a student-created newspaper and read it. Discuss how these interests should be reflected in a school newspaper.

4. Determine what the main sections of the newspaper will be, and divide students into groups accordingly. The sections may include, for example, world, national, and local news, entertainment, editorials, special featrures, and sports. Each group should decide what stories or features they could create or gather for that section. Have each group then report to the class as a whole for feedback.

5. Give students a few days to complete writing their articles or other entries. Students should put their articles on to a computer for editing and for later merging into one document. Each section should have a section editor, who ensures that the articles are written. Section editors should collect the articles and redistribute them within the section in order for them to receive critique and feedback. Encourage students to rework their articles. Next, collect all the articles.

6. From among the various methods for compiling the articles into a newspaper, have students determine what is feasible in their school. Some teachers have access to computer programs for doing a real newspaper layout; others may assemble the articles in the form of a newsletter.

7. Have students design an audience feedback questionnaire to include with the newspaper to gather information about how well their newspaper responds to a diverse audience.

8. Duplicate and distribute the newspaper; collect as many feedback questionnaires as possible. Analyze feedback questionnaires. Have students examine the results and write recommendations for how to improve the newspaper.

Evaluation

1. Evaluate each section of the students' newspaper for its reflection of purposes of that section of the newspaper.

2. Evaluate each student's written contribution for effective communication and use of correct writing conventions.

3. Evaluate the newspaper for how well it interests readers in the school.

Creating a Newspaper

AFTER

Subject Areas: English, Journalism
Grade Level: 8–12
Time: Four weeks

Objectives

1. Students will describe the purposes and forms of various parts of the newspaper.

2. Students will communicate effectively, using correct writing conventions.

3. Students will analyze the diverse interests and viewpoints of a multicultural community and issues of concern to them.

4. Students will recognize biases in the media.

5. Students will critique relationships between institutional power, economic power, and media.

6. Students will create a newspaper that effectively serves a multicultural community and advances its interests.

Suggested Procedures

1. Find out the extent to which students use the newspaper and, if they do, which section(s). Distribute several community newspapers and, if possible, school newspapers from several schools. Have students skim them, discuss why people use newspapers, and identify the common sections in newspapers. Tell students that they will be creating a newspaper for their own community, as a way both of learning about newspapers and of creating something that serves a diverse community well.

2. Invite a panel of guest speakers who work for local newspapers (both free and commercial newspapers), magazines, and TV stations. Try to get speakers who represent a diversity of sociocultural groups. Have them talk about the purpose of the newspaper or TV station they work for, who the audience is, how knowledge of the audience influences stories and coverage, how closely they pay attention to the audience, and how much advertisers influence stories and coverage. Also ask about how much they investigate controversial issues beyond what the major news services provide.

3. Decide who will be the audience of the newspaper the class will create: It might be the school, the local neighborhood, or both the school and neighborhood. Gather information about the racial and ethnic composition of the audience, the socioeconomic composition, languages spoken, the age composition, and any other demographic variables that might be significant in terms of audience.

4. Assign students to analyze a TV show or a section of a newspaper. Divide the class so that a group of students is assigned to examine one of the reader demographics described above. For example, a group of students may examine the representation of Asian American adults and children.

5. Have students share their findings and determine which sociocultural groups are best represented and best served by the media they analyzed. Which group is invisible? Is any group represented negatively? Whose perspectives predominate? Whose issues are discussed and advanced?

6. Gather several alternative media (media produced by groups other than the dominant society, such as African American newspapers or magazines, Latino news media, feminist media, gay and lesbian media), or locate alternative media Websites. Distribute them; after students have browsed through them, discuss how the viewpoints represented are similar to or different from those in the media they examined earlier and the degree to which issues discussed in them are different and investigated differently. Discuss why alternative media arise.

7. Have older students examine relationships between power and media by exploring how advertisers affect the content and substance of media. View the first half of the video *Manufacturing Consent*, which presents Noam Chomsky's theory of propaganda. Then have students in small groups create a poster, skit, or short essay expressing what they learned. Use their work to discuss how one can find out in one's own community the degree to which advertising affects the substance of news.

8. Have each student interview one or two people in the target audience to find out (a) what they would like to see in a newspaper, (b) what they don't like in a newspaper (or on TV), (c) what would make them want to pick up a student-created newspaper and read it, and (d) their suggestions for making the newspaper respond well to a diverse audience. Make sure people from all subgroups in the target audience are interviewed. Have students share their findings.

9. Based on these various investigations (of the audience, of biases in media, and of alternative media), have students develop a purpose for the newspaper they will create. Their purpose may be partially to entertain and respond to consumer demand; it might also be to educate and to examine issues and address the concerns of a multicultural community.

10. Determine what the main sections of the newspaper will be, and divide students into groups accordingly. The sections may include, for example, a main section, entertainment, editorials, and sports. Each group should decide what stories or features they could create or gather for that section. Have each group then report to the class as a whole for feedback, paying particular attention to how well their ideas fit the expressed desires of the audience. The desires of groups that are numerically small often get lost at this point; draw students' attention to any such groups in their audience, and have them consider how to make the newspaper relevant to these groups. If students are not sure at this point, they may need to do a few more interviews.

11. Give students a few days to complete writing their articles or other entries. Students should put their articles on to a computer for editing and for later merging into one document. Each section should have a section editor, who ensures that the articles get written. Section editors should collect the articles and redistribute them to group members responsible for the section to read and provide feedback. Encourage students to rework their submissions. It is up to the section editor to determine when each article is finished.

12. From among various methods for compiling the articles into one document, have students determine what is feasible in their own situations. Some teachers have access to computer programs for doing a real newspaper layout; others will assemble the articles in the form of an informal newsletter.

13. Have students design an audience feedback questionnaire to include with the newspaper to gather information about how well their newspaper responds to a diverse audience. The questionnaire should include the most important

demographic variables so that responses can be grouped according to who the respondents are (such as by sex).

14. Duplicate and distribute the newspaper; collect as many feedback questionnaires as possible.

15. Analyze feedback questionnaires, dividing them for analysis by key demographic variables. Have students examine the results to find out how well their newspaper served the various subgroups in the audience. Have the class write recommendations for how to create a newspaper that serves a diverse community audience. If they wish, their recommendations may be sent to local news media.

Evaluation

1. Evaluate each section of the students' newspaper for its reflection of its purposes.

2. Evaluate each student's written contribution for effective communication and use of correct writing conventions.

3. Evaluate the newspaper for how well it addresses and reflects the diversity, viewpoints, and interests of its audience.

Creating a Newspaper

WHY THE CHANGES?

Modeling Diversity

In the "Before" lesson, while audience is acknowledged, the diverse perspectives and interests of the audience are not necessarily addressed. The "After" lesson focuses on diversity within the audience. Students may at first feel uncomfortable with that focus, until they realize that there are some real differences in perspectives among people in the audience, which they cannot necessarily anticipate without finding out specifically about their audience.

The "After" lesson also attempts to make sure guest speakers are diverse. Not only does this present a diversity of role models, but issues related to diversity are much more likely to be discussed when the speakers are diverse.

Analyze Systems of Oppression

Newspapers are a great way to examine what bias there is in the media, whose viewpoints predominate in the media, and how media connect with power and control issues. The "Before" plan does not address these issues at all. The "After" plan has students examine media they consume and then use the results of their examination to attempt to create a newspaper that is more inclusive. Using alternative media (such as ethnic or feminist media) helps students to see limitations in the perspectives of mainstream media and to see what it means to advocate for interests other than those students may be used to seeing advocated. It is particularly effective to find different treatments of the same event or issue, such as immigration.

The "After" plan also suggests examining relationships among economic power, advertising, and media content. This is a complex issue that can become an entire unit in and of itself. However, even a short lesson, such as using the suggested Chomsky video to help analyze local newspapers, can raise students' level of awareness about the power of advertising and cause students to examine their advertisers critically.

Encourage Social Action

Part of social action entails learning to build new institutions that work for everyone. The entire focus of the "After" lesson is on building a newspaper that actually works for everyone in the community, based on some analysis of why newspapers often exclude or distort parts of their audience. In addition, in the "After" plan, students are encouraged to communicate their recommendations based on an analysis of their own newspaper, for building a newspaper for a wider audience.

Resource

Achbar, M., & Wintonick, P. (Directors.) (2002, 1992). Manufacturing consent [Motion picture]. (Available from Zeitgeist Films, Ltd., 247 Centre Street, New York, NY 10013)

▶ LESSON PLAN[7]

Twentieth-Century Social Change Movements

BEFORE

Subject Area: Social Studies
Grade Level: 8–12
Time: Two weeks at the end of the year

Objectives

1. Students will describe and appreciate the social change movements that impacted the United States during the last century.

2. Students will gain experience in conducting research, analyzing primary sources, and evaluating secondary sources, including Internet sources.

3. Students will develop skills in note taking and report writing.

4. Students will develop skills in working with and presenting to groups.

Suggested Procedures

1. Referring to the U.S. history textbook and other materials, students will identify a twentieth-century social change movement to study in more depth. They will reread the materials that pertain to their chosen topic and generate a list of questions about the social, political, and economic aspects of the movement. Possible movements can include but are not limited to civil rights, feminist, labor, American Indian, Chicano/Latino, disability rights, and gay/lesbian/bisexual/transgendered rights.

2. For several days, students will gather materials about the social movement they have chosen, attempting to find information to answer the list of questions they generated. Basic information gathered about the movement will include the time period, goals, strategies and approaches, outcomes, leaders, cultural impact, and the current agenda of the movement (if it still exists). Sources should include at least one first-person account. Teachers will find that, increasingly, students

[7]*Source:* Cheri Sistek, Marina, CA.

are using the Internet as a reference source. Students may need to be reminded that just because something is on the Internet does not mean that it is correct or includes points of view from different groups of people. Some Web resources that teachers may wish to suggest to students are those associated with museums and other recognized institutions: for example, the Smithsonian Institution in Washington, DC, at www.si.edu; Museum of Science and Industry in Chicago at www.msichicago.org; and the Field Museum in Chicago at www.fmnh.org. Many cities have museums and galleries that students have been visiting over the years that will provide useful information about social changes during the twentieth century.

3. Students will write short reports based on their research.

4. Students who have researched the same social change movement will form groups in order to share resources and develop a short classroom presentation about the key aspects of the movement they have studied. They will develop visual aids to enhance their presentations.

5. In their groups, students will present their research. They will write responses to their peers' research and share them with their peers. They will engage in discussions of each group's research presentation.

Evaluation

1. By evaluating their written reports, assess students' abilities to gather and organize information.

2. Through their presentations and their participation in the discussions, evaluate students' understanding of the details and impact of the social change movements.

Subject Area: Interdisciplinary (Social Studies, Language Arts)

Grade Level: 8–12

Time: Three weeks

Objectives

1. Students will describe and appreciate the social change movements that have impacted the United States during the last century.

2. Students will gain experience in conducting research, analyzing primary sources, and evaluating secondary sources, including Internet sources.

3. Students will use interviewing techniques.

4. Students will examine the ways in which participation in social change movements impacted individuals' lives.

5. Students will write for an audience by weaving together facts and fiction.

6. Students will present their own written work for an audience.

Suggested Procedures

1. Referring to the U.S. history textbook and other materials, students will identify a twentieth-century social change movement to study in more depth. They will reread the materials that pertain to their chosen topic and generate

a list of questions about the social, political, and economic aspects of the movement. Possible movements can include but are not limited to civil rights, feminist, labor, American Indian, Chicano/Latino, disability rights, and gay/lesbian/bisexual/transgendered rights.

2. For several days, students will gather materials about the social movement they have chosen, attempting to find information to answer the list of questions they generated. Information gathered about the movement will include the time period, goals, strategies and approaches, outcomes, leaders, cultural impact, and the current agenda of the movement (if it still exists). Sources should include at least one first-person account.

3. Students will interview one person who was personally involved in the social change movement they studied. (If the movement took place early in the twentieth century, they can interview a descendant of a person involved in the movement or a younger friend of a person who was involved.) Interviews will focus on the personal aspects of being involved in the movement (e.g., choices the person made about his or her involvement, consequences of being involved, feelings about being involved).

4. Students who have researched the same social change movements will form groups to compare notes and gain a deeper understanding of the impact of the social change movement on individuals, groups, and the greater American culture. They will discuss and plan an approach they can take as "experts" who will teach the rest of the class about their social change movements through their upcoming dramatic monologue presentations.

5. Drawing on their research and interviews, students will write a short (3–5 minute) dramatic monologue to read or perform for the class. In the monologue, the student will invent a fictional character involved in the social change movement. The character will be struggling with a conflict in his or her life that is connected to or a result of an issue the movement is addressing. The monologue will either show how the conflict will be resolved or hint at the possible avenues for resolution of the conflict. The dramatization of the monologue will illustrate for the audience some of the key aspects of the social change movement as well as a personal perspective on it. Since monologues can be set in the middle of the movement or in a period of time subsequent to the movement, the student performer will identify the setting (the time and place) and the age of the speaker. Costumes and visual aids may be used to enhance the performance.

6. After each dramatic monologue performance, students will jot down on index cards two to three things they appreciate about the monologue. These will provide the foundation for a brief discussion about each of the research projects/monologues and movements.

7. Each student will write a brief reflection about what it was like to perform the monologue for the class. Possible questions for reflection include, What was particularly challenging about it? What was the most positive aspect of doing it? What would you wish to do over again if given a chance?

Evaluation

1. Assess students' abilities to gather information through written and human sources.

2. Evaluate the students' understanding of social change movements through their own dramatic monologue presentations, their written comments about their peers' presentations, their reflections about their own performances, and their participation in the discussions.

Twentieth-Century Social Change Movements

WHY THE CHANGES?

Perspective

The "Before" lesson encourages understanding of the actions of a particular group of people but only requires the reading of one first-person account. By contrast, the "After" lesson promotes a deeper understanding by bringing a student face to face with a person who was (and possibly still is) directly involved in a social movement. Incorporating an interview into the research allows students to actively engage in a discussion about the movement on an intellectual and personal level. Furthermore, talking with a person helps the student understand what the group's view of itself was or is. In the "After" lesson, students also gain perspective as a result of putting themselves in the place of another person through the creation and performance of the dramatic monologue.

Encourage Social Action

The "book learning" approach of the "Before" lesson is less likely to promote students' understanding of the group they were studying than the "After" lesson, which encourages students to gain a fuller understanding of the day-to-day life of the people engaged in the social change movement. By talking with a person who has been involved in the group being studied, a student can understand more about the ways in which people related to one another, the cultural aspects of their lives during the movement, and what it is like to act as a change agent.

▶ LESSON PLAN[8]

Principles of the U.S. Legal System

BEFORE

Subject Area: Social Studies
Grade Level: 9
Time: One day

Objectives

1. Students will determine the principles of the U.S. legal system.

2. Students will analyze how the judicial system functions.

Suggested Procedures

1. Introduce due process as one of the principles of the U.S. legal system by presenting the following situation: John was arrested and thrown into jail. He

[8] *Source:* Kristen Buras, University of Wisconsin–Madison.

was not informed of the charges against him and was denied bail. He was held in jail until his trial, which took place three years later. Because he could not afford a lawyer, he had to defend himself. During the trial the judge forced him to testify against himself. John was found guilty and sentenced to life in prison. Ask, Could this scenario take place in the United States? Why or why not? What principle of the U.S. legal system protects us from situations like John's?

2. Have students identify the principles of the U.S. legal system by having them read the social studies textbook. Using a corresponding worksheet, direct students to provide a summary of each of the following principles:
   - Equal justice
   - Due process—substantive and procedural
   - Adversary system
   - Presumption of innocence

   Ask, How do the key principles of the legal system provide justice for all?

3. Reinforce understandings of the principles by referring students to the school district student behavior handbook. Ask, Why do we have a student handbook? What are some examples of the principles of our legal system found in the handbook?

Evaluation

Assess students' abilities to apply the principles of the U.S. legal system by having them complete this workbook activity (see *Government and You*, by Killoran, Zimmer, & Fischer, 1995):

1. Read information that defines "due process of law."

2. Review the facts of a hypothetical case from Anytown, USA, in which a poor Eskimo woman is accused of "causing city property to become ugly" by clipping roses planted around a courthouse. Wearing attire similar to that described by a witness of the rose decimation, Mary Toka is arrested and read her rights. Unable to afford an attorney, she is questioned by police without the presence of one. Toka pleads innocent, but bail is set at $100,000—a sum that she cannot afford to pay. After several days in jail, Toka signs a confession and is put on trial with a jury made up of six men of European ancestry. During the trial, she is criticized for refusing to testify in her own defense. The jury ultimately mandates that Toka serve two years in prison at hard labor.

3. Consider a list that summarizes former Supreme Court cases that might apply to the hypothetical case.

4. Fill out a legal brief that is worded: My client has a constitutional right to _____. Her right was violated when _____. This protection was established in the case of _____. Conclusion: _____.

It should be noted that, although the hypothetical case has class, race, and gender dimensions, the activity offers little opportunity to explore these aspects. While students may be encouraged to think about when particular rights were violated and which former cases apply to certain circumstances, they are not asked to focus on why such violations occur. (pp. 90–93)

Resource

Baltimore County Public Schools. (1999). *American government curriculum guide*. Towson, MD: Author.

The U.S. Legal System: Justice for All?

Subject Area: Social Studies

Grade Level: 9

Time: One to three days

Objectives

1. Students will determine and examine the meanings of various principles of the U.S. legal system.

2. Students will analyze the degree to which the judicial system upholds those principles by considering issues of class, race, gender, and disability in relation to the judicial system.

3. Students will identify ways of challenging the unequal forms of power that facilitate violations of those principles.

4. Students will organize to address one such violation by the judicial system.

Suggested Procedures

1. Begin class by having students complete a reflection on the functioning of the judicial system (see Figure 6.3). Each statement corresponds to one of the legal principles; students are asked to think about the validity of each statement, indicate agreement or disagreement, and offer a reason for their position.

2. After students have completed the reflection, facilitate a class debate regarding each of the statements. Students should be encouraged to share their perspectives and to respond to the perspectives of others.

Read . . . Read each statement below.

Think . . . Does the statement appropriately describe the judicial system? Can you think of evidence that supports or weakens the validity of the statement?

Write . . . Indicate whether you agree or disagree with the statement. Explain the reason for your position.

Statements

1. In a court of law, all people are treated alike.

2. The process of law enforcement ensures that a person's rights are protected.

3. All parties involved in a trial have an equal opportunity to prepare and present their cases.

4. During judicial proceedings, a person is considered innocent until proven guilty.

Figure 6.3 Reflections on the Judicial System

3. Distribute a worksheet that will help students organize the principles and their meanings. Referring back to the statements on the reflection, the teacher may ask students to determine—using their own words—the significance of and principle underlying each statement. As the class develops ideas, the teacher can draw explicit connections between those ideas and the formal names given to the legal principles. Each principle and associated details may be recorded on the worksheet.

4. Have students, who have now developed a vocabulary for particular principles and their meanings, reconsider the earlier debate by analyzing a variety of legal scenarios (see Figure 6.4). Have students volunteer to read the scenarios to the class. After each scenario is read, have students share their assessments of which legal principle was involved and whether or not the principle was upheld or violated.

- Three Latino youths are walking down a street one evening in a predominately White neighborhood. A police car slowly follows them, then suddenly pulls over. Two officers get out of the car and command them to put their hands behind their heads. The three young men are taken to police headquarters and interrogated about several cases of vandalism in the area.

- The mayor of a city is accused of stealing government funds. The judge assigned to the case has known the mayor for years. As the trial proceeds, the judge allows the defense to harass witnesses testifying against the mayor. On the other hand, the prosecution is frequently disciplined by the judge for badgering the mayor's witnesses.

- A working-class woman is busted for possession of illegal substances. She is given the maximum jail time allowed. A wealthy and well-known businesswoman is charged with drug possession. It is mandated by the court that she attend rehabilitation for her substance abuse problem.

- A mentally retarded man admires a group of tough and influential drug dealers in his neighborhood. Often humiliated because of his disability, the man hopes to earn their acceptance and friendship. On one occasion, his "friends" give him a gun and tell him to go into a store and get money, "only shooting if necessary." The man eventually enters the store, but becomes frantic and forgets his instructions. He shoots the clerk and forgets to rob the store. In criminal court, he is convicted of murder and receives the death penalty (Human Rights Watch, 2001).

- The owners of a business are charged with not paying taxes—nearly $250,000. They hire a team of private lawyers from a highly respected law firm to defend them. Ultimately, the case is settled, and they avoid prosecution for evading their taxes. In a separate case, a man is accused of robbing a store of $5,000. He cannot afford a lawyer, so one is appointed by the court. The court-appointed attorney spends only an hour preparing for the trial. The man is found guilty and is sent to prison.

- A woman is arrested for prostitution. In court, she is given time in jail. The man who solicited the woman and paid her money was never charged with violating the law.

- Jury members gather to decide a case. During their deliberation, a member of the jury comments, "When I first entered the courtroom and saw the accused, I just knew he was guilty. All 'those' people do is cause problems."

Figure 6.4 Legal Scenario Examples

During the examination of the scenarios, the teacher should assist students in identifying the ways in which class, race, gender, disability, and other forms of unequal power impact the workings of the judicial system.

5. To extend the discussion further, ask the students to consider a brief reading from Mumia Abu-Jamal's (1995) *Live from Death Row*, "No Law, No Rights." In the piece, Abu-Jamal discusses the brutalization of nineteen Pennsylvania prisoners by guards and concludes:

> All found out how fragile the very system that stole their very freedom was when the state committed crimes against them. All found out that words like "justice," "law," "civil rights," and, yes, "crime" have different and elastic meanings depending on whose rights were violated, who committed what crimes against whom, and whether one works for the system or against it. (p. 105)

Students may be asked to write about the reading and share their responses in pairs or small groups while the teacher circulates around the classroom; the class may then reconvene as a whole to discuss the relationship of Abu-Jamal's piece to claims that the judicial system provides "justice for all."

6. Conclude class by giving each student an index card. On one side, ask students to briefly explain which principle of the U.S. legal system they think is most important and why. On the other, ask students to explain whether or not the principle they chose is generally honored by the judicial system.

7. In preparation for the next class meeting, give students a homework assignment that requires them to bring in documentation of a recent case in which one of the legal principles was either upheld or violated. Thus, students will be seeking evidence to support the conclusions they recorded on their index cards.

8. Next class, have students share their findings. Develop a class project that addresses one of the cases.

Evaluation

1. Have students write an editorial to a local paper, magazine, attorney, or judge regarding a particular case.

2. Have students plan a presentation for another social studies class.

3. Have students attend a meeting of a local grassroots organization focusing on judicial injustice, then write a report or offer assistance.

4. If your school has the technological resources, create and update a website that highlights cases in which principles are violated and provides information on related political mobilizations.

5. Have students create political cartoons that make a statement about one of the legal principles and the degree to which it is upheld. Display these on a bulletin board, or encourage students to submit them to school publications.

Resources

Crowe, C. (2003). *Getting away with murder: The true story of Emmett Till*. New York: Phillis Fogleman.
Maayers, W. D. (1999). *Monster*. New York: HarperCollins.

The U.S. Legal System: Justice for All?

WHY THE CHANGES?

Practicing Democracy

In the "Before" plan, students are primarily asked to define principles using the textbook and identify illustrations in the handbook. Classroom instruction is organized around teacher questions and "correct" student responses. Likewise, the evaluation of student learning is structured around using information to appropriately fill in a legal brief. In the "After" plan, students are asked to formulate opinions, offer evidence, share, listen, and debate—activities fundamental to genuine democracy. In this way, an evolving dialogue is established, rather than a Q&A session.

Analyzing Social Inequalities

In the "Before" plan, students are asked how the key principles of the legal system "protect us" and "provide justice for all." They are further asked to locate examples of the principles in the student handbook. Although the lesson does conclude with a hypothetical case that alludes to issues of class, race, and gender, the circumstances of the case appear inauthentic. Furthermore, students are limited in their ability to analyze such issues due to the structure of the legal brief. Injustice within the U.S. legal system is thus a fiction not worthy of extensive examination. In comparison, the "After" lesson does not open with the assumption that principles provide justice for all. Instead, it subjects that assumption to debate and scrutiny. And it offers opportunities for students to examine principles in relation to both hypothetical and actual cases in which such ideals were betrayed. Most important, all cases allow for an in-depth discussion of inequalities within the legal system.

Encouraging Social Action

In the "Before" plan, social action is a distant possibility. On one hand, the opening premise of the lesson indicates that there are virtually no inequalities to be addressed. On the other hand, the violation of principles is presented only hypothetically, and the course of action favored is the writing of a legal brief for appeal. In the "After" plan, students are provided with a range of ways to address existing injustices within the judicial system. These possibilities allow students to engage in activities central to their development as citizens and crucial to changing multiple forms of oppression.

▶ LESSON PLAN

Heredity

BEFORE

Subject Area: Biology

Grade Level: 10–12

Time: Two or three days

Objectives

1. Students will describe Mendel's experiments and their significance.
2. Students will define the terms *dominant trait, recessive trait, genes, genotype, phenotype,* and *hybrid.*
3. Students will differentiate among theory, hypothesis, and fact.

Suggested Procedures

1. Discuss with students the types of traits that seem to run in families. Ask them to name the traits that seem to run in their families.
2. Have students read the pages in a textbook or Internet on Mendel's work.
3. Discuss the concepts from the material students have read illustrating them in terms of human eye color. Use a chart depicting several generations to illustrate dominant and recessive traits.
4. Have students construct a chart depicting the crossing of yellow and green peas. The chart should illustrate dominant and recessive traits, hybrids, genes, genotypes, and phenotypes.
5. Through discussion of students' charts, make sure students understand the distinction among theory, hypothesis, and fact. Point out that Mendel never saw chromosomes or genes; his theory of dominant and recessive traits started as a hypothesis based on casual observation and was later tested through scientific experimentation. Make sure students understand that theories are accepted only as long as they explain observations; when new evidence contradicts a theory, the theory is reconstructed.

Evaluation

Through the charts they construct and through a quiz, assess students' understanding of Mendel's work and of the terms.

Biological Determinism

Subject Area: Biology
Grade Level: 10–12
Time: Three days

Objectives

1. Students will explain the term *biological determinism* and differentiate it from alternative interpretations of scientific findings.
2. Students will describe political biases that can be embedded in scientific findings.
3. Students will appreciate how biological determinism is used to support political interests and social relations.

Suggested Procedures

1. Distribute the worksheet shown in Figure 6.5. Ask students to mark the statements on the worksheet that they believe to be scientific fact. After students have completed the worksheet, point out that none of the statements has been

Check the statements you believe are true and supported by scientific research.

_____ 1. Men are innately stronger than women.

_____ 2. Low intelligence is caused by some sort of brain deficiency.

_____ 3. Brain deficiency is more prevalent among the lower class than the middle class.

_____ 4. Women are more emotional than men because of hormones.

_____ 5. As a group, African Americans are innately stronger than European Americans.

_____ 6. A sense of musical rhythm is inherited genetically and is more prevalent among some races than among others.

_____ 7. Homosexuality is caused mainly by hormone imbalance.

_____ 8. Aborigines are lower on the evolutionary scale than Caucasians.

_____ 9. Learning disabilities are caused by minor impairments to the brain or nervous system.

_____ 10. Males, especially Asian males, are genetically better disposed to think quantitatively and spatially than are females.

Figure 6.5 Biological Determinism Worksheet

conclusively proven by science, although research exists that both supports and refutes most of the statements.

2. Discuss with students that science is often thought to proceed in the following manner:

   a. The scientist develops a hypothesis.
   b. The scientist designs a perfect, definitive experiment to test the hypothesis.
   c. The scientist carries out the experiment, which works the first time and thereafter.
   d. The hypothesis is proven and is now fact.
   e. The fact is now presented in textbooks (Whatley, 1986, p. 187).

3. Tell students that they will role-play scientists and attempt to verify the following hypothesis: "A sense of musical rhythm is inherited genetically and is more prevalent in some races than in others." Stress that they should pretend this is really true and expect to confirm it. Have the class suggest a procedure that could be used to test the hypothesis and that will probably confirm it. The class may wish actually to conduct the experiment.

4. Have the class brainstorm biases built into their experiment that help them reach the desired conclusion. Have them suggest alternative interpretations for the findings of such an experiment. Explain that the same sorts of biases are built into most research on biological determinism. Biases such as the following are common:

   • Scientists conducting research are almost always members of the group that is "proved" superior.
   • A fairly limited repertoire of behavior (such as answering verbal questions) is often generalized to represent a global ability (such as intelligence).
   • What is usually published or reported are experiments finding differences between groups, differences that readers of scientific research tend to support; research that does not find differences often is not reported.

- Scientists sometimes repeat an experiment, modifying the procedure until the desired results are found.
- Data can be analyzed statistically to support a variety of conclusions; which data are analyzed using which statistical tests can depend partly on the results one is seeking.
- Findings often can be interpreted several different ways, not just the way the experimenter interprets them.

5. Provide students with an account of research on at least one aspect of biological determinism, such as the inheritability of intelligence. Helpful source materials include those by Barton (1998), Gould (1996), and Selden (1999) listed in Resources.

6. Discuss with students how biological determinism is used to support some groups' interests. For each item on the worksheet, discuss the roles and social relationships that are reinforced if the statement is considered to be true.

7. Discuss the implications of this lesson for students, including (a) the need to think critically about what one reads; (b) the need to be aware of how science is used for political purposes; and (c) that students could aspire to become scientists who provide alternative viewpoints. If issues involving biological determinism are in the media, these can be studied and discussed as well.

Evaluation

In a description of a real or hypothetical research study, students are asked to suggest potential biases in the research, potential political uses of the findings, and alternative interpretations of the findings. Evaluate student responses.

Resources

Barton, A. (1998). *Feminist science education*. New York: Teachers College.
Gould, S. J. (1996). *The mismeasure of man (3rd ed.)*. New York: Norton.
Selden, S. (1999). *Inheriting shame: The story of eugenics and racism in America*. New York: Teachers College.

Biological Determinism

Critical Questioning

The "After" plan teaches students about the social aspects of scientific inquiry. Social, human, and political biases are built into any field of scientific investigation, a fact that students should be aware of. This does not mean that human behavior has no biological basis, but students should have tools for critically questioning claims that it does. The lessons taught about science in the "After" plan can be extended to an examination of scientific research in any current social area. The plan can be taught as a sequel to rather than a replacement of the "Before" plan. The two are not mutually exclusive, but the teacher may not have time to teach both.

Analyze Systems of Oppression

The ideology of biological determinism continues to be used to rationalize social inequality. Often people simply accept it in the form of unexamined, assumed stereotypes. The traditional curriculum usually does not directly examine this ideology and the stereotypes and inequalities it supports. However, this lesson replaces or supplements the closet curriculum concept—heredity—with a critical examination of biological determinism. The study of heredity as it usually appears in biology tends to support the ideology of biological determinism. Some teachers present only the biological inheritance of obvious physical features, such as eye color, and do not address more complex things, such as intelligence, whereas others explain that the connections between biology and intelligence, ability, and personality are not clearly understood. In either case, students' beliefs relating to biological determinism are left unexamined.

▶ **LESSON PLAN**

African American Literature[9]

BEFORE

Subject Area: English
Grade Level: 9–12
Time: Over the course of one month

Objective

While reading the case work *Black Boy*, by Richard Wright, students will become familiar with three additional literary works dealing with the African American experience.

Suggested Procedures

1. Have students read the novel *Black Boy*, by Richard Wright. There are many issues raised in this novel that students probably have limited understanding of; while reading the novel, have them also read and discuss works such as those listed in Resources.

2. Have students read aloud "After You My Dear Alphonse," by Shirley Jackson, as a Readers' Theater. Afterward, have students identify Johnny's mother's problem. She makes assumptions based on the fact that her son's friend Boyd is Black; these assumptions cause Mrs. Wilson to stereotype Boyd. Students will easily identify the stereotyping. Johnny's mother is apparently kind but is disappointed when Boyd doesn't fit her stereotype. Discuss this, and examine why these stereotypes are harmful even though the mother wants only to help Boyd.

3. Have students read "Everyday Use," by Alice Walker. After reading, ask, Why doesn't the mother want Dee/Wangero to have the two old quilts? Have students brainstorm this issue in groups and then share their answers with the class for discussion.

4. Have students read "Thank You M'am," by Richard Wright, and come up with questions for the class to answer, in an individual quiz or in groups.

Evaluation

1. Through their participation in class discussions, informally assess students' understanding of the main ideas in the stories.

2. Give and grade a follow-up quiz on all four stories.

[9]*Source:* Anne Fairbrother, Del Norte High School, Albuquerque, New Mexico.

Resources

Jackson, S. (1991). After you my dear Alphonse. In S. Jackson, *The lottery and other stories*. New York: Noonday.

Walker, A. (1991). Everyday use. In *Braided lives: An anthology of multicultural American writing*. St. Paul: Minnesota Humanities Commission, Minnesota Council of Teachers of English.

Wright, R. (1978). *Black boy: A record of childhood and youth*. London: Longman.

Wright, R. (1993). Thank you m'am. In A. Mazer (Ed.), *America street: A multicultural anthology of stories*. New York: Persea Books.

Taking Action Against Discrimination

Subject Area: English

Grade Level: 9–12

Time: Over the course of one month

Objectives

1. Students will become familiar with three or four literary works dealing with diverse U.S. American cultural experiences.

2. Students will recognize and identify similarities and differences among the various cultural experiences.

3. Students will see that discrimination and racism affect relations between other groups besides European Americans and African Americans.

4. Students will see that stereotyping and discrimination may or may not be related to issues of color or culture.

5. Students will examine their own experiences and look at issues of prejudice and discrimination in their school or community, devising and implementing strategies for combating the problem.

Suggested Procedures

1. Have students read the novel *Black Boy*, by Richard Wright, over the course of one month. There are many issues raised in this novel that students probably have limited understanding of. To help, students could watch *Patch of Blue*, identifying themes of physical and mental abuse, of prejudice and discrimination, and of goodness and love. An essay identifying the major theme might be assigned. In addition, have them read and discuss works such as those listed in Resources.

2. After reading a portion of Part 1, Chapter 7, from the story "Chicano" (excerpted in *From the Barrio* by Vasquez) aloud in class, have students in groups answer discussion questions that lead them to show an understanding of, and an evaluation of, the issues raised in the story.

3. Have students then do a free write on the questions, Do you think Sammy was treated fairly? What wider social and racial issues are shown here? Can you relate to any of his experiences? These questions can then be discussed as a class. There is stereotyping and racial and cultural discrimination in this story. (If "Chicano" cannot be found, two other stories dealing with Latino experiences could also be

used: "The Scholarship Jacket," by Marta Salinas, or Chapter 13 from *George Washington Gomez*, by Americo Paredes. Both deal with discrimination and issues of culture and class. Another suggested work to parallel *Black Boy* is *Living Up the Street*, by Gary Soto.)

4. Have students read the story "The Stolen Party," by Liliana Heker (set in Argentina), aloud in class; then, in groups, they will answer comprehension and interpretive questions. The students will discuss if there is prejudice here. (It is a matter of class and color—not race, culture, or country.) As a class, students will discuss this story and what is happening and why, identifying parallels between the experiences of Hosaura and Richard: stereotyping as well as class, cultural, and racial discrimination.

5. Have students read aloud "An Awakening . . . Summer 1956," by Nicholasa Mohr (a Puerto Rican author) and, in groups, come up with one interpretive and one evaluative question about the story.

6. Have students send one person from one group to write the questions on the board. The teacher will go over the questions, but only to establish whether they are truly interpretive and evaluative. Students will then answer the class's questions in groups. If the following questions are not generated, they can be added to the questions on the board:
   - Why had the young woman come to Texas? (interpretive)
   - How does she feel when she sees the sign in Nathan's Food and Groceries, and why? (interpretive)
   - Why does Nathan give her a Pepsi after refusing to serve her? (interpretive)
   - Do you think she did the right thing in breaking the bottle as she did? What would you have done in her position? (evaluative)
   - How did she feel afterward? Why? (interpretive)
   - What does she mean by, "A reminder . . . should I ever forget"? (interpretive)
   - What does she mean by, ". . .now she was more than ready for the challenges"? (interpretive)

7. Have students write about their own experiences that relate to the literature and about parallels and contrasts among the different novels and stories.

8. Have students work in groups to identify problems involving prejudice and discrimination in their school or community. Have groups share their ideas with the class. As a class, discuss each problem and brainstorm solutions.

9. Have students decide on one or more problems in the school or the community that they are prepared to try to solve, then decide on strategies, timelines, and measures of success. Depending on the situations being tackled, set up time for feedback, written reports, and assessment of the results.

10. After finishing *Black Boy*, have students watch *Mask*, where the issue of discrimination and stereotyping pertains to disabilities. A quiz, to be taken in pairs, could be assigned to assess students' grasp of the plot and issues raised in the movie and similarities to the issues raised in *Black Boy*.

11. Have students discuss how various forms of discrimination affected characters in *Black Boy*. If action had been taken in a manner similar to the strategies students

have proposed for addressing discrimination in their own school or community, how much better would the lives of the characters have been? Have students pretend they are Richard Wright and write an evaluation of the strategies they are undertaking in their own communities.

Evaluation

1. Students' familiarity with the main themes of the literature and videos will be assessed through their essays and free writes.

2. Students' identification of similarities and differences between the different cultural experiences, and their analysis of discrimination and racism, will be assessed informally during class and group discussions.

3. Students' ability to identify and change perceived social injustices in their school or community will be assessed through the effectiveness of the action strategies they develop and implement.

Resources

Print

Heker, L. (1986). "The stolen party." In A. Manguel (Ed.), *Other fires: Short fiction by Latin American women*. New York: C. N. Potter.

Mohr, N. (1994). "An awakening … summer 1956." In Virginia Seeley (Ed.), *Latino Caribbean literature*. Paramus, NJ: Globe Fearon.

Paredes, A. (1990). *George Washington Gomez*. Houston: Arte Publico.

Salinas, M. (1984). "The scholarship jacket." In R. A. Anaya & A. Marquez (Eds.), *Cuentos Chicanos: A short story anthology (Rev. ed.)*. Albuquerque: Published for New America by the University of New Mexico Press.

Soto, G. (1992). *Living up the street: Narrative recollections*. New York: Dell.

Vasquez, R. (1973). "Chicano." In L. O. Salinas & L. Faderman (Eds.), *From the barrio*. San Francisco: Canfield.

Wright, R. (1978). *Black boy: A record of childhood and youth*. London: Longman.

Audiovisual

Bogdanovich, P. (Director). (1985). *Mask [Motion picture]*. United States: Image Entertainment.

Green, G. (Director). (1965). *A patch of blue [Motion picture]*. United States: Metro-Goldwyn-Mayer.

Taking Action Against Discrimination

Curriculum

In both the "Before" and "After" lessons, students read multiple works by African American authors to deepen their understanding of African American experiences. Obviously, one could teach a whole course focusing on African American literature! One novel does not fully represent any group, and in both plans, the teacher recognizes that issues in a novel such as *Black Boy* are complex and will not necessarily be understood simply through reading this one novel by itself. Furthermore, instead of just hearing of the brutality of slavery, often written by White European American historians, students need to read of the events in books such as *Before the Mayflower*, by Lerone Bennett Jr. Then, to further focus on the struggle and courage of African American history, rather than the stereotypes of submission, students should read *Narrative of the Life of Frederick Douglass, an American Slave* (written by Douglass in 1845) or other slave narratives. At some point, especially if this course is integrated with U.S. history, students should read poems from the wealth of Black poetry from the 1950s and 1960s so that they can see how the issues of heritage and assimilation were addressed. Books such as *The Autobiography of Malcolm X* would be important supplemental reading for students, along with at least one book written by one of the many prominent modern African American women writers.

Analyze Systems of Oppression

African American literature, as well as the literature of any other group, can be taught with a multicultural perspective. The problem in the classroom with a traditional curriculum on African American works is that students often only hear of racism and discrimination when reading African American literature, such as *Black Boy*, and this perpetuates a stereotype that racism is only a Black-and-White racial issue as well as the stereotype that African American experiences do not have additional dimensions. Only when students examine prejudice involving other groups in society can they clearly examine the underpinnings and extent of discrimination and racism. Only then can they see it in their communities and work at trying to change it. Of course, a view of social injustice should include issues involving other peoples and groups not mentioned here: Native American and Asian American experiences, gender inequities, people with disabilities, ageism, heterosexism and homophobia, restrictions on youth, and so on.

Encourage Social Action

All students know that problems involving prejudice and discrimination exist. To help them understand those problems more fully and to work to effect changes is an empowering process, which will probably cause the students to grow to be active and involved citizens.

Resources

Bennett, L., Jr. (1987). *Before the Mayflower: A history of black America* (6th ed.). Chicago: Johnson P.

Bishop, R. S. (1993). Multicultural literature for children: Making informed choices. In V. J. Harris (Ed.), *Teaching multicultural literature* (pp. 39–53). Norwood, MA: Christopher Gordon.

Douglass, F. (1845). *Narrative of the life of Frederick Douglass, an American slave*. Boston: Published in the Anti-Slavery Office.

Freire, P. (1970). *Pedagogy of the oppressed*. New York: Seabury.

Freire, P. (1973). *Education for critical consciousness*. New York: Seabury.

Grant, C. A., & Sleeter, C. E. (1996). *After the school bell rings* (2nd ed.). New York: Falmer.

Lee, E., Menkart, D., & Okazawa-Rey, M. (Eds.). (2002). *Beyond heroes and holidays: A practical guide to K–12 anti-racist, multicultural education and staff development*. Washington, DC: Network of Educators on the Americas.

Shirts, G. R. (1977). *BaFa BaFa*. Del Mar, CA: Simile II.

Sleeter, C. E., & Grant, C. A. (2009). *Making choices for multicultural education: Five approaches to race, class, and gender* (5th ed.). Hoboken, NJ: Wiley.

Smith, N., Greenlaw, M., & Scott, C. (1987). Making the literature environment equitable. *The Reading Teacher, 40*(4), pp. 400–407.

X, Malcolm (with Alex Haley). (1992). *The autobiography of Malcolm X*. New York: Ballantine Books.

▶ LESSON PLAN

Westward Emigration[10]

BEFORE

Subject Area: Social Studies
Grade Level: 4–6
Time: Two weeks

Objectives

1. Students will identify on a map the trails used by wagon trains traveling west and the geographic features of the land they traveled across.

2. Students will describe why emigrants went west, how their trips were organized, and how they handled obstacles and problems during their travels.

3. Students will appreciate the importance of the early emigration and the impact the emigrants had on the peoples already inhabiting the lands.

Suggested Procedures

1. Using a large map, review the locations of the main American Indian tribal settlements during the early 1800s between the West Coast and the Mississippi River.
   a. Point out the Oregon Territory, and give a few reasons why the emigrants may have been drawn to this land and other Western lands.
   b. Have student study the map and suggest hazards or problems that American Indian tribes faced because of the emigrants' movement west and vice versa.

2. Read a textbook about the westward movement of emigrants. As the class comes to each topic (i.e., such as why the emigrants decided to head west, planning for the trip, etc.) in the text, explain and discuss the following questions:
   a. What are some goals of people wanting to move west?
   b. What did the emigrants need to take with them?
   c. How did they organize themselves for travel?
   d. What did each person on the trip do, or what roles did he or she fulfill (e.g., wagon master, cook, etc.)?
   e. What main routes did they take? Why? How did they know these routes?
   f. What were some possible solutions to the geographic hazards discussed in (1b)?
   g. What kinds of threats did the emigrants pose to American Indian tribes?
   h. What kinds of threats did the American Indian tribes pose to emigrants?
   i. What health hazards did American Indians face? How did they respond?

3. Show a film that portrays an account of the emigrant's trip west. Deconstruct images used in the film (for instance, show portions of the Public Broadcast Service (PBS) series *The West*, an eight-part documentary series that premiered on PBS stations in September 1996).
   a. Where were the American Indian tribes living at the time of the Oregon Trail?
   b. What perspective does this film take (that of the emigrants or Native peoples)? Does this make a difference of what story is told in the film?

[10]*Source:* Derek Jennings, University of Wisconsin–Madison.

4. Have students construct a wall mural of a westward bound wagon train.
    a. As a class, decide what should go on the mural; each student should participate in the drawing and coloring.
    b. Help students to properly place the locations of American Indian tribes as well as the Oregon Trail route of the emigrants.

Evaluation

1. Through a test, assess students' ability to do the following:
    a. Identify tribes and their locations
    b. Describe geographic features the wagon train passed as it traveled west
    c. Describe reasons for westward movement.
    d. Explain the process of westward movement, such as why the emigrants went west, how they planned for the trip, and the interpersonal relationships between those emigrating and those already there—Native tribes.
2. Through their contributions to the mural, assess students' knowledge of American Indian tribes located along the Oregon Trail and the route of the emigrants on the trail.

Resource

Westward Emigration

Subject Area: Social Studies
Grade Level: 4–6
Time: Two weeks

Objectives

1. Students will identify on a map the trails used by wagon trains traveling west and the geographic features of the land they traveled across.
2. Students will describe why emigrants went west, how their trips were organized, and how they handled obstacles and problems during their travels.
3. Students will appreciate the importance of the early emigration and the impact the emigrants had on the peoples already inhabiting the lands.
4. Students will examine attitudes and skills for cooperation and problem solving in various contexts.
5. Students will solve the problems and threats faced by the American Indians living in the area and show how this movement affects them today (e.g., interpersonal relationships, working to reach goals similar to those encountered by the emigrants going west, and homesteading concerns).
6. Students will examine the stereotypes and negative attitudes associated with sex roles and American Indians.
7. Students will develop skills in writing paragraphs.

Suggested Procedures

1. Using a large map, review the locations of the main settlements of White European Americans, American Indian tribes, and Mexican Americans during the early 1800s between the West Coast and the Mississippi River.

2. Point out the Oregon territory on a map, and explain why the emigrants were drawn to the West.

3. Discuss which groups were considered emigrants (White European Americans and also Black emigrants).

    a. Have the students read a short account of Black emigrants, such as George Washington Bush, whose son was elected to the Washington State legislature and who sponsored legislation that led to the establishment of Washington State University.

    b. Have the students read an account of a woman emigrant traveling west, such as Helen Carpenter who kept a journal about the daily chores that a woman performed during the trip.

4. Divide the class into groups of five or six students.

    a. Make sure each group contains students mixed on the basis of academic skill level, race, sex, and social class.

    b. Assign each of the groups to role-play those who already lived in the territory that the emigrants are wishing to settle (Group A) or the emigrants (Group B) moving west. (Depending on the number of student groups, you may have several Group As and several Group Bs.)

    c. Read the following background information on each group and/or print out on a sheet of paper for each group as determined by their assigned role-plays:

Group A. Current groups living in the area	Group B. Emigrant groups moving toward the West
✓ This group already lives in this area and is observing the immigration of emigrants into their homelands. ✓ This group is wealthy, having ample food and knowledge of the land and environment. • The roles of each member are important in building, caring for the home; hunting for food, storing and preparing the food, and in discussing how to negotiate with the new emigrants coming to your homelands.	✓ This group is entering new territory. They are eager to settle and begin a new life. ✓ Leaders and guides were usually men, but women could perform this role as well • The roles included wagon master, mule skinner or bullwhacker (assistant leader), journalist (keeps logs of daily activities), trail guide (plots routes on a map).

    d. Explain that each group will have a log, with each student-journalist rotating roles and maintaining the log.

    e. Explain that the log will be used to help evaluate each group. Thus, the student-journalist of the day has the main responsibility to see that each log is completed. However, all group members may pitch in. The log need not be straight narrative: Letters, pictures, and diaries may also be entered. If computers are available, ask students if they would like to keep their logs on computers or if they would prefer to use pen and paper. This choice gives students another opportunity to be decision makers.

    f. Explain that each group (as assigned to Group A or B) will consider the following:

Group A. Current groups living in the area	Group B. Emigrant groups moving toward the West
✓ Each group has ample food and supplies to live and full knowledge of how to live well in their homeland. For example, • They know which animals are plentiful for food and how to fish. • They know what types of material are available for constructing homes. • They have group leaders and people assigned to different roles and responsibilities. • The roles of men, women and children are established.	✓ Group should organize for the trip west. ✓ Each group is given money to spend; members must decide on the following: • destination for the trip • the supplies needed • how the roles on the wagon train are allocated • Whether women and men perform different roles. Why?
✓ Have the group describe their reaction when they see a large group of emigrants arriving. ✓ Have each group decide how they will greet the emigrants (will they help them or will they turn them away?).	✓ Show pictures or have students read a description of a rainy day with the wagons mired in mud. ✓ An axle is broken trying to free the wagon, and one team member injures a leg. Each team must decide what to do, and how to do it.
✓ Ask the group to describe any fears they have when they see/meet the new emigrants.	✓ What fear do the emigrants have of the persons already living on the land which they want to cross or to establish homes?
✓ Ask the group to consider what possible resources or trading opportunities the new emigrants bring.	✓ What possible conflicts may occur when the two groups meet? ✓ What opportunities are available to them from the groups already there?
✓ Explain that each group notices that the trees are in short supply after the new emigrants have arrived as they are being used for home construction and fuel. ✓ Also, their major food source for the buffalo has become depleted because the emigrants' cattle are overgrazing the lands. The buffalo are being shot for sport. ✓ New diseases have also been brought by the emigrants, causing some of the group members to become ill and die. • Ask the groups if their perspectives of the emigrants are changing and how can they address these problems.	✓ Explain to each group that they have decided to settle in this new area and must make a plan for settlement in a way that fosters cooperation and good relationships with the groups already there and minimal sex-role assignments.
✓ Each group should then discuss the depletion of resources and other concerns with the emigrants. • What actions should they take as they work together?	✓ Each group will consider how they will continue to live on the land now that the resources have been depleted and their cattle require more grazing grass. • Ask the students what actions they should take with the other group living in the area and how they can work together.
✓ The groups receive notice that they must vacate their homelands because the new emigrants need more room for their cattle to graze. • Each group should reflect how they feel about being told to leave their homes when they have been accommodating to the emigrants.	✓ This group has gotten federal support in making treaties to remove the original peoples living on the land so that they can have more land for the cattle. • Each group should discuss and consider how they would react to the other groups moving because many may have been friends and helped them establish their homes. But the decision for them to move has become "legal."

5. Have each group read textbook accounts or reputable online accounts of the immigration west and the American Indian tribes who lived along the Oregon Trail.

   a. This may include the accounts of most encounters between the emigrants and American tribes as being friendly, with the tribes helping the emigrants settle.

   b. Also, the class can discuss the conflicts of the Gattan Massacre (in which a misunderstanding around a Siouxan tribe eating a lost cow led to the massacre of the tribal people without them fighting back), the Rocks Incident Massacre (in which eight emigrants were killed), or the Bear River Massacre (in which four hundred Shoshone men, women, and children were brutally massacred in a genocidal attempt to extinguish the tribe).

   c. Relate these readings to the experiences of the groups who role-played Group A, taking the perspective of the American Indian tribes and the groups who role-played Group B, taking the perspective of the emigrants.

6. Have each group locate at least one tribe (Pawnee, Cheyenne, Lakota, Dakota, Chinook, Hidatsa, etc.) to read about their past location along the Oregon Trail and their current location within the United States (unless they are no longer a single tribe, such as the Multnomah, whose tribe of eight hundred died from disease).

7. Show a film of a current Native tribe who was involved with the Oregon Trail and how they live today, such as segments from the PBS miniseries *Indian Country: Native Americans in the 20th Century.* Discuss how their lives changed after the westward emigration.

Evaluation

1. Review the logs, making sure that each student participated in the writing process and was able to write a paragraph for the logs.

2. Review the participation of each student as based on their academic skill level, and assess how well each was able to explore his or her own ideas and engage in exploring other perspectives.

Resources

Westward Emigration

WHY THE CHANGES?

Curriculum Contents

The "After" plan shows how the impact of past history is affecting American Indians today. It is more inclusive of other cultural groups (Blacks and Mexican Americans) and women. Also, the "After" plan gives students more responsibility in learning activities.

Multiple Perspectives

Having students examine the effects of the emigrant group on the group living in the area allows students to better understand that the concept of "Manifest Destiny" produced many causalities, problems, and issues for both groups.

Instructional Strategies

The "After" plan makes use of many more instructional strategies and provides more ways for students to learn about westward emigration.

Evaluation

The "After" plan gives more attention to the assessment of each individual student's academic skill level and each student's own ideas.

▶ KNOWLEDGE IS POWER UNIT

> *Subject Area*: Career Guidance, Home Room Activity
>
> *Grade*: 9–12
>
> *Time*: Ongoing: This plan does not include a before plan; proceed directly working on it each month of the semester.

Lesson 1: What Is Student Success in a Global World? (September)

Objectives

1. Students will develop a comprehensive definition of personal success.
2. Students will develop and understanding of the significant relationship of knowledge to success.
3. Students will identity reasons why it is becoming increasingly important for them to attend and complete college and/or a vocational school.
4. Students will compare how success is defined today with how it was defined forty or fifty years ago.

Suggested Procedures

1. Have students write out on an index card their definition of personal success. (Prompt: *Describe what your financial life style, where you will be living and the kind of work you will be doing ten years from now.*)
   Ask students to keep the index card in a safe place because they will need to refer to it and add more information to it.

2. Share with students a story from your own experience about how knowledge enables you to be successful. If possible, give an example that does not include your success in schooling.

3. Have students relate a story about how by having knowledge someone was able to achieve success. As the stories are being told, have students take notes on how success is defined within the stories.

4. Provide students with materials from a variety of sources about the meaning of success in the twenty first century. For example, read passages from the following

   > Thomas Freedmans; *The World is Flat*
   > Sandy Lenthal and Joy Brady, More Conversations With Remarkable Women
   > National Women's History Project, *Women Pioneering the Future.* http//www. feminist.com/resources/antspeech/genwomen/womnepioneer.html

5. Have students respond to Kuh's (2006) statement that student success includes, not only academic achievement but the following seven factors: "engagement in educationally purposeful activities, (personal) satisfaction, acquisition of desired knowledge, skills and competencies, persistence, attainment of educational objectives including graduation and post-college performance (p. 3).

6. Have students identify ten people they consider successful. Encourage students to select people of both genders and from different cultural groups. Students should determine to what extent the people they identified display the seven areas in Kuh's statement.

7. Place students into groups for a discussion of the people they identified, paying particular attention to their areas of success.

Evaluation

1. Assess students' definition of success and the extent to which they define success broadly, in keeping with Kuh's statement (in procedure 5).

2. Assess whether students' definition of success is narrowly focused, such as on economy and financial achievement, or more comprehensively focused, such as on having a flourishing life in many areas (e.g., art, music, civic service).

Resources

Lesson 2: Preparation for Success in the Twenty First Century (October)

Objectives

1. Students will develop a definition of what it means to be prepared both personally and professionally.

2. Students will identify (and assess) their overall ability to prepare for activities and events in their lives.

Suggested Procedures

1. Have students share their favorite life story about the importance of "being prepared" and what getting prepared must take into account.

2. Have students review their index card where they wrote out what they would like their financial life style, *where they will be living, and the kind of work they will be doing to be ten years from now.* Use the information on the card to help each student assess his or her goal(s) as well as the preparation he or she will need to accomplish the goal. Caution: The author discovered that boys sometimes are in the fantasy world about their career goals, thinking they will become great pro athletes. If you encounter a similar situation, have students investigate what percent of high school and college athletes make it into the pros. If possible, have some former athlete come in to talk with the students about this point.

3. Have some students read material that compares preparation for everyday life in the nineth or twentieth century with preparation for life in twenty first century. Possible sources include Ann McGovern's *If You Lived 100 Years Ago* and Winifred G. Helmes's *Notable Maryland Women.*

4. Have students working in groups read material that compares and contrasts preparation for everyday life in twenty first century in Western countries to how people prepare for everyday life in Third World countries. Ask them to address how the preparation is similar and different and why so. Encourage students to use the Web to collect information. Suggest websites such as UNESCO, Bureau of Census.

Evaluation

Assess the quality of information students collect and the seriousness and realism they bring to the discussion, including the extent to which they support their comments with statistics and anecdotal information.

Resources

McGovern, A. (1999). *If you lived 100 years ago*. New York: Scholastic.

Helmes, W.G. (Ed.). (1977). *Notable Maryland Women*. Cambridge, MD: Tidewater, 1977.

Lesson 3: Handling the Truth About Who Is Usually Prepared and Who Is Not for Success in College?—Remember, Knowledge is Power! (November)

The expectation for this lesson is that by now you have developed an excellent rapport with your students, they can talk honestly with you, and you can do the same with them.

Objectives

1. Students will learn which students statistically are least prepared to achieve success in our global society.

2. Students will begin to develop strategies that will prevent them from becoming one of the negative statistics.

3. Students will identify reasons why some students have difficulty attending college after high school.

Suggested Procedures

1. Tell the class the "good news" about students' achieving success: Many more high school students today say that want to attend college; increasingly many women are attending college—and they now outnumber men. Also, many more students of color are attending college, and at a few colleges they are in the majority (Kuh, 2006).

2. Give students the "bad news": Use your best bedside manner to let them know that THEY do not have to be one of the statistics below:
   - Only 68 out of every 100 ninth graders graduate from high school.
   - Only 18 of that 100 complete any type of postsecondary education within six years of graduating high school.
   - Low-income students, African American, Latino, and Native American students, and students with disabilities lag behind White and Asian American students.
   - Just over half (51%) of high school graduates have high school reading skills.
   - Over 25% of four-year college students who take three or more remedial classes leave college after the first year.
   - College costs are increasing faster than family income.

- The vast majority of poor young people cannot imagine going to college.
- Delaying postsecondary enrollment, for whatever reason, reduces the likelihood that the student will persist and complete a degree program.

3. Have students discuss what surprises them most about the statistics.

4. Have students write a short essay on what they are doing to make certain they will not "be a statistic."

5. Hold a class discussion in which each students has three minutes to report on what they are doing to prevent becoming a statistic.

Evaluation

Assess to what extent students demonstrate a seriousness and a willingness to engage in discussions about the good and bad statistics, which includes acknowledging the implications of the statistics for their life.

Lesson 4: Two Keys to Students Success in College (December)

Objective

Students will learn about the significance of academic and social integration for achieving success in college.

Suggested Procedures

1. Explain to students the meaning of academic and social integration.
   a. Academic integration includes satisfactory compliance with both explicit norms, such as earning passing grades and attending class, and the normative academic values of the institution, such as a school of education that values the arts.
   b. Social integration includes the extent to which a student finds the institution's social environment to be congenial with his or her preferences and lifestyle, including the university community's having available stores and shops (e.g., beauty shops) that can serve the personal needs of the students.

2. Discuss with students the importance of learning how to develop new friendships and to negotiate new environments.

3. Have students form triads including students they do not usually socialize with, and have the triad work on getting to know about one another, including their academic and social behavior such as favorite subjects, hobbies, and interests.

4. Set up an activity that will have students meet with their other subject matter teachers during office hours outside of the formal classroom in order to practice their communication and human relations skills.

5. In many high schools students have to do community service projects as a requirement. Have students identify social skills they will work on during the community service project that will facilitate their social integration.

Evaluation

Assess the extent of students' ability to discuss the academic and social integration knowledge, skills, and attitude they will need to be successful in the college or the postsecondary school they plan to attend.

Critical Questions

The plan is designed to challenge students to raise critical questions within themselves about themselves, both alone and with the help of peers and teachers. It raises questions about what success is and provides students with a comprehensive definition, one that may be more satisfactory in helping them to move forward.

Analyze Systems of Oppression

The plan has students examine the results of and/or negative statistics that come from students' not understanding and/or strongly resisting the different types of oppression that work to keep them down.

Encourages Social Action

The plan encourages students to take social action for themselves. It teaches them about power and pulls no punches when it introduces them to reasons why some students drop out. It informs them about keys to success in college—academic and social integration—and helps them to develop strategies to be successful.

▶ LESSON PLAN

Globalization

Subject Area: Social Studies, Economics, Global Studies.

Grade: 8–12

Time: One week

Objective

1. Students will examine definitions of globalization.
2. Students will explain the major features of globalization.
3. Students will learn that the current and future progress of the United States depends on the citizens' level of global literacy, which includes academic knowledge, technology skill, and a cultural disposition that facilitates communicating and working with people who are different.

Suggested Procedures

1. Have students to write out a definition of *globalization*.
2. Present students with the following definitions of globalization, and ask that they compare and contrast the definitions: How are they similar and how are they different? What do they address? What don't they address?
   - Jill Blackmore (2000) sees globalization as "increased economic, cultural, environmental, and social interdependencies and new transnational financial and political formations arising out of the mobility of capital, labor and information, with both homogenizing and differentiating tendencies".
   - Malcolm Waters (1995) argues that "globalization is the direct consequence of the expansion of European culture across the planet via settlement,

colonization and cultural mimesis. It is also bound up intrinsically with the pattern of capitalist development as it has ramified through political and cultural arenas" (p. 2).

3. Have students do a computer search of definitions of globalization and discuss what each suggests about their education.

4. Have each student write a short essay on the influence of globalization on their life career goals.

Globalization

Subject Area: Social Studies, Economics, Global Studies

Grade: 8–12

Time: One week

Objective

1. Students will examine definitions of globalization.

2. Students will explain the major features of globalization.

3. Students will explain how cultural diffusion can be a product of globalization.

4. Students will discover how for students is narrowly defined in discussion of education for the global society.

5. Students will explain how major world issues are influenced by globalization and how globalization influence's major world issues.

6. Students will explain how female rights have become a central issue in discussion of the influence of globalization.

7. Students will discover the role immigration plays in globalization.

Suggested Procedures

1. Have students to write out a definition of *globalization*.

2. Assign students to search the media for two days and report on how globalization is defined and discussed and in what context (e.g., economic, politics, immigration, the role of women).

3. Present students with the following definitions of globalization, and ask that they compare and contrast the definitions: How are they similar and how are they different? What do they address? What don't they address?
   - Jill Blackmore (2000) sees globalization as "increased economic, cultural, environmental, and social interdependencies and new transnational financial and political formations arising out of the mobility of capital, labor and information, with both homogenizing and differentiating tendencies".
   - Malcolm Waters (1995) argue that globalization is the direct consequence of the expansion of European culture across the planet via settlement, colonization and cultural mimesis. It is also bound up intrinsically with the pattern of capitalist development as it has ramified through political and cultural arenas" (p. 2).

4. Have students compare and contrast the different definitions of globalization and list the features that are common and different.

5. Have students discuss whether any of the following may be brought on by globalization: boom in the technology field, outsourcing, world trade, unemployment, raising gas prices, immigration, military armaments, international political instability and upheavals.

6. Present the observations on globalization by John Gray (2006) in "Global Delusions" from *The New York Review of Books* and ask students working in groups to research the accuracy of the observation.
   - Globalization dates backs to the sixteenth century, with the conquistadors, and continued in the nineteenth century with British imperial free trade.
   - Nineteen-century globalization involved large-scale movements of people to new lands.
   - The present phase of globalization involves mainly commodities and images.
   - The reason poor countries stay poor is that they have little that rich countries want or need, and the poor of the world are not so much exploited as neglected and forgotten.
   - Globalization involves an information technology revolution that makes it possible to digitize the boundaries between design, manufacturing, and marketing and to locate these functions in different places.
   - Globalization includes having the availability of large numbers of workers and engineers in low-wage countries.
   - The fundamental forces driving globalization is a great free-up of trade and capital flows, deregulation, the shrinking cost of communication and transportation.

   Students will find additional information in Michael Bordos "Globalization in Historical Perspective," in *Business Economics* (January 2002, pp. 20–28).

7. Present students with Karen Lurie's (1998) "Eleven Big World Issues," and have them discuss how they are influenced by cultural diffusion and globalization and/or how they influence cultural diffusion and globalization.

   War and peace
   Population
   Hunger and poverty
   Political and economic refugees
   Environmental concerns
   Economic growth and development
   Human rights
   World trade and finance
   Determination of political and economic systems
   Energy: Resources and allocation
   Terrorism.

   Resources that students use may include in their search for research material:

   Roger Lowenstein, "The Immigration Equation," in *The New York Times Magazine* (July 9, 2000)

Bruce R. Scott, "The Great Divide in the Global Village," in *Foreign Affairs* 80(1) (January/February 2001, pp. 160–177)
The Far, Poor, and Muslim Find Themselves Hurt the Most, *Financial Times*

8. With students working in groups have them point out—based upon all that they have read—"what seems to be missing" or narrowly defined in the discussion of globalization. During the discussion, especially if the students have difficulty coming up with "education" as a prime topic, ask them to what extent is education discussed and what is the nature of the discussion.

Ask students if the following three points dominate the discussion regarding education and globalization:

a. How to prepare a work force to function in our technological society

b. How education/schooling lags far behind the "world outside of schools"

c. Whether education should help engender a new way of thinking about the relation between people. In other words, education would contain an ethical component and argue for knowledge of, and respect for, the culture and spiritual values of different civilizations; it would therefore serve as a counterweight to globalization advocated in economical or technological terms.

Have students write a letter to the periodicals listed as resources to inquire as to why education is not more broadly defined (e.g., discussion of a flourishing life, learning for the sake of self-improvement).

For research material students may wish to retrieve the following:

"Globalisation and Its Critics: A Survey of Globalisation," in *The Economist* (Retrieved September 29, 2001, from http://www.economist.com/surveys/displayStory.cfm?story_id = 795995
Robert Keohane and Joseph Nye, "Globalization: What's New? What's Not? (And So What?)," in *Foreign Policy* (Spring 2000, pp. 104–18).
"Measuring Globalization" *Foreign Policy* (2001)

9. Share with students a definition of cultural diffusion or the following statement: Cultural diffusion occurs when different cultures share with or influence each other and is promoted by trade, aid, migration, conquest, slavery, war and entertainment (Lurie, 1998). Working in groups, have students identify evidence of cultural diffusion from the media, mall movies, etc.

10. Have students write a short essay about the affect of cultural diffusion on their lives.

11. Have students do a Web search of "globalization and gender" in order to discover how the role and identity of females are affected by globalization. In order to start the discussion, share with students and get their reflections on President of the American Sociological Society Cynthia Fuchs Epstein's (2007) statement in her presidential address, "Great Divides: The Cultural, Cognitive, and Social Bases of the Global Subordination of Women." Pay attention to see if the boys assess the statement differently than the girls, and if so, work out a plan with the girls and interested boys to take action against sexist attitudes in the class.

Categorization based on sex is the most basic social divide. It is the organizational basis of most major institutions, including the division of labor in the home, the workforce, politics, and religion. Globally, women's gendered roles are regarded as subordinate to men's. The gender divide enforces women's roles in reproduction and support activities and limits their autonomy, it limits their participation in decision making and highly-rewarded roles, and it puts women at risk. Social, cultural, and psychological mechanisms support the process. Differentiation varies with the stability of groups and the success of social movements. Gender analyses tend to be ghettoized; so it is recommended that all sociologists consider gender issues in their studies to better understand the major institutions and social relationships in society. (p. 1)

12. Students will discover the role that immigration plays in globalization.
Have students search the Web and media for articles, such as the following, that discuss immigration and globalization

> Roger Lowenstein, "The Immigration Equation," *The New York Times Magazine* (July 9, 2000)
> Bruce R. Scott, "The Great Divide in the Global Village," in *Foreign Affairs*, 80(1 (January/February 2001, pp. 160–177
> "The Far, Poor, and Muslim Find Themselves Hurt the Most," *Financial Times*

Resources

Evaluation

1. Students' are able to define globalization and identify its major features.

2. Students are able to point out that education receives a narrow perspective in many discussions of globalization.

3. Students are able to define cultural diffusion and tell how it comes about.

4. Students can explain why female rights have become central in the discussion of the influence of globalization.

5. Students can explain why immigration is often a major point during discussion of globalization.

WHY THE CHANGES?

Curriculum

According to business executives, politicians, and academic scholars, globalization is the mantra of our times. It is arguably the most powerful force shaping international and domestic politics today. When the media and other observers discuss the effects of globalization, they refer to many different facets of globalization, such as the economic, political, social, and environmental. However, globalization is often the object of both misplaced criticism and adulation and is poorly understood. In order for students to be knowledgeable, critical citizens and actively participate in democracy, as well as advocate and take action for those penalized by globalization, they must understand its history, the ideologies promoting it, and the practices used to put it in place. The "Before" plan addressed globalization, but mainly to offer students a definition that highlights major features. The "After" plan addresses many more topics (e.g., immigration, sexism, economic inequality).

Analyze System of Oppression

The "Before" plan is mostly silent about how globalization influences systems of oppression such as sexism and economic inequality or is influenced by those systems of oppression. The "After" plan addresses and contextualizes sexism, economic inequality, and immigration to globalization.

Encourages Social Action

Students are encouraged to write letter to the periodicals listed as resources to inquire why education is not more broadly defined. Girls and interested boys are encouraged to develop take action-activities to help the boys in their class understand sexist behavior.

▶ LESSON PLAN

The United Nation: Declaration of Human Rights

BEFORE

Subject Area: Social Studies
Grade 6–12
Time: One week

Objectives

1. Given the increased discussion of social justice and human rights in the media, students will examine definitions social justice and discover why after World War II the United Nations advocated for and adopted the Universal Declaration of Human Rights.

2. Students will review the definition of human rights presented in Universal Declaration of Human Rights adopted by the United Nations General Assembly in 1948 (see wwwun.org/rights).

Suggested Procedure

1. Have students read the Universal Declaration of Human Rights adopted by the United Nations General Assembly in 1948 (wwwun.org/rights). Explain to students that the Declaration is considered the foundation of modern international human rights defense and promotion. Human rights are based on the inherent dignity of every person. This dignity, and the rights to freedom and equality that derive from it, are undeniable.

2. Using a search engine, have students to key in "What is social justice?" They should compare and contrast the definitions they receive, especially noting commonalities and differences.

Evaluation

Have students write out a definition of *human rights and social justice.*

Human Rights Is Social Justice

AFTER

Subject Area: Social Studies

Grade: 6–12

Time: Two weeks

Social Justice, Democracy, and Dignity in the Global World

Objectives

1. Students will examine definitions of social justice to discover why after World War II the United Nations advocated for and adopted the Universal Declaration of Human Rights.

2. Students will review the definition of human rights present in Universal Declaration of Human Rights adopted by the United Nations General Assembly in 1948 (wwwun.org/rights).

3. Students will develop a definition of social justice and identify the social conditions that often inspire actions for human rights and social justice.

4. Students will learn that the world's wealthier economies control the global economy, sometimes to the detriment of poor countries.

5. Students will explore whether wars and conflict—though still a scourge of too many communities—perhaps no longer pose the greatest threat to human rights. Rather, increasing wealth inequalities within and among nations now represent the most immediate attacks on human dignity.

6. Students will examine the argument that human rights should be allocated equally, in discussions of civil/political rights and economic rights.

Suggested Procedures

1. Have students read the Universal Declaration of Human Rights adopted by the United Nations General Assembly in 1948 (wwwun.org/rights).
   a. Explain to students that the Declaration is considered the foundation of modern international human rights defense and promotion.
   b. Human Rights are based on the inherent dignity of every person. This dignity, and the rights to freedom and equality that derive from it, are undeniable.

2. Have students discuss which rights or civil liberties—such as freedom from repression, freedom of expression, freedom of association or economic security, the right to work, free choice of employment, just and favorable conditions of work, and protection against unemployment—are the more significant rights or civil liberties.

3. Have students, using a search engine such as Google, key in "What is social justice?" and compare and contrast the definitions they receive, especially noting commonalities and differences among the definitions.

4. Have students take the definitions of social justice they find and debate which definition is best for them and their class.

5. Have students research on the Web statistics on poverty and inequality in the world. For example, Prime Minister Bertie Ahern of Ireland stated at the United Nations' "Millennium Summit":

> Half the world's population struggling on less than $2 a day, over half a billion on less than $1. A Quarter of a billion children of 14 and under are working, sometimes in terrible conditions. Death from preventable and treatable diseases—10 people will die of malaria in the five minutes I take to address you (p. 1).

6. Have students read the Rights of the Child: wwwunicef.org/crc/
   Ask students to keep a journal of their thoughts and reactions to the readings. Near the end of the week, ask students to share two comments with the class.

7. Point out to students that "51 of the 100 largest economies in the world are corporations, not countries; and that company managers are just as likely as dictators to brutalize people.

8. Have one half of the students research a large corporation with which they are familiar (e.g., Nike, Adidas, Gap, etc.), and have the other half of the students research low-wage factories. Next, have the students share their findings with the total class and then communicate with the companies for additional information.

9. Have the students to determine whether they (and you) are recipients of goods from low-wage factories and thereby benefit from social injustices.

10. Have students discuss whether they will continue to be recipients or whether they are going to take action for social justice and, if so, what type of action.

11. Have students research and discover why people/workers organize unions. Students may wish to research the development of: the Knights of Labor, the American Federation of Labor, and the Industrial Workers of the World. In addition, students may wish to web search "The history of the development of unions."

12. Have students identify companies that deny or resist the formation of unions.

Evaluation

1. Have students write-out a definition of human rights and social justice.

2. Have students identify in a short essay of actions against social justice and human rights in their community.

3. Have students working in groups develop an essay that addresses human rights allegations and social justice actions taken to correct the allegations

Critical Questioning

The "After" lesson plan is designed to help students learn not only about human rights and social justice, including some of its history, but also about the debate concerning what should be the focus of human rights: political rights or economic rights.

Practice Democracy

The "Before" lesson plan pays little attention to directly connecting human rights and social justice to principles of democracy, such as fairness. The "After" lesson plans have both the teacher and students to examine if they benefit from the social injustice of others.

Analyze Systems of Oppression

The In the "Before" plan, social justice is not given meaning in peoples' lives nor is it personalized to the lives of the students. In the "After" plan, however, social justice is allowed to take shape and have meaning at the local, national, and global level. The class discussion of human rights and social justice is also important in that the teacher helps students to identify the oppressors and the oppressed as groups. The teacher must decide the extent to which race, class, gender, and disability dynamics are reflected in the discussion of human rights and social justice.

Encourage Social Action

The "After" plan encourages social action. It challenges students and the teacher to take action if they are beneficiaries of social injustice done to others.

What Is Poverty and Who Does It Effect

BEFORE

Subject Area: Social Studies and Language Arts

Grade: 5–8

Time: Two periods

Objectives

1. Students will examine their attitudes and beliefs about poverty and the working poor.
2. Students will examine stereotypes, prejudice, and discrimination related to people in general, and students specifically, who are of low-income status.
3. Students will develop sensitivity toward people who are impoverished.

Suggested Procedures

1. Have students define poverty and list its characteristics and effects.
2. Have students analyze their attitudes (e.g., they are lazy, they need to lift themselves up) and beliefs (e.g., society dealt them a mean blow, they need help) about individuals who are in different economic conditions.
3. Have students read *The Rag Coat*, by Lauren Mills.
4. Have students volunteer to serve food at a homeless shelter.

Resources

Mills, L. A. (1991) *The Rag Coat*. Boston: Little, Brown.

Human Rights, Social Justice, and Poverty

AFTER

Subject Area: Social Studies and Language Arts

Grade: 5–8

Time: Two periods

Objectives

1. Students will examine their attitude and beliefs about poverty and the working poor.

2. Students will examine stereotypes, prejudices, and discrimination related to people in general, and students specifically, who are of low-income status.

3. Students will develop sensitivity based upon statistical information toward people who are impoverished.

4. Students will identify the characteristics of poverty.

5. Students will examine the interrelated causes of poverty among low-income earners, women, and children.

6. Students will identify nonprofit organizations that act against poverty and impoverished living conditions and study the reasons why each organization was started.

7. Students will examine the Universal Declaration of Human Rights as related to poverty.

Suggested Procedures

1. Have students define poverty and identify people who make up the working poor.

2. Place students into groups, and have them compare their definitions of poverty and those who make up the working poor. Have each group list on the chalkboard what they believe are the conditions that foster poverty. The teacher should decide based upon the class if it is wiser to address students' misconceptions in the moment or take note and make sure to address them through the lessons. In addition, the teacher will want to be alert how the discussion may be affecting any student in the class who lives in poverty conditions.

3. Have students interview community members who help people in poverty. If it is in keeping with the rules of the school, encourage students to volunteer so they can learn about the effects of poverty firsthand and take action on behalf of the people.

4. Have students discuss the causes of poverty and what circumstance may cause impoverishment. (Responses should reflect a variety of causes: poor quality of education or lack of education, racism and discrimination, lost of job, condition of the economy, size of family in relation to family income, family members with disabilities and/or mental illness, natural disasters) Teachers may wish to visit the National Center for Children Poverty (NCCP) website (www.neep.org/publication/pub_762.html) and the EdChange website (www.EdChange.org) for statistical information and resources about poverty.

5. Have students read the Articles of the Universal Declaration of Human Rights, identify the part that addresses poverty, and write a short essay commenting on what they read.

Give students the following information from the World Bank:

- 110 million primary-school-age children in developing countries are not in school
- Of these, 60 percent (66 million) are girls.
- More than a billion people in the world continue to live on less than $1 a day.
- Poor economic conditions in developing countries often lead to the inability of governments to provide clean water, health care, public education, and other services.
- Some countries sacrifice the rights of its workers in order to attract foreign investors and companies who can offer jobs. Such conditions lead to limit opportunities for the poor and make it hard to meet their basic needs.

6. Have students discuss poverty in the United States and in developing countries. Students may wish to visit the Economic Policy Institute website (www.epi.org). Remind students that websites often are helpful in that they suggest link to other websites. In addition, remind students that they should be aware of how the original data was collected and not simply accept everything they read as absolutely factual.

7. Have students visit the websites listed in the Resources that report poverty statistics in the United States. Students should pay attention to the identification of poverty in different areas (e.g., urban, rural, suburban) and regions (e.g., North, South, East, West) and the causes of poverty in the areas.

8. Have students, in their analysis of poverty in the different areas and regions, pay attention to issues of race, gender, and language and inquire if these issues are related to causes of poverty.

9. Have students identify organizations—both for-profit and nonprofit—that work to eliminate poverty and aid impoverished and homeless people. Have students write letters to them congratulating them on their efforts and asking the organization what they can do to help.

10. Have students' identify how governments respond to their people in poverty. It may be useful for students to review the message of the 2008 presidential candidates on poverty and people living in improvised conditions. In addition, have students select their "favorite" country other than the United States and to research how the government deals with poverty.

11. The following passage by Michael Harrington from his 1962 book *The Other America: Poverty in the United States* may be a bit dense for some eighth-grade students. On the other hand, if the students are given some help in understanding the passage it, will serve to anchor their historical, social, and political understanding of poverty in the United States. Harrington states:

> There are mighty historical and economic forces that keep the poor down; and there are human beings who help out in this grim business, many of them unwittingly. There are sociological and political reasons why poverty is not seen; and there are misconceptions and prejudices that literally blind the eyes. The latter must be understood if anyone is to make the necessary act of intellect and will so that the poor can be noticed. (p. 21).

Evaluation

1. Students who have met the objectives will understand how race, gender, and language may influence the cause of poverty and/or place people in impoverished living conditions.

2. Students who have achieved this object will write a one-two essay that compares the causes of poverty in the United states and developing countries.

Resources

Websites

www.bread.org/hungerbasics/domestic.html This is the website of Bread for the World Institute.

www.un.org/Pubs/CyberSchoolBus/humanrights/resources/plain.asp: The plain language version of the Universal Declaration of Human Rights was taken from this site.

www.udhr.org/index.htm: This is the Franklin and Eleanor Roosevelt Institute's website for the Universal Declaration of Human Rights.

www.un.org/Overview/rights.html: This is the official United Nations website which includes the Universal Declaration of Human Rights.

Shipler, D. (2004). *The working poor invisible in America*. New York: Alfred A. Knopf.

WHY THE CHANGES?

Critical Questioning

The "Before" plan teaches about poverty without doing much to get students to challenge their own personal thinking. The "After" lesson plan engages students in a variety of questions and issues ranging from questions about the self to poverty in the United States as well as poverty in developing countries.

Analyze Systems of Oppression

The "Before" plan provides limited opportunity for students to analyze oppression. The "After" plan has students analyze oppression at several levels, including the causes of poverty in different areas and regions, how it is discussed in several prominent international documents, and how it is addressed by the World Bank and scholars who conduct research on poverty.

Encourage Social Action

Both the "Before" plan and the "After" plan encourage social action; however, the "After" plan provides more opportunities and encouragement for social action.

References

Killoran, J., Zimmer, S., & Fischer, J. (1995). *Government and you*. New York: Amsco School Publications.

Abu-Jamal, M. (1995). *Live from death row*. New York: Addison-Wesley.

Human Rights Watch. (2001). Mental retardation: An overview. Retrieved, 2008, from http://www.hrw.org/reports/2001/ustat/ustat0301-01.htm

Whatley, M. H. (1986). Taking feminist science to the classroom: Where do we go from here? In Ruth Bleier (Ed.), *Feminist approaches to science* (pp. 181–190). New York: Pergamon.

George D. Kuh, Student Success in College

Lurie, Karen (1998). *Global studies*. New York Random House.

Harrington, M. (1962). *The other America: Poverty in the United States*. New York Macmillan.

Subject Index

Lesson Plan Index

BY GRADE LEVEL